EGYPT'S FOOTBALL REVOLUTION

EGYPT'S FOOTBALL REVOLUTION

EMOTION, MASCULINITY, AND UNEASY POLITICS

CARL ROMMEL

University of Texas Press   Austin

Requests for permission to reproduce material from this work should be
sent to:
  Permissions
  University of Texas Press
  P.O. Box 7819
  Austin, TX 78713-7819
  utpress.utexas.edu/rp-form

♾ The paper used in this book meets the minimum requirements of ANSI/
NISO Z39.48-1992 (R1997) (Permanence of Paper).

Library of Congress Cataloging-in-Publication Data

Names: Rommel, Carl, author.
Title: Egypt's football revolution : emotion, masculinity, and uneasy poli-
  tics / Carl Rommel.
Description: First edition. | Austin : University of Texas Press, 2021. |
  Includes bibliographical references and index.
Identifiers:
  LCCN 2020054711
  ISBN 978-1-4773-2317-5 (cloth)
  ISBN 978-1-4773-2318-2 (library ebook)
  ISBN 978-1-4773-2319-9 (ebook)
Subjects: LCSH: Soccer—Political aspects—Egypt. | Soccer—Social
  aspects—Egypt. | Sports—Anthropological aspects—Egypt.
Classification: LCC GV944.E3 R66 2021 | DDC 796.3340962—dc23
LC record available at https://lccn.loc.gov/2020054711

doi:10.7560/323175

For Karin
In memory of Jagger

Any social project that is not imposed through force alone must be affective in order to be effective.

William Mazzarella, "Affect: What Is It Good For?"

Everything has become politics; there is no fun left.

Hamada, passionate fan of the Cairo club al-Zamalek since the early 1990s, March 2013

CONTENTS

ILLUSTRATIONS

ACKNOWLEDGMENTS

This book is the end result of a decade of researching, thinking, discussing, and writing, and a large number of people have supported me along the way.

First and foremost, I want to thank all my friends and interlocutors in Cairo—fans, players, coaches, journalists, state bureaucrats, entrepreneurs, coffee shop owners, and many more—who told me the football stories that I retell in this book. By sharing generously what you knew, thought, and felt about your lives, your country, and your favorite sport, you are the ones who made me grasp the weight and scope of Egypt's football revolution. The vast majority of you are not identified by your real names in the pages that follow. Your anonymity does not change the fact that I am forever grateful.

This project grew out of a doctoral dissertation in social anthropology at SOAS, University of London. At SOAS, I met many people to whom thanks are due. My supervisor Stephen Hughes's careful way of steering me—loosely at most times, firmly when needed—gave me the confidence to find my own way through readings, fieldwork, and writing. My examiners Walter Armbrust and Will Rollason pinpointed strengths as well as limitations and convinced me that I should rework my thesis into this book. Kit Davis, Caroline Osella, Richard Fardon, Caitlin Robinson, and Matt Fish read and commented on drafts at the Post-Fieldwork seminar. Among many lovely peers, I especially like to mention Alessia Costa, Giulia Zoccatelli, Nadeem Karkabi, Safitri Widagdo, Andrea Pia, Seamus Murphy, and Helena Pérez Niño for friendship, debates, dinners, drinks, and lodging. A special thank-you goes to Vale, Diego, Michele, and Alessandra, who cared for me during the last destructive months before submission.

In Cairo—my hometown for five of the last fourteen years—countless friends pushed me and my research along: Adam Almqvist and Helena Hägglund; Ben Prestel, Nora Danielson, Sarah Wessel, and Steve Thorpe in the soon-to-be-famous Cairo League; Marine Poirier, Marie Vannetzel, Sixtine Deroure, Youssef El Chazli, and Giedrė Šabasevičiūtė, without whom I would not have survived New Orleans; Ilka Eickhof and Taha

Belal; Aymon Kreil, Dalila Ghodbane, Naïma Bouras, Jakob Lindfors, and
Maria Malmström; Amro Hassan, Sherif Hassan, and Ahmad Saied; Dalia
Abdel Hamid; and Riham Hamada, the best language teacher one could
ever imagine.

When a book project is ten years in the making, a vast number of colleagues have inevitably commented on chapter drafts and presentations.
With the risk of forgetting some of them, I would like to thank Samuli
Schielke, Aymon Kreil, Alice Elliot, Fuad Musallam, Ben Prestel, Moritz
Buchner, Benno Gammerl, Michele Serafini, Sarah Green, Birgit Meyer,
Lucie Ryzova, Joseph Viscomi, Phaedra Douzina-Bakalaki, Ronnie Close,
and Sanaa Alimia. My editor Jim Burr at the University of Texas Press
offered precisely the combination of enthusiasm and direction that I
needed to see the project out. At the Press, I am also thankful to Sarah
McGavick and John Brenner. I want to direct a special thanks to Johan
Wollin for god knows how many late-night readings and edits, and for
his insistence that language and style are serious matters. Without Jessica
Winegar's encouragement and advice at a critical moment and superb sug-
gestions at a slightly later stage, this book would not have taken the shape
and form it eventually did.

Money was always going to be needed to live a life and write a book.
As a doctoral student, I was given financial support by the SOAS Research
Fellowship, the SOAS Fieldwork Grant, Birgit och Gad Rausings Stiftelse,
Anérstiftelsen, Stiftelsen Lars Hiertas Minne, Helge Ax:son Johnsons Stiftelse, the Swedish Society for Anthropology and Geography, and Sixten
Gemzéus Stiftelse. Later on I received a writing grant from the Camel
Trust and held fellowships at the Zentrum Moderner Orient in Berlin and
the Walter Benjamin Kolleg in Bern. The University of Helsinki has been
my home institution during the final three years of research and writing. I
am indebted to my brilliant colleagues in the Crosslocations project, most
especially to Sarah Green—who always made sure there was time to finish
what needed to be finished—and to Philippe Rekacewicz and Lena Malm,
who drew maps and took photos. I am also thankful for institutional support provided by CEDEJ in Cairo and the Department of Social Anthropology at Stockholm University, and for Karim and Natha's idiosyncratic
perspectives on all things Swedish.

My family in Sweden constitutes the bedrock on which this project was
built. From an early age, Mom and Dad taught me that the world is large
and enchanted, and they encouraged a life-long desire to look, listen, and
learn. I also want to thank my brothers Olof and Jacob. I know that they
will always be there, no matter where and what; to me that is a very precious

thing. The male members of my family have been instrumental for the cultivation of my passion for football, the best game there ever was and the subject matter of this book. For decades, we have shared long periods of despair and brief moments of ecstasy together with IK Sirius, our blue-and-black heroes. And still we do dream; 2027 is just around the corner.

And last, my love and thanks to the person who for two decades has journeyed beside me through the worlds and words that became our life. Things have not always been easy, and who knows what the future will hold. But we have been two and we have had fun, and for me that has made all the difference. To my most persistent reader, fiercest critic, and very best friend. To say that this book would not have been possible without you, Karin, would be the most futile understatement.

NOTE ON TRANSLITERATION

In my transliteration of Arabic into English, I have used a simplified version of the *International Journal of Middle East Studies* conventions. While I have not marked emphatic consonants or long vowels, I have indicated *'ayns* (') and *hamzas* ('). Transliterations of Egyptian dialect have been adjusted to reflect the colloquial pronunciation. Names have been transliterated following the same principles, with the exception of cases where an established English spelling already exists.

EGYPT'S FOOTBALL REVOLUTION

Emotions, Politics, and Egypt's Changing National Game

*If signification and representation (what things mean) are
no longer the only primary realm of the political, then bodily
processes (how things feel) must be irreducibly central to any
notion of the political.*

Jasbir K. Puar, "Coda: The Cost of Getting Better: Suicide,
Sensation, Switchpoints"

*The boundaries between what is and what is not political are
an important part of reality.*

Matei Candea, "'Our Division of the Universe': Making a
Space for the Non-Political in the Anthropology of Politics"

In the early hours of 3 February 2006, the Egyptian passenger ferry
al-Salam 98 sank on its way from Duba in Saudi Arabia to the Egyptian
port at Safaga. More than one thousand people, many of them returning Egyptian labor migrants, drowned in the Red Sea. The tragedy happened just as the Africa Cup of Nations was in full swing in Cairo; later the
same day, the host country, Egypt, was to play the Democratic Republic
of Congo in the quarter-final. Rather than dedicating his energies to crisis
management, President Hosni Mubarak stuck to his original plans for the
day. He attended the national football team's morning training session as
well as the match at a sold-out Cairo Stadium in the evening. The Egyptian team won the game comfortably by four goals to one. Surrounded
by an elated home crowd, the president celebrated in the stadium's VIP
lounge with family members and political allies.

In the days that followed, all Egyptian eyes were on the male national
football team. As the "Pharaohs" defeated Senegal in the semi-final and

Ivory Coast after a dramatic penalty shootout in the final, Egyptian media beamed out football, football, football. Following the title-winning penalty kick—scored by the beloved playmaker Muhammad Abu Treika—the president and his two sons, Alaa and Gamal, were all smiles as they hobnobbed with the players and coaching staff on the stadium tribune. When Hosni Mubarak handed over the gold medals and the cup trophy, the veteran team captain, Hossam Hassan, insisted on kissing the president on his forehead. Later that evening, Egyptians from all walks of life poured into streets and squares across the country. In Cairo, Tahrir Square overflowed with euphoric fans, Egyptian flags, and honking cars. The festivities continued into the early morning; singing, laughter, and proud chants filled the winter night. It was only seven days since *al-Salam 98* had gone missing. Who could have predicted that a week that began with one of the worst tragedies in the country's modern history would end on such an upbeat note?

The 2006 Africa Cup of Nations victory marked the beginning of an unlikely Egyptian winning streak. In 2008 as well as in 2010, the team won the biannual tournament again and then again, completing an unprecedented hat trick of continental titles. The national team's successes were paralleled by those of al-Ahly Club from Cairo, which brought home three African Champions League titles between 2005 and 2008. Still, the great results on the football field were just one part of the extensive hype. Boosted by exploding media coverage, the celebrity status of Egypt's football idols reached well beyond the confines of any stadium. Players intermingled with businessmen and politicians; some married pop stars and actresses; the sport featured as the theme in pop songs and movies. In the latter half of the 2000s, Egyptian football was not only turning into an unstoppable winning machine and the preferred pastime for millions of fans across the nation. The game was also becoming a primary concern for the country's political, economic, and cultural elites.

The story I am about to tell takes off in the thick of this sports boom at the tail end of the Mubarak presidency. Conceptualizing the football hype as an emotionally charged and highly politicized *bubble*, I will delineate an inflated coming together of finance, media, match results, and pop culture that encapsulated the Egyptian nation, propagated particular structures of feelings, and suggested how normal Egyptian men should act, behave, talk, and feel. At its peak, the bloated football bubble spawned an affective and discursive texture that permeated and defined late Mubarak Egypt. The sport and everything that came with it became vital components of the regime's soft power.

But Egypt's emotional-political football boom would prove to be fleeting. Beginning in the final year or two under Mubarak and accelerating in the wake of the 25 January 2011 Revolution that ousted him, the sports bubble burst. Spectacularly worsening results expedited the demise,[1] although they were not the sole or most decisive catalyst. With revolutionary developments dominating public life, millions of Egyptians found it difficult to keep paying attention to clubs, players, and tournaments. Then, in early 2012, a horrendous stadium massacre took place in the city of Port Said. Shortly after the final whistle of a league match between the local team, al-Masry, and al-Ahly from Cairo, thousands of home fans broke through security barriers, invaded the pitch, and attacked the stadium's visiting team section. Seventy-two young Ahly supporters were killed that night. Some were strangled, others were stabbed; many victims perished in a stampede as they tried to escape but found the stadium exits locked.

The Port Said disaster ushered in a profound football crisis in Egypt. Domestic tournaments were suspended for a full twelve months; many fans expressed repulsion toward a game that had taken so many lives. At the same time, the massacre catapulted football into the revolutionary-political limelight. Since the victims were all members of a relatively new type of fan group—the so-called Ultras, who had played a central role in recent protests and street fights—the event was widely interpreted as a setup by the police and the ruling military council. The Ultras supporters soon launched an impressive campaign for rights, retribution, and radical football reforms. As a result, Egyptian football was both nowhere and ever-present in 2012 and early 2013. While stadiums stood empty and fans left matches and club rivalries behind, the history, future, and sociopolitical function of the game were debated more than ever before.

This revolution inside the realm of sports constitutes a central interest of this book. Several chapters detail Ultras supporters, club officials, media pundits, and politicians doing their utmost to (re-)mold the crisis-ridden game at their own discretion. The window for radical alteration proved brief, though. Just as the Egyptian security state and Mubarak's crony capitalists found ways to regroup after the July 2013 military coup, the old football establishment regained control over Egypt's sports institutions. At the time of writing, the game's popularity has also begun a resurgence: the league is up and running; Egyptian teams are once again competing for Africa's finest club titles. In October 2017, the national team, led by the new superstar, Mohamed Salah, qualified for Egypt's first World Cup appearance in twenty-eight years. Still, memories of the past hover over the present. A couple of days after Salah sealed Egypt's World Cup qualification with an iconic, last-minute penalty kick at Burg el-Arab Stadium outside Alexandria, I caught up with my friend Mahmoud,[2] a pious gym instructor, father of two, and supporter of Cairo's second-biggest club, al-Zamalek. His mixed feelings that day exemplify a widely shared mood:

> Of course, I'm happy that we reached the World Cup. Finally, after all these failures! It's something that makes us all happy [*di haga tifarrahna kullina*]. It's good. There are so many problems in Egypt. But to be honest, no one really likes this team. Salah is great of course, amazing [*maluhsh hall*], but Cuper [the national team's Argentinean coach] . . . The team plays defensively. Boring football. Not like the team of Hassan Shehata [the national team's charismatic coach between 2005 and 2011]. And then . . . There's also a risk. I mean, if people start loving football again, they might forget our real problems. The regime would like to utilize it politically [*yistaghillha siyasiyyan*]. Like Mubarak, when that ferry sank, remember? Football can be dangerous, Carl. This people loves football very much.

On the most general level, my aim in this book is to chronicle and elaborate this Egyptian football saga. Drawing on several years of ethnographic fieldwork with fans, players, journalists, and coaches in Cairo and extensive analyses of football media, I tell a number of stories—some more general, others more intimate—that follow the game from boom to bust to cautious rebuilding. It is important to stress at the outset that these are narratives about male discourses, male feelings, and male experiences. In Egypt, such a bias is all but inevitable; it is widely taken for granted that football is played by men, watched by men, and discussed in male-only television studios. My storyline kicks off with the Egyptian national team's participation in the World Cup in Italy in 1990 and closes in the summer of 2019, when Egypt once again hosted the Africa Cup of Nations. That said, the main emphasis is on a few especially eventful years between November 2009 and the summer of 2013, a relatively brief period that revolutionized Egyptian football.

Analytically, my ethnographies and arguments pivot around a dialectic between football feelings and football politics. On the one hand, I examine how emotions elicited by football have interfered in, and shaped, Egyptian national politics over the last three decades. What I call the Egyptian football "bubble," a metaphor originally formulated by a close interlocutor, is central to this story. Initially, I describe how the bubble came together, the emotions and subjects it gave rise to, and how and why it took on a political role in the late Mubarak era. Later chapters elucidate why the bubble burst, and how it has given way to alternative emotional-political projects, masculinities, and struggles—radical, progressive, or reactionary. These emotional-political developments pertaining to the country's most popular sport provide an unconventional narration of Egypt's (counter-) revolutionary transition.

But the relationship between football and politics is not a one-way street. The book's second analytical leg takes interest in how conversations about and lived experiences of *siyasa* (politics) have proliferated in and around Egyptian football since the late 2000s, and how such discourses and sentiments have affected the game's transformation. Much like the gym instructor, Mahmoud, many Egyptians have come to see football's descent into *siyasa* as reason never to embrace the game without reservations. Similarly, a prevailing understanding of the revolutionary years as an era dominated by *siyasa* rendered football curiously obsolete. Paying close attention to anxieties about *siyasa* among football supporters, activist fan groups, and journalists, I argue that the term connotes an uneasy mix of divisions, intrigues, uncertainty, and selfishness in contemporary Egypt. Controversies over what *siyasa* is and who is *siyasi* (political) pop up at each twist and turn of Egypt's emotional-political football revolution. In particular, an intrinsic tension between Egyptian nationalism and all things *siyasi* gave rise to a contradiction that permeated and eventually thwarted Egypt's revolutionary moment. This unease is especially visible in the case of football, Egypt's indisputably *national game*.

EGYPT'S NATIONAL GAME

Football is Egypt's national game by all conceivable measures. The sport is the country's most popular by a mile both in terms of the number of players and spectators. It is played and watched by millions of men in large cities and small villages across the nation. And it occupies an overwhelming majority of all sports media coverage. The game is also deeply embedded in the history of Egyptian nationalism. Since British colonial officers and army conscripts brought football to Egypt in the late nineteenth century, the sport has functioned as a vehicle for nationalist mobilization and aspirations. An early case in point is the founding of al-Ahly Club in Cairo in 1907. As the first sports club set up by and for Egyptian nationals only, al-Ahly formed part of an explicit anticolonial project to mold healthy and strong national male bodies (al-Mistakawi, 1997; Jacob, 2011:84–89).[3] The establishment of the Egyptian Football Association (EFA) in 1921 constituted another landmark. Falling between the 1919 popular uprisings against the British and the declaration of nominal independence in 1922, the formation of a domestic association wrested power over the game away from the colonizers and confirmed football's status as an Egyptian national affair.

Another period of especially close entanglements between football and nationalist politics occurred after the Free Officers' Military Coup in 1952. President Gamal Abdel Nasser's Arab Socialist regime invested heavily in sports infrastructure and sports media. Colonial clubs were Egyptianized; football institutions were tied closely to the military elite (Di-Capua, 2004).[4] Nasser's engagement with football contributed to his ambitious pan-African project. Egypt was one of the initiators of the Confederation of African Football (CAF), established in 1957, as well as the organization of the first Africa Cup of Nations the same year (see Ayoub, 2010). Most of all, though, the game advanced a populist nation-building effort that brought people and politicians together (Di-Capua, 2004; Tawfiq, 2010:59–68; Thabet, 2010:88–100). Football under President Nasser in this sense resembled what would unfold in the latter half of Hosni Mubarak's presidency (see chapters 1 and 2).[5]

Egypt is certainly not the only country where football has bolstered nationalist attitudes and politics. The Egyptian game's trajectory—from colonial pastime, via mobilizer in the anti-imperialist struggle, to instrument for authoritarian control—is recognizable across the Global South.[6] Still, for several reasons, Egypt's *national* game stands out. First and foremost, football has rarely perpetuated separate identities or sociopolitical divisions *inside* the Egyptian nation-state.[7] By contrast, and as I will elaborate in the pages that follow, the Egyptian game has always been unusually inward-looking and nondivisive. Most fans direct their attentions to domestic club competitions rather than the big leagues in Europe.[8] It is widely taken for granted that football tournaments and matches should bring men across the nation together.

To characterize football in Egypt as distinctively nondivisive might seem counterintuitive to some readers. After all, the country's football universe has for more than a century orbited around a well-known rivalry between the two Cairo clubs, al-Ahly, established in 1907, and al-Zamalek, founded in 1911. Since the 1920s, these two antagonists have not only completely dominated Egypt's domestic football competitions but also constituted a most visible societal rift.[9] The Ahly-Zamalek enmity has long divided Egyptian men into two distinct groups: red-shirted *Ahlawiyya* (al-Ahly supporters; singular, *Ahlawi*) and *Zamelkawiyya* (al-Zamalek supporters; singular, *Zamelkawi*) sporting al-Zamalek's classic white jersey with two red stripes.

Even so, as conspicuous as the al-Ahly versus al-Zamalek rivalry might be, it is arguably not as profound as it appears. Despite distinct historical and ideological origins (see below), it is today hardly relevant to map divisions between *Ahlawiyya* and *Zamelkawiyya* onto sociological variables such as class, political opinions, ethnicity, or religion. In contemporary Cairo, one finds boys and men supporting both al-Zamalek and al-Ahly among all social strata and in any given neighborhood. Moreover—with the important exception of the Suez Canal region, where Ahly fans are few and the local clubs, al-Ismaily and al-Masry, enjoy strong support—Egyptian club support does not propagate a lot of regional differences and local patriotism. Provincial clubs do not attract the crowds that they used to attract a few decades ago. Al-Ahly and al-Zamalek are the two dominant clubs in most parts of the country.

Egyptian football might not reinforce many social or regional divisions, although that should not make us assume that the game lacks political purchase. By contrast, precisely because the game has been perceived as national and unifying by default, football has recurrently arisen as a projection of and battleground for what the Egyptian nation is and should be about. The national team's participation in four Olympics and one World Cup in the 1920s and 1930s constituted one early, exemplary moment. As Wilson Chacko Jacob (2011:127–141), Shaun Lopez (2009), and Mahmoud Elassal (2018) have detailed, the team's performances in those tournaments were followed with great anxiety among what was then an emerging national public: victories were portrayed as evidence of national progress; losses led to heated debates in the press about the young nation's backwardness and image on the world stage. The question of who the Egyptian people really are also imbues a seemingly never-ending quarrel between *Ahlawiyya* and *Zamelkawiyya*. In stark contrast to al-Zamalek Club, which was established on the initiative of foreigners, al-Ahly was founded by anticolonial campaigners and retained close ties to the Egyptian nationalist movement throughout the first half of the twentieth century.[10] For Ahly supporters, this legacy proves, once and for all, that their club represents a progressive force for the national good. Zamalek fans, however, like to characterize al-Ahly as a club propped up by the establishment and all kinds of political and economic elites. At least since the Nasser era, they maintain, supporting al-Zamalek has therefore constituted an oppositional stance in sync with the true interests of normal Egyptian citizens.[11]

Acrimonious conflicts over Egypt's national game and national formation have sprung up on multiple occasions in recent decades. First, in the late Mubarak era, football carved out a particular male and normal national subject that proved favorable for the country's political and popular culture elites. Second, this football nationalism was challenged by Islamists and secular intellectuals in the wake of two feverish matches against Algeria in late 2009. Third, the Ultras movement proposed alternative scripts for being and acting as a revolutionary Egyptian football supporter before and after the 2011 Revolution. And fourth, attachments to the sport were transformed after the revolution and the Port Said tragedy, a period when the national game's position in Egyptian society was fundamentally altered.

My decision to employ the national level as a principal frame of analysis results from this history as well as from the ethnographic encounter: my interlocutors might all be sports people, but they discuss the Egyptian nation all the time. Football is by no means the only realm where this is the case. Whether in the case of film (Armbrust, 1996, 2002a), television (Abu-Lughod, 2005), music (van Nieuwkerk, 1995; Danielson, 1997), the fine arts (Winegar, 2006), physical exercise (Jacob, 2011), mass media (Fahmy, 2011), the so-called marriage crisis (Kholoussy, 2010), discussions on urban emotions (Prestel, 2017), or tourism development (Ahlberg, 2017), historians and ethnographers have demonstrated how the identity, essence, and image of the Egyptian nation have constituted prevailing concerns for a century and more. Indeed, as Lila Abu-Lughod argues in her ethnography of the politics of Egyptian television, the national frame seems to take on a special obviousness and primacy in Egypt (2005:1–27).[12] My research on Egyptian football intervenes in this long conversation. Taking on an immensely popular phenomena and a type of mass politics that has thus far largely evaded the academic spotlight, I tell a hitherto untold story about the contestation and reconfiguration of the Egyptian national formation over the last three decades. In addition, I offer a novel thematic too, for the national politics that we find in and around football is never confined to narratives, media, images, and pop cultural expressions. A spectator sport overflowing with feelings and sentiments, football politics is always also *emotional politics*.

THE EMOTIONAL POLITICS OF EGYPTIAN FOOTBALL

Wherever and however one looks at Egyptian football history, one sees emotions and politics: thrilling victories and devastating losses; hyperbole followed by cool abjection; authoritarian regimes doing their utmost to contain and control; animated Ultras fans rebelling at stadiums and in the streets. Football in Egypt, in other words, is a social field where emotionality must be highlighted to properly illuminate the politics at stake. A story attending to emotional-political developments pertaining to Egypt's national game provides an alternative account both of statecraft in the late Mubarak era and of the subsequent (counter-)revolutionary process.

Critical analyses of the intertwining of football, feeling, and politics have thus far proceeded along two broad tracks. First, it has long been standard practice to associate the political potency of spectator sports with a capacity to stir emotions that tempt and lure. The Romans talked about *panem et circenses*—bread supplemented by circuses—as effective means of domination and obedience. And since the late nineteenth century, when sports emerged as the favorite pastime of the European male working classes, Marxists have likened football to a reactionary "opiate of the masses" that brushes over the more significant concerns associated with realpolitik (see Bromberger, 1995; Elias and Dunning, 1986; Kuhn, 2011). Depictions of political elites cunningly mobilizing football feelings to hide and cover are common in more recent scholarly and journalistic writings too (e.g., Goldblatt and Nolan, 2018; Mason, 1995; De Waele et al., 2018). In Egypt, as I flesh out in the next section, fans and journalists habitually resort to such tropes when contemplating the history of the national sport.

The second prevailing way to think through football's emotional politics academically is more optimistic and leaves more space for resistance. It is premised on a portrayal of matches as "rituals" within unique "liminal" spaces afforded by stadiums and their immediate surroundings.[13] Liberated from otherwise dominant social structures, the argument goes, the stands allow for extraordinary fan practices, for "carnivalesque" ruses, and for reflexive discourses rarely found anywhere else.[14] Further, as Victor Turner has famously showed (1969), rituals, regardless of original intentions, always encompass the potential for social transformation. The person entering a stage of liminality might come out of it forever altered. The emotionality of a ritualistic football game, in other words, is inherently difficult to control. Again and again, we learn how the sport turns into a socioemotional space for radical subversion—of norms, identities, and the most potent of power structures (e.g., Bromberger, 1995; Finn, 1994; Giulianotti, 1991; Montague, 2020; Pearson, 2012; see also Besnier, Brownell, and Carter, 2018:159–165).

My research in Egypt takes its cue from these two approaches. Over seven ethnographic chapters, a conclusion, and a postscript, I repeatedly depict how actors in power have exploited football emotions for political reasons, and how the game's unique affectivity has provided openings for sociopolitical resistance. But my vantage point is also distinctive. Instead of portraying the game now as intoxicating domination, now as liberating ritual, I demonstrate that such divergent outcomes constitute two sides of what is ultimately one and the same emotional-political coin. Liminal thrills at stadiums, after all, *are* the opiate that tempts and lures the masses. To this end, I engage scholarly traditions not commonly encountered in studies of sports. The opening chapter, for instance, mobilizes Ann Stoler's concept of "affective states" (2004) when delineating a particular kind of visceral football nationalism that permeated Egyptian society before January 2011. Stoler's work on Southeast Asian colonial regimes spawning such states spotlights a type of power that regulates and distributes affect among the subjects. At one point she writes: "Critical analyses of colonial authority have often treated the affective as a smokescreen of rule, as a ruse masking the dispassionate calculations that preoccupy states, persuasive histrionics rather than the substance of politics" (Stoler, 2004:6). This is an explicit call to treat the emotional-affective as more than just a clouding "opiate" or "smokescreen" concealing some "true" *realpolitik*. Instead, anthropologists should attend to "redistributions of sentiments" and "reformatting[s] of the visceral" (ibid., 7)—over time and across space—as the very "substance of politics" (ibid., 6). Such processes, Stoler insists, might be less overt but ultimately more enduring reasons why emotionality is such a potent political tool.

In Hosni Mubarak's Egypt, football turned into a compelling emotional-political force for precisely the reasons that Stoler pinpoints. Especially in the four years that followed the *al-Salam 98* tragedy and Africa Cup of Nations victory on home soil in early 2006, an unprecedented wave of football excitement redistributed a variety of visceral sentiments among the nation's male subjects. I have chosen to call this moment in history the Egyptian football bubble—a singular constellation of new legislations, semipublic financing, booming football media, popular cultural productions, an especially talented generation of players, and unprecedented triumph, which all came together at the same time. At its most inflated apex, this world of football *encapsulated* the Egyptian nation and *sealed* it off from the world outside. The successful national sport also *circulated* a range of nationwide affective patterns, akin to what Raymond Williams has called "structures of feelings" (Williams, 1977): exhilarating happiness, boisterous pride, a rare sense of possibility, and collective feelings of victory. Retrospectively, friends of mine have described these years as a great party that never seemed to end. Others have told me about a heady feeling of being unbeatable. That these were sentiments in rare supply in late Mubarak Egypt—an era otherwise dominated by frustration, humiliation, and despair (see Ismail, 2012; Schielke, 2008; Sobhy Ramadan, 2012)—added to football's attraction and appeal.

The Egyptian football bubble also delineated distinctive emotional subjectivities. In her groundbreaking intervention, *The Cultural Politics of Emotions* (2004), Sara Ahmed teaches us how and why emotions so often interfere in processes of subjectivation. Feelings, claims Ahmed, are inherently "sticky" objects: "they move, stick, and slide. We move, stick and slide with them" (Ahmed, 2004:14). By this she means that emotions have a propensity to mark and accentuate boundaries between people—fearful vs. fearing, lovable vs. hated, crazy vs. sane—boundaries which habitually translate into gendered, racialized and classed distinctions between us and them, self and other. The collective effervescence surrounding Egyptian football performed a great deal of such boundary work in the late 2000s. Being a passionate football supporter came to index a successful and upbeat masculine normalcy which, while excluding its abnormal others, occupied a pivot of the national formation. The book's first chapter argues that this affective football state constituted an indispensable dimension of the social fabric in Mubarak's Egypt. Football demarcated both who the national male subject should (and should not) be and how he should (and should not) feel. Incidentally, the ethos and aesthetics of the normalized football subject—moderately Muslim, not overly intellectual, and somewhat brutish and chauvinistic—happened to be well in line with the public persona of President Mubarak and his two sons, Gamal and Alaa. As a result, football turned into an instrumental part of the regime's statecraft.[15]

And yet this most vigorous modality of power—a football politics operating through emerging structures of feelings and sticky emotional subjectivities—was by necessity a fragile one. The football bubble's affective pervasiveness would over time turn into a source of great weakness. To grasp the nature of this instability, William Mazzarella's book, *The Mana of Mass Society* (2017), is useful to consider. In this text—a historical exposé of social theory's struggle to account for "mana," i.e., vital energies and collective effervescence—Mazzarella returns, time and again, to an ambivalence inherent to the emotional-political. On the one hand, he writes, "mana appears as a name for the transcendent force guaranteeing a moral order" (Mazzarella, 2017:4); affect, as in Mubarak's Egypt, has an unmatched capacity to regulate collectives, carve out subjects, and sustain *"meaning that matters"* (ibid., 3, italics in original). On the other hand, mana "is also a mark of excess, of the super-natural, the sur-plus, the 'surcharge'" (ibid., 4); what cannot be properly confined and described is impossible to fully control. Thus, Mazzarella claims: "Mana, in one version, is the substance that holds worlds together and yet leaks out so as to blur the boundaries between one thing and the other. [. . .] Mana is [. . .] at once the palpable authority of canonical order and the volatile force that troubles order" (19).

This leakiness in the midst of emotional holding-together constitutes a keynote in the story of why the football bubble eventually deflated. Just as I argue that football feelings defined a particular Egyptianness that suited the Mubarak regime, I also suggest that it has been possible to re-emotionalize the nation and its subjects for oppositional, sometimes even revolutionary, purposes. Egypt's Ultras supporter movement constitutes the outstanding example. As I show throughout part II of this book, the Ultras groups cultivated a subcultural "emotional style" (Gammerl, 2012) from 2007 onward. This style consisted of new ways of relating to and feeling for football—novel fan practices, elaborate flags, fireworks, bold chants, and strict principles—that came across as modern and international, connoted fun as well as freedom, and appealed to large numbers of Egyptian youths. Posing a generational challenge to the affective statecraft promulgated by the football bubble, the Ultras fans found themselves persecuted by security forces and demonized by the football media. However, when revolutionary winds swept Egypt in 2011 and 2012, the old establishment's classist slurs no longer stuck. The Ultras not only turned into one of the revolt's most adored vanguards. For a moment, they also managed to redefine both what it meant to be an emotional-revolutionary Egyptian football fan and what should count as a progressive and respectable citizen in postrevolutionary Egypt.[16]

Finally, I should make clear that while this section has mostly discussed football's *emotional* politics, *Egypt's Football Revolution* is just as concerned with the politics of *affect*. Both the Mubarak era's football bubble and the Ultras' alternative emotional style rested on eclectic coming-togethers: on the one hand ideologies, symbols, and mediation; on the other hand materiality, infrastructures, and singular match events. The sensations that Egyptian football has propagated and politicized over the last few decades are thus neither clear-cut cases of culturally contextual, semiotic emotionality nor of the presymbolic, immediate intensities analyzed by scholars of affect. In fact, and as I describe in chapter 6, feelings for football most often take shape within emotional-affective *circulations*, encompassing infrastructures, spaces, discourses, media, match events, and habituated bodies, all at the same time. The attentive reader will find that I alternate between vocabularies of emotionality and affectivity in the chapters that follow. On occasions when the feelings discussed are particularly direct, I tend to describe them as affect; at other times, I speak about emotions. However, at no point do I insist on a strict distinction between the two. In this regard, my orientation is similar to that of a number of anthropologists and social theorists who in recent years have proposed a blurring of an emotions-affect divide that they, and I, find ultimately unproductive.[17]

FOOTBALL AND *SIYASA*

The emotional politics of Egyptian football is a kind of politics that is not confined to state relations, government institutions, and political parties and elections. The sport's political significance is instead broadly Foucauldian: a distributed power that molds affective-discursive genres and calls subjectivities into being; a politics that neither limits nor restricts nor hides the real world behind smokescreens, but instead constitutes Egyptian men as emotional subjects (see, for example, Foucault, 1977, 1978, 1980). At the same time, whereas Foucault analyzed a power that is dispersed to a point where agents *having* power become secondary, this is no doubt a book about actors acting politically. It depicts a range of men challenging or defending dominant fan practices and discourses. It delves into supporter groups claiming previously inaccessible virtual and physical spaces. And it accounts for club officials and journalists attempting to rewrite and resignify how supporters speak, act, and feel. Put simply, mine is a storyline replete with Egyptian football characters—friends as well as foes—who intervene in their own and others' affectivity and subjectivity to advance specific interests. It is by casting such a fairly traditional—we might call it Weberian or Schmittian—view of political action in a poststructural, emotional-affective mold that I am able to tell an overlooked tale about the role of football in Egypt's revolutionary transition.[18]

But my interest in the political goes beyond politics such as I happen to define it. My ethnography also attends to emic conceptualizations of *siyasa*, and to how conversations about phenomena rendered *siyasi* have interfered in the game's revolutionary and counterrevolutionary transmutations.[19] Given the time period considered, such an orientation has been indispensable; for if there is one thing that my interlocutors in Cairo all revel in, it is to talk about and problematize intrusions of football in *siyasa*, and vice versa. Especially in the months and years immediately after January 2011—a time when most aspects of the recent past were critically reexamined in Egypt—the history, sociopolitical function, and future of the national sport became a topic of unceasing evaluation. Many football people came to appreciate that the country's politicians (*siyasiyyin*) had not only groomed but also cynically exploited (*istaghall*) the ecstatic football hype of yesteryear. Retrospectively, the moment stands out as one of radical revelation. Suddenly, critical conversations about football and *siyasa* became commonplace among journalists, activists, and supporters alike.

To exemplify these discussions' themes and tonality, I momentarily return to the drama on 3 February 2006: to the *al-Salam 98* ferry disaster, which caused more than a thousand deaths, and to President Mubarak's decision to attend a football game the same night. The day's stark disparity—on the one hand, a devastating tragedy; on the other hand, triumphant festivities—has rendered it a memorable archetype. During field trips to Cairo five, ten, or twelve years after the event, countless people have told me the story about the awful calamity and the regime mobilizing national sports euphoria to gloss over its own responsibility. With time, the *al-Salam 98* episode has turned into an epitome of a football-mad era when affective manipulation was the unfortunate norm. As the public intellectual Yasser Thabet has documented, the late 2000s saw a whole series of political crises (*azmat siyasiyya*) diluted with football emotions. A trial of the ferry's owners—the wealthy Ismail family, one of Mubarak's cronies—was for instance scheduled on the same day as an Ahly-Zamalek derby match in March 2009 (Thabet, 2010:125–126). And as security forces were fighting back a huge strike at the textile plant in el-Mahalla el-Kubra in April 2008, the media were obsessing over the "betrayal" of the star goalkeeper Essam el-Hadary, who under turbulent circumstances was leaving al-Ahly for the Swiss club Sion (ibid., 128).

The Mubarak regime's purported misuse of the national game has sometimes been injected in a more extensive *longue durée*. As friends of mine like to point out, the Egyptians have for more than a century developed a particularly strong love (*hubb*) for football, giving way to a special chemistry (*kimiya*) between themselves and the sport. Because of its closeness to the hearts of the Egyptian people, my interlocutors claim, the game has *always* held the potential for political exploitation (*istighlal siyasi*). Indeed, Egyptian football histography suggests that most if not all of the country's modern rulers have used football feelings to divert people from politically sensitive issues. The British colonizers used the sport to simultaneously distract (*ilha'*) and humiliate (*idhlal*) the subjects (Tawfiq, 2010:53); the corrupt and flamboyant King Faruq to "drag the people [. . .] away from what happened in his royal palace or in the lands of Palestine" in the aftermath of World War II (Tawfiq, 2010:54);[20] and Gamal Abdel Nasser's military-led regime, which invested heavily in sports and propped up a football boom in the 1960s, to diffuse more authentic political antagonism with stirred-up passions for al-Ahly and al-Zamalek (al-Mistakawi, 1997:164–170; Tawfiq, 2010:59–68).[21]

Now, what we see here is of course a pervasive vernacular discourse on football as an "opiate of the masses." In post-2011 Egypt, most people are acutely aware that their leaders used to exploit the game as a way to vent emotions. The happiness (*farha, sa'ada*) that football engenders is understood to have acted as replacement (*badil*), drug (*mukhaddarat*), or concealment (*taghyib*) of more pressing concerns. My friend Mahmoud expressed this sentiment well in the book's opening vignette: "Football can be dangerous, Carl. This people loves football very much."

At the same time, these clichés often come with a twist. There also exists a strong conviction that the game is an addiction that the people have been able to *overcome*. "I think the Egyptians have finally woken up from that weird, passionate football dream," my journalist friend Amro Hassan told me in spring 2012. "Football is done with (*al-kura khalas*), people can now see the real world, and football cannot trick them to look the other way anymore," sports journalist Tarek Mourad explained during a March 2013 interview. These snippets of quotes exemplify an atmosphere of sober reawakening, which was especially prevalent during the revolutionary period (2011–2013). Because of the uprisings, many Egyptians felt that a progressive national project had been restored after thirty years of regression and emotional football manipulation. Football as an addictive drug or cunning replacement for the Real might have spoken volumes about the past, but it made much less sense in the present. In fact, I often heard people say that the causality had been reversed. Many would argue that the revolutionary struggle had now *replaced* their former passions for football.

If the book's first aim is to explore the emotional politics of Egyptian football over the last three decades, the second is to examine *siyasa* as an ethnographic category at this moment of revelation and revaluation (see Candea, 2011). How, I ask, have supporters, club officials, and sports journalists in Cairo talked about and felt *siyasa* inside and around Egypt's national game before as well as after January 2011? How can such conceptualizations, perceptions, and experiences be contextualized and historicized? What role did they play in the country's revolutionary process? One overarching objective is to demonstrate that debates about the sport's *siyasa* have been interwoven with and deeply implicated in the larger emotional-political football story that I am also telling: how such discourses *evaluate* subjectivities, *discredit* particular initiatives and projects, and *impede* feelings for the game that they at the same time describe. In other words, Egyptian fans' reflections about the game's politicization (*tasyis*) do not just chronicle political developments past and present. Critical accounts about football and *siyasa*—or about football being (or not being) *siyasi*—have also worked *performatively* and by extension *politically* in accordance with *my* usage of that term.

The terms "politics" and "the political" of course evoke an intricate conceptual legacy. Within political theory, broadly defined, towering figures from Carl Schmitt (2015), Max Weber (2005), Michael Oakeshott (2006), and Hannah Arendt (2006) to Antonio Gramsci (2011), Michel Foucault (1980), Jacques Rancière (2004), and Wendy Brown (1995) have all weighed in on a conversation about how the discipline's foundational concepts should be defined, analyzed, refined, and thought anew. Needless to say, I make no attempt to intervene in this conceptual debate through my anthropological research. Nor do I seek merely to extend political science's limited conceptions to purportedly nonpolitical fields (see Candea, 2011:310–311). My ethnography of emic notions of *siyasa* pertaining to football in Egypt is not primarily concerned with what politics *is* or *ought* to be, but with a specific Egyptian genealogy that has informed how my interlocutors think, discuss, and experience the political. The argument that I will make is essentially the following: the question of what *siyasa* is and is not has long been a contentious one in Egypt. The term lacks a well-established definition; what actions, actors, institutions, and emotions should or should not be labeled *siyasi* is inherently uncertain and persistently questioned, contested, and debated. At the same time, most Egyptians approach *siyasa* as something troubling. The political might be experienced differently by different actors and in different contexts, but a general antipathy is almost always present. Phenomena rendered *siyasi* are instinctively understood as entities that one should stay away from. *Political* actors are by default suspicious: self-centered, divisive, and not concerned with the common, national good. To be considered *mish siyasi* (nonpolitical; not related to politics) or someone who *maluhsh fi siyasa* (has no interest in politics; apolitical) is by contrast a virtue. Consequently, when distinctions are drawn between the political and the nonpolitical, these delineations tend to have emotional-political effects.[22]

In the sequence of chapters, the problematic of *siyasa* first surfaces within the hysteria surrounding two World Cup qualifying matches between Egypt and Algeria in November 2009 (chapter 2). Especially as Egypt lost the decisive second match and failed to qualify for the World Cup, strong voices were raised describing the sport as a cause of exaggerated fanaticism, divisions, and intrigues. At the heart of these debates was a revelation of problematic imbrications between football and *siyasa*. The football criticism unearthed a deep-rooted contradiction between political initiatives forwarding *partisan* interests and the historical constitution of Egyptian nationalism as a valorized, progressive, and self-evidently *unitary* project. In November 2009, many fans realized that the immense popularity football had enjoyed in the recent boom years had rested on a tacit but ultimately untenable assumption about the national game being neutrally nonpolitical. Now, the same football nationalism was widely dismissed as "lazy," "divisive," or "vulgar." In short, the national sport appeared to be *siyasi*. And so the affective bubble that the game had brought together began to fall apart.

The 2009 Algeria games unleashed something, but it was only the beginning. In the wake of the January 2011 Revolution and the stadium tragedy in Port Said in early 2012, conversations about the national game's politicization intensified further, along the revelatory drugged-but-sober lines accounted for above. The immediate context was now Egypt's (counter-) revolutionary transition, a period, it is crucial to stress, that was saturated with acrimonious antipolitical sentiments. For many young working-class men who fought the security forces in the streets of Cairo, the true revolution was embodied, highly immediate, and thus by definition not "political" (Ryzova, 2020). Among middle-class activists, politicians, and journalists, the struggle at hand was perceived as an axiomatically national one carried out by the whole Egyptian people for the common good (see Agrama, 2012:224–235; Sabea, 2014; Schielke, 2015:191–216; Schielke, 2017; Winegar, 2016). One consequence of this premise was that all political leaders with ambitions—Islamist, radical, military, or reactionary—ensured their nationalist credentials and *apolitical* intentions. *Siyasa* based on factional demands (*matalib fi'awiyya*) and personal interests (*masalih*) was widely dismissed (see, for example, Makram-Ebeid, 2014; Shenker, 2016).

I will argue that this antipolitical atmosphere impacted directly on the power struggle that raged over Egypt's national sport. The Ultras supporters' challenge to the establishment might have been an emotional-political one, but the battles were often lost and won over the question of whether the fans should be considered *siyasi*. While the Ultras themselves always insisted that their actions and campaigns were located outside of *siyasa*, however defined, establishment actors depicted the young supporters as self-centered and merely fighting for their own, *political* demands. As spelled out in part II, the male subjectivity of the Ultras took a 360-degree turn between early 2011 and summer 2013: first the young men were widely dismissed as rowdy and partisan thugs; then the supporters became heralded as respectably nationalist and revolutionary-masculine role models; later they once again came across as self-serving, vulgar, and a threat to national stability. All things considered, the story of the rise and fall of Egypt's revolutionary Ultras highlights a paradox hovering over the Egyptian Revolution: the socially enforced imperative of shunning *siyasa* and retaining an apolitical aura for any actor aspiring to a say and a role on the national-political stage.

Finally, the revelation that Egyptian football had been exploited politically also impacted millions of ordinary (non-Ultras) fans. The Port Said massacre in particular ushered in a sense of gloom and crisis that continues as this book goes to press. Part III examines lived experiences of *siyasa* in this moment of affective detachment. From 2011 to 2013, *siyasa* took many shapes in the lives of my interlocutors: on the one hand, discourses about football being or having been *siyasi* prevailed; on the other hand, there was a feeling that "political" events, rhythms, and uncertainties were ever-present. When this proliferation of *siyasa* intruded in times and spaces that had previously been reserved for sports, it became difficult for Egyptian football fans to stay in touch, emotionally, with the national game they had used to love. At the same time, international matches and football as a recreational game remained relevant. As these activities were perceived as "just football"—neither national nor political—troubling questions were never asked. The labeling of a phenomenon as *siyasi*, then, might be detrimental for its emotional charge. The Egyptians' deep-seated unease over *siyasa* has rendered football somewhat irrelevant and toothless as an emotional-political force.

AN EVENTFUL SETTING

To call the first few years of the 2010s a uniquely eventful period in Egypt's modern history is an understatement. The wave of popular protests that erupted on 25 January 2011 was merely a spectacular beginning. Between the fall of President Mubarak in February of that year and the counterrevolutionary summer of 2013, the Egyptians would witness a full election cycle,[23] two constitutional referenda,[24] the dissolution of parliament by the judiciary, a presidential declaration limiting the powers of said judiciary, numerous cabinet reshuffles, and a military coup enjoying significant popular support. After the presidential elections in the summer of 2012, executive power was transferred from a military council to the Muslim

Brotherhood-affiliated President Muhammad Mursi, only to return to the army a year later. Large and small demonstrations, strikes, and sit-ins were legion in streets, squares, and workplaces all over the country. At regular intervals, protests developed into bloody clashes between demonstrators, police, and military forces. With thousands of people killed and many more injured, violence and martyrdom turned into all-too-common facets of everyday life.

It is important to emphasize that the bulk of the developments this book examines unfolded during these eventful two and a half years. It is also important to stress how and why this setting mattered. The game's emotional politics—as well as conversations about football, emotions, and *siyasa*—were fundamentally transformed as a result of, and in tandem with, the revolutionary period's dramatic events. The reinvigoration of a national-revolutionary project on Tahrir Square in early 2011 and the wholesale revaluation of the Mubarak era that ensued *dampened* emotions for football clubs and enthusiasm for former heroes. The clashes on and around Muhammad Mahmoud Street in November and December 2011 *shifted* public opinions vis-à-vis male protesters, among them the Ultras fans. The election of President Mursi in June 2012 *emboldened* the same fans. These critical events and many others were instrumental in plunging Egypt's biggest spectator sport into its worst crisis since the war years in the late 1960s and early 1970s.[25]

It is useful to think of this revolutionary-political context as what David Scott would call an "exceptional time" of "radically condensed contingency" (Scott, 2014:33-65). Just like the Grenada Revolution (1979–1983), which constitutes Scott's object of analysis, Egypt in 2011–2013 exemplified a revolutionary moment of "crisis and dislocation in which human action, in its capacity to intervene, [stood] out starkly against established patterns" (ibid., 34).[26] Within the world of Egyptian football, this exceptionality implied that circumstances were volatile and important matters were at stake. As contingent events proliferated and unpredictability reigned, the discursive-material ground beneath the sport shifted constantly. Previously unthinkable spaces were opened up for exceptional actors to change worlds.

And yet momentous moments of revolutionary politics have not been alone to influence the national game's trajectory. One reason why football makes such a rich and evocative research topic is precisely that it *expands* conventional understandings of 2011 to 2013 as an epitome of exceptional eventfulness and *recasts* perceived ideas of what constitute truly decisive historical events. After all, a host of football-specific events have mattered a great deal too. A number of these events—the Port Said stadium massacre in February 2012 and the demonstrations and court cases that followed it are all good examples—have already been included in mainstream narrations of Egypt's revolutionary process.[27] Other critical occasions, such as the Africa Cup victories in 2006, 2008, and 2010 and the loss to Algeria in the 2009 World Cup qualifier, are likewise well known and spectacular, although their timing and character have rendered them parts of a different set of stories (e.g., Rommel, 2014; Thabet, 2010; Tawfiq, 2010). Still other more mundane occurrences—league and cup matches watched at stadiums or in coffee shops, pick-up matches played in a square—have not been given much scholarly attention at all (but see Hussein, 2011; Rommel, 2018a).

My research seeks to contemplate this multitude of events—pertaining to football as well as to (counter-)revolutionary politics—along the same line of vision. Tracing links between a multiplicity of contingencies over several decades, I provide an integrated narrative that interrogates, on the one hand, the role of football events in Egypt's revolutionary transition and, on the other hand, how revolutionary events have imbued the world of football. Events—of all scales and kinds—add indeterminacy and open up hitherto unseen futures. A popular uprising might spoil a long-standing affective buildup on a whim. An unfavorable match result could turn debates about the values and sociopolitical function of sports inside out. A stadium massacre might irreversibly transform young men's experiences as football-loving and political subjects. In this sense, my story about football feelings and football politics both unsettles the timeline of Egypt's so-called revolutionary transition and poses questions about what should count as contingent events, exceptionality, ordinariness, and agency. A heightened, multifaceted, and nested eventfulness is both a context that frames my account and an actor propelling my emotional-political narrative forward.

THE ANTHROPOLOGIST AND THE FIELD

This research project constitutes the culmination of a life-long passion for football as a game, spectacle, and world unto itself. For some thirty years now, I have been a devoted supporter (the club of my heart is IK Sirius, Sweden), a compulsive media consumer, and an aficionado of fan cultures and stadiums. In the second half of the 2000s, I spent a year and a half in Cairo just as Egypt's fervent football hype peaked, and the way the game's presence seemed to be everywhere—in coffee shops, in the media, in everyday conversations, and in popular culture—made a lasting impression. Plain and simple, I had never visited a place as football-mad. A couple of years later, this experience formed the nucleus of a proposal for doctoral studies in social anthropology. The emotionality of the game, I was convinced, constituted an obvious but also original entry point for an ethnography of everyday masculinity in Cairo.

My graduate studies at SOAS, University of London, commenced in October 2010. Less than four months later, revolution shook Egypt, and my field site transformed beyond recognition. My initial fieldwork in Cairo was conducted during twenty exceptionally eventful months from August 2011 to March 2013. It has been followed by several longer and shorter research stints between 2015 and 2019.[28] Throughout this period, rupture and crisis have often seemed the only true constants. The predictable, everyday rhythms of football matches and tournaments—so dominant in the pre-2011 Cairo that I first knew—have receded to background noise at best. Instead, I have followed in real time as interests in, feelings for, and conversations about Egyptian football have faded away, transformed, and, more recently, slowly recovered.

To write a classic anthropological monograph in a timeless ethnographic present has under these circumstances never been an option. Instead, I have envisioned my project as what Jean and John Comaroff would call a "historical ethnography": an anthropology of the emotional politics of Egyptian football that combines interrogations of the past with studies of the present, and which seeks to illuminate "how realities become real, how essences become essential, how materialities materialize" (Comaroff and Comaroff, 1992:20).[29] This ambition has translated into a methodologically eclectic and inherently multi-sited field research. When possible, I have joined friends watching their favorite teams play at Cairo International Stadium, at Burg el-Arab Stadium outside Alexandria, or at smaller stadiums elsewhere in Cairo.[30] I have also watched hundreds of televised football matches in coffee shops (*ahawi*; singular, *ahwa*). In the first half of 2012, I was a regular in one *ahwa* in Cairo's centrally located neighborhood Abdeen, where I met many of my closest interlocutors. In Abdeen I also played football myself in a large square. Moreover, between 2011 and 2013, I frequented demonstrations, sit-ins, and manifestations organized by the Ultras fan groups in different parts of Cairo. Finally, friends and interviewees have brought me to many official spaces with ties to the sport: the Egyptian Football Association's headquarters on el-Gabalaya Street, al-Ahly and al-Zamalek's club premises, the Division for Youth and Sports at Cairo Governorate, and the sports desks of some of the country's biggest newspapers.

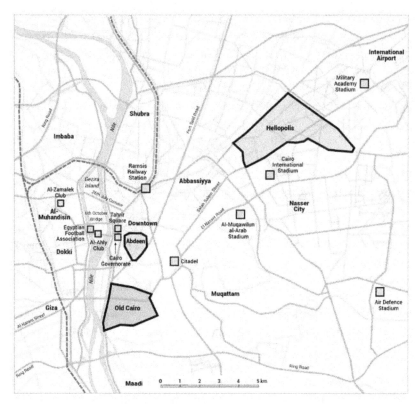

Fig. 0.1. Cairo's football geography and my main field sites. Map: Philippe Rekacewicz.

To make sense of football feelings, discourses, and events that are not just fleeting and shifting but disappearing or no longer existing, I have supplemented participant observation with extensive media analyses,[31] newspaper archives, football-themed feature films and pop songs, and Arabic-language secondary literature.[32] Such a media-heavy research design has been indispensable. Egyptian football media actors—especially star pundits on satellite television—need to feature as key protagonists in any story about Egyptian football in recent decades. Furthermore, through daily media consumption and archival studies over nine years, my knowledge of past and present Egyptian players, clubs, matches, goals, and incidents has expanded exponentially. As I learned the hard way in the initial months of my fieldwork, there are literally hundreds of references that one must master to partake in a meaningful way in discussions about Egypt's national game, its media, and its history.[33]

That being said, the lion's share of my ethnographic material has been provided by the wide range of football people whom I have met in Cairo. Since autumn 2011, I have conducted more than fifty long sit-down interviews with football journalists and writers, club officials and bureaucrats, players and coaches, and Ultras and more ordinary supporters.[34] While I met most of my interviewees only once or twice, some have turned into acquaintances, and a handful have become close friends. With time, a number of primary circles of interlocutor-friends crystallized: the *ahwa*-owner Sayed, his waiter Abdu, Abdu's brother Muhammad and their friends in Abdeen; Mahmoud, who works at the gym that I used to frequent; Hamada, a pharmacist and passionate *Zamelkawi* from Old Cairo (*masr al-qadima*); the journalist Amro Hassan and his former colleagues at the football website FilGoal.com; and a group made up of people who know Mido, a member of Ultras Ahlawy (Ultras fans supporting al-Ahly) from the upscale neighborhood Heliopolis (*masr al-gadida*). Mido has been my most important gatekeeper to the exclusive world of the Ultras. He introduced me to the hierarchies and history of the groups, and he explained the rationales behind their various tactical moves. Between 2011 and 2013, I also met regularly with Muhammad, a member of al-Zamalek's Ultras White Knights, the Ahly Ultra Shadi, and Sherif Hassan, a journalist who has written extensively about the group. In the chapters about the Ultras, material from these personal relationships is supplemented by press sources, secondary literature,[35] social media activities, and participant observation at matches, demonstrations, and other public events.

My interlocutors stem from a variety of socioeconomic backgrounds and many different parts of Cairo, but they all have one thing in common: all are men. This one-sidedness has been all but unavoidable. In Egypt, it is presumed (by men and women alike) that the national game constitutes a strictly demarcated "male preserve" (Dunning, 1986; see also Besnier, Brownell, and Carter, 2018:143–151). Football is overwhelmingly played by male players, supported by male fans, and covered by male-only football media. Supporter organizations, such as the Ultras, are exclusively male milieus (see Ibraheem, 2015:42–47). Egyptian media might love to point out that girls and women also play the game (Hakim, 2019) and that women have taken part in celebrations after national team victories since the mid-2000s (see, for example, *al-Misri al-Yum*, 15, 16 November 2009). Still, the percentage of female players and spectators remains extremely low, and in coffee shops where people gather to watch games on television, it is zero. Most certainly, there are thousands of Egyptian girls and women out there who follow football fanatically in their homes, although, unfortunately, these locations are inaccessible to an unmarried male researcher like me. Be that as it may, not a single one of the Egyptian women I know considers herself particularly interested in football.[36] For men, on the contrary, it is all but mandatory to support either al-Ahly or al-Zamalek.

Given this overwhelming gender bias, it cannot be stressed enough that I will tell stories about *male* phenomena and *male* developments. When I describe how football provides a space to define and contest the Egyptian nation, it is a male version of the nation that is being delineated. On occasions when football constitutes a battleground between different emotional-political subjects, the subjects at stake are masculine by definition. If football accentuates experiences of and debates about *siyasa*, these are all male experiences and debates. It is also striking to note how often unease over politics surfaces as a masculinized problematic. As we will see, what Egyptian football people fear is not necessarily *siyasa* per se, but its materialization in suspicious male figures: the fanatical fan, the vulgar television pundit, the rowdy football Ultra.[37]

CHAPTER OUTLINE

This book contains seven ethnographic chapters, divided into three parts. Part I, called "Bubble," takes on emotional football politics in the latter half of the Mubarak era. The first chapter traces the Egyptian football bubble's scaffolding and inflation. Depicting first how a national football boom came together in the late 2000s—through money, media, pop culture, and victorious teams—I then move on to the bubble's emotional-political effects: the positive feelings it elicited, the masculine subjects it defined, and how football became a central part of the regime's statecraft. Chapter 2 focuses on two frenzied World Cup qualifying matches against Algeria in 2009, a critical event which constituted both the peak of the bubble and the moment when it began to burst. The chapter highlights how the loss in the second match initiated a wave of criticism of football as *muta'assib* (fanatical) and *siyasi* (political). As a result, the sport's national status and emotional-political function were seriously in question a good year before 25 January 2011.[38]

Part II, "Ultras," consists of three chronological chapters about the Ultras supporter movement. Egypt's spectacular Ultras fans have gained a lot of scholarly and journalistic attention over the last decade. The young men's unique dedication, their strict principles and discipline, their radical aesthetics, their capacity to mobilize thousands of young men at an instant, and their brave fights with security forces before and during the January 2011 Revolution have been examined in great detail and from a variety of angles.[39] Taking a somewhat different approach, one primary objective of part II is to include the emotional politics of these relatively new supporters into the longer story about the inflation and deflation of the Egyptian football bubble. Another overarching aim is to highlight how discourses circulating about the Ultras' "politics" have impacted directly on the fan groups' actions, projects, and existence.

Chapter 3 deals with the period from the establishment of Egypt's first Ultras group in 2007 until January 2012.[40] It examines the fans' unique emotional style and demonstrates how it came to pose a serious challenge to the affective statecraft of the football bubble. Initially, the Ultras constituted a somewhat marginal phenomenon, although after January 2011 their style was increasingly accepted and appreciated, and football took center stage in the revolutionary struggle. The role of the Ultras on the national-political stage became even more prominent in the year that followed the February 2012 Port Said massacre, a period elaborated on in chapter 4. Zeroing in on a spectacular campaign for justice and football reforms launched by al-Ahly's biggest Ultras group, it illustrates how Ultras Ahlawy momentarily managed to evade classist slurs about thuggery to take control over developments inside Egypt's national game. In particular, a balanced employment of violence turned the football fans into masculinized, revolutionary role models. And yet, as I make clear in chapter 5, it did not take long for this respectable masculinity to once again become problematized. The subjectivity of the Ultras transformed fundamentally at the time of the Port Said court verdicts in winter 2013, and it continued to appear problematic in the years of counterrevolutionary resets that followed. Altogether, part II tells a rise-and-fall story that mirrors the Egyptian Revolution more broadly. One thing that its ethnography highlights repeatedly is the imperative yet nearly impossible feat of keeping a strictly nonpolitical profile on Egypt's national-political scene.

The theme of part III, "Aftermath," is football in the wake of the 25 January Revolution and the Port Said tragedy. My ethnography here changes gear as well as scale. The larger emotional-political contests accounted for in parts I and II are left behind; instead, the perspective is more personal, spotlighting how and why emotions for football were reconfigured among a handful of interlocutors between 2011 and 2013. Chapter 6 concentrates on how and why one close friend of mine lost his ability to feel for football in an era dominated by various kinds of *siyasa*. Paying attention to shifting discourses, occasions, rhythms, and expectations, I suggest that phenomena experienced as *siyasi* had many affective-structural similarities with football in the recent past. As such, the two realms overlapped in numerous ways; football emotions were recurrently compared to, and overshadowed by, political sensations. However, as chapter 7 shows, some kinds of football remained unscathed throughout this period of crisis. Shifting the ethnographic focus to televised football from Europe and football as a recreational game, I argue that these football practices stayed emotionally charged, because they were considered "just football" and "mere entertainment." In contrast to the bursting football bubble, nobody considered these activities part of the national sport; they were thus nonpolitical by default and not affected by the ongoing revolutionary transformation. The two chapters in part III provide ethnographic substance and nuance to tensions that have long existed between Egyptian nationalism and *siyasa*. It illuminates when the political does or does not arise as a problem, how it is experienced, and why it has had such wide-reaching effects on the national game's popularity and appeal.

The book's ending is twofold. The conclusion pulls out bridging arguments about football's emotional politics and *siyasa* as a perennial problematic, and suggests how my research contributes to scholarships on sports, revolutions, and contemporary Egypt. I also argue that my research about *siyasa* as a lived experience can help us understand why the immensely popular and strictly *nationalist* Egyptian uprising could not effectively mobilize around radical demands understood to be "political." The postscript continues the story to the time of this writing. Its ethnographic emphasis is on the revival that Egyptian football has witnessed between 2017 and 2019, a surge linked closely to Egypt qualifying for the 2018 World Cup in Russia, the Egyptian player Mohamed Salah turning into one of the global game's very brightest superstars, and Egypt hosting the 2019 Africa Cup of Nations. I also note that the era has been characterized by a deep ambivalence. Lessons from the recent past, I argue, make current attachments and debates markedly different from those of the football bubble that encapsulated Egypt prior to 2011.

PART I

BUBBLE

CHAPTER 1

Normal Nationals
and Vulgar Winners

*Consent is made possible, not through some abstract process of
"internalization," but by shaping appropriate and reasoned
affect, by directing affective judgements, by severing some
affective bonds and establishing others, by adjudicating what
constituted moral sentiments——in short, by educating the
proper distribution of sentiments and desires.*

Ann L. Stoler, "Affective States"

On a hot afternoon in June 2012, I met for the first time with Amro Hassan
in an upmarket coffee shop in Cairo's Nasser City neighborhood. Now
serving as a correspondent for the *Los Angeles Times*, Amro had previously
worked as a journalist at the Egyptian football website FilGoal.com. Over
the following years, he would become a dear friend. It was just a couple
of weeks before the runoff of the presidential elections, and much of our
conversation revolved around the prospects of either the Muslim Brother,
Muhammad Mursi, or Hosni Mubarak's former prime minister, Ahmed
Shafiq, becoming Egypt's first postrevolutionary president. While not particularly enthusiastic about Mursi, Amro was more worried about Shafiq
coming into power. He feared that much of the past eighteen months of
change for the better in Egypt—politically, socially, and in terms of "mind-
set"—would be turned back to the "old ways of the Mubarak era" that he
despised. Asked to elaborate on what he detested about how Egypt used to
be, Amro began to talk about a "suffocating bubble," within which everyone had had exactly the same preferences:

> I tell you how it was. It was a bubble and we all lived inside it. When
> I was in school, Amr Diab [an Egyptian pop star] used to come out
> with a new album every summer. All sixty million Egyptians would

buy and listen to this album the whole summer, and they would all like it, even before it was released, since Amr Diab, he was like a music god. I didn't, so I was considered crazy. There was no difference in opinion. You *are* crazy. It's not a matter of preferences or taste. If you don't like Amr Diab, it's something really wrong with you. You should get yourself checked. It was the same with movies, television series, ambitions. When I was that young and I tell someone that my ambitions were to study abroad and then try to live abroad, everybody was always like: "Go to Europe? You're not gonna make much money there." And I would be like: "I just want to go there and live there." And they would go: "No, no, no, the best place in the world if you have money would be Egypt. You should become an engineer, because that is the good proper job for all of us. Then you go to the Gulf and make some good money there, and then you'll come back and be the king of Egypt with the money that you have." Among my closest group of friends, nine out of eleven became engineers. The other two became police officers.

We ordered another coffee. Then Amro continued:

Inside this bubble, football became a crucial part, especially with all our successes in the last decade. Everyone was supposed to support the team that was winning, whether it was al-Ahly or al-Zamalek, and everyone should cheer for the national team like crazy. [. . .] If [Shafiq] comes to power he'll do everything he can to re-create this fake bubble of football games, Amr Diab, Adel Imam [a famous Egyptian actor], the television series in Ramadan, the summers in Marina [a posh beach resort on the North Coast]. [. . .] All of this was part of the same politically nondangerous bubble of the former regime. It's no coincidence that all famous artists—*all of them*—as well as our football players were against the revolution. They all want Shafiq. The bubble was their heaven. They were supported, they were praised, they reached a sort of stardom that they would never have dreamt of considering their talents. It was all connected to each other: football, music, television, and business. It made people dream of the same things, aim for the same things. We all dreamt of being singers or football players.

Amro's experience of the Mubarak era as a homogenizing bubble surely resulted from his particular social background—"just slightly above middle class"—his journalistic profession, and his age (he was born in the early 1980s). Even so, his depiction would resonate with many of the Egyptian men I know. Contrasting the past to the dramatic political and social developments that have unfolded after 25 January 2011, another good friend, Abdu—a waiter and gym receptionist from the Abdeen neighborhood— has often talked about the prerevolutionary period as stagnant and "without any movement at all." Half-jokingly, he once told me that during his youth there was not much in life but "boredom, football, Rotana [a Saudi television channel showing music videos], and drugs (*mukhaddarat*)." In a similar vein, Egyptians from all walks of life would insist that "everyone" (meaning all Egyptian *men*) was obsessed with football in the late 2000s. "There wasn't much going on in those days," Mahmoud, the *Zamelkawi* gym instructor mentioned in the introduction, once explained, "but we had football. We all talked about football, all the time."

The notion of the late Mubarak era as a football-crazed bubble sits at the heart of part I of this book. The way I have come to mobilize the metaphor may have drifted away from Amro Hassan's original intentions. Still, his portrayal of the pre-2011 nation as a peculiarly sealed-off social space where everything was "connected to each other" remains crucial to my inquiry.[1] In this chapter, my concern is with how the Egyptian football bubble came into being and how it gained emotional-political resonance. The initial sections describe how a new "professional system," a substantial influx of indirect public funding, new media infrastructures, popular-cultural productions, a talented generation of players, and unprecedented success on the pitch gradually fell into place in the 1990s and early 2000s. My analytical vision is here broadly Latourian. I picture the bubble as a social assemblage of qualitatively distinct mediators—humans, symbols, objects, and texts—that all mattered, and which worked on and off each other (see Latour, 2005).

This perspective on the bubble's constitution imbues my understanding of its affect and political effects. During its boom years, football brought together individuals, infrastructures, and discourses that together composed what Ann L. Stoler would call an "affective state" (2004). As the latter parts of the chapter show, the Egyptian football bubble fostered a compelling and appealing "redistribution of sentiments" (ibid., 6) that permeated the nation, circulated thrills in the midst of hardship, and defined how normal Egyptian men should—and should not—behave, talk, and feel. Between 2006 and 2010, Egypt's national game was located at the very center of the national formation despite, or perhaps because of, its masculine, victorious, and vulgar aesthetics. The sync between this successful-and-chauvinist national normality and the ethos of President Mubarak and his family rendered the sport a highly political affair. Allowing Hosni, Gamal, and Alaa Mubarak to partake in a buoyant, normalized, and victorious version of the national community, the affective football bubble turned into a key component of the regime's statecraft.

A NEW PROFESSIONAL SYSTEM

In June 1990, the Egyptian national football team participated in the World Cup in Italy. After a promising 1–1 draw versus Holland, the team failed to score in their remaining two matches—a dull 0–0 stalemate with the Republic of Ireland and a 1–0 loss to England—and Egypt was consequently one of eight countries to return home after the group stage. It was the first time since 1934 that the national team had qualified for the tournament, and interest was enormous throughout Egyptian society: friends of mine—some were not older than five or six at the time—are still able to recall exactly where and with whom they watched the games in 1990. Even today, thirty years later, many Egyptians remember in detail the collective ecstasy when Magdi Abdelghani scored Egypt's one and only goal from the penalty spot in the Holland game.

The 1990 World Cup is widely considered the beginning of the modern era of Egyptian football. When meeting fans, sports journalists, and club officials in Cairo, I have made a practice of asking what my interviewees deem the most important developments in the sport's history. Almost without exception, their answers begin with the summer of 1990. Whereas many people argue that the World Cup shaped sentiments for the sport for a whole generation (see Tawfiq, 2010:37–42), some point to a more specific transformation. Upon returning from Italy, the immensely popular national team coach, Mahmoud al-Gohary, convinced the Egyptian Football Association (EFA) to introduce a professional system (*nizam al-ihtiraf*), which was implemented when the league restarted in the autumn. In retrospect, this reform stands out as a crucial catalyst, simultaneously liberating Egyptian football from its amateur past and propelling it into the future. In an interview at the sports desk of the state-owned evening newspaper *al-Masa'* in March 2013, the senior sports editor Tarek Mourad recalled the transition with some nostalgia:

> After the wars [against Israel] in 1967 and 1973, there was a football crisis in Egypt. All the big stars of the Nasser era had retired. So in

the 1970s everything was small-scale and the players were young. In the 1980s, this generation grew up. Personally, I think they were the best we ever had: Hassan Shehata, Mustafa ʿAbduh, Farouk Gaafar, and Mahmoud al-Khatib. [. . .] You know that this was when we began to win titles in Africa? And at the same time, these players had morals and manners [*ikhla' wi sulukiyyat*]; the fans loved them; the atmosphere at the stadiums was great. [. . .] It changed a bit in the 1990s when the professional system arrived. But at the same time, it was of course the system for the future [*nizam al-mustaqbal*].

According to Mourad, the professional system set off a "fundamental change in the very concept of football and of the player. [. . .] The commitment of the player was no longer primarily to the club and the color of the shirt, but to the constitution of his monetary contract." Egyptian football clubs had previously only paid their players "result-based bonuses (*mukafa'at*), which didn't make anybody rich"; now professional players were suddenly entitled to "monthly salaries (*murattabat*), which turned our footballers into wealthy celebrities." In combination with spiraling transfer fees, the increasing salaries changed the economics of the game beyond recognition.[2] Although money had been a key concern for Egypt's football clubs already in the days of amateurism, it had been possible to launch competitive campaigns on a relatively small budget. Surely, al-Ahly and al-Zamalek had been by far the most consistent clubs prior to 1990. But smaller teams with local fan bases—al-Ismaily, al-Mansoura, al-Tersana, or al-Masry—had always known that a particularly talented generation of youth, or a tactically ingenious coach, could be enough to beat the odds and grab a surprising league or cup title. As the dynamics of professionalism took full effect in the latter half of the 1990s, such upsets became increasingly rare.[3] Drastically boosted revenue streams were now a necessity merely to stay afloat.[4]

For Egypt's biggest club, al-Ahly, rising costs did not turn out to be a problem. In the 1990s and 2000s, the club signed a series of lucrative sponsorship contracts, primarily with companies in Egypt's telecommunications sector. According to my *Zamelkawiyya* friends, these deals were by and large a result of corruption (*fasad*), made possible thanks to the position of al-Ahly's president between 2002 and 2014, Hassan Hamdy, who was chairman of the state-owned advertisement agency, al-Ahram Advertising. Others—above all *Ahlawiyya*—rather viewed their club's appeal among sponsors as a reflection of its superior market value, in turn a consequence of al-Ahly's famous stability, principled nationalist ethos, and great popularity.

Be that as it may, there is no doubt that al-Zamalek's sponsorship deals were not able to match those of its great rival. Cairo's second-largest club instead found itself forced to look for alternative revenue streams to stay competitive. Explanations as to how permanently crisis-ridden al-Zamalek has managed to finance their expensive players in the professional era are manifold.[5] Yet most Zamalek fans I know accept that the club has been bankrolled by its often very wealthy presidents. As my *Zamelkawiyya* friends bitterly accept and concede, however, these revenues have been neither large nor steady enough to properly compete. As is painfully evident from al-Ahly's dominance on the football pitch, al-Zamalek has not been able to keep up with al-Ahly financially since the onset of the professional system in the early 1990s.[6]

Al-Zamalek was not the only Egyptian football club to become dependent on donations from wealthy businessmen-cum-fans as the costs for players' salaries increased. As Yasser Thabet has documented, all of Egypt's famous clubs have at times been presided over by business tycoons channeling private assets into the football teams (Thabet, 2010:251–262).[7] But private subsidies from elected club presidents on limited tenure are unlikely to yield long-term financial stability. A lost election is all it takes for the money to dry up. Consequently, as Thabet noted during a May 2012 interview, it was really only al-Ahly and (to a lesser extent) al-Zamalek with their huge fan bases that were able to permanently meet the inflated monetary demands that professionalism put on Egypt's football clubs. In the 1990s, the two Cairo clubs signed all the best talents in the country, and the gap between them and smaller clubs from the provinces widened significantly. By the early 2000s—the decade when the Egyptian football bubble really inflated—this process had produced a clear outcome. The dominance of al-Ahly and al-Zamalek was more comprehensive than ever before in the stands and on the pitch as well as in the mass media.

A GOVERNMENTAL PRIORITY

The professionalization of Egyptian football, spurring widening financial inequalities, is congruent with a continental trend. Commercialization and privatization have translated into similar scenarios in many parts of sub-Saharan Africa in recent decades. It is generally acknowledged that neoliberal policies and structural adjustment after the 1973 oil crisis incited this development. Government-owned companies and institutions, which had previously funded many of Africa's best football clubs, were now either privatized or significantly weakened financially (Alegi, 2010:104–114; Hawkey, 2010:205–211). The withdrawal of the state opened up space for men of fortune either to take control of already existing community-based clubs, or to establish new one-man show football enterprises; a growing number of Africa's dominant clubs came to rely on the patronage of Big Men (Pannenborg, 2012). Just as in the Egyptian case, this dependence on individual owners bred instability, power struggles, and increasing divides between haves and have-nots. As more and more players migrated and fans shifted their allegiances to clubs in England, Italy, or Spain (Akindes, 2011), the popularity of domestic leagues fell sharply (Alegi, 2010:106–112; Pannenborg, 2012:35–41).

In a few important regards, however, Egypt's professionalization departs from the general African trajectory. Al-Ahly, for one, has been able to reinforce its position as the country's, and arguably the continent's, biggest football club through lucrative sponsorship deals rather than by digging into the pockets of wealthy owners. The Egyptian game also displays unique features with regards to the ownership of its top division clubs. In the last decades, historically prominent "popular clubs" (*andiyya sha'biyya*: membership-based clubs with popular support), such as al-Mansoura, al-Tersana, and Baladiyyat el-Mahalla, have vanished from the top tier; in their stead, financially strong "company clubs" (*andiyyat sharikat*) with no or very few supporters have emerged. The new teams are outgrowths of the social clubs that Egyptian enterprises and government agencies have long run to provide employees and their families with recreational facilities and spaces.[8] From the 1970s onward, a handful of these clubs increased their expenditures on football teams dramatically. The teams advanced quickly through the league system: before long, company clubs found themselves competing at the top of Egypt's and Africa's club tournaments.[9]

Football clubs run by companies or state bodies proliferated even more in the late 1990s and early 2000s. According to Ahmad Saied, chief editor at FilGoal.com between 2008 and 2014, the development was a logical consequence of Egypt's professionalized football economics. In a spring 2012 interview, he explained:

> When professionalism was introduced in 1990, prices spiked and football turned a bit commercial. Initially, the money came from basic sponsor deals, nothing huge, and millionaire fans, like the owners and chairmen of British clubs. [. . .] This was the case in every popular club: al-Ahly, al-Zamalek, al-Ismaily, al-Masry from Port Said, and al-Ittihad from Alexandria. [. . .] At this time, our

football league had fourteen teams: al-Muqawilun al-Arab belonging to a company, the rest, thirteen popular clubs. [. . .] Then at the end of the 1990s, it started to shift towards companies, because when money started to kick in really big, individual businessmen couldn't afford it anymore. So, clubs like ENPPI [a government-owned engineering contractor in the petroleum sector] went up [to the top division]; clubs belonging to the military went up.

Why could company clubs afford the spiraling costs if millionaire owners could not do it? One reason is found in the legal frameworks that regulate Egyptian sports clubs. As Ahmed Abdel Satir, a football reporter at the newspaper *Ruz al-Yusif*, explained in an interview, Egypt's popular clubs are closely tied to the Ministry of Sports.[10] Not only is the minister entitled to appoint a portion of each club's board members, but as it is prohibited for clubs to separate their budgets for football activities and social activities, it is not possible for private investors to invest in football teams "like in any other business." According to Abdel Satir, this legislation has made Egypt's membership-based popular clubs financially dependent on the goodwill of the state, both in terms of direct state support (which has dwindled since the 1990s) and in that state-appointed board members have to approve any plan for external financing. Indirectly, the same law has benefited clubs run by companies. Operating under a different law, Egypt's company clubs are not subjected to the same degree of political interference. The restraints on budgets are also more lax for clubs that are not based on membership. As only a relatively small fraction of the companies' significantly more extensive turnover is earmarked for their football teams, expenses on players and coaches can be adjusted more or less irrespectively of the revenues generated by the actual sports activities.

The development in the 1990s and 2000s toward financially strong company clubs with less governmental control always contained a peculiar paradox: a majority of the mushrooming *andiyyat sharikat* were in fact owned by Egyptian state entities. The last Premier League season before the fall of President Mubarak provides a telling example. Of the sixteen teams that participated in the 2010–2011 competition, three belonged to the military, one to the Ministry of Interior, two to companies controlled by the Ministry of Petroleum, and two were part of other government-owned companies. Among the remaining eight teams, two were run by private enterprises, leaving only six member-owned, popular clubs of the type that completely dominated the scene before 1990. Most of the fans and journalists I know would consider this a pattern of ill-concealed state support for the national football industry. When we met in 2013, Tarek Mourad at *al-Masa'* summarized the development:

> During the 1990s, the general level of Egyptian football dropped when small clubs lost their biggest stars to al-Ahly. Here, the state entered the picture and opened the door for clubs belonging to ministries and companies. The Ministry of Petroleum got into football with ENPPI and Petrojet; the Ministry of Defense opened the door for Tala'i' al-Gaysh, Haras al-Hudud, and al-Intag al-Harbi, and the Ministry of Interior entered with al-Shurta and later al-Da-khiliyya. The introduction of these clubs led to a type of balance [*nu' min al-tawazun*], since these clubs had great financial power and the ability to keep their stars. [. . .] The state paid hundreds of millions of pounds for this, to assure the level of the players, which had collapsed in the 1990s, when al-Ahly monopolized everything. [. . .] They did this to ensure that there was a proper competition, because without competition in the league, the level of players and the national team cannot be sustained.

With hindsight, it is easy to see that this extensive state sponsorship constituted a fundamental pillar of the national football boom that Egypt witnessed in the last years before 2011. The influx of hundreds of millions of Egyptian pounds ensured proper competition in a league plagued by financial inequalities, and it allowed a whole generation of Egyptian players to continue playing in Egypt instead of making their money abroad.[11] The growing involvement of the Egyptian state is even more striking when contrasted to the dismantling of government involvement in the sport, which unfolded in other parts of Africa. While the new money significantly raised the level of the Egyptian league and the Egyptian national team, the *relative* lift compared to sub-Saharan Africa was hence even more pronounced.[12]

In later sections of this chapter, I will elaborate on how this competitive edge translated into a variety of emotional-political effects in the period that I have called the Egyptian football bubble. For now, let me note that the configuration of this funding dovetailed with the character of the Mubarak era's neoliberal crony capitalism. As scholars such as Timothy Mitchell (2002), Ulrich G. Wurzel (2009), and Samer Soliman (2011) have argued, the neoliberal reforms that the regime began to push through in the late 1980s did not solely stimulate privatizations and shrinking government. What most of all characterized Egypt's neoliberal experiment was rather a "merger of the old (military-technocrat-bureaucratic) state class with the class of regime-connected big businessmen" (Wurzel, 2009:119), in parallel with a process of "fiscal fragmentation" of the state itself (Soliman, 2011:54–75). Whereas the regime prioritized the security sector (in particular the Ministry of Interior) and certain domains within the "propaganda machinery" (cultural productions and the state media apparatus), other state institutions were neglected and obliged to raise "their own" revenues. Not surprisingly, some sectors were more successful at this than others. The Egyptian military, for example, controlled a vast industrial empire that generated enormous surpluses. Similarly, for state bodies in control of rentier incomes, such as companies owned by the Ministry of Petroleum, bringing in revenues would never pose much of a problem (ibid.). Given the character of this fragmentation, it is hardly a coincidence that the state-controlled football clubs that flooded the Egyptian league were bankrolled by either the prioritized Ministry of Interior or wealthy, self-funded government sectors such as the military or the Ministry of Petroleum.[13] Just as it is symptomatic that the military-led Nasser regime brought football into the orbit of the Egyptian Army and used the sport as a vehicle in its ambitious pan-African project (see Di-Capua, 2004), the contribution of cash-rich governmental units to the financial scaffolding of the Egyptian football bubble closely mirrored the Mubarak regime's financial-political infrastructure.

A NEW FOOTBALL MEDIA LANDSCAPE

The influx of state resources significantly boosted the quality of the Egyptian Premier League in the early years of the 2000s. Following a decade when the league (at best) had been a two-horse race, moneyed company clubs provided al-Ahly and al-Zamalek with new sparring partners that sharpened the league's overall competitiveness. But the new revenues did not manage to draw the masses to Egypt's football stadiums. The propagation of governmental clubs totally devoid of fans, at the expense of popular clubs with local support, resulted in many matches being played at all-but-empty stadiums. Ahmad Saied at FilGoal.com and Tarek Mourad at *al-Masa'* were among those lamenting this development when I interviewed them. In the 2000s, both journalists made clear, the only chance to experience the vibrant atmosphere of a crowded Egyptian stadium was either at international fixtures or on the few occasions each season when two of the handful of surviving popular clubs faced each other.

Even so, the emptiness at Egypt's football stadiums did not equal an atrophy of engagement. On the contrary, in the years leading up to January

2011, football arguably played a more dominant part than ever in Egyptian men's lives, although they engaged with it in front of radios, newspapers, and television sets more than in the stands. A number of shifts within Egypt's (sports) media landscape fueled this development. As late as the end of the 1990s, the Egyptians' consumption of football media had looked more or less the same for over three decades: fans followed the game via terrestrial television, radio broadcasts, and state-owned newspapers.[14] In the early 2000s, though, Egyptian media as a whole developed rapidly. Following deregulation measures of the industry and the launch of the Egyptian satellite Nilesat 101, private newspapers and satellite television channels emerged (Halabi, 2015; Sakr, 2013:325–326). The new satellite television channels (*fada'iyyat*)—typically owned by crony capitalists loyal to President Mubarak—soon recognized the financial potential that the country's most popular sport presented. The transformation that followed was swift. Already by the mid-2000s, private satellite television had taken over as Egypt's most influential football media platform.

Egypt was by no means the only country to experience such shifts. About a decade earlier, liberalized television markets and new pay-to-view business models had caused a veritable explosion of the market for televised live sports in Europe and the United States (see, for example, Besnier, Brownell, and Carter, 2018:178–180). The rise of football television in Egypt was similar but also distinct. First, the emerging Egyptian media sphere was always a national one. Lacking the financial muscle to challenge channels operating from the Arabian Gulf in the rat race for international broadcasting rights, Egypt's *fada'iyyat* directed their attention almost solely to domestic football: al-Ahly, al-Zamalek, and the national team. Second, the monetizing of the market was hampered by a law granting the state-owned Egyptian Radio and Television Union (ERTU) a monopoly of the "signal" (*ishara*) of all matches in the Egyptian League and Cup. Somewhat ironically given the overall social politics of the era, which forced Egyptian citizens to pay for more and more state services, the ERTU claimed that it was the inalienable right of all Egyptians to watch domestic football free of charge. In contrast to European leagues and the World Cup that were locked into pan-Arab pay-to-view networks in the 2000s, Egyptian football tournaments thus continued to be broadcast for free on private national television channels.

The broadcasting rights that the ERTU put on the market were initially relatively affordable. The journalist Sherif Hassan, a longtime colleague of Ahmad Saied at FilGoal.com, recalled in a 2012 interview that before the market "took off" in 2007 and 2008, the price for broadcasting the Egyptian League was approximately 1.5 million EGP per season. In those years, three satellite channels and terrestrial state television showed the games, leaving the clubs in the league with total revenues of approximately five million pounds per year. In the last three years before January 2011, prices skyrocketed. In autumn 2011, to mention one example, the EFA demanded 160 million EGP for the rights to broadcast the 2011–2012 season (Ahmedhassan17, 2011).[15] The booming prices reflected a rapidly surging demand; by the end of the 2000s, Egyptian football television had become a highly lucrative business. Numerous channels devoted more and more programming to football, and a handful of football-only satellite channels even came on the air. Because of the ban on pay-to-view, however, the business model that had proved so profitable in Europe since the early 1990s could not be replicated. Instead, all revenues had to be raised from advertising.

This particular constellation of infrastructure, popularity, competition, and legislation resulted in a uniquely Egyptian type of football television that defined a whole era. Doing all they could to keep people watching for as long as possible, the channels centered programming on extensive pre- and postgame studio analyses (*studio tahlil*), supplemented by up to six-hour-long talk shows that mixed football results with populist politics, scandals, and light entertainment. While also featuring telephone call-ins from players, coaches, and fans, the shows' most characteristic feature was a monologue by a star host who, seemingly without any script or time constraints, discussed the latest trade rumors, the everlasting financial crises in al-Zamalek Club, and al-Ahly's latest victories. Although lengthy talk shows have been widespread throughout Egyptian private television since the early 2000s (see Sakr, 2013; El Khachab, 2016), these programs stood out for the way they turned football into such an all-encompassing topic. As Ahmad Saied put it in an interview, the best way to understand the business model of Egypt's sports channels might not be as football journalism, but rather as a type of sensation-seeking "tabloid TV," to which "football games only matter in so far that they provide the opportunity to make more tabloid content and sell more advertisements."

Regardless of their most appropriate label, the football talk shows were immensely popular in the last years under President Hosni Mubarak, and they constituted a fundamental component of the football bubble encapsulating the country. In parallel with other booming media genres such as political talk shows (Sakr, 2013), reality television (Kraidy, 2010), and media platforms tied to the Islamic revival (Moll, 2010; Hirschkind, 2006), the football *fada'iyyat* circulated a variety of pervasive debates, emotions, and sensibilities across the Egyptian nation. Millions of men of all ages watched and discussed the shows each day with friends and family. One of my closest friends in Cairo, Mahmoud—the *Zamelkawi* gym instructor—has in recent years often pondered on his intense relationship to football in general and football television in particular before 25 January 2011. He once described his earlier dedication in the following terms:

> Shalaby's and Shoubair's [Medhat and Ahmed; two famous talk show hosts] shows were what everyone talked about before the revolution. We all watched them: at home, at work and in the *ahwa* [coffee shop]. I didn't really like their style, but to be honest, I cared a lot about what they said. I got very angry when they insulted al-Zamalek, and I loved when they made fun of al-Ahly. It's strange to think of it now, but they were very big. Very important people.

THE WINNER TAKES IT ALL

By the second half of the 2000s, most components required to turn football into a nationwide emotional-political bubble were in place: a new type of financial scaffolding, based on rentier incomes and the wealth of the military's business complex, rendered the league the most powerful in Africa; stadiums had been renovated in preparation for the 2006 Africa Cup of Nations; a booming private satellite-television industry disseminated the sport through everyday spaces, quotidian discussions, and popular discourse. To fully grasp the immense impact that football came to exert in the final years of the Mubarak era, however, the Egyptian teams' outstanding international performances must also be factored in. The financial and infrastructural strength of the league constituted a precondition for the impressive results. But, as anyone who knows the game will understand, money and infrastructures alone could never guarantee that al-Zamalek and al-Ahly would bring home five African Champions League titles between 2001 and 2008, and certainly not that the Egyptian national team would win three consecutive Africa Cup of Nations in 2006, 2008, and 2010. At each of these occasions, the team's strongest opponents fielded players from the top leagues in Europe. In 2008, for example, Egypt outclassed an Ivorian side including Didier Drogba, Salomón Kalou, and Kolo and Yaya Toure in the semi-final before defeating Cameroon, featuring FC Barcelona's superstar Samuel Eto'o, in the final. The Egyptian squad, by contrast, was heavily dominated by players from the local league.

A generation of extraordinarily talented players, born in the late 1970s and early 1980s, were instrumental in turning Egyptian football into this unstoppable winning machine. Athletes like Muhammad Abu Treika, Mohamed Barakat, Ahmed Hassan, Amr Zaky, Essam el-Hadary, and Hosny Abd Rabo, whose careers all peaked in the late 2000s, were a unique group. From an African perspective, it is intriguing to note how many in this golden generation spent the best years of their careers in Egyptian clubs; among the handful of players who tried their luck abroad, many failed to make their mark and soon returned home to al-Ahly or al-Zamalek.[16] The relatively high salaries in Egypt was one reason for this tendency. Another, several friends and interviewees have insisted, is the well-known "fact" that Egyptians never really feel at home anywhere else in the world, and that there would be no point for an Egyptian to make money if he had no chance to show off his wealth before his friends in Cairo.[17] Be that as it may, a majority of Egypt's biggest football stars played together in al-Ahly during most of the 2000s. This unique concentration not only led the club to seven league wins and four African Champions League titles in ten years, but also may have helped the Egyptian national team establish its collectively efficient and organized style of play. Finally, it allowed the national team to run unusually long training camps prior to each big international tournament, since the EFA suspended the league for several weeks to prioritize the team's preparations.

Two other individuals must also be included in this unrivaled success story: Manuel José, al-Ahly's Portuguese manager in the periods of 2001–2002, 2003–2009, and 2011–2012, and Hassan Shehata, the national team coach between 2005 and 2011. Ahly fans can talk for hours about the changes that the club underwent after *Guse* (José) took over in the early 2000s. The Portuguese coach aligned discipline, training regimes, and diet with more professional standards that ensured al-Ahly's superiority in Egypt as well as on the African continent. For his part, Hassan Shehata's legacy was a mentality of never being satisfied with anything less than victory. Shehata's coaching star first rose as he led the Under-20 national team to great successes in the early 2000s. After winning the Egyptian Cup with the second division club al-Muqawilun al-Arab in 2004 (beating al-Ahly and al-Zamalek en route to the final), he took over the national team in 2005. His dominant and self-assured coaching style proved to be a perfect match with a talented group of players just entering their prime. Through deeds and ambitions, the two trainers thus both contributed to and incarnated Egypt's unparalleled football victories in the last years of the Mubarak presidency.

Egypt's famous string of victories was launched during the 2006 Africa Cup on home soil. Prior to this tournament, one friend of mine recalled, the national team had shown a frustrating habit of coming up short whenever it mattered the most. "We had an *'uqda* [knot, psychological complex]," he explained. "Especially when we played Arab teams from North Africa, they always beat us. Because of that, when we won our group ahead of Morocco in 2006, it was very important. We started to believe in ourselves. Everything changed, and we began to win important games instead of losing them. The team felt unbeatable, especially in 2008 and 2009."

While such an accumulation of triumphs might have enthralled any nation, it was perhaps especially potent in the Egyptian case. During the same Nasser City interview in which he first talked about football as a bubble, Amro Hassan drew parallels between the centrality of victory and a distinguishing feature of Egyptian football fandom. "The whole community here was raised on the fact that you should win everything you can," he told me. "So, let's just win in football, otherwise there's no point. You are not gonna waste your time watching a football team that is losing, even if they are playing well." In Hassan's opinion, this obsession with winning is why an overwhelming majority of Egyptian fans support either the most successful club, al-Ahly, or their only real competitor, al-Zamalek. In contrast to elsewhere in the world, where emotions tied to sporting losses bind communities together (Kelly, 2004; Swyers, 2007), supporting an underdog or a weaker local team neither makes much sense nor connotes any hipness or authenticity in Egypt. Here, perhaps even more than in other contexts, the lure of football *is* the lure of winning. It was above all this feeling of superiority that rendered the football bubble so attractive in the last years before 2011.

It should come as no surprise, therefore, that celebratory practices and discourses have come to epitomize the sport in those heady days. In retrospect, many Egyptians have singled out the huge street parties that swept Cairo after the three consecutive Africa Cup titles as emblematic of the immense attraction that the game enjoyed. Living in Cairo at the time of the 2008 tournament, I experienced firsthand the intensity and magnitude of the collective exhilaration. Back then—before I made Egyptian football the object of my research—I watched Muhammad Abu Treika score the decisive goal in the final against Cameroon in a packed coffee shop in the working-class district, Shubra. Later on, I followed tens of thousands of jubilant fans as they sang and danced their way downtown to Tahrir Square, where fireworks, honking cars, and waving flags filled the cold winter night until the early hours. At a time when even the most insignificant public gathering was tightly regulated by security forces, the sight of so many happy Egyptians of both genders and from all walks of life partying in the streets was remarkable. The night in the square seemed to prophesize that a different, more joyful, and less cynical national community was possible.[18]

At least as impressive as the nocturnal celebrations was the media's coverage in the days that followed. Satellite television broadcast hour after hour of footage and interviews, not only with players and coaches, but with ordinary citizens who filled streets and squares across Cairo and the provinces. The printed press published countless images, interviews, and commentaries from the festivities. In this way, the media both sustained the elated atmosphere and delineated the national community caught up in celebrations. Through a positive feedback loop, television and the press relayed, recycled, and extended the upbeat vibe for days on end, prolonging the event and bolstering feelings of a victorious nation and a nationwide football bubble.

As everyone who has attended a tense football game will know, similar but more short-lived circuits of reinforcing affect sometimes materialize at the stadium. Momentum might suddenly build between players and the home crowd, coursing like electricity between the stands and the pitch as pressure mounts against the visiting team. Football as an emotional spectacle relies on such dialectical circuits, and in Egypt they came in a variety of shapes and forms in the final years of the Mubarak era: short-term loops at some stage during a match, in the stands, or in front of a television set; medium-term waves during a particular tournament, built up collectively by optimistic media coverage, good results, and ever-increasing expectations among the general public; and long-term emotional momentum, amassed from the mid-2000s onward, by booming satellite television coverage, the succession of victories for the national team and al-Ahly, and politicians stressing the nationalist impact of the triumphs. Seen from this perspective, the Egyptian football bubble might have been scaffolded by infrastructure, money, and media, but it manifested primarily as an ever-increasing pile of jubilant parties and street celebrations. "Football was happiness and party [farha wi hafla] in those days," as my friend Abdu from Abdeen once put it, not without a hint of bitterness and nostalgia.

Needless to say, exhilaration was not the only emotion prevalent in Egypt in the late 2000s. As we recall from this chapter's opening, Abdu also remembered this time as stagnant, frustrating, and boring. He was not alone in recognizing these significantly less-upbeat structures of feeling. Considering the abundance of gloomy emotions and temporalities that saturated late-Mubarak Egypt—desperate humiliation and loss (Ismail, 2012), passive frustration (Sobhy Ramadan, 2012), hopeless boredom (Schielke, 2008), and undreamy pragmatism (Mittermaier, 2011:1)—it is the football bubble's ecstatic happiness that stands out as odd, surprising, and discordant. And yet, at particular times and in certain spaces, the sport's sentiments of victory and tempting possibility were also prominent, real, and highly accessible. The football euphoria ran beside the well-documented frustration, humiliation, and despair, and it turned the game into something like a joyful haven: a rare source of immediate pleasures paired with a prophecy for a better Egyptian society.

A BUBBLE FOR THE NATION'S NORMAL

The Egyptian football boom might have been embodied by the nation's successful teams and players, yet it was never only a matter of matches and results. In the first decade of the new millennium, the game recurrently overlapped with other domains of Egyptian popular culture. The Egyptian film industry constituted one interface: football figured in the plot of several movies; players appeared as actors in feature films; and movie stars were often present at the stadium. The hype around the national football team also revitalized a battery of nationalist songs that had been mainly associated with military victories. Tunes like "Yi habibti, yi masr" (Oh My Darling, Oh Egypt), "Bahibik yi masr" (I Love You, Oh Egypt), "Masriyyatna wataniyyatna" (Our Egyptianness Is Our Patriotism) and "Masr hiyya ummi" (Egypt Is My Mother) frequently played on television and radio before and after important matches. Furthermore, some of the Arab world's most famous pop stars recorded new patriotic songs that soon became very popular: "Law sa'altak inta masri, ti'uli eih?" (If I Asked If You Are Egyptian, What Would You Tell Me?), by the Lebanese superstar Nancy Ajram; "Masharibtish min nilha" (Didn't You Drink from the Nile?), recorded by Ajram's Egyptian rival, Sherine; and "Wallahi 'amiluha al-rigala" (I Swear, the Men Made It), sung by Hamada Helal.

In a book chapter titled "Every Epoch Resembles Its Heroes" (*kull 'asr yushbih abtaluh*), Muhammad Tawfiq reflects on these connections between football, popular culture, and nationalism. He argues that whereas earlier eras in Egyptian history had been personified by the likes of the academic Taha Hussein, the singing diva Umm Kulthum, or President Gamal Abdel Nasser, the most heralded heroes in Mubarak's Egypt were the country's football stars (Tawfiq, 2010:15–21). Celebrity media, music, and film turned players and coaches into role models for the nation. The mass celebrations that followed national football victories were widely portrayed as expressions of pure and authentic patriotism (ibid., 37–40). As a result, the sport turned into a main stage for anyone aspiring to fame and glory. Football was a social field where national subjectivities were at once visibly reflected, feverishly debated, concretely embodied, and mundanely practiced.

Depictions of football in Egyptian feature films shed instructive light on the national and male subjects that the game propagated in this period as well as how they changed over time. As Walter Armbrust (1996) and Lila Abu-Lughod (2005) have shown, mainstream Egyptian popular culture promoted a relatively coherent national ideal for more than half a century. In Armbrust's readings of films, television, and music from the 1930s to the early 1990s, this idealized modern and male Egyptian subject is characterized as middle-class in the making: an appropriate blend of rural, *ibn al-balad* authenticity (literally "son of the country"; for details, see El-Messiri, 1978), refined through urban modern education, without ever being *too* westernized or losing touch with his humble origins (Armbrust, 1996:25–29, 75–86, 95–105). Similarly, Abu-Lughod discerns what she calls a genre of "developmental realism" in many of the Ramadan television series she parses. In these shows too, the down-to-earth urban middle classes are valorized, and interventions to educate and morally reform the rural backwardness of Upper Egypt constitute a recurrent theme (Abu-Lughod, 2005:55–108).

Early football-themed Egyptian movies typically adhere to this recognizably modernist genre. Comedies from the 1980s—such as *Gharib fi bayti* (A Stranger in My House, directed by Samir Sayf, 1982) and *4-2-4* (Ahmed Fu'ad, 1981)—dramatize Cairo's football industry as a glitzy realm of quick cash, celebrity cults, and passionate ruses that the honest but somewhat naive *ibn al-balad* cannot resist. For players, spectators, and club owners alike, the game deflects rural and working-class men's attentions from education, the arts, or a morally sound family life. True to their era's developmental ideals, however, the films typically close by pointing to the progressive values that sports also potentially entail. By highlighting youth development, female care, or education, this early generation of Egyptian football movies suggests that football *could* be a productive force in the shaping of modern national men, albeit only after sweeping reforms.[19]

What particularly interests me here is how this portrayal of football exerting a baleful influence on men and morals is played down in films from the 1990s and 2000s. In movies from this period—the years just before and during Egypt's inflated football boom—the sport instead appears as a positive force for national unity. The 1994 blockbuster *al-Irhabi* (The Terrorist, Nadir Galal) is one good case in point.[20] In line with the developmental realist genre, the plot once again revolves around an uneducated man from Upper Egypt moving to Cairo. However, Ali, played by the mega-star Adel Imam, has not come to the capital to join the football industry. He is an Islamist extremist on a mission to execute a vicious terror attack. After assisting in the killing of a senior police officer, Ali is run over by a car and coincidentally taken care of in the home of a cultivated Cairene upper-middle-class family with three university-aged children. In a pivotal scene toward the end of the movie, the entire family, Ali, an intellectual (*muthaqqaf*) family friend, and the family's Coptic neighbor come together in front of the television to watch the national football team play a crucial World Cup qualifier. Initially, both Ali and the intellectual are resistant to the spectacle: Ali because of his fundamentalist beliefs, and the *muthaqqaf* because of the irrational fanaticism (*ta'assub*) he associates with the sport. But as the match progresses, their hesitation is gradually dismantled. After a decisive late goal, everyone in the living room celebrates wildly, and Ali even hugs the Coptic man he is meant to hate. The message is clear: the feelings of nationalist belonging brought forward by football are too strong to resist; they override differences of class, religion, gender, and generation. When the national team plays, everybody is simply Egyptian, and it is the game of football that makes this untainted national unity possible.

Al-Irhabi was but one of several movies representing football as a neutral, national sphere of emotionality in the final two decades that preceded January 2011. Over and over, the Egyptian film industry established that it was normal and natural for Egyptian men (and, to a lesser degree, women) to feel strongly about football and, by extension, their beloved nation. By the same token, men who did *not* care for the game—for example, religious extremists and the overly intellectual—were rendered marginal, even abnormal. Shunning football in this way became a narrative shorthand for eschewing the national collective.[21]

This distribution of normality and otherness no doubt exceeded cinematic representations. In an interview in April 2012, the football author Muhammad Tawfiq insisted that the only two groups of male Egyptians he could think of who (stereo)typically had *not* loved football in the pre-2011 era were "the sheikhs in the religious television channels, and the professors at the university." Amro Hassan told me something similar that day in May 2012 when he first talked to me about football as part of a bubble: people who did not like football (or pop star Amr Diab) had been considered "crazy." They needed to "get themselves checked." And yet, as *al-Irhabi* illustrates, even the oddest anti-sport deviant could not help but be carried away by the emotional force of momentous national victories. No Egyptian man was *that* abnormal. In addition to being a sphere of upbeat emotionality, victory, and possibility, then, the feelings propagated by the football boom constituted a neutral and largely positive center point for the Egyptian nation. All normal Egyptian men cared about the national sport. The football hype was a bubble for the nation's normal.

"MANY MEN WITH MONEY, BUT FEW WITH MORALS AND CULTURE"

Yet normalcy, victories, and elation notwithstanding, the Egyptian football bubble always included an inherent sense of ambivalence. To delineate this tension, the works of Armbrust (1996) and Abu-Lughod (2005) are once again helpful to consider. As mentioned, these scholars argue that Egyptian popular cultural productions have long idealized a particular modern Egyptian subject at the intersection of rural or working-class authenticity and urban-educated, cultural refinement. Even so, both Armbrust and Abu-Lughod also highlight a shift *away* from this middle-class balance since the late 1980s. Armbrust describes this transition as the rise of "vulgarity" in films lacking smooth endings. Narratives in which (morally) corrupt nouveau riche personas become filthy-rich and powerful, whereas hard-working, ordinary men stay poor and humiliated regardless of education, ambition, and conduct, proliferated in the 1990s (Armbrust, 1996:165–210).[22] Similarly, Abu-Lughod identifies a change in genre from "developmental" to "capitalist" realism in Egyptian television series. This adjustment, she suggests, is reflected in a dramaturgy that increasingly accepts consumerism, glossy lifestyles, and stardom as celebrated and sought-after ideals (Abu-Lughod, 2005:193–245). Both writers depict this shift as hugely popular with the Egyptian public. The audience may not have endorsed the new and grimmer depictions of society, but they appreciated the vulgar realism. After all, since at least the 1990s, many Egyptians have recognized that cunning indecency—not diligence and formal education—is what it takes to succeed in a society saturated with neoliberal reforms, labor migration to the Gulf, and widespread corruption (see also Schielke, 2015:173–179; Shechter, 2018).

A tension of the kind that Armbrust and Abu-Lughod describe starts to become discernible in football-themed movies from the years just before 2011. In contrast to the national-progressive and unifying work that the game performs in *al-Irhabi* and even as late as in *Ana mish ma'hum* (I Am

Not with Them, Ahmed al-Badri, 2007), more critical and distinctly vulgar depictions of the social world of sports now became common. The characters in *Wahid Sifr* (One Zero, Kamla Abu Zakri, 2009)—a tragic tale of a number of life destinies intersecting during the night when Egypt beat Cameroon to win the 2008 Africa Cup of Nations—showcases a spectrum of problematic subjectivities that football likewise encapsulated. A morally corrupt television presenter with alcohol problems runs a talk show before and after the game; a good-looking female singer with limited talent desperately tries to get her five minutes of fame by promoting her latest single live on television; doctors at a hospital forsake their lifesaving duties, since all they care about is the match; and all around the city, people are drawn into a sporting event that is shown to benefit only the already powerful and wealthy. In a similar manner as a number of slightly later productions,[23] *Wahid Sifr* alludes to the football bubble's darker facets: mass hysteria, a corrupt media industry, a noxious combination of hope and despair, and an idealization of victory at any cost.

The treatment of football in a film such as *Wahid Sifr* reflects how most Egyptians talk about the game in the period after January 2011. When I have asked friends of mine to describe what football represented before the revolution, the words used are not only "happiness" (*farha*), "party" (*hafla*), and "success" (*nagah*), but also "corruption" (*fasad*), "connections" (*wasta*), "remnants of the old regime" (*filul*), and *sububa* (which loosely translates as immoral grabbing for quick gains). More or less everyone involved—from players and coaches to people in the media and the millionaires and army officers who bankrolled the clubs—are understood to have embodied some, if not all, of these unflattering traits.[24] Among those succeeding within Mubarak's football business, there were "many men with money, but few with morals and culture," as my friend Omar—a kind-hearted father of two and passionate youth coach—once summarized it. He explained:

> The players were our heroes, of course, because of everything they won. We dreamed about being like them, even though we of course saw that their behaviors [*sulukiyyat*] weren't ideal. Now it's clear that this wasn't good. Especially the media, and all the money and politics. I don't think football will ever be as big and important again in Egypt.

In making his complaints about "many men with money, but few with morals and culture," I know that Omar was referring to a particular category of football men that for him, as well as for many other fans, epitomized

Fig. 1.1. Ahmed Shoubair hosting his talk show *Aqarr wi A'tarif* on the sports channel Modern, 29 July 2012.

the sport's pre-2011 bubble. The most emblematic manifestation of this sports masculinity was (and to a degree still is) found on Egyptian football television. The middle-aged men who populated the various studio programs and talk shows—immensely popular prior to 2011, but subsequently swept away by the game's popularity crisis—were generally referred to as *kabatin* (captains). Most often former players, these figures tended to sport pitch-black, obviously dyed hair, impossibly shiny suits, and heavy golden watches. In the late 2000s, a handful of them emerged as some of Egypt's most famous television personalities. Their contracts were worth millions of pounds per year.

The profile of two of Egypt's most (in)famous *kabatin*—Ahmed Shoubair and Medhat Shalaby—illustrate the personality in question. Each of them requires a brief introduction. Shoubair, a former Ahly and national team goalkeeper, started his career as a commentator on Egyptian state television. After a switch to private satellite television in the early 2000s, he turned into *the* mega star of the booming football media industry. In the late years of the Mubarak era, his immensely popular talk show changed networks several times. Yet regardless of platform, Shoubair remained famous and much discussed for his stern loyalty to al-Ahly as well as for his impassioned rants against adversaries in the clubs and the media as well as in politics. That he was a member of parliament for Mubarak's National Democratic Party between 2005 and 2010 is telling. He has always enjoyed close connections within the EFA (see Tawfiq, 2010:170–171).

In contrast to the irascible Shoubair, Medhat Shalaby owes his charisma to an eloquent wittiness. Unlike most of his colleagues, Shalaby is

Fig. 1.2. Medhat Shalaby on the talk show *Masa' al-Anwar* on the sports channel Modern, 25 September 2012.

not an old player but a retired police officer who began his media career as a humorous commentator. His constant smiles, benign jokes, and mild appearance notwithstanding, Shalaby's talk shows have always been known for a tough political line. A frequent and outspoken supporter of the Mubarak family as long as they stayed in power, he relentlessly promoted "stability" and law and order throughout the turbulent revolutionary years, and has continued to support those in power ever since. As many of my friends like to point out, Shalaby is, in this sense, not really a sports journalist. He is first and foremost a police officer, who for obscure reasons has been allowed to vent his reactionary opinions in daily monologues on prime-time football television.

Shoubair and Shalaby have constituted constant points of reference as friends of mine have tried to explain to me what football expressed and represented under Mubarak. The two pundits' characteristic appearance, political profile, and enormous media presence make them impossible to ignore as well as inevitable targets for scorn and criticism. Once when we met, Amro Hassan stressed that he "utterly despise[d] this rotten side of Egyptian football." For him, pundits like Shalaby and Shoubair had "destroyed the beauty of the game" and actively manipulated the audiences. And it was not only an issue of political opinions. What truly disgusted Amro was the football media's blatant display of the dubious values that they stood for. "It is not only that they were corrupt and rich and completely part of the politics of the former regime. They did not even try to hide their corruption, power and wealth! I mean, that was rather something they were proud of, the thing that made them popular!"

As Amro helped me understand, this masculinity at the intersection of wealth, victory, and superiority was paradoxically detested and popular at one and the same time. Similar to the vulgar and immoral characters that Armbrust (1996) identifies in post-1990s movies, the values that Shalaby and Shoubair represented were never truly loved. Still, their monetary success and unyielding ruthlessness awed and impressed; millions of viewers flocked to their programs. Furthermore, iterations of this vulgar masculinity were embodied by thousands of football coaches and supporters across the nation as well as by many of Egypt's best players. Most football stars enjoyed being part of the sport's great bubble. They gladly combined training and matches with a life of glamor, marrying pop stars and actresses, and frequenting celebrity parties in posh resorts along the North Coast. The prevailing masculinities that took shape within the Egyptian football bubble in this way reflected and promoted a multilayered constellation of success, national normality, and vulgar-chauvinist aesthetics. In spite of—or perhaps because of—this ambivalence, the sport developed into one of Egypt's all-dominant popular cultural spheres in the years before 2011.

THE BUBBLE AND THE MUBARAKS

President Mubarak's blatant efforts to form ties to the country's successful football teams have been thoroughly documented and much discussed. Writings on Egyptian football in the 2000s rarely fail to draw attention to the grand receptions, at which the president and the players celebrated each African triumph at the presidential palace "as sons with their father" (Tawfiq, 2010:75–81, quote on 75; Thabet, 2010:115–151). Moreover, as Muhammad Tawfiq has noted, summaries of Mubarak's achievements during his presidency have often confounded subject and spectator. Phrases such as "*the president* reached the World Cup [in 1990] and took five Africa Cup of Nations titles" are not uncommon (Tawfiq, 2010:76, emphasis added). When I interviewed Tawfiq in spring 2012, he provided another telling example. Following Egypt's third straight African title in Angola in 2010, he told me, every Egyptian television channel had showed images of the players celebrating in the dressing room together with the president's two sons, Gamal and Alaa. Exhilarated after the victory, they had all come together in a catchy, rhyming chant addressed to their father back home: *zay ma'al al-rayis, muntakhab masr kwayis* (Like the president said, the Egyptian national team is great).

Coverage in the state-owned weekly newspaper *al-Akhbar al-Yum* from the final week of the 2008 Africa Cup of Nations provides lucid exemplification of imageries and tropes applied in the press. The entire front page of the 9 February issue—the day before the final against Cameroon and shortly after Egypt's 4–1 thrashing of the favorites, Ivory Coast—was dedicated to the nationalist festivities sweeping the country, with President Mubarak depicted at the very center. Under a bold, over-sized headline stating "Oh our country, your sons will always be men" (*tul 'umr wiladik yi biladna . . . rigala*) was a large photo of the president and his wife, Suzanne, happily waving and giving the thumbs-up sign. The picture was surrounded by eighteen smaller photos of star players and coach Hassan Shehata in action during the match, the EFA president Samir Zahir, the president of the National Council of Sports, Hassan Saqr, and jubilant fans with flags and match shirts partying in the streets of Cairo. The page offered a patriarchal vision of a glorious nation: the leader and father-figure with his wife, his heroic player-sons, and the masses, all united in celebration after a momentous victory in foreign lands (see fig. 1.3).

In the same issue of *al-Akhbar al-Yum*, as well as in the special supplement released on 16 February to celebrate the triumph in the final, the newspaper consistently reiterated President Mubarak's importance for the team's performance. His telephone calls to the team in Ghana throughout the tournament were said to have raised the spirits of coaches and players (9 February); pictures of the celebrations at his palace after the team's return to Cairo filled several pages (16 February); the golden generation of players was described as "brought up in the spirit of the October war" (ibid.), i.e., the 1973 war against Israel, in which Mubarak famously participated as Commander of the Air Force. The 16 February supplement also included seven full-page advertisements, in which semi-private and state-owned banks, real estate companies, and travel firms offered their congratulations. In most of these ads, the first line of congratulation was directed neither to the players nor the coaches, but to "our leader, President Muhammad Hosni Mubarak."

Being a state-owned newspaper, it is likely that *al-Akhbar al-Yum* would be particularly prone to portray President Mubarak as intrinsic to the team's victories. Indeed, in the oppositional newspaper *al-Dustur's* coverage of the same Africa Cup, the focus was on players, matches, and tactics, and the tournament was depicted as a nonpolitical sporting event. Given these diverging press voices, it is difficult to assess with precision if, how, or to what extent the propaganda worked and was efficient. Did Egyptian football fans really perceive Mubarak's role in the football bubble as a leading one? Did they, like Syrians in Hafiz al-Assad's Syria, rather act "as

Fig. 1.3. The football-saturated front page of *al-Akhbar al-Yum*, 9 February 2008. The subheadings read "The throne of Africa is near" and "The Pharaohs are ready to hunt the Lions [Cameroon] after slaughtering the Elephants [Ivory Coast]."

if" they believed in the glorifying stories that circulated about the nation's leader? (Wedeen, 1999:67–86.) Did they not care much at all about the reporting? How, if at all, did the media's persistent association of football with President Mubarak grant the regime legitimacy and popularity?

One way to interrogate these questions is to look beyond the media's most blatant attempts to bolster the president's virtues while concealing his vices. For the extravagant—yet ultimately unbelievable—spectacle around Mubarak-the-leader was not the only aspect of football that worked to the regime's benefit in the five years before January 2011. In those years, Egyptian media also featured numerous narratives about the Mubarak family's *passions* for football, as fans as well as players. The president's oldest son Alaa's dedicated support for al-Ismaily Club, for instance, was instrumental for the down-to-earth image that he enjoyed at the time (Tawfiq, 2010:80–81). Similarly, when footage of the president's two sons playing five-a-side football with a group of friends in a Ramadan tournament circulated on television as well as on social media, it reconfirmed an image of the ruling family as in touch with the game's grass roots (see Thabet, 2010:148). The *al-Akhbar al-Yum* Africa Cup of Nations supplement from 16 February 2008 is illustrative also in this regard. On the first page, the paper's editor-in-chief, Mumtaz al-Qatt, reported on an exclusive telephone interview that he conducted with the president shortly after the final whistle. Al-Qatt wrote:

> I asked President Hosni Mubarak about his feelings at the moment when Egypt scored the decisive goal in the Africa Cup of Nations and he told me: "My emotions were like the emotions of every Egyptian citizen. I almost jumped off the chair and I could almost hear my heart beat. I raised my hand to praise God at a moment when millions were shouting the name of Egypt."

These less-bombastic stories of football and feeling add important nuance to the politics that the Egyptian football bubble exerted. As these narratives piled up, they carved out an image of the presidential family as ordinary, football-loving Egyptian citizens. In one sense, this was not an overly difficult feat; in terms of ethos, appearance, and persona, the Mubaraks were all-but-perfect incarnations of the not-too-intellectual, not-too-Islamist normality that the national sport propagated. And yet the mundanity of the reports made a difference. While extravagant receptions at his palace would inevitably associate the president with the football bubble's ambivalent-yet-popular aesthetics of vulgarity, stories of his and

his sons' untainted football passions evaded this moral gray zone. Anecdotes of this kind instead effectively connected the ruling family to the
much less ambivalent emotional registers of national normalcy that the
game put in circulation. At the stadium, on the pitch, or at home in front
of the television, the Mubaraks were, perhaps more than anywhere else, in
touch with their subject-citizens and the joyful national community that
football made possible. They were as passionate and dedicated as everyone else in those years when a victorious football bubble encapsulated the
Egyptian nation.

CONCLUSION: A VULGARIZATION OF POWER

In one chapter of his 2010 book *Life as Politics*, Asef Bayat identifies a peculiar difference between Iran and Egypt when it comes to the politicization
of the countries' youth. In Iran, shows Bayat, the generation coming of age
in the 1990s, in the wake of the devastating war with Iraq, was possibly the
most subversive that ever was. In the cities, drug consumption, wild parties, illicit sex, and Western music came together in a joyful youth habitus
that was everything the Islamic Republic abhorred. In Egypt, however, the
situation was the opposite. The ruling elites managed to foster a range
of benign entertainments and desires that captivated large sections of the
youth. Alluding to an unholy alliance between the notionally secular Egyptian state and Islamist revivalist tendencies, Bayat coins these respectable
and moderately religious amusements Hosni Mubarak's "secularreligious
state." It was epitomized by the Muslim pop-preacher Amr Khaled, an
immensely popular figure, who advocated a balanced message of "faith and
fun," self-responsibility, and charity as roads to moral and material fulfill-
ment (Bayat, 2010:115–136; see also Winegar, 2014).

As I have shown in this chapter, football constituted another popular-cultural phenomenon distributing upbeat yet ultimately nonsubversive
emotions in the late Mubarak era. Akin to the NGO's, youth centers, television sermons, and charities that Bayat discusses (2010:131–135), Egypt's
national sport accommodated dreams, aspirations, and desires within a
sealed-off emotional bubble assembled by money, media, popular culture,
and great success on the pitch. The normal masculinity that football propagated during its boom years at times overlapped the secularreligious block
that Bayat sketches. The Egyptian national team under Hassan Shehata
cultivated a distinctive Muslim identity that was highly compatible with
neoliberal ideals of individual self-fulfillment. And unlike more orthodox

sheikhs and preachers, Amr Khaled himself was a dedicated football player and supporter who enjoyed frequenting the same social circles as Egypt's football stars, sports pundits, and Alaa and Gamal Mubarak (Tawfiq, 2010:153–158). Due to its flirtation with vulgar aesthetics and a nonelitist normality, however, the football bubble was significantly more influential than pious preachers or neoliberal NGOs could ever be. As the sports hype peaked in the late 2000s, its structuring of feelings reached well beyond Khaled's upper-middle-class fans and followers. To properly understand Egyptian society and politics in the late Mubarak era, this "affective state" (Stoler, 2004) spawned by the national football industry needs to be considered too.

The affective football state encompassed much more than distraction and benign entertainment. In the last years before 2011, the sport inflated a bubble of affect and subjectivities that was both grand and alluring, and which became incredibly difficult to resist. In an ethnography about media and urbanism in northern Nigeria, Brian Larkin has illustrated how large-scale infrastructures acted as what he calls a "colonial sublime" during the British colonial rule. By this term, Larkin highlights the feelings of awe and powerlessness that glorious and exalting technological constructions, such as bridges and movie theaters, induced among the colonized subjects (Larkin, 2008:35–47). The big business, satellite television, stardom, and victories that assembled in the Egyptian football bubble had a similarly awesome, perhaps even sublime, function. It was one of few spheres in an otherwise dull and desperate historical present to be widely adored and revered, and which still glimmered brightly. In contrast to colonial Nigeria, however, Mubarak's football was not separated from the people; it did not shine down on the masses from an estranged and unattainable universe. By contrast, football in Egypt became politically potent because of the way it *appended* Mubarak and his family to its appealing world of nationalist normality and upbeat emotionality. The bubble spawned by the nation's successful football teams encompassed the people *as well as* the political regime. The mundane national football subjects conflated the ethos and aesthetics upheld by the president of the republic.

The emotional politics of football, then, hinged on a historically contingent bubble of affect and subjectivity, wherein the people partook spontaneously, side by side with their masters. Political scientist Achille Mbembé has written extensively about this modality of power in postcolonial Africa. Identifying a trend he calls the "vulgarization of power," Mbembé suggests that since the 1980s, rulers and ruled have come to occupy one and the same "episteme" and a shared set of aesthetic codes. At one point, he writes:

To my mind—and in fidelity with the Latin origins of the term *vulgus*, which refers to the crowd, or throng—"vulgarity of power" [is] meant to allude to the cultural and political "work" (*travail*) by which State power "comes down to the level" of the greatest number of people [. . .], becomes "down-to-earth" (*terre à terre*); spreads the knowledge of itself and its habits, renders them accessible to a society (1992a:129).

These sentences capture the essence of the Mubarak regime's exercise of football statecraft. By staking out what Mbembé calls a "master-code" and an "imaginary of an époque" (1992b:2) shared by the ruling family and millions of ordinary Egyptians, the football bubble formed a rare realm of unity between the citizenry and an otherwise widely unpopular regime. While the state as the "organizer of public happiness" (Mbembé, 2001:31) played a part in this process (recall the extravagant spectacles at the Presidential Palace), media reports about Mubarak and his sons playing the game and cheering like "any other citizen" were at least as influential. After all, what football first and foremost made legible and sustained was a peculiar emotional normality that harmonized with a victorious version of the Egyptian nation. In so far as President Mubarak and his family were understood to be congruent with this structure of feeling and subjectivity, the bubble provided the president with a platform to join the celebrations of the people, of the country, and in effect also of himself. At a time when it was utterly difficult to find any other social phenomena in the country to point to as exemplary, football thus became a nodal point of the regime's hopes and aspirations.

And yet this down-to-earth state power, tied to the nation's most popular sport, was not without risks. As I have indicated, the aesthetics that the Mubarak family shared with the football bubble were not only immensely popular: they also connoted troubling vulgarity. In addition, the sport's popularity was dependent on an extraordinary string of successes that in the late 2000s seemed never-ending. As the next chapter will illustrate, these contingencies would eventually force the bubble's burst. The process was initiated when Egyptian football encountered its most painful backlash, at a stadium outside the Sudanese capital Khartoum, in November 2009.

CHAPTER 2

Fanatical Politics and Resurging Respectability

It is commonplace that violence erupts between fans at football games, but what happened in Khartoum far exceeds football violence. The Algerian Air Force planes transported thousands of armed Algerian thugs to Khartoum and assigned them with one particular mission: to assault and insult Egyptians.
Egyptian author Alaa al-Aswani, *al-Shuruq*, 24 November 2009

Laziness is the most appropriate rubric for the state of nationalist revival around football. For it is a nationalism that does not demand anything from you.
Egyptian intellectual Hani Shukrallah, *al-Shuruq*, 21 November 2009

On 14 November 2009, the Egyptian national team played Algeria at home in the final round of the qualifications for the 2010 FIFA World Cup. With the qualifier group extremely tight, the stakes were high and absolutely clear: if Egypt won the match by three goals or more, they would be going to South Africa the following summer; a two-goal win for the Egyptians would leave the two teams deadlocked in terms of points, goal difference, and head-to-head results, forcing an unprecedented replay on neutral soil; all other results would send Algeria to the World Cup. The buzz around the game was by all measures enormous. In the Egyptian daily newspaper *al-Shuruq*, the national football team had already been a leading story for several weeks; on match day, the paper devoted sixteen out of twenty-four pages solely to football. Several articles recalled episodes of tension and violence that in recent decades had surrounded Egypt-Algeria matches.[1] Readers were also reminded that although Egypt had won the last two

Fig. 2.1. The Egyptian player Ahmed Eid Abdel Malek and fans celebrate Emad Moteab's last-minute goal against Ageria at Cairo Stadium. Photo: Reuters/Goran Tomasevic, 14 November 2009.

Africa Cups of Nations and made an impressive display in the Confederations Cup the previous summer,[2] they had failed to qualify for the last four World Cups. For the current, beloved generation of players, the tournament in South Africa was likely the last chance to get the international recognition they so well deserved. Consequently, as the newspaper's front page plainly stated, the match that evening was the most important in the history of Egyptian football.

The magnitude of the occasion was apparent in more than just the bombastic press coverage. When the Egyptian Football Association (EFA) released the match tickets a week in advance, they sold out within hours, and riot police were called in to disperse the agitated crowds. For the lucky ones who managed to get a ticket, the fight in the queue could prove lucrative; tickets were soon sold on the black market for up to a hundred times the original price (*al-Shuruq*, 8, 12, 15 November 2009). The buildup in the final days was extraordinary: Egypt's biggest football satellite channels coproduced a one-off, twenty-four-hour studio show; President Hosni Mubarak paid a visit to the team's training camp; the Coptic Pope Shenouda III prayed for a good result in the Sunday mass. In the hours prior to kickoff, a mix of Quran recitations, Sufi-inspired prayers, and nationalist songs ensured that the sell-out crowd at Cairo Stadium was at a boiling point (*al-Shuruq*, 15, 17 November 2009; Thabet, 2010:159–160).

As the match got under way, it did not disappoint. Egypt's Amr Zaky scored a first goal early on, but although the home team put the Algerians under intense pressure for the ninety minutes that followed, creating a vast amount of chances, frustration turned to despair as it looked like the second goal needed was not meant to be. But then, in the ninety-fifth minute—deep into injury time—a final opportunity appeared: a fine cross from the right back Sayed Moawad, was followed up by a precise header from striker Emad Moteab. As the ball found its way into the bottom-left corner of the Algerian goal, Cairo Stadium erupted with some of the most ecstatic jubilation ever witnessed at any football arena.[3] In the following days, the media could not get enough of footage and articles establishing the game and its aftermath as *the* occasion for national, all-Egyptian celebrations and success. Men and women, young and old, rich and poor, Muslims and Christians, everyone was out in the streets that night, coming together—as political analyst Wael Qandil expressed it—in a "hug of national unity" (*al-Shuruq*, 16 November 2009; see also *al-Misri al-Yum*, 16 November 2009).

Egypt's two-goal win was of course no all-out victory. As mentioned, it was merely enough to force a decisive play-off. A few days later, the same two teams thus faced each other again, this time in Omdurman outside the Sudanese capital Khartoum, in an even more feverish show-down. It is no exaggeration to say that these two football matches animated the Egyptian nation more than any other games before or after. The matches spurred wild jubilation, intense anger, deep shock, and, slightly later, agitated debates over the sport's sociopolitical role and function. In this chapter, I take a close look at this episode and locate it within the wider context of the emotional politics of football in late-Mubarak Egypt. Drawing on retrospective interviews with supporters and press material from the time of the event,[4] I show how the Algeria games constituted the moment when the football bubble first reached its peak and then, abruptly, began to show signs of cracks and decline. Just about every Egyptian football person I know would single out November 2009 as the time when the frenzy around football was the most intense in their lifetimes. At the same time, I have often been told that football "lost something" after Algeria won the second match and Egypt missed the much-anticipated World Cup.

The chapter examines this defeat of all Egyptian football defeats as what Michel Foucault once called an "incitement to discourse" (Foucault, 1978). After the loss in Sudan, football in general and football emotions in particular were suddenly debated in a radically new and much more critical language. Commentators lashed out at the sport's vulgar aesthetics and complained about how it had become entwined in affective registers called *ta'assub* (similar to fanaticism) and a particular notion of *siyasa* (politics) connoting toxic divisions and partisanship. Expanding on the inter-related genealogies of these two terms, I argue that they have long been considered inherently incompatible with Egyptian nationalism. Therefore, as soon as football became perceived as political and fanatical, its emotion-ality had to be separated from the axiomatically progressive and unitary national project. In the process, football lost its inflated popularity. A dif-ferent set of more respectable, less vulgar, and ostensibly nonpolitical sub-jectivities took hold within the Egyptian national formation. In examining this fraught relationship between football and *siyasa*, the chapter identifies a conundrum that I will return to and elaborate in several subsequent chap-ters. The more Egypt's national game has been rendered *siyasi* (political), the more it has lost its ability to act as a national-political force.

THE FOOTBALL BUBBLE AT ITS PEAK

The euphoria that Emad Moteab's late goal at Cairo Stadium unleashed spilled over into the following days. Although the decisive play-off game—scheduled only four days later—was fast approaching, the Egyptians could not stop celebrating. In hindsight, several of my friends have admitted that they felt overly self-assured in the days between the matches. The way the Egyptian team had dominated the Cairo match assured them that the follow-up game would be an easy ride. The self-confidence was boosted further by the location of the upcoming match. Due to the realistic pros-pects for a replay, FIFA had made plans for the hypothetical tiebreaker in advance. Whereas the EFA had wanted the match to be played in Sudan, the Algerians had preferred Tunisia, and the final decision had come down to a lottery draw. As Khartoum was the destination drawn from FIFA's tombola in Zürich, many Egyptians consequently considered it good news; on 13 November, *al-Shuruq* described Sudan as a "brother coun-try," forever tied to Egypt through their common history. Friends of mine recall that Egyptian media insisted that Khartoum would be like a sec-ond home game. This, apparently, was also what many of the Egyptian elite were thinking. In the early morning before the match, large numbers of politicians, business tycoons, and celebrities set course for Khartoum in airplanes chartered by the ruling National Democratic Party (Tawfiq, 2010:180). The game in Sudan promised to be the culmination of the victorious national bubble built up around football over the previous years, and which had reached another crescendo after the dramatic victory in Cairo. The plan was to celebrate like never before once the World Cup spot had been secured, and the Mubarak regime and its allies made sure to be present at the party.

But there was another side to the game in Cairo that was left out of most Egyptian media reports. This story—which made big headlines in Algeria, Europe, and the United States—was not about jubilant Egyptian masses dancing in streets, but about ugly acts of violence. The Algerian team's bus had been pelted with stones on its way from Cairo Airport, leaving a handful of players injured. There were also reports of fans clashing in the streets before and after the game and of tens of (mostly Algerian) supporters being severely hurt (Thabet, 2010:160). In his book *Hurub kurit al-qaddam* (The Football Wars), Yasser Thabet illuminates the difference between Egyptian and Algerian press coverage at the time. He suggests that whereas Egyptian journalists ignored all incidents of violence,[5] Algerian newspapers exaggerated the brawls, claiming inaccurately that the hosts had systematically assaulted Algerian fans, and that a handful had been killed (Thabet, 2010:165-166). As a result of these divergent perspectives, the atmosphere in Algeria was completely different from the festive mood that reigned in Egypt between the two matches. The Algerian government imposed additional taxes on Egyptian companies, episodes of retaliation against Egyptian residents were widespread, and the Algerian media spilled over with angry, anti-Egyptian sentiments. As far as the upcoming game in Sudan was concerned, it was primarily framed as a chance for revenge, both on and off the pitch (ibid., 165–170).

In retrospect, commentators have noted that the Algerians who ended up attending the match in Khartoum came from a social background different from that of the Egyptians making the journey to Sudan. Whereas most Egyptian supporters were reasonably wealthy sports journalists, entertainers, and politicians, the Algerians were—in Thabet's phrasing—"non-educated elements [*'anasir ghayr muta'allima*] and groups who perhaps do not adhere to civilized manners" (2010:187). During a May 2012 interview, Sherif Hassan at the football website FilGoal.com pondered on the differences in slightly different terms. For him, most Algerians in Khartoum seemed to have been "quite normal football fans from the lower and lower-middle classes." He also asserted that, in his view, the Algerians had good reason to be agitated. "Of course, I understand their feelings," he told me: "they were angry because of the injustice they felt had been done to them in Cairo and excited because they could reach the World Cup. Remember, they had waited even longer than us. Algeria had not participated [in the World Cup] since 1986."

Regardless of aims and intentions, the presence of 8,500 Algerians was clearly enough to leave many in the smaller group of 3,500 Egyptians shocked and scared upon arrival. In *al-Shuruq*, press reports and interviews with celebrity fans portrayed Khartoum as a hellish, dirty, and undeveloped place full of aggressive Algerian thugs (*baltagiyya*) or mobs (*ghugha'*) who spoke incomprehensible Arabic and approached the Egyptians with indecent gestures and threats of slaughtering (20 November 2009). Moreover, contrary to the assumption that the Sudanese would support their "brother country," the Egyptian delegation was stunned to find thousands of Sudanese waving Algerian flags in the streets. *Al-Shuruq*'s correspondent reported on this scene with great disappointment. In a lengthy piece, he suggested that the Algerians had bought the feelings of the poor and humble Sudanese. Cunningly, they had drowned Khartoum in Algerian flags in the days prior to the game, and paid local citizens up to 100 US dollars each for changing their allegiances (20 November 2009).[6]

When the football match itself kicked off inside al-Marikh Stadium in Khartoum's twin city Omdurman, it turned into an Egyptian disaster. The national heroes underperformed badly when it mattered the most, and Algeria deservedly won by a score of 1–0. For the Egyptian fans in the stands, though, the crushed dream of a World Cup appearance was soon overshadowed by a more acute trauma. As Egyptian buses made their way back to Khartoum International Airport on the opposite side of the Nile, Algerian fans allegedly attacked several of them. In one famous case, a group of Egyptians had to hide inside an industrial estate for several hours after their bus had been completely destroyed (Saied, 2009). Among the people hiding was the renowned actor and singer Muhammad Fouad. His desperate phone calls from inside the factory to Egyptian television stations and to the Sudanese foreign minister begging for help indicated that the situation appeared quite desperate.[7] Furthermore, the chaotic conditions and haphazard treatment that the Egyptian celebrities, politicians, and businessmen received once they reached the airport was clearly very different from what they were used to. In the middle of the night, and in the midst of rumors of violent attacks from Algerian mobs, people had to wait for up to seven hours inside crammed planes that for some felt like "microbuses" before being allowed to take off (*al-Shuruq*, 20 November

2009). In the days that followed, these unpleasant experiences became a common theme in eyewitness reports of close-to-death encounters with hostile Algerians that flooded Egyptian media (see Thabet, 2010:174–175).

What had been merely a football game now escalated into a full-blown diplomatic crisis. When the Algerian government imposed Egyptian-specific taxes and Egyptian residents felt forced to return home from Algeria in the wake of the first game, the Egyptian media had widely condemned the Algerians as bad losers (Thabet, 2010:161–162). In the chaotic days that followed the loss in Sudan, however, Egyptian politicians and journalists found themselves discussing similar measures to defend "the dignity of the Egyptians" (*karamit al-misriyyin*) (Thabet, 2010:171). A few hours after the game, President Mubarak apparently contemplated sending army troops to Sudan to protect Egyptian citizens from the Algerians' attacks (ibid., 140). Several prominent public figures demanded that the Egyptian ambassador to Algeria should be recalled (*al-Shuruq*, 20 November 2009). Angry demonstrators attacked the Algerian embassy in Cairo; there were multiple incidents of mobs targeting Algerian citizens residing in Egypt (*al-Shuruq*, 26 November 2009).[8]

In the midst of disappointment, resentment, and violence, a host of actors jumped on the anti-Algerian bandwagon: the Egyptian Olympic Committee suspended all sports exchange with Algeria (*al-Shuruq*, 22 November 2009); al-Ahly Club contemplated selling their only Algerian player as a matter of principle (ibid.); the doctors, lawyers, and engineers syndicates published statements demanding the expulsion of the Algerian ambassador to Cairo (*al-Shuruq*, 23 November 2009); Egyptian singer Khalid Salim recalled an album because it included a song sung in an Algerian accent (*al-Shuruq*, 24 November 2009); and the popular artist Shaaban Abdel Rahim released a new single titled "Al-sha'b kulluh thayir" (The Whole People Is Furious) that he described as taking a "serious and strong stance against the terrorism" that the Egyptian fans had been exposed to in Sudan (*al-Shuruq*, 23 November 2009).

The tumult in Khartoum also prompted a qualitative shift in Egyptian media coverage. What had previously been reported as a hugely important football match and an occasion for national celebration turned into a major national crisis. For several days, it was *al-Shuruq*'s biggest news story by far, with coverage reaching far beyond the sports pages. Meanwhile, the match itself received hardly any reportage at all, as nobody seemed interested in analyzing what had gone wrong on the pitch. Instead, the paper published page after page of eyewitness reports about "barbaric" acts of extreme violence, photos of evil-looking Algerians in Sudan, and speculations about how the vile Algerian government had planned the "massacre" in advance (particularly 20, 21, 22 November 2009). Even *al-Shuruq*'s senior sports columnist, Hassan al-Mistakawi, who in the run-up to the matches had called repeatedly for calm and reason (e.g., 3, 4, 9 November 2009), joined the chorus. Pointing to the long history of unacceptable Algerian behavior at football games, al-Mistakawi argued that the violence in Sudan was no isolated incident. Instead, the event had to be understood as the result of the Algerian people's "deep and piled up hatred toward the Egyptians" (*karahiyya makhzuna lil-misriyyin*) (20 November 2009).

Similar opinions were common among football experts and political analysts on television too. On talk shows and studio programs, several pundits lashed out at what one commentator called an "Algerian culture of armed terrorists" (Thabet, 2010:188–189). Famously, President Mubarak's eldest son, Alaa, telephoned into a couple of these shows. In one call-in, fuming with anger, he accused the Algerians in Sudan of being mercenaries (*murtaziqa*) and criminals (*mugrimin*) who had viciously attacked Egyptian fans that he depicted as well-mannered and friendly families. Alaa—who had attended the Omdurman match with his brother and presidential-hopeful Gamal—also depicted Algerians as incapable of speaking proper Arabic, and he portrayed the Algerian media as corrupt and solely preoccupied with insulting Egypt and the Egyptians (Thabet, 2010:137–141).[9] Alaa Mubarak's media appearances proved very popular with broad layers of Egyptian society. His passionate reaction in defense of Egyptian honor came across as authentic. A widely held opinion was that his thoughts could have been expressed by any other Egyptian citizen (see, for example, Ibrahim Eissa in *al-Dustur*, 21 November 2009; Hassan, 2009). Like so often during the late 2000s, the presidential family's emotions pertaining to the realm of sports struck a chord with a widespread, perhaps even nationwide, structure of feeling. In this agitated moment of rage and humiliation, Alaa said what "everybody" in the country felt. His masculinized aggressions vis-à-vis the Algerian insults both incarnated and epitomized the emotional-political football bubble at the time of its most expansive inflation.

THE FOOTBALL BUBBLE UNDER ATTACK

In the heated atmosphere that reigned, it was difficult not to get carried away. With a few years' distance, many Egyptians would admit that their reactions had been embarrassing: one interviewee told me that he "could have killed an Algerian at the time, I have no idea why"; a journalist and friend, who in 2009 was working for a large western newspaper, revealed that an article of his "thankfully" had been turned down by his editor the day after the Khartoum match. The text had gone too far in its criticism of the Algerians' behavior. He would have "regretted it massively" had it been published.

But the scale and intensity of the anti-Algerian outcry were not the only things making November 2009 unique. Even more remarkable is how this nationwide wave of affect and antagonism quickly developed into something markedly different. A few days after the alleged "massacre" in Khartoum, a realization dawned on the Egyptian public that perhaps events had not been as terrible as they had first seemed. When all supporters had returned to Cairo, and it was established that no Egyptians (but two Sudanese) had been killed in the brawls, and that the injuries sustained were relatively minor, more and more commentators began to criticize the media (*al-iʿlam*: referring to television, not the printed press) and leading politicians for having blown it all out of proportion. Earlier, scattered voices in the press had called for calm and moderation: Ibrahim Eissa, for example, wrote such pieces in the regime-critical *al-Dustur* (13, 16 November 2009), as did Fahmy Huwaydi in *al-Shuruq* (14 November 2009) and Hassan al-Mistakawi in his sports columns in the same newspaper (3, 4, 9 November 2009). Yet as November drew to a close, this criticism grew at pace. An increasing number of public intellectuals began to critically debate the excessive violence and politicized madness that the two football matches had instigated (see Abdel Shafi, 2010:127–141).

One recurring theme in these conversations was football's detrimental impact on Egyptian nationalism. Notions of the game as a "drug" or "replacement" for a "real nationalist cause"—tropes that I have come across frequently during my post-2011 field research (see the introduction and chapter 6)—started to gain purchase in the press. The 21 November issue of *al-Shuruq* featured a series of articles of this kind. In an op-ed, famous economist Galal Amin portrayed the unfolding football craze as the pinnacle of a culturally deprived, celebrity-focused "age of mass audiences" (*ʿasr al-jamahir al-ghafira*). This period, which had been initiated in the Nasser era and sustained by President Sadat as well as by Mubarak, was, according to Amin, inherently "superficial" and sadly devoid of any "real love" for the nation. Football and its inflated media in this sense epitomized a depraved and ultimately empty nationalism.

Another column in the same paper, penned by public intellectual Hani Shukrallah, focused on the skewed national identity that the sport propagated. Analyzing the causes behind the recent crisis, Shukrallah claimed that the problem with sports is that it appeals to people as supporters rather than citizens. This, he argued, was both destructive and petty. As he put it: "Laziness is the most appropriate rubric for the state of nationalist revival around football [*li-halit al-ba'th al-watani kurawi al-tabi'*]. For it is a nationalism that does not demand anything from you, and which invests all your ambitions and hopes as well as the entire 'nationalist dream' on eleven individuals."

Other intellectuals depicted football as a threat to Egypt's pan-Arab relations. In the same 21 November issue of *al-Shuruq*, Fahmy Huwaydi devoted his daily last-page column to Egypt's television pundits. For Huwaydi, these unscrupulous figures were to blame for having "instigated and provoked hatred and bitterness" (*baghd wi marara*), and for "poisoning the relations between Egypt and Algeria." In the following days, this theme was picked up by several commentators—Ibrahim Eissa, Hassan al-Mistakawi, and Mustafa Kamil al-Sayd among others—in articles that self-critically depicted Egyptian journalists and politicians as smug and overly superior (see, for example, *al-Dustur*, 22, 25 November; *al-Shuruq*, 24 November 2009). To overcome the noxious and violent rift that football had opened up between two "brother countries," these writers insisted, Egyptian pundits and politicians needed to stop boasting about Egypt's natural leadership status in the pan-Arab struggle. To reclaim a sound nationalism and good relations with the country's Arab neighbors, the fanaticism and chauvinism propagated by the football bubble had to be replaced by humility and moderation.

On 26 November, eight days after the decisive Khartoum match, the mood in Cairo shifted further with the beginning of Eid al-Adha. The Eid is one of the two most significant Muslim holidays of the year, and it fundamentally reorders the city's rhythms. For a few days, workplaces are closed, people stay home with their families, and those who can afford it slaughter an animal and distribute the meat among relatives and the poor. The 2009 Eid put a definite end to the most intense buzz around the Algeria matches. In the press, the reporting shifted toward the religious rituals that were performed en masse all over the city, and football largely retreated to its previous location on the sports pages. At the time of the Eid, *al-Shuruq* provided editorial space to an unusually large number of Muslim scholars and Islamist activists, many of whom used the opportunity to voice critical opinions about the inflated role of football in Mubarak's Egypt. On 25 November, for instance, a long article reported on an Islamist lawyer who intended to take the president of the National Council for Sports, as well as President Mubarak himself, to court for their lavish public spending on national team bonuses instead of much-needed medical equipment. And two days later, the paper covered the Islamist group al-Jama'a al-Islamiyya launching an initiative to bring an end to the fanaticism (*ta'assub*) that the football matches had brought about, and which had led to violent animosity between two Muslim countries.

It is important to note that Islamist scholars in Egypt and elsewhere have a long tradition of criticizing sports in general and football in particular. For many pious believers, the positive effects that sports undeniably have for creating a "healthy soul in a healthy body" must be carefully measured against the risks of stirring exaggerated emotions that divert Muslims from God (Shavit and Winter, 2011:257). My friend Mahmoud, the devout gym employee and *Zamelkawi* mentioned in previous chapters, has often pondered on this intricate balance. Mahmoud, a gym instructor, would of course argue that football, like any physical activity, could be a positive force in society. At the same time, in light of Mahmoud's Salafi-leaning piety, the excessive importance that he and his fellow Egyptians attached to the sport before the 2011 Revolution has rendered football increasingly problematic. "The problem," he once told me,

> is when people prioritize football over the family, or over one's prayers, or even over *Allah*. It is like other Western things that distract us [*bitishaghghalna*], like music, belly dancing or film. They do not have to be bad, but when your feelings for them become too strong [*lamma ahsasak tab'a ufer*], then there is a problem. That is fanaticism [*ta'assub*].

That Islamists would be critical to football as a mass spectacle was thus neither new nor particularly surprising in late 2009. Nonetheless, the ample space given to a terror-associated group such as al-Jama'a al-Islamiyya to articulate this position in a newspaper such as *al-Shuruq* is striking, and it must be understood within the context of the veritable wave of football-critical commentary flooding Egypt at this point in time. It should also be noted how this religiously grounded sports criticism stressed football's fostering of secular-nationalist, i.e., inherently anti-Muslim, sentiments as a main concern. For the spokesperson for al-Jama'a whom *al-Shuruq*'s piece quotes, the recent craze around football was evidently a coordinated plan by the secular media in Algeria and Egypt to sow divisions within the Muslim *Ummah*. The ingenuity of the secularists was that they had managed to "turn football from a game we pass our free-time with [*nilhu biha fi awqat faraghna*] into a national project, which the people rally around [*yltiff hawluh al-sha'b*]." As such, football had taken on an exaggerated role of diversion, division, and violence, against which all true Muslims had to stand up (*al-Shuruq* 27 November 2009).

Even so, in the midst of this media storm, the argument that the sport had been toxic for the nation, Arabism, or the *Ummah* was not readily accepted by everybody. Instead, a rift opened up within the Egyptian intelligentsia (see Abdel Shafi, 2010:127–141). At the same time that Galal Amin, Fahmy Huwaydi, Hani Shukrallah, and many Islamist sheikhs denounced football feelings as "empty," "divisive," "fanatical," or a "replacement," other prominent figures dismissed this conversation as hopelessly elitist. A column by the internationally renowned novelist Alaa al-Aswani in *al-Shuruq* on 24 November is the most famous case in point. In this article, al-Aswani situated the assault (*i'tida'*) and indecency (*sifala*) directed against the Egyptians in Sudan within a series of historical-heroic events—the nationalist struggle against British colonialism and the Arab-Israeli war in 1973—when Egyptian citizens had paid with their lives for "raising the Egyptian flag." He also argued vehemently for the Egyptians' cultural superiority vis-à-vis its Arab neighbors:

> Egypt is the biggest Arab country and the biggest source of human talent in the Arab world. The Egyptians have had the honor of contributing in building the renaissance of many Arab countries: the universities were established by Egyptian professors; the newspapers were established by Egyptian journalists; the institutions for the arts, cinema and theater were established by Egyptian artists; the cities and buildings were built by Egyptian engineers. The hospitals were erected by Egyptian doctors, even the laws and constitutions were often put in place by Egyptian legal scholars. Yes, even the Algerian national anthem was composed by the Egyptian Mohamed Fawzi. This Egyptian excellence shaped the relations between the Egyptians and the Arab peoples.

Hence, al-Aswani continued, it was completely understandable that common Egyptians felt "humiliated" by the Algerians' shameful treatment in Khartoum. In contrast to those intellectuals who argued that Egypt had to tone down its rhetoric and show more modesty toward its Arab brother country, al-Aswani insisted that "normal people's feelings" constituted a progressive, "truly nationalist" force that had to be taken seriously (*al-Shuruq*, 24 November 2009; see also Abdel Shafi, 2010:130–133; Thabet, 2010: 227–228).

And yet in time, Alaa al-Aswani would also join the football-skeptical consensus. By late November and early December 2009, arguments such as his became increasingly rare and the criticism against the Mubarak regime's fanatical football nationalism all the more unified. Across the board, the focus shifted from boastful aggression to damage control and reconciliation. Many of those who, in the first days after Khartoum, had stood firmest against everything Algerian now turned increasingly self-critical. Youssef Ziedan—another prominent novelist who had expressed chauvinist opinions in the press (*al-Misri al-Yum*, 25 November 2009)—released a public apology for the unfortunate "anger that conquered him" after the loss (quoted in Abdel Shafi, 2010:136). Both the Egyptian government and the Egyptian Olympic Committee backtracked on earlier threats of boycotts against Algeria (*al-Shuruq*, 26 November 2009), and the EFA gradually gave up on its campaign to force FIFA to punish the Algerians and have the decisive match replayed (see Rommel, 2014).

Within Egypt's satellite television football channels—the target of much of the criticism and accusations—a blame game developed: the owners accused the talk show hosts of exaggeration and propagating hatred; the hosts, in turn, argued that they could not be held responsible for reflecting a general atmosphere in society. However—as Yasser Thabet convincingly argues—the public did not buy the trick. Instead, the "crisis resulted in a big crack [*sharkh*]," not only between Egypt and Algeria, but also between the Egyptian media and their viewers (Thabet, 2010:214–217). In an interview in April 2012, football author Mohammed Tawfiq depicted the moment as an abrupt awakening. "After the games against Algeria in 2009," he told me, "everybody suddenly understood what was going on. People realized that [the pundit Ahmed] Shoubair was trying to use the popularity of football to promote Gamal Mubarak's inheritance of power [*tawrith al-sulta*]. It became clear, because it was too much. And then people stopped believing in it."

FOOTBALL FANATICISM AND FOOTBALL POLITICS

To what extent did disputes in the Egyptian media resonate with Egyptian football fans? How deep a crack did these variegated attacks on the national sport really cause within the assemblage of money, media, sports, and glamor that I have called Egypt's emotional-political football bubble?

To examine these questions, let me for a moment focus on a particular set of affective registers and subjects indexed by the Arabic term *ta'assub*. *Ta'assub* is most often translated as "fanaticism" in English, although the Arabic concept is more semantically loaded, with denotations as varied as creation of a team, clique, or coalition; plotting against someone; taking sides; chauvinism; bigotry; zeal; partiality; and racial or national pride.[10] As the previous section illustrated, *ta'assub* surfaced as a primary anxiety for close to every protagonist partaking in the football debates raging in Egypt in late 2009. Whether secular intellectuals, football journalists, or Muslim sheikhs, everyone agreed that football fandom and football media had become more "fanatical" (*muta'assib*) in recent years. The Algeria crisis proved that the sport's *ta'assub* had spiraled out of control. Something clearly had to be done to combat it.

By late 2009, the preoccupation with *ta'assub* as a symptom of football gone awry was nothing new. Already in the mid-1990s, the grand old man of Egyptian journalism, Mohamed Hassanein Heikal, had used the term to depict the unrest and violence that ravaged Egyptian football stadiums in the final years of the Nasser era. For Heikal, this 1960s wave of exaggerated football *ta'assub* had not emerged in a vacuum. On the contrary, it was a direct result of the Nasser regime precluding the "necessary human impulse" to experience a more authentic *ta'assub* for political parties in a pluralist democracy (see Tawfiq, 2010:60-62).

The question of how to understand and tame *ta'assub* had also been a long-standing favorite topic among Egyptian sports researchers. In a representative book from 2002 solely devoted to the topic, sports psychologist Muhammad Yusif Hagag portrayed *ta'assub* as a worsening problem within Arab spectator sports, ultimately resulting from "lack of objectivity" and "automatic, unfounded passions" (Hagag, 2002:21–22). As an antidote, Hagag stressed the importance of "education [that] spreads tolerance and love between people" (ibid., 95). He also suggested a series of media reforms to stop the spreading of the nonobjective, partial propaganda (*da'aya*) on which false ideas, prejudice, and *ta'assub* thrive (ibid., 101-111).

The football criticism that ensued in the wake of the Algeria games rested on these earlier conversations. Like Heikal, many commentators depicted football *ta'assub* as a replacement for more profound national-political feelings. And the media were habitually spotlighted as the primary cause of the problem, just as in Hagag's book. At the same time, it is important to note that the concept does not always connote troubling demise. *Ta'assub*, as well as the partly synonymous *'asabiyya*, have for centuries elicited overlapping, often even contradictory, associations. In the Arab historian Ibn Khaldun's *Muqaddimah* from 1377, for example, *'asabiyya* is discussed at length, although not as a problem, but as a necessary bond bringing communities and societies together. Similarly, some of the most important figures in Egypt's late nineteenth and early twentieth-century nationalist awakening highlighted collective feelings of *'asabiyya* as a foundational and progressive building block for broad and vital national solidarity (Geer, 2011:407–408). The football debates that erupted in November 2009 thrived on this equivocation. Indeed, one way of reading the sudden discursive shifts that took place after the match in Sudan is to say that the latent ambiguity at the heart of the *ta'assub/'asabiyya* couple was revitalized and turned on its head. Whereas the positive role of the game to foster progressive emotions of national solidarity—*'asabiyya*—had largely overshadowed the problems of the same emotional ruses in previous years, the fanatical, chauvinist *ta'assub* that the football business and satellite media stimulated now came to dominate the conversation.

Furthermore, *ta'assub* is a remarkably malleable derogatory label. One intriguing aspect of the debates examined in this chapter is how the presumed instigators of fanaticism and those rendered *muta'assibin* (plural form of fanatical) kept shifting as matches were played and the crisis unfolded through its different stages. Initially, many commentators pointed to the Algerian people's historic inclination toward *ta'assub* as a main reason behind their outrageous behavior in Sudan, often with reference to past incidents of stadium violence (see, for example, *al-Shuruq*, 20 November 2009). Later, as critical scrutiny came to be directed inward, it was Egyptian politicians and football media pundits poisoning "normal nationalist feelings" and relations between two "brother people" with "blind *ta'assub*" that was lamented (*al-Shuruq*, 23, 24, 29 November 2009). No matter the angle, however, the feelings of normal Egyptian football fans were never singled out as the root cause of the rot. It was always some internal or external Other that led the sports-loving Egyptians astray, from sound collective jubilation toward the ills of *ta'assub*. Whether zealous Algerians, secular sports journalists, or even the president's own son ranting on prime-time television, the troublemakers took on different shapes depending on the ideological stances of particular commentators. Regardless of who he happened to be, though, the threatening *muta'assib* was invariably understood as a violent and fanatical fringe figure threatening key values at the core of the Egyptian nation.

Historian Benjamin Geer's examination of the early genealogy of Egyptian nationalism does not only highlight tensions between troubling *ta'assub* and (potentially) progressive *'asabiyya*. He also identifies a parallel and likewise unresolved overlap between sound *'asabiyyat* (group solidarities) and separatist *ahzab* (political parties) in several of the canonic nationalist texts that he parses. While both of these terms index tightly knit groups, the attributes of the groups in question differ. Whereas *'asabiyyat* could potentially be a positive force that brings the nation together, Geer suggests that *ahzab*, almost exclusively, were viewed as a troubling concern. Sowing rifts and divisions among the people, parties, and partisanship were by definition perceived as threats to the nascent national unity (Geer, 2011:407–411).

The anxieties that many Egyptians felt vis-à-vis football's *ta'assub* in the wake of the Algeria matches mirrored this subtle yet crucial distinction. Indeed, what the football critics ultimately feared was that potent feelings of potentially progressive togetherness were spinning out of control into fanaticism for one's cause, zealous partisanship, and narrow-minded tribalism. Depending on the commentators' ideological affiliations, the precious entity under threat could be the Egyptian nation, pan-Arabism, or the Muslim *Ummah*. Regardless of what unity needed to be protected, however, there was a wide consensus that *ta'assub* risked causing detrimental divisions.

This concern with rifts and partisanship speaks to a more generalized unease permeating Egyptian nationalism. Nationalism might constitute Egypt's hegemonic political project, but it has been and still is instinctively hesitant to *siyasa* (politics) of all thinkable kinds. To contextualize and historicize these prevailing antipolitical sentiments—to which I will return in subsequent chapters—let me first note that Egyptian nationalism is built on a premise that bestows to all "members of the nation [. . .] a shared moral duty towards their country," a country, in turn, which is conceptualized as unitary and "inevitably personified" (Geer, 2011:21). Every citizen, in other words, is by default called upon to work for the common national good and to foster solidarity, togetherness, and unity among a highly idealized Egyptian people (*al-sha'b al-misri*). It is not difficult to envision how *siyasa* could surface as fundamentally at odds with such suppositions. Projects forwarding political group demands—partial, limited, fanatical—will always risk causing divisions and disintegration within the unitary nation. Unsurprisingly, then, Egypt's nationalist intellectuals and leaders have long depicted *siyasa* as something to avoid, or as a necessary evil at best. Already the movement's pioneers in the nineteenth and early twentieth centuries looked upon political factions and partyism (*hizbiyya*) with suspicion (Geer, 2011:144, 309–310, 408); the messy intrigues connoted by *siyasa* did not have a place in the modern nation that was emerging (Fahmy, 2018:81–132).[11]

Fast-forward to the Nasser era (1954–1970) and what Alain Roussillon has aptly called an "innate illegitimacy of the political field" (*illégitimité native du champ politique*) (1996:25) turned into official state policy. Nasserism was first and foremost a kind of nationalist populism, and the unity of the people was both idealized and valorized (Podeh and Winckler, 2004; Ikram, 2018:143–144). Consequently, the pluralist parliamentary system was castigated, only one explicitly nonpolitical party was permitted, and the Army—presumably superpolitical—gained unmatched influence over vast sections of the state apparatus (Roussillon, 1996:20–25).[12] This outright abolishment of party politics might have been softened gradually under Gamal Abdel Nasser's successors, Anwar Sadat (1970–1981) and Hosni Mubarak (1981–2011). But even during the Mubarak era, when a limited range of parties was allowed and semi-democratic elections organized, nationalist-unitary ideals stayed strong and *siyasa* remained an object of deep hesitation within regime-friendly and oppositional circles alike.[13] Fittingly, President Mubarak worked hard to craft an image of himself as an apolitical, all-national father figure in the course of the 2000s. Promising above all to deliver stability (*istiqrar*), he made a point of hovering above the petty intrigues and divisions that played out in the parliament and his own cabinet (see Makram Ebeid, 2012). Together with his son and potential inheritor, Gamal, he also brought people from the business sector into the state apparatus, his party, and the government in an effort to render the regime more professional, more technocratic, and in effect less *siyasi*.[14]

As demonstrated in the previous chapter, football provided a formidable vehicle in the crafting of President Mubarak's nationally normal subjectivity. Especially in the final years of his reign, the game staked out a unique realm of untainted nationalist pride and joy in an era otherwise steeped in gloom and despair, and it attached the presidential family seamlessly to a victorious version of the people. What is more, despite the government's extensive financial and infrastructural support for the football industry, the game was by and large discussed as a self-referential universe in which players, clubs, and tournaments were evaluated with reference to internal measures unique to football: titles, goals, revenue streams, and stadium attendance. As a result, the national sport was also perceived as strictly delineated from intrigues and divisions conjured as *siyasa*. The Egyptian football bubble was always a national one, encompassing a vast majority of the people. To think of it as political was accordingly something like a contradiction in terms.

One thing that we have seen in this chapter is how this spell was broken in the weeks following the Algeria games. The matches in Cairo and Khartoum in November 2009 prompted a sweeping reevaluation of football in general and a revelation of the sport's latent emotional-political purchase in particular. Suddenly, external, politically connoted concepts—progressiveness, fanaticism, nationalism, and pan-Arabism—were drawn on in a wide range of conversations about the game's social role and function. The separation between the world of sports and the realm of *siyasa* looked increasingly untenable, a conflation which necessarily tarnished the apolitical image on which President Mubarak—the down-to-earth football man—had built his legitimacy. As 2009 drew to a close, the game of football and the bubble that had been assembled around it appeared more and more as a source of violence, bad manners, and division. The sport had started to look highly political, leaving its national status in a great deal of doubt.

THE REVENGE OF THE RESPECTABLE

The Algeria matches not only altered *how* football was talked about in Egypt, but also changed *who* participated in conversations about the game. Concerns about the game's empty nationalism, excessive *ta'assub*, and propensity for political divisions were raised primarily by two distinct camps: people within the cultural and academic intelligentsia, and more or less conservative Islamist scholars and politicians. That these two groups spearheaded the attacks should not come as a surprise. As mentioned, pious Muslims have long held an instinctive ambivalence for the distracting emotions that spectator sports stir among the masses. Similarly, as Muhammad Tawfiq has noted, Egypt's intellectuals had by the 2000s developed an antagonism to football, as they saw how the more refined activities that they represented and endorsed—be it the arts, literature, or theater—lost influence and popularity to the evolving football boom (Tawfiq, 2010:125–131). Furthermore, the particular variety of Egyptian nationalism that football carved out in the late Mubarak era had never favored those seen as overly intellectual, or religious in problematic or extreme ways. Highlighting football as a sphere of emotional normality uniting the nation and its leader, the national football bubble had systematically left out precisely these two groups, portraying them as abnormal Others for whom football did not matter (see chapter 1).

The disapproval of football by Egypt's intellectuals and Islamists might appear as a straightforward class issue. The Algeria games crisis provided an opportunity to claim back a social status that the two groups had either lost or never had, but which they had always somehow felt entitled to. Such a reading makes a lot of intuitive sense. The attacks that followed the match in Sudan were a reaction to lost class privileges and diminishing cultural capital; the critical targeting of the "uncultivated," "unaware," and "uneducated" pundits in football television, for instance, reveals a great deal of elitism and disdain for a particular habitus that aligned sports with the country's emerging nouveau riche.[15] Yet given that not all Egyptian intellectuals—and by no means all Islamists—are wealthy, *economic* class alone does not suffice as an explanation. Even more illuminating, arguably, is how football critics from *both* groups self-identified as "respectable" (*muhtaram*). The ordering principle of "respectable" versus "not respectable" has an enormous purchase in contemporary Egypt. While the category denotes very different characteristics in different regional and gendered contexts—wealth, piety, education, morals, or courage—to be respectable ultimately means to be *someone*, and it is as such of utmost importance (see, for example, Abu-Lughod, 2005; Ghannam, 2013; Schielke, 2015). As is well documented, voices propagating particular notions of respectability dominated many public discourses and institutions in the 1990s and 2000s. Calls for morality, purpose, and cultural refinement frequently saw Egypt's nationalist-secular elites and certain sections of the Islamic revival unite in all-out attacks against the ills associated with disreputable *sha'bi* culture and folk religion (see, for example, Amar, 2011b; Ismail, 2006b:58–81; Schielke, 2008, 2012; Winegar, 2014; van Nieuwkerk, 2013).

The respectability that the football critics in late 2009 claimed to embody harkened back to these societal fault lines. Preaching moderation, calm, and restraint, they called for a reformed national subjectivity based on education, religious morality, and refinement that turned its back to the game's vulgar emotionality, and which was everything but folk or *sha'bi*.[16] At the same time, when Egypt's Islamists and intellectuals lashed out at football as not respectable, *muta'assib*, and a lazy nationalism without real purpose, they did not merely reiterate well-rehearsed discourses and interventions. Striking back against vulgar politicians, businessmen, and entertainers who had used football to define how the Egyptian nation should be represented, lived, and felt, they also staked out a partial reordering of the nation's respectable and not respectable subjects. For in contrast to the powerful respectability bloc that scholars such as Abu-Lughod (2005:163–191), Salwa Ismail (2006b), Samuli Schielke (2008), Jessica Winegar (2014), and Asef Bayat (2010:128–136) have analyzed, the respectable actors fighting the battle against football in November 2009 were neither sheikhs at *al-Azhar*, nor state-aligned ideological functionaries, nor glitzy American University–educated New Preachers. In fact, as noted in chapter 1, the benign religiosity, superficial consumerism, and regime support that such elite actors embodied were rather representative of the nationally normal masculinity carried by the football bubble. Instead, the eclectic anti-football front consisted of outspoken oppositional intellectuals like Ibrahim Eissa and Fahmy Huwaydi, as well as Islamists belonging to the Muslim Brotherhood and the country's Salafi movement. One thing that distinguished these individuals from many other celebrities highlighted as epitomes of respectability in Mubarak's Egypt was that they were significantly more antagonistic to the ruling regime. In many ways each other's opposites on the ideological spectrum, the football adversaries were united in their opposition to the government's vulgarization of power and an emotional-political football bubble that they had never felt part of. As the football nationalism spun out of control, these new actors found space to articulate their own particular notion of respectability. In this sense, November 2009 constituted the revenge of the respectable against the ethics and aesthetics of Egyptian football, as well as against the Mubarak regime more broadly.[17]

CONCLUSION: THE BEGINNING OF THE END OF AN ERA

In retrospect, the two matches against Algeria stand out for many Egyptians, both as the pinnacle of the Mubarak era's football hype and as a moment when something was revealed, irreparably broken, and lost. Take my friend Bilal, a sincere and somewhat eccentric man, born in the mid-1980s in the lower-middle-class neighborhood Abdeen. The last time we met in late 2019, Bilal was living in a new housing development close to the Pyramids in Giza with his wife and five-year-old daughter; when I first got to know him in late 2012, he was about to get married. One night in January 2013, I visited Bilal in the old one-bedroom flat in Abdeen, where he had grown up with his now-deceased grandparents, and where he was temporarily residing at the time. As usual that winter, Bilal had gone straight from his office job in Maadi to do refurbishment work on his new Giza flat. When he finally made his way home, it was already well past midnight, but Bilal seemed undisturbed by the fact that he had to drive to work again in less than six hours. He invited me for a late supper of instant noodles, mango juice, and sweet tea, and while flipping between football channels on his small television set, he told me about the emotional roller-coaster ride that November 2009 had constituted. "I always watched football here, in this room with *giddi* [my grandfather], *Allah yirhamuh* [God bless his soul]," he said, and looked up at the photo of the old man on the wall.

We watched every Ahly-match and of course also the national team. *Giddi* used to record the games on VHS, so the big games, like the Cairo derby or the final of the Africa Cup of Nations, we watched maybe ten times. But the Algeria games were something very, very special, because the biggest dream of all Egyptians was the World Cup. I was so nervous during the first game here in Cairo. I couldn't watch. The last ten minutes, I was in the bed in the reception, out there, under a blanket and cried because we were losing. But then of course, Moteab scored that goal, and you see, our television is a bit slower than the ones at the *ahwa* [coffee shop] down in the street—it must be something with analogue and digital—so I heard people screaming in the street, and when I came into the room, I watched the goal live with *giddi*. It was the biggest happiness, and I cried, I cried a lot. But then of course, four days later [the game in Khartoum], we sat here again—me and *giddi*—and we couldn't say anything. We were shocked, because we were so sure of winning. I remember that for the first time in my life, Abdeen was completely silent outside the window. No cars, nobody said anything. Nothing.

For Bilal, the game in Sudan marked the end of an era. Directly after the defeat and the turbulence that followed, he had promised himself never to watch football again. He had felt tired and disgusted, he told me; it had been madness; things had gone too far. Of course, he did not keep his vow. But as he explained later the same night, something changed nonetheless.

For example, the cup in Angola [the Africa Cup of Nations in early 2010, which Egypt won] was nice, but mostly because we beat Algeria [in the quarter final]; actually, that felt better than winning the final. And in 2010, I started to miss Ahly games for the first time. And then *giddi* died, and then came the revolution, and now I've too much to do with the flat and the wedding. Football isn't what it used to be, not at all [*ya'ni, al-kura mish zay ma kanit, khalis*].

Bilal was by no means the only Egyptian man to reconstitute his relationship to football from late 2009 onward. His more restrained attachments matched the general sentiment; not even a third consecutive Africa Cup of Nations victory in February 2010 was able to fully reignite the previous passion. As Egypt's new Africa Cup of Nations qualification campaign got underway the following autumn, the shifting mood was reconfirmed painfully on the pitch. A disappointing draw at home to Sierra Leone was followed by a shocking loss in Niger. Hassan Shehata's unbeatable Pharaohs had by this point—some three months before 25 January 2011—clearly passed their zenith.

Meanwhile, the sport lost its favored position at the heart of Egypt's national project. Extending the football-skeptical momentum of November 2009, accentuations of football's latent but long-neglected links to immoral *ta'assub*, divisive *siyasa*, and vulgarity proliferated. Let me once more take Egyptian feature films as an example. Already in Kamla Abu Zakri's *Wahid Sifr*, released in early 2009, the sport was no longer depicted as axiomatically normal and nationally unifying. A host of troubling questions were raised about the Egyptians' media-driven football obsession (see chapter 1). A similar theme is legible in Mohamed Diab's *678* from 2010, a dark tale about Egypt's endemic problem of sexual harassment. In a key scene in this movie, a crowd of football fans sexually assault a female protagonist after yet another national team victory. As the camera zooms out, capturing a mass of people celebrating in the street where the rape has just happened, the mob turns into a chilling metaphor for the tail end of the Mubarak era: a masculinized, hysterical, and ultimately blinded nation where brute force rules, women never feel completely safe, and football is a phenomenon on which everything else pivots.

When I conducted my fieldwork a couple of years later, the break was even more blatant. During a November 2012 interview, I asked the journalist and football author Yasser Thabet to reflect on the drastic change of mood that the Algeria games had incited. For him, the shift was best understood in terms of a "depression" that had struck the people as well as the elites who had invested heavily in Egypt reaching the World Cup. Thabet also emphasized the fact that Egypt *lost* the game in Khartoum as a crucial but sometimes overlooked reason for what had happened.

> The World Cup in 2010 would have been the main stage for Gamal Mubarak both internationally and here in Egypt. Therefore, [the regime] put all their cards into the games, and they got very upset to miss out on this opportunity. [. . .] Everyone was getting ready to celebrate, to make use of it, to justify the popularity of Gamal Mubarak [to succeed his father as president]. This is why it hurt them a lot. This was mainly a propaganda story for Gamal Mubarak and his businessmen friends who went with him to the game in Omdurman. It was a big party, like going to the opera. Like any other dictator, they should have known better. I think it

was Goebbels who once told Hitler: "Do not put us in any propaganda situation which we might lose." It was a risky investment that worked well as long as Egypt was winning. But when the team became inconsistent, it was over.[18]

Winning and winning again had been a defining feature of the soaring emotionality, positive national community, and boastful subjectivity that football had been associated with, and which had made such a good match with the ethos of the Mubarak family. Consequently, when Egypt *lost* the match that had been singled out as the most important ever played, the sense of endless possibilities was broken, and the affective football bubble was no longer possible to sustain. Media, money, and infrastructure alone could not do it. Seen in this light, one thing that the craze that followed the Egypt-Algeria showdown illustrates is how singular football matches sometimes are able to take on transformative agency; how a game might expand into a "generative moment" (Kapferer, 2015) or "critical event" (Das, 1995) that splits history into a before and an after, reshapes affect and temporality, and incites new dominant discourses and subjects. In social scientific studies of sports, this ground-shaking potential has typically been ascribed to the liminality that the game as a spatiotemporally confined ritual engenders (see Besnier, Brownell, and Carter, 2018:159–165). In November 2009, this was certainly part of the story. The weeks that followed Egypt's World Cup exit were everything but ordinary; they encompassed an unlikely multitude of exhilaration, performances, and reappraisals. And yet what we also see surfacing amidst the transformations of discourse, emotion, and subjectivity is how particular *match results*—a late goal in Cairo, a 1–0 loss in Khartoum—play pivotal roles in the multidimensional social assemblages that popular spectator sports spawn. After all, as Joshua Rubin (2014) has noted, one thing rendering the world of sports so unique is the inherent unpredictability of the game itself: what unfolds on the pitch has a certain autonomy and agency that businessmen, politicians, and television pundits can only ever partly control.[19] In the waning days of the Mubarak era, this was clearly the case. As Egypt moved toward the momentous year of 2011, the bubble that had been built around football had already begun to burst, and one particular match result had done much of the damage. In view of this—as many of my friends in Cairo like to speculate (see also Gabr, 2013)—a different result in Omdurman might have given the Mubarak regime the boost required to survive for another year or two.

PART II

ULTRAS

CHAPTER 3

A Revolutionary Emotional Style

*In the beginning, nobody in the clubs or the media took us
seriously. They considered us some small guys and crazy
ones and left us alone. This changed in 2009 and 2010.
As we became really big, al-Ahly Club started to use us in
negotiations with sponsors and for TV rights: "Look at our
fans, they're the biggest and most passionate in Egypt, we
should get more money." They also started to use our culture
in their official merchandise. [. . .] Just before the revolution,
the club helped us once when fifteen members were arrested at
a match in Asyut [in Upper Egypt]. But other times when we
got into trouble, they said some bullshit like "they're not part
of us, not real Ahly fans." Only after Tahrir, people changed
their minds. Now, they've begun to understand that youth in
Egypt can do something really big.*
Shadi, longtime member of Ultras Ahlawy, May 2012

Cairo International Stadium is the centerpiece of a vast complex of sports
facilities located between two busy thoroughfares and rows of sand-colored
apartment buildings at the fringes of the Nasser City neighborhood.
Constructed in the late 1950s as part of the Nasser government's large-
scale investments in sports, the stadium area has since undergone multiple
renovation schemes and extensions. For more than half a century, this is
where al-Ahly, al-Zamalek, and the Egyptian national team have played
a vast majority of their home games. Consequently, the arena has been
the showground for most of the memorable events in Egypt's modern
football history.

For anyone attending a game at Cairo Stadium in the aftermath of
Egypt's January 2011 Revolution, however, it could be difficult to take in

that it had been a recent site of national euphoria. On dark winter nights, when the cold, dry wind from the north blew across the concrete and only a fraction of the seventy-five thousand seats were occupied, watching football at the arena could be a surprisingly forlorn activity. On one such night in January 2012, al-Ahly hosted Smouha—a small club from Alexandria—in the Egyptian Premier League. Possibly because of the cold, I failed to convince any of my *Ahlawiyya* friends to join me, but I decided to go to the game anyway, preparing myself with gloves, a hat, long johns, and multiple sweaters. After a quick taxi ride to the stadium, I bought a third-class ticket for ten pounds from a hawker, passed a swift security check, and climbed the stairs to a seat at the top of the northeastern upper tier. The view was breathtaking: the steep, gray, and sparsely settled stands formed a giant bowl below me; red and yellow figures drew geometrical patterns on the green field during the two teams' warm-up session. The lack of regulation was also eye-catching. While hundreds of police officers congregated behind fences on the running tracks encircling the pitch, not a single security guard could be spotted in the stands. Fans moved around as they pleased, crossing barriers into stadium sections where their tickets were not valid. Behind me, a dozen supporters had scaled a board decorated with motifs of ancient Egypt that crowned the top of the eastern stands. High up there in the wind, they had attached Ahly flags and scarves to murals depicting the Giza pyramids and the Sphinx. The loudspeakers around me were all defunct, and the kiosks were closed. Unlicensed vendors moved up and down the steep steps, offering tea, crisps, biscuits, and *kushari*.[1]

At first glance, only one stadium sector stood out, an exception to the reigning informality. Opposite from me, in the center section of the western stands, were neat rows of black-clad police officers encircling a lone section of a markedly different order. Over there, club officials, former players, and potentates from the football association mingled with journalists and supporters prepared to spend several hundred pounds on first-class tickets. When the two teams came marching in and everyone rose to sing the national anthem, all activities took place in front of this small VIP section: the advertisement placards surrounding the pitch faced its direction; television zoomed in on its celebrities; functioning loudspeakers relayed the voice of the stadium's public announcer; at halftime there were refreshments to enjoy from well-staffed kiosks. One year after January 2011, and two years after the World Cup qualifiers against Algeria, this seemed a telling image of what Mubarak's football bubble had shrunk down to: a choreographed, commercial, and condensed spectacle for television and the rich in the middle of a cold and uninspiring football wasteland.

But the media-covered VIP event was not the only activity taking place at the stadium. On the lower tier, behind one of the goals, a very different spectacle was unfolding. Down there, where the view of the pitch is the worst, some five thousand young men amassed, standing tightly together on top of the seats. Many were dressed in red T-shirts with hoodies underneath to protect against the cold. Behind them, on the railings of the upper tier, they had hung red and black flags with messages like *a'zam nadi fil-kun* (the greatest club in the universe), *Together Forever*, and *Ultras Ahlawy*. At the very bottom, right in front of the security fence, two young men in skinny jeans and T-shirts had scaled a couple of three-meter-high loud-speakers. Ten minutes before kickoff, the two men rose to their feet. Balancing on the narrow speakers, they turned toward their friends in the stands, like conductors of a symphony orchestra. From that moment until well after the final whistle, the youngsters sang without interruption— about their club, their stadium section *talta shimal*, their freedom, their martyrs, and their revolution.[2] Led by the *capos* on the speakers, who urged them to keep it up whenever the energy briefly flagged, Ultras Ahlawy filled the *curva* with a strictly choreographed mix of songs, dance, flags, and burning flares (*shamarikh*) in red, pink, and orange.[3]

Just as the players entered the stadium and lined up in front of the VIPs, television cameras, and advertisements, Ultras on the upper terrace unfolded a huge flag that fell down over their friends below. On the flag, they had painted a head of a black and red devil, alluding to al-Ahly's nickname, Red Devils. Simultaneously, everybody in the all-male crowd raised pieces of black, red, white, or yellow plastic. Meticulously arranged in advance, the combination of colors provided the devil with a body that stretched out across the lower tier. Neither this impressive display—tonight's *dakhla* (entrance scene)[4]—nor the young men's singing and dancing were given any attention in the mainstream media. Yet a couple of Ultras behind the opposite goal filmed everything that was happening. Later that night, they published photos of this parallel stadium event on Facebook, and videos were released on YouTube. The clips circulated widely on social media; tens of thousands of Egyptians watched them in the days that followed.

At the time of this match in early 2012, it was almost exactly five years since Ultras fans had first appeared at Egypt's football stadiums. In this relatively short time span, their popularity and influence had grown remarkably. What had initially constituted small congregations of particularly dedicated football supporters had developed into a well-organized subculture. In this chapter—the first of three charting the history of the Egyptian

Ultras from 2007 to 2019—I examine these first five years. Why did the new fan organizations grow so quickly? How did they become a serious challenge for the emotional-political statecraft propagated by the Egyptian football bubble? How were they caught up in the revolutionary momentum that swept Egypt after 25 January 2011? As I show, the Ultras were not only vehemently opposed to the way football had been financed, organized, and covered in the media. Through discourse, practice, and collective hard work, they also embodied a novel "emotional style" (Gammerl, 2012)—a unique repertoire of songs, flags, and fireworks fostering emotional registers of fun and freedom—which struck a chord among broad sections of Egyptian youth. The story about this style adds an affective layer to Egypt's January 2011 Revolution. It spotlights an inherent instability in the Mubarak regime's emotional football statecraft and demonstrates how Egypt's national game became an arena for a younger, internationally oriented, and much more radical kind of emotional football masculinity. Given the new fans' challenge to the powers that be, it should come as no surprise that they faced intense scrutiny from the security forces and a great deal of media condemnation. The Ultras were repeatedly framed as rowdy, politically partisan thugs not fit for the respectable national community. However, after January 2011, the image of the groups was redrawn. Previous derogatory labels no longer seemed to stick. As the Ultras found ways to strike a balance between radical action and class-based ideals of nationalist unity, they turned into central actors in Egypt's revolutionary struggle.

PRINCIPLED PURITANS

The Egyptian Ultras movement's first five years are no doubt a remarkable success story. The first two groups—Ultras Ahlawy (UA07), who support al-Ahly, and Ultras White Knights (UWK), who cheer for al-Zamalek—were both established in the spring of 2007.[5] Shortly thereafter, Ultras groups supporting clubs outside Cairo emerged, but UA07 and UWK would remain the largest and most influential;[6] already in 2009, they were capable of mobilizing many thousand young men on especially important match days. By the time I observed UA07 in action at the Ahly vs. Smouha game in January 2012, their presence had expanded well beyond the stadiums. In the press, in everyday discourses, and especially in social media, Egypt's new fan groups had become a phenomenon that spurred attention, awe, opinions, and debates.[7]

The Ultras' appeal among Egyptian youth has most often been attributed to the fan groups' radical ideology. In a 2011 book by the blogger and former UWK member Muhammad Gamal Bashir, *Kitab al-ultras* (The book of the Ultras)—the most comprehensive account of the fan movement's formative years—large sections are devoted to the groups' founding principles of organizational and financial independence. When UA07 and UWK came into being, Bashir tells us, a handful of similar fan associations already existed in Cairo. Organizations such as al-Ahly Fan Club (AFC, established 2005), Ahly Lovers Union (ALU, 1996) and Zamalek Lovers Union (ZLU, 2005) all targeted youths and tried to introduce new ways of cheering. As a result of hefty membership fees and close relationships with the boards of the clubs, however, these fan groups never attracted any significant numbers of Egypt's football-loving youth. Their activities were widely considered too controlled, too commercialized, and too expensive (Bashir, 2011:35–67).

Many of the founding members of Ultras Ahlawy and Ultras White Knights had previously been active in AFC, ALU, or ZLU. The new groups that emerged in spring 2007 were their attempt to break free more radically from the clubs' control, and to establish truly independent fan organizations (Bashir, 2011:35–67). One episode, often referred to as pivotal, was al-Ahly's centennial match versus FC Barcelona in April 2007. As many older Ultras would tell me, the club allocated tickets to this historic event almost completely to sponsors and VIPs rather than to ordinary fans. This blatant instance of corruption constituted a moment of revelation. For many *Ahlawiyya*, the Barcelona game made it evident that a new type of independent and more oppositional fan culture was needed (see also Bashir, 2011:59-60).

But autonomy from the clubs was not the only novelty. To establish a contrast to the rigid hierarchies of former supporter organizations, the Ultras also made a point of adopting decentralized structures of command. Local *sikashin* (UA07; singular, *sakshin*, literally "section") or *dawal* (UWK; singular, *dawla*, literally "state") organized most day-to-day activities. It was here, locally, that *capos* and other group leaders were elected (Bashir, 2011:84–86; see also Ibraheem, 2015:82–88).[8] Furthermore, to make the groups accessible to young Egyptians of all classes, compulsory membership fees were scrapped.[9] Financial support from the clubs was also ruled out, to ensure that the movement stayed independent. Instead, the economy of UA07 and UWK came to rely on sales of T-shirts, scarves, CDs, and other merchandise, all of which were designed, produced, and distributed through informal networks, by and among the members and via social media (Bashir, 2011:163–166; Ibraheem, 2015:49).

When it comes to actual fan practices at the stadium, Bashir depicts UA07 and UWK's novel approach as based on a few nonnegotiable principles: cheer for ninety minutes no matter the result on the pitch; stand up throughout every game; travel to every match, home as well as away; stand in the cheapest stadium section behind one of the goals (2011:78–81). These basic rules take inspiration from Ultras elsewhere in North Africa. As a result of trips to matches in the Maghreb in the years of AFC, ALU, and ZLU, the founding members had firsthand experience of the Ultras associations that had sprung up around the biggest clubs in Tunis and Casablanca in the first half of the 2000s. The impressive *dakhlas*, organization, and dedication of these Maghrebi pioneers provided a blue-print for UA07 and UWK, and the relationships between Ultras across the Arab world have been strong ever since (Bashir, 2011:35–67). Notably, the groups in Morocco and Tunisia had, in turn, drawn a lot of their inspira-tion from Ultras in southern Europe, fan groups who had played import-ant roles at stadiums in countries like Croatia, Italy, and France since the mid-twentieth century (Bashir, 2011:31–34; Thabet, 2013:12–13; see also Kuhn, 2011:159–177; Montague, 2020). From the outset, the Egyptian Ultras thus constituted a branch within a loosely connected international supporter movement.

Another outstanding facet of Ultras' self-identification is that they think of themselves as different from other types of football fans, whom they consider less dedicated and pure, more controlled and corrupted. In contrast to the "passive millions" who would rather watch football on television, for instance, Ultras insist on always being present at the sta-dium. Ultras also like to stress that—unlike hooligans in England or Bara Brava in Latin America—they are unconnected to criminal networks and never violent unless provoked (Bashir, 2011:18–30). Furthermore, an Ultra would never support only the team that wins, and his loyalty to the club transcends the worship of any individual player. Finally, as many Ultras in Cairo have told me, the groups have found it important to distance them-selves from the charismatic cheerleaders (*hatifin*) who used to animate the stadium crowds in the pre-Ultras era (Bashir, 2011:57; Thabet, 2013:16–17). My friend Shadi, a journalist and longtime member of Ultras Ahlawy, once explained the difference like this:

> There used to be *hatifin* at the stadiums, like al-Khawaga at al-Za-malek's matches who's really famous. They created a nice but a bit silly atmosphere. Their chants were much simpler than ours, but many people liked them. They were often paid by some board member or businessman. It happened that they incited the crowds against certain players, the coach or other members of the board

that the one who paid them disliked. We would never do anything like this. We're independent. Today, the days of the *hatifin* are over.

The oppositional ethos of Ultras—in Egypt and elsewhere—is often summarized in the catchphrase "against modern football": a loathing for the commodified, globalized, and media-saturated spectacle that the sport has become, paired with nostalgia for a more local game, played in front of fans who really care (for example, Bashir, 2011:170–184; Hamzeh and Sykes, 2014; see also Kuhn, 2011; Montague, 2020). For Egyptian Ultras, the international movement's famous against-the-media stance has translated into a more particular aversion to the pundits who populate the country's football television. In Egypt, the media are not problematic only because they lure football fans away from the stadiums. As I will return to throughout this chapter and the two that follow, television is also a business conglomerate that the Ultras have accused of corruption, regime bias, and spreading negative images of the groups' ideals and activities.

FUN AND FREEDOM

Independent, principled, and dedicated—the image of the Ultras that emerges in books, articles, and manifestos alike is one of a disciplined movement of young football puritans. Among broad layers of Egyptian football fans, this oppositional ethos was much welcomed, and it was key to the groups' rapid growth in the years before January 2011. When I have asked UA07 and UWK members to describe what made them join the Ultras in the first place, they have often cited the organization's "principles" (*mabadi'*) and praised the "freedom" (*hurriyya*) that the fan community has provided them. As Ultras, they have told me, they have been allowed to support their football teams in their own way, independent of the hypocritical media and corrupt big business, which so much of football in Egypt has turned into.

But the popularity of UA07 and UWK was never solely a result of principles and ideals. For my close friend Muhammad—a UWK member from the lower-middle class neighborhood al-Sayyida Zaynab—being an Ultra has also afforded an attractive emotional experience contingent on united efforts. I first became acquainted with Muhammad while he was still a teenager. It was spring 2012, the Port Said tragedy had just taken place, and the league had been suspended indefinitely. As a result of the ban on supporters at Egyptian stadiums that followed, it was not until spring 2019 that Muhammad and I were able to watch a live match together.[10] Nonetheless, before and after playing football, when having dinner at his parents' place, or while watching a Zamalek match on television, he has often spoken about the years in the not-too-distant past when his life revolved almost exclusively around the group and the *curva*. "For me, the basic thing was always to work hard every week in the local *dawla* preparing for the match," he told me one of the first times we met:

> Sometimes we wrote new songs, sometimes we designed or sold T-shirts, sometimes we tagged graffiti in our neighborhood, sometimes we prepared a *dakhla*, sometimes we recruited new members, sometimes we collected money for *shamarikh*. There are many things to do, and when everybody in all *dawal* do their best, the songs, flags, and *dakhlas* that the *capos* decide to use at the match become better, more professional. Because the match at the stadium is the best thing in the world. I wish you can join me one day; I can't explain it to you. When everyone is together in *talta yimin* [UWK's section at Cairo Stadium], and we sing about al-Zamalek, and we dance, and then comes the *shamrukh* and then aaaaaaah!!! [pumping his fist up and down in the air and laughing]. We just continue for ninety minutes; we never stop. All of us together, my friends in the *dawla* and 15,000 more people. You feel strong and you feel free, and it is so much fun. I love it a lot.

When Muhammad talks about his experience with Ultras White Knights, the group comes across as a dispersed and well-oiled machine, channeling hours of hard work by each and every *dawla* into collective effervescence at the stadium. In an insightful analysis of the possibilities and limitations of the Egyptian Ultras as a sociopolitical force, journalist Mohamed Elgohari has argued that it is this ever-ongoing collective project, as much as the movement's abstract principles, that holds the groups together (2013). But the joint efforts of painting flags, composing songs, organizing trips to away games, choreographing *dakhlas*, and propagating it all through social media do more than provide the groups with common goals and a sense of community through repeated practice (see also Close, 2019:115–126). What Muhammad's story also alludes to is the magic of collectively assembled *emotionality* in the *curva*, where feelings of "fun and freedom" are elicited and circulated as a result of physical space, material objects, clever chants, bodies in motion, and a great deal of hard work. Late one night after a game of pick-up football on a local five-a-side pitch, Muhammad elaborated on this experience:

I can't understand young people who go to the stadium and sit down. OK, if you are old and weak, of course you can't jump and sing. But when you're young, you miss the point if you only watch the game. I mean, you can see the match better on television, but it's only at the stadium that you can sing, burn *shamarikh*, jump and do *dakhlas*. If you don't do that, you miss what's special about real football. Honestly, you miss the fun and the freedom [*bi-siraha al-mut'a wi al-hurriyya fatitak*].

The affective distinctiveness of these occasions is striking and impossible to disregard. Indeed, whenever I have had the chance to observe Ultras dancing, singing, and burning *shamarikh* at an Egyptian stadium, one thing that has always been palpable is that the young men are having a great deal of fun. Shadi, the UA07 member and journalist who spelled out the distinction between Ultras and *hatifin*, once described the experience in the *curva* like this:

> There're so many strong feelings, so much adrenalin. You just let go. If I watch a match on television, I usually get nervous that we'll concede a goal or that we'll lose. But when I'm at the stadium, together with the other boys, the result becomes secondary. Sure, we care about winning, but there's so much more going on: flags, *dakhlas*, new songs, and ninety minutes of sweat and jumping. Even if we lose, we've still achieved something. Do you understand my point? We're still doing our thing.

Amro Hassan, the *LA Times* journalist who first talked to me about Egyptian football as a bubble, would most probably agree with Shadi. Slightly too old to join the Ultras in 2007, he has nonetheless followed them closely as a devoted Ahly-fan as well as through his profession. Once when we met, he portrayed the younger fans' feelings and actions as "more organized and somehow more modern and international" than those of older fans like himself. Not without a sliver of envy, he told me: "Ahly fans on the section where I usually sit never do anything creative. [We] basically just go to the stadium to swear at al-Zamalek for 90 minutes. [. . .] The Ultras have a completely different style."

If Cairo's Ultras bring together "a completely different style" at the stadium—a style that, as much as principles and ethics, shapes the appeal of being an Ultra—what precisely renders this style emotionally distinctive? In a comparative research project about emotional variabilities across

Fig. 3.1. Al-Zamalek's Ultras White Knights performing a *dakhla* at Cairo Stadium minutes before kickoff of an African Champions League match between al-Zamalek and AS Douanes from Niger. Photo: Ahmed Gawad, 9 February 2014.

space and time, historian Benno Gammerl has argued for the usefulness of the analytic "emotional styles," i.e., communities of more or less coherent discourses and practices tied to specific emotional registers. Similar to what Pierre Bourdieu would call habitus, styles in Gammerl's sense encompass "the experiencing, fostering, and display of emotions [. . .] discursive patterns and embodied practices as well as [. . .] common scripts and specific appropriations" (2012:163). The registers of fun and freedom that the Egyptian Ultras embody take shape precisely at such an intersection of collective fostering, display, discourse, and embodiment. Through a constellation of disciplined organization, flags, fireworks, songs, clothing, social media, and more, the new fans have come to shape a whole new style for football emotionality that is more intense, more condensed, and more tightly scripted than any previously existing template for acting and feeling as an Egyptian football supporter. The emotional style of the Ultras is at the same time *less* dependent on what is happening on the pitch; as long as everyone comes well prepared and is dedicated enough to sing and dance for ninety minutes, affect is circulating in the stands regardless of match results.

A number of studies of Egypt's new football fan groups have highlighted this centrality of the emotional. Whereas Muhammad Gamal Bashir has depicted the Ultras as "organizers of anarchy" (interviewed by Dorsey, 2016:49), Dalia Abdelhamdeed Ibraheem calls the fans "pleasure-oriented fraternities" (2015:47), and Ronnie Close characterizes the body of the Ultras as a utopian site of visceral energies and aesthetic "dissensus" (2019:71–103). In an often-quoted essay from 2012, sociologist Ashraf el-Sherif, drawing on Asef Bayat (2010:116–158), stressed the political potency of these feelings, as he assigned the new football fans to a novel and rebellious "paradigm of fun." Through an embrace of "joyful liberation from the shackles of social and institutional norms to create gratifying chaos," the Ultras were set up in opposition to a ruling "paradigm of depression, control and normalisation of apathy" that dominated Egypt in the years before January 2011. For el-Sherif, it was this emotional-political paradigm shift that most of all boosted the new fan groups' popularity among the youth in the late Mubarak era (2012; see also Ibraheem, 2015:89–90).

El-Sherif's characterization of the Ultras as a ground-breaking emotional community is apposite, and it resonates with Muhammad's and Shadi's stories about a unique style of fun and freedom that they sought and found at the stadium. As I showed in chapter 1, however, it is not entirely correct to depict the late Mubarak era as *only* depressive and apathetic. The victories, pride, and jubilation pertaining to the Egyptian football bubble brought forward a range of upbeat and exhilarating emotional registers in an otherwise rather gloomy era. In other words, the Ultras' emotional style was not the only kind of fun around at football stadiums in pre-2011 Egypt. Rather, what the new fans' festive joy at the stadiums facilitated was a parallel realm of football fun which, to many young men, seemed more international, more exhilarating, freer and more appealing. Even so, just because this alternative emotional style for football fandom combined great fun with elating freedom, it did not come with an individualist do-what-you-will absence of regulations and constraints. In contrast, the feelings of freedom that made the Ultras so attractive were something to be learned and crafted through strict organization, internal discipline, independent media channels, and decentralized hard work (for comparison, see Mahmood, 2005:29–30). Through these means, Cairo's Ultras groups manufactured a highly particular social-emotional experience in Egypt's football stadiums in the years just before January 2011. Structuring feelings around football in a unique and innovative way, the Ultras' masculine emotional style composed what Raymond Williams would call an emergent "sense of a generation" (1977:131).

Fig. 3.2. Al-Zamalek's Ultras White Knights in action in Cairo Stadium's *talta yimin* during an African Champions League match between al-Zamalek and AS Douanes from Niger. Photo: Ahmed Gawad, 9 February 2014.

DISCOVERED IN TAHRIR SQUARE

The Ultras supporters' relationship to the Egyptian security forces was tense and conflict-ridden from the outset. During a couple of long interviews in May 2012, Sherif Hassan, a journalist who has written extensively about fan cultures across North Africa, explained that the real troubles began in 2008, when the police started to monitor and regulate activities, equipment, and messages in the *curvas*. The Ultras deemed these control measures unacceptable infringements on their rights and countered any attempt at enforcement with violent resistance inside and outside the stadiums. The more the police challenged them, Hassan told me, the more the fans made a point of increasing the activities that the authorities wanted to regulate. When Ultras Ahlawy took their usage of flares and fireworks to a new level at an infamously smoky match in Ismailia in January 2009, the conflict escalated. A few days later, security forces arrested several *capos* from both UA07 and UWK in a coordinated raid on their homes. The arrests were carried out a couple of days before the derby game between al-Ahly and al-Zamalek, and to protest the capture of their leaders, both Ultras groups decided to either boycott the match or attend without their red and white T-shirts and without cheering. Accordingly, Cairo Stadium was eerily silent during the game. Since both *curvas*, where the Ultras usually stand, were only sparsely filled with people dressed in normal clothing, the match has been remembered as the Black Derby (see also Thabet, 2013:38–40).

Shortly after the Black Derby, the arrested *capos* were released, although this was not enough to deescalate the conflict. As the Ultras defied every regulation that the police imposed on their activities, as well as on the controversial pro-Palestinian rhetoric that now appeared in the stands, violent clashes erupted on numerous occasions in 2009 and 2010 (Sherif Hassan, interview, 17 May 2012). The Ministry of Interior even established a special office tasked with monitoring the capital's Ultras groups (Elgohari, 2013). As Hassan described it, the Ultras won several incremental victories during this period; by the end of 2010 they had managed to carve out a unique space for free expression in Egypt's football stadiums (see also Goldblatt, 2010; Ibraheem, 2015:93–96). To some extent, the police regulations were counterproductive. The way the groups proved able to take on the dreaded security state through witty provocations as well as in street fights only increased their appeal among the youth. Indeed, over time the cockiness and violent resistance was incorporated as an intrinsic dimension of the Ultras' masculine style and ethos: a facet of the groups' popular style, which contributed to the fun and guarded their freedom.

The last couple of years before the 25 January Revolution were also the time when Egypt's mainstream football media began to take an interest in the Ultras movement. As Yasser Thabet has analyzed in some detail (2013:37–46), the fan groups' new ways of cheering and defiant resistance against the police became a serious issue for the commentariat. In an article in *al-Misri al-Yum* on 5 January 2009, for instance, famous television presenter Ahmed Shoubair described the Ultras as "solely concerned with firing rockets and taking all sorts of drugs; hence the only reasonable thing is for them to be hit and arrested, since they are out of their minds [*fi ghayr wa'ihim*]" (cited in Thabet, 2013:39). Two years later, senior football journalist Hassan el-Mistakawi devoted a column in *al-Shuruq* to the new manners that the Ultras had brought to Egypt's football stadiums (27 December 2010). After making clear that his belief, hope, and dream had always been that the groups' songs and colors would constitute a positive addition to the stadium atmosphere, he lamented that the young supporters' energy too often was channeled into hatred (*karahiyya*), insults (*sabab*), harm (*idha'*), and animosity (*'ida'*) incongruent with the spirit of sports. Mimicking the dichotomy between fanatical partisanship versus unitary nationalism that had shaped conversations about football in the wake of the Algeria games a year earlier (chapter 2), *al-Shuruq*'s most respectable sports columnist concluded that harsh measures were required to deal with the problem that the Ultras had become for the sport, the police, and, indirectly, the stability of the Egyptian nation-state. As he put it: "When chaos becomes apparent, the solution must be the hard and strict law. History tells us that. All social reforms are based on the sword of the decisive law [*sayf al-qanun al-hasim*]. This applies to everyone without exception; football fans are not immune to the law" (ibid.)

The Ultras who I know would all insist that the Egyptian media have intentionally tarnished the groups' image. When looking back at the time when al-Mistakawi wrote his article, this suspicion seems well-founded. In late 2010, press reports about the Ultras consistently relayed and confirmed the police's derogatory narratives, focusing almost solely on troubles, unruliness, fanaticism, and violence. The 25 January Revolution, which broke out less than a month after al-Mistakawi's publication, fundamentally altered this perception. It is crucial to stress that none of Egypt's Ultras groups explicitly encouraged their members to join the demonstrations at Tahrir Square. While Ultras Ahlawy issued a Facebook statement declaring that they were "a sports group only, which has no political inclinations or affiliations of whatever kind," Ultras White Knights publicly denied that the group participated in any political events (Gibril, 2015:324). At the same time, it is well known that thousands of leaders and rank-and-file members participated in the uprisings. The groups' songs, flags, clothing, and *shamarikh* were visibly and audibly present throughout the eighteen days of protests that culminated with President Mubarak stepping down on 11 February (Hassan, 2012a; Dorsey, 2016:60–61; Ibraheem, 2015:71–72). Due to their experience of on-the-ground organizing and street fights, Ultras played prominent roles in the protection of the sit-in on the square, particularly on 28 January, the so-called Day of Rage, and the 2 February Battle of the Camels (Dorsey, 2011; Zirin, 2011).[11] While this discrepancy between statements and deeds might seem contradictory, it must not be read as such. Like many Egyptians—especially men belonging to impoverished social strata (see Ryzova, 2020)—some Ultras I spoke to did not want to call what happened at Tahrir "politics" (*siyasa*). The notion that members joined the struggle as individual citizens is crucial in this regard. If the Ultras had decided to enter as groups, the movement would inevitably have been embroiled in the divisions, games, and self-interested intrigues that characterize *siyasa*.[12]

In the months that followed, the Ultras were discovered by a wide range of revolution-inclined activists and journalists well beyond the realm of sports. Their years of struggle against the police became a central component of a narrative of the revolution as a liberal quest for freedom, run by different groups of youth, and primarily combating the hated Ministry of Interior. Invariably, these accounts highlighted the international Ultras movement's aversion to the police, summarized in the abbreviation A.C.A.B.—All Cops Are Bastards—which can be found on Ultras flags and graffiti all over the world. The fans' pre-2011 clashes with the security forces were at times portrayed as something akin to a laboratory for the revolution to come. Many commentators noted how this experience had prepared the groups for street fights and fostered the discipline and organization necessary for pushing the police back from Tahrir Square (e.g., Bilal, 2011; Elkayal, 2011; Lindsey, 2011; see also Bashir, 2011:95–103; Elgohari, 2013; Dorsey, 2016:25–91; Gibril, 2015).[13] Another often-mentioned episode was when Ultras Ahlawy had shouted "Tunis, Tunis" and illegally put up a banner with the text "Freedom" at a match on 23 January 2011. Occurring nine days after the ousting of President Ben Ali in Tunisia, the event has been read with hindsight as a prophecy of what was to be unleashed in Egypt only two days later (Hassan, 2012a; Thabet, 2013:63).

One episode revealing how the tide of media coverage and public opinion was turning unfolded in the aftermath of an Egyptian Cup game between al-Ahly and Kima Aswan in September 2011. This was, incidentally, the first match I ever attended at Cairo Stadium, and as I had heard and read a lot about the Ultras, I made sure to get a seat with a good view of their singing, dancing, and *dakhlas* in the *curva*. Throughout the game, I observed Ultras Ahlawy reminding the Central Security officers positioned by their section of their humiliating defeat at Tahrir Square in January, and they repeatedly insulted their antagonists' former boss, the imprisoned former Minister of Interior, Habib el-Adly. Right after the final whistle, the police had had enough. On a given order, they launched a surprise attack against the fans. Police officers chased Ultras supporters up the steep stands and out through the narrow exit, indiscriminately arresting, kicking, and hitting the fleeing youth with their batons. As I got home, somewhat shocked, and turned on the television, I watched the clashes continuing for hours in streets and alleyways outside the stadium.

In the following days, the brawls were a major topic in Egyptian news media. Images of well-equipped police officers hitting and dragging young football supporters at Cairo Stadium filled newspapers, television, and the internet. As Sherif Hassan later confirmed, this coverage was not only significantly more extensive, but also much differently framed than during similar episodes in the past. The sports websites Yallakora.com (Dayf Allah, 2011) and FilGoal.com (Saied, 2011), as well as many private newspapers such as *al-Tahrir* (Abu Bakr and Al-Hamid Sharbani, 2011) supported and reconfirmed the Ultras' view of the incident as an unreasonably violent and unprovoked attack. Many journalists criticized what seemed like completely arbitrary arrests of nine UA07 members. Only state newspapers such as *al-Ahram* (7 September 2011), and Medhat Shalaby's talk show on the network Modern—both infamous for their anti-Ultras stance—echoed the Ministry of Interior's official narrative of "infiltrators inciting violence" and the police showing an "utmost degree of self-control." In contrast to earlier years, then, the media coverage was more favorable to the Ultras' case and cause. At least among the growing number of media outlets self-identifying as "revolutionary," the Egyptian police were by September 2011 an institution to dislike and discredit. Ultras Ahlawy fighting policemen in stadiums and in the streets came across as part and parcel of an ongoing progressive-nationalist struggle for freedom and self-determination.

RESPECTABLE REVOLUTIONARIES OR BRUTAL *BALTAGIYYA*?

In a long article published in *al-Misri al-Yum* on 19 April 2012, my journalist friend Sherif Hassan looked back at the first five years of the Egyptian Ultras movement. Among other things, the text reflected on the clashes that had followed the Kima Aswan match six months earlier. Hassan read the event as both a turning point and an indication of developments to come. On the one hand, the arrests of nine Ultras leaders had united UA07, UWK, and the broader revolutionary movement against the security state. The joint front had won several important victories. It had only taken a short period of outrage—at the stadiums, in demonstrations, and in the media—to get the young men released. New regulations had likewise been introduced, stipulating that the police forces should be positioned not among the Ultras in the stands, but on the running tracks behind the security fences. This constituted a most tangible achievement; the Ultras had demanded such a separation for several years. On the other hand, Hassan stressed that these incremental improvements did not add up to an outright triumph. The Kima Aswan clashes had merely triggered a change in tactics among the forces that wanted to thwart the Ultras' rise to power. As he wrote: "The regime [*al-nizam*] realized that they could not oppress these groups in the traditional way of violence only. Therefore, they once again resorted to the media, which portrayed the youth as *baltagiyya* [thugs], who were paid to unsettle the country's stability."

Hassan's observations are no doubt to the point. Throughout autumn 2011, when Cairo's Ultras groups campaigned for their right to use *shamarikh* at the stadiums, they were consistently met by accusations of being *baltagiyya* (singular, *baltagi*) by football media pundits, club officials, the police, and the Egyptian Football Association (see, for example, al-Din Muhammad, 2011). The Ultras were by no means the only group of young Egyptians to face this accusation at the time. By contrast, moral-political conversations about *baltaga* (thuggery) played a central role throughout Egypt's revolutionary process, and especially so in late 2011.

The emergence of *baltagiyya* as *the* issue to address that first revolutionary autumn harkened back on a long tradition. As several scholars have noted, since the Ottoman era the *baltagi* has signified an ambivalent masculine subject associated with physical strength, social marginalization, criminality, and drugs (Ghannam, 2013:121–132; Jacob, 2011:225–262; Ziedan, 2011; see also Rommel, 2016; Wahba, 2020). Thuggery was further emphasized in the late 1990s, when *baltaga* efficiently replaced Islamist terrorism as the primary imagined threat to the Egyptian nation. A public focus on poor young males now occasioned increased security measures and middle-class moral panics (Ismail, 2006:139–145). From this moment on, the regime also began to mobilize *baltagiyya* as part of its statecraft, as the security apparatus recruited former prisoners as plainclothes thugs. More generally, as Paul Amar has showed, dangerous masculinities were "hypervisibilized" in demonstrations as well as in public space (2011b, 2013).

During the bloody protests and street fights that took place on and around Cairo's Muhammad Mahmoud Street, Tahrir Square, and, slightly later, the Cabinet building in autumn 2011, this historically complex phenomenon surfaced as a dominant discursive figure and a political tool applied by the regime. As thousands of young men took to the streets, distinctions were repeatedly drawn between nonviolent "revolutionary youth" (*shabab al-thawra*) and bad elements—*baltagiyya*—who sought to destabilize the nation and derail what had so far been achieved. Friends of mine who had previously been largely positive toward popular power and demonstrations now began to question the usefulness of more protests. With the country's first free parliamentary elections approaching, more and more Egyptians considered it time to clean up the streets and enter a new phase of a more institutionalized type of revolutionary politics.

The tendency to draw separations between the revolution's good and bad elements inevitably came with problematic side effects. Political scientist and leftist activist Rabab El-Mahdi early on pointed to the strong class connotations of the *baltagiyya* discourse. In her view, the focus on thuggery created a counterproductive split between "respectable" middle-class revolutionaries and the "vulgar" lower classes, who were often the most vulnerable to Mubarak's neoliberal reforms and police violence (2012). In a similar vein, historian Lucie Ryzova has observed the strict spatial division between working-class men on the front lines of the Muhammad Mahmoud clashes and middle-class protesters who more often stayed in the relative safety of nearby Tahrir Square (2011; 2020). Coming into downtown from Cairo's informal neighborhoods on "cheap Chinese motorcycles" while sporting "a particular dress code and hairstyle that often involve copious quantities of gel," the men who Ryzova saw fighting at the frontier had for many years been portrayed as troublemakers, sexual harassers, and threats to public order (2011). Consequently, the label *baltagiyya* would always come in handy as middle-class Egyptians tried to make sense of what was going on. And yet it was precisely these discredited men who threw rocks at the police, carried the injured to hospital on their motorcycles, and paid with their blood as the security forces retaliated with birdshot and sharp ammunition. Somewhat paradoxically, therefore, the young men labeled *baltagiyya* were simultaneously the villains and the unsung heroes of Egypt's revolutionary struggle (Ryzova, 2020).

The obsession with *baltagiyya* throughout Egyptian public discourse inevitably affected the stance taken by Egypt's Ultras groups toward the Muhammad Mahmoud uprising. While I have talked to members of both groups who participated actively in the protests in late 2011, Ultras Ahlawy and Ultras White Knights took the same position as in January: none of the groups publicly called on their members to join the fights (see also Ryzova, 2020:292–294). For UWK, this attitude changed somewhat when one of theirs—Shihab Ahmed from the informal (*'ashwa'i*) neighborhood Bulaq al-Dakrur—was killed on the third day of the clashes. Thereafter, the group's criticism of the police and the military became fiercer, and the *capos* encouraged all UWK members to attend the martyr's funeral. But not even at this point did UWK directly tell its rank-and-file to join the struggle en masse. Instead, group representatives, as well as Shihab's family, had to face aggressive questions about the dead man's history, morals, and motives. In an interview published on the football website alforsan.net five days after Shihab's death, his mother struck back against those who questioned that her son was a proper revolutionary martyr (*shahid*). Understandably traumatized and pressured by the media questioning her dead son's role in the street fights, she claimed that "the one who goes to a protest prepared to sacrifice his life (*musta'id lil-tadhiyya bi-ruhi*) cannot possibly be a *baltagi*. He is a hero and a man and not a tramp (*mutasharrid*) as some people claim." The title of the article was indicative of the mood in the country and the defensiveness of the protesters: "The mother of the martyr: 'Those who die in Tahrir are not *baltagiyya*'" (Diyab, 2011).

The longer the unrest continued, the more difficult it became to rid the protests of allegations of *baltaga*. After a short period of calm in early December, the fighting downtown resumed, after military police broke up a sit-in outside the Cabinet building. The scenes of tear gas, Molotov cocktails, stone-throwing teenagers, and armed policemen firing rubber bullets, birdshot, and live ammunition at this point felt like a ghastly rerun of an all-too-familiar script. But a distinct change in attitude was also noticeable. One taxi driver shouted at me: "The police must hit them harder, to save the revolution!" At the grocer's, I overheard: "The state must defend itself against those criminals." My friend Hamdi, an *Ahlawy* in his early thirties with Islamist sympathies, was one of many to reconceptualize events unfolding around him. Only a few weeks earlier, Hamdi had been outraged by the "unacceptable" violence committed against protesters by the military and the police. Three days into the second wave of violence—and a mere twenty-four hours after footage of Egyptian military police dragging and beating a veiled woman in Tahrir Square, famously revealing her bare belly and blue bra, had spread across international media—he told me:

> Have you seen those who camp in Tahrir Square? I pass them every day, and I can tell you, they aren't good people, not respectable [*mish muhtarama*]. Probably they are paid by Gamal Mubarak to destroy the elections. By the way, that woman [in the blue bra] wasn't a real *munaqqaba* [woman wearing the full-body veil, *niqab*]. You could see it on the type of underwear she wore. [. . .] This is a Muslim country, Carl. It can't be run this way. But *Insha'Allah*, it'll be rebuilt step by step through elections and institutions. All of them are *baltagiyya*! Honestly, it doesn't matter to me if they die or not.

At least in its official channels of communication, the Ultras' attitude toward what was going on in downtown Cairo was cautious and in line with the general mood; a couple of days into the second stint of clashes, both UA07 and UWK posted public statements on their Facebook pages stressing their nonpartisan profile and disassociating themselves from the skirmishes. One of UA07's *capos*, Ahmed Idris, even made a rare appearance in the mainstream press, denying rumors that one of the men killed had been a member of his group. Instead, he made clear that UA07 was against "any action that hurts the interest of the country and its institutions [*maslahit al-balad wi munsha'atiha*]" and that all individuals present at the protests were there as "citizens only and not as members of any kind of group" (*al-Shuruq*, 21 December 2011). In one sense, this careful positioning was neither new nor particularly surprising: the Ultras had always claimed their struggle to be a "nonpolitical" one, limited to football-internal issues and to the protection of their own "rights" (Bashir, 2011; Gibril, 2015; Shenker, 2016:375–376). Moreover, as groups of young, loud, and rowdy men, they would always be susceptible to accusations of *baltaga*. At the same time, the urgency with which the Ultras distanced themselves from *this* particular episode of violence is noteworthy. Clearly, this was not a case of working-class street fighters shunning the "insincere game" of middle-class "politics" (see Ryzova, 2020:34). In a discursive climate where many Egyptians associated the protests with *baltaga*—a classed and purportedly destructive modality of politics that in turn was singled out as the main threat to the interests of the nation—the Ultras did all they could to side with the respectable common good against the troublemakers, whoever they might be.

In the end of December, the fighting finally subsided. The Ministry of Health reported twelve people dead and 815 injured. Crucially for this story, one of the casualties—a young student named Mohamed Mustafa or "Karika"—was a well-known member of Ultras Ahlawy. When Karika was shot dead on Qasr al-Ainy Street on 21 December—incidentally the same day that Idris's cautious statements appeared in *al-Shuruq*—the football fan group he had been part of was abruptly pushed straight back into the revolutionary struggle. Suddenly, there was no other way to go. The group's own interests were now in conflict with those of the Egyptian security state. Two days later, al-Ahly played Misr lil-Maqqasa at Cairo Stadium, and UA07 turned the entire match into a tribute to the martyr and a protest against the state violence that had killed him. Most Ultras present were dressed in black instead of the normal red, the *dakhla* before kick-off covered *talta shimal* with a huge black-and-white portrait of their dead friend, and al-Ahly's legendary Portuguese coach, Manuel José, showed his sympathies by wearing a "RIP Mohamed Mustafa" T-shirt under his tweed jacket. Throughout the game, the fans' chanting against the ruling military council and the Ministry of Interior was more explicit than ever before; high up above the *curva*, they had hung an enormous banner with a message that read: "The engineer Mohamed, martyr of freedom. The *baltagiyya* killed him with live ammunition" (see Ultras Ahlawy's Facebook page, 23 December 2011).

The banner's contrast between the martyred "engineer" (Mohamed

Mustafa had been an engineering student) and the *baltagiyya* who killed him—referring not so vaguely to the Ministry of Interior and the military—had an important rhetorical function. In the days that followed, Mustafa's educational qualifications and the fact that he had been one of the country's best tennis players were reiterated constantly by Ultras Ahlawy as well as in the media (see, for example, Maher, 2011). This framing of the dead supporter effectively disrupted the narrative of the ongoing protests as lawless, destructive *baltaga*, because as every Egyptian would instantly recognize, an engineering student who also played an expensive sport like tennis was not just anybody, but a member of the respectable upper-middle classes. In this way, Karika's martyrdom—in striking contrast to working-class Shihab Ahmed's death a month earlier (see Rommel, 2016)—testified that the protesters and Ultras Ahlawy were not *baltagiyya* but real, respectable *shabab al-thawra* (revolutionary youth).[14] Well-established rifts between fighters and demonstrators, violence and reason, partisanship and nationalism, and differently classed notions of political action all came to nothing. As a result, Ultras Ahlawy's emotional style was more self-confident than ever when they honored Karika at Cairo Stadium that December night. It made perfect sense for them to reflect the discourse of the establishment back onto the police and the military. Singing from the stands their most provocative song about Egypt's policemen as failures in school and corrupt "crows" that destroy the fun and freedom for the youth, the Ultras returned over and over again to a rhyming chant that was as simple as it was effective: *al-dakhiliyya—baltagiyya* (The Ministry of Interior—are *baltagiyya*) (Ultras Ahlawy 07 Media, 2011).

CONCLUSION: BREAKING FREE FROM THE BUBBLE

With ten minutes remaining of the January 2012 game between al-Ahly and Smouha, I had had enough of the cold and decided to climb down to the Ultras on the tier below me. With the home team winning 3–1, the mood among the fans was upbeat. Upon entering the stands and passing under the red-and-black Ultras Ahlawy banner, I felt the warming presence of a few thousand young males jumping around. The two *capos* on the loudspeakers leaned toward us, pumping their open palms in the air and urging the group to sing even louder, to jump even higher. The concrete walls of *talta shimal* were covered in graffiti, mostly simple tags of Ultras Ahlawy, UA07, or Ultras Devils, but also A.C.A.B. slogans, insults directed at the football association, and stencils of the martyred Karika's smiling face. Many members carried flags with messages critical of the ruling military council, the police, the football media, and modern football; all around me, people were shouting insults at the state security personnel, now positioned at safe distance on the running tracks behind high fences. Finally, it seemed, the Ultras' distinctive aesthetics and fandom had gained absolute control in their sector of the stadium, something they had always insisted to be their inalienable right. The young men were not merely guests, accepting the rules of the stadium hosts. They were the de facto owners of the *curva*, in charge of a parallel football event that had grown into something quite substantial.

As this chapter has illustrated, the self-confidence that Ultras Ahlawy radiated this night was one of many dramatic outcomes of Egypt's revolutionary transformation. The Egyptian Ultras had both shaped and were shaped by a series of reconfigurations initiated in the late 2000s, and which came together in a perfect storm after 25 January 2011. In some regards, the aims and objectives of their struggle were easily recognizable. Like many other groups of rebellious Egyptians in 2011 and 2012, the Ultras fought a battle ultimately focused on *hurriyya* from the clubs that they despised, from journalists who understood nothing, and from police interventions in the *curva* that they claimed as theirs. But the freedom that the supporters had demanded and gained was visceral as much as ideological. It rested on lofty principles, surely, but it also manifested in an emotional style of self-sovereignty and control over the match event's affective timespace. Put simply, the story of the Egyptian Ultras' rise to fame and power demonstrates that January 2011 was not only a struggle over political representation, recognition, ideals, and resources, but also a revolt of and through emotions and affect.

What exactly was the emotional style of the new football fans a rebellion against? According to political scientist Salwa Ismail, it was first and foremost a matter of settling scores. In an article spotlighting the Ultras' teasing songs about the idiocy of the security forces, Ismail locates the football fans within a broad affective revolution by lower-class Egyptian men against the humiliation that the police's systematic, semimilitary surveillance campaigns had long caused (2012; see also Ryzova, 2020). Others, like Ashraf el-Sherif (2012), have rather pointed to a generational "politics of fun": an affective resistance against a hegemonic block of Islamist and secular elites that since the 1990s had looked down on "purposeless" amusements and regulated youthful joy in Egypt (for comparison, see Ismail, 2006b:58–81; Schielke, 2012:81–110).[15] Ismail and el-Sherif no doubt identify central layers of the Ultras' affective revolt. Provoking the police was both thrilling and subversive, and their ecstatic fun at the stadiums did break hegemonic norms. At the same time, it is worth reiterating that Hosni Mubarak's Egypt did not *only* limit, repress, and ban emotions. Football, as demonstrated in chapter 1, brought together a powerful constellation of upbeat and successive affect, emotionality, and subjectivity within a benign, regime-friendly bubble. To see the full scope of the emotional revolution unleashed by the Ultras, this other emotional football politics must be considered too. For if the distribution of sentiments that football circulated in the late Mubarak era sustained a hegemonic crafting of the state and the nation, then parallel emotional styles of fun and freedom challenged this modality of statecraft. Much more than a struggle *for* fun and *against* power, the rising popularity of the joyful Ultras coincided with a period when the media, popular culture, and Egypt's football-political establishment sanctioned, even encouraged, markedly different registers of football-related joy and fun.

For many middle-aged men with power, the emotional style of the Ultras was not only difficult to comprehend, but also a challenge to what they believed that Egyptian football fandom, and in effect the Egyptian nation, should be about. Similar to the unruly ecstasy found at Sufi *mulids* (Schielke, 2012) or the destabilizing fun manifested by other youth movements (Bayat, 2010:137–160), the Ultras' independence, energy, affect, and freedom reshaped and challenged a particular affective state disseminated by the national game, which the old regime had propped up and relied on. The new fan groups' carefully assembled style of decentralized organization, material equipment, and collective hard work constituted a different type of fun, and embodied an alternative form of power (for comparison, see Schielke, 2012:7). It should come as no surprise, then, that the state's security apparatus made wholehearted efforts to curb what the young men were doing and feeling at Egypt's football stadiums. The establishment media's more or less successful attempts to accuse the Ultras of *baltaga*, partisanship, and violence must be understood in the same light.

Yet the Ultras' alternative vision for football and fandom was not the only criticism of the status quo gaining momentum in Egypt in 2010 and 2011. As the previous chapter illustrated, a distinctive set of public conversations around the national game's fanaticism and politicization had likewise been in sway since the national team's defeat to Algeria in late 2009. By early 2012, the Mubarak era's bubble of football, celebrities, media spectacles, and emotionality was thus squeezed from two directions: from the increasingly powerful Islamists and anti-Mubarak intellectuals, who considered the recent football hype a vulgar and unrespectable distraction from more pressing concerns, and who wanted to expunge sports from the national project; and from the young Ultras groups, inspired by like-minded fans in the Maghreb and Europe, that despised the bubble for being dated, corrupt, and hopelessly boring. The two flanks did not agree on everything. Many older "respectable" voices would consider the Ultras part of the problem, yet another proof of the sport's fanaticism and function as an opiate of the masses. And in contrast to the anti-football block forming in November 2009, the Ultras were of course by no means anti-football. While highly critical of the sport as it had been run, they also staked out a concrete alternative for the national game and a possible way forward.

By January 2012, UA07 and UWK's emotional style was in other words a singular sphere of football fandom that was picking up momentum in a football-skeptical Egyptian society. Even so, troubling questions loomed. To what extent could the Ultras' project thread the fine line between unifying nationalism and partisan-political interests that had been debated so fiercely at the time of the Algeria games, and that had sprung up again at the time of the Muhammad Mahmoud clashes? Would they be able to *combine* youthful energy and radicalism with class-conscious scripts for order and respectability? As I will show in chapters 4 and 5, this balancing act would not go away in the years that followed. As the Ultras intensified their campaign for a revolutionary kind of football in revolutionary Egypt, their masculine subjectivity would at the same time become more questioned and more celebrated than ever. The inherent tension between Egyptian nationalism and politics would likewise arise again and again. Before that, however, a dreadful event in Port Said would shake and shock Egyptian football. How this tragedy impacted on the Ultras movement is the topic of the next chapter.

CHAPTER 4

A Respectable Revolution Measures Its Violence

I think they understand that they have a problem. Football is dying after Port Said, but the Ultras are really strong. We have shown that we can do things; whatever we want to do, we do it. But they don't understand us. They're old and thinking in old ways. It's the same everywhere: in the clubs, in the media, and even among proper football journalists, like Hassan al-Mistakawi [columnist at al-Shuruq*]. They cannot understand us, but also, they cannot stop us. Maybe it sounds strange after all that happened, but I'm sure that the future of Egyptian football belongs to the Ultras.*

Shadi, longtime member of Ultras Ahlawy, May 2012

On Wednesday, 1 February 2012, just as another golden sunset faded into an inescapably cold winter's evening, a gruesome event of death and violence marked Egyptian football irreversibly. In a football league with just half a dozen popular clubs (*andiyya sha'biyya*) with supporters, the matches this night were as spectacular as could be: at 5 p.m., al-Masry from Port Said was hosting al-Ahly from Cairo; immediately thereafter, al-Zamalek was to take on al-Ismaily Sporting Club at Cairo Stadium. During my morning Arabic class, I noted an unusual level of anticipation among the school's administrative staff members, Basam and Hani. They discussed tactics, asked me to predict results, and took turns explaining how a combination of history and geography had made football fans in Port Said and Ismailia the country's most loyal. "It was always like that along the Suez Canal," Basam told me:

They say it has to do with the way that region was at the front line in all the wars. In '56, '67, and '73, Israeli attacks destroyed the canal cities. The people had to move, also the football clubs. This made them very proud of their cities and of their football. Much more than in Beni Suef [Basam's hometown 140 km south of Cairo], where everyone supports al-Ahly or al-Zamalek.

Hani added:

> In the war period, when al-Ismaily Club had to be based in Cairo, they asked al-Ahly if they could use their facilities to train and play matches. To be hosted temporarily, you know [*istidafa mu'aqqata, ya'ni*]. But al-Ahly said no, so they asked al-Zamalek, and they said yes. Ever since, people in Ismailia hate al-Ahly. It's the same in Port Said.

Al-Ahly's refusal to host al-Ismaily when the canal zone was evacuated (1967–1973) is an often-told story. I had heard it several times before February 2012, and it would come up again in countless conversations with interviewees and friends in the following years. Details about how and with whom the canal clubs spent the war years vary.[1] Yet it is an indisputable fact that al-Ahly has far fewer fans along the Suez Canal than in other parts of the country. For many decades, al-Masry against al-Ahly has constituted one of Egypt's fiercest football rivalries. Consequently, this was a match that both Basam and Hani would be sure to watch. "You know that I'm *Ahlawi* [an al-Ahly supporter]," Hani told me as I got ready to leave. "But I tell you what, the most passionate supporters in Egypt come from Port Said. You should go to a game there some day, for your research. There is much more enthusiasm [*hamasa*] up there than here in Cairo; those guys are really crazy [*maganin bigad*]."

The game that evening constituted one of the season's highlights for al-Ahly's Ultras supporters too. Earlier the same morning, a few thousand members had met outside the club's compound in central Cairo and several hundred more had set out for Port Said from Alexandria. Because of a strike among the bus drivers who usually drove Ultras Ahlawy (UA07) to away games, the trip from Cairo had been reorganized at the last minute; the fans had eventually boarded a slow northbound train. The last time Ultras Ahlawy had traveled to a game in Port Said, some eight months earlier, there had been clashes between Ahly and Masry supporters outside the stadium. The skirmishes resulted in several injuries and a lot of damaged property. Possibly to avoid another altercation, the train carrying the Ahly fans was stopped by the army some twenty kilometers before reaching its final destination. Here, a mere thirty minutes before kickoff, all Ultras were ordered to disembark and board buses that drove them directly to the arena. The escort by police and military personnel did not hinder home fans from hurling stones and firecrackers as the buses approached the stadium in Port Said. Yet as one Ultra clarified in a widely circulated eyewitness account, "all of this was still very normal and happens everywhere we travel" (The Art of Chaos, 2012).

The scenes outside the stadium might have looked "normal," but inside, the atmosphere was unusually edgy. As I planned to attend the subsequent Zamalek match at Cairo Stadium with a friend, I ended up watching the Masry-Ahly game in a small *ahwa* (coffee shop) inside a community center in nearby Nasser City. The establishment's small television set was enough to convey the tensions reigning in Port Said. During the warm-up session, home fans threw firecrackers at the Ahly players, and the kickoff was delayed to allow the crowds time to calm down. At halftime, more than a dozen Masry fans scaled the security fences and ran around on the pitch with little interference from police or security personnel. In the second half, with the home team turning a 1–0 deficit into a surprising 3–1 victory, events really spiraled out of control: someone threw an unknown object that hit the head of al-Ahly's Portuguese coach Manuel José; people in the stands launched fireworks directly toward the players on the pitch; and the referee interrupted the game numerous times, as home fans repeatedly made their way over the security barriers. For a couple of older men next to me in the *ahwa*, the scenes playing out on the screen were completely unreasonable (*mish ma''ul khalis*). The lack of organization at the stadium was a scandal, the home fans' behavior a sign of *ta'assub* (fanaticism), for which Port Said had long been infamous. "Look at our players, José and the referee," a middle-aged *Ahlawi* behind me complained. "They all look scared; this is not right; this is not football."

Just before full-time, I dragged myself away from the coffee shop and the televised drama to catch the kickoff of the Zamalek-Ismaily game. In the crowds lining up outside the stadium entrance, news reached us that the match in Port Said was over. Al-Ahly had lost; a win for al-Zamalek would see them leapfrog their rivals at the top of the league standings. As a result, the atmosphere among the home fans was very cheerful as we took our seats. God willing, several people in my section assured me, this was going to be the season when al-Ahly, the winner of the last seven league titles, would finally prove beatable.

The start of our match was promising too. It was a fast-flowing encounter between two of the country's best teams, both seeking to capitalize on al-Ahly's surprising slip-up. At halftime, with the score tied 2–2, a young guy with a transistor radio a few rows behind me suddenly spoke up:

"Listen folks, two from al-Ahly's supporters are in the morgue in Port Said. They say there might be more [*asma'u yi gama'a, itnayn min gumhur al-ahli fil-mashraha fi bur sa'id. Biy'ulu mumkin tiktir*]." Instantly, rumors started to spread. Everyone tried to find reliable news. People congregated around radios; men with smartphones frantically updated Twitter. Someone said there were six dead, then we heard fifteen, then twenty-two. Just like the people around us, my friend and I could not believe what we were hearing. But when our match was called off, and the players and al-Zamalek's coach, Hassan Shehata, entered the field crying, we realized that something really terrible had taken place in Port Said. In the taxi on my way back downtown, the driver and I sat quietly and listened to the radio report that just would not stop the awful count: twenty-six, thirty-two, thirty-eight. Later in the night, I got a better sense of the scale of it all. The attack had been broadcast live on television, and through the night the dreadful images rolled over and over again on every Egyptian football channel: several thousand exhilarated spectators from the home stands storming the pitch upon the final whistle; the police mysteriously stepping back, doing nothing; the Ahly players desperately fleeing, barely managing to take cover in the dressing room; hundreds, perhaps thousands, of Masry supporters continuing across the field up to the Ahly Ultras sections without any police interference; the lights in the stadium suddenly going out; fires burning on the terraces; the glimmering of what looked like long, sharp weapons; chaos; panic, death, and horror.[2]

The death toll in Port Said finally stopped at seventy-two, making the carnage by far the deadliest stadium disaster ever in Egypt and the fourth-worst football tragedy anywhere in the world. All victims were members of Ultras Ahlawy or its Alexandrian sister-group Ultras Devils, and all of them were young: the youngest—Anas—was only fifteen years old. Some of the victims were stabbed to death with sharp objects; some were strangled; several were burned with blazing *shamarikh*. Still others were pushed or forced to jump from the top of the stadium, falling down on the pavement some fifteen meters below. Many of the casualties were suffocated in a stampede as people tried to flee down a narrow corridor toward the exit, only to find that the iron gate facing the streets was locked.[3] One supporter passed away inside al-Ahly's dressing room among the shocked players. Somehow, he had been brought in to get first aid by the team's medical personnel, but it was too little, too late.

At half past three the next morning, a train from Port Said pulled in at Cairo's Ramsis railway station. On board were many injured and

Fig. 4.1. Stencil of the youngest Port Said martyr, Anas Mohyeldin on a wall in central Cairo. The text underneath Anas's face is UA07's famous slogan: *yi nigib haqquhum, yi nimut zayhum* (either we will bring their rights, or we will die like them). The smaller print above reads: "Parking forbidden except for at the nation's borders." This slogan demands that the army go back to the barracks (at the borders), that is, that the military stay away from politics. Photo: Gigi Ibrahim, 10 February 2012.

traumatized supporters who had been lucky enough to survive the blood-bath. The train's arrival was broadcast live on several television channels. The main hall, the platforms, and even most of the tracks were packed with relatives, friends, political activists, and members of both Ultras Ahlawy and Ultras White Knights (UWK). As the train slowly made its way through the crowds, a persistent chant echoed throughout the spacious nineteenth-century building: *yi nigib haqquhum, yi nimut zayhum* (either we will bring their rights [i.e., bring them justice], or we will die like them).

The determination showed that night was a first indication of actions to come: in the weeks and months that followed, al-Ahly's Ultras (with some support from UWK) came out in the streets in an impressively organized, highly visible, and emotionally charged campaign for *al-qasas* (justice, ret-ribution) and *haqq al-shuhada'* (the rights of/justice for the martyrs).[4] The next afternoon a large demonstration with songs, chants, flags, and fire-works proceeded from al-Ahly Club on Gezira Island across Qasr el-Nil bridge to Tahrir Square. The event was both a solemn occasion for grief and mourning and an effort to pressure the judiciary and the newly elected parliament to ensure fair trials and harsh penalties. As many participants blamed the security forces' inaction (or complicity) for the death of their friends, demonstrators soon spilled over into the streets surrounding the Ministry of Interior. Over the next few days, clashes resembling those at Muhammad Mahmoud Street two months earlier filled downtown Cairo. Protesters threw rocks at the security forces. The police retaliated with tear gas, rubber bullets, birdshot, and live ammunition. The spiral of violence drew thousands of young protesters into the unrest. Ultras and non-Ultras alike braved the security forces in the streets, adamant about claiming back the rights of their killed friends.

But Ultras Ahlawy would also seek retribution by other means. After the tragedy, the Egyptian Premier League was suspended, and international matches were played without fans. Ultras Ahlawy and Ultras Devils formally called off all stadium-based activities to mourn their dead and to seek justice, and their rivals in Ultras White Knights followed suit in a gesture of support. The Egyptian Ultras' activities now changed character. What had been tightly organized football fraternities acting out a distinctive emotional style at Egypt's football stadiums increasingly took the shape of dedicated activist organizations. Throughout the winter and spring of 2012, the groups were busy attending funerals and visiting the families of their martyred friends. Graffiti with the names and faces of the Port Said martyrs spread on walls all around Cairo. Leaders from the group also made appearances in some of Egypt's most prominent political talk shows,[5] and they published a sequence of strongly worded declarations and evidential material on their Facebook page, outlining their version of what had happened in Port Said and who was to blame (4 February 2012). UA07 made clear that they held three groups responsible for the massacre: al-Masry's Ultras fans, who had carried out the killings; the police, who had failed to intervene; and the Military Council, Egypt's executive rulers at the time. Across these statements, Ultras Ahlawy alluded to a ghastly hunch shared by many revolutionary journalists and activists at the time: what had happened in Port Said had not been an outburst of "normal" fan violence. It was a set-up by the remnants of the old regime, intended to punish a group of youngsters that in the last year had become too bold and provocative.

The focus of this chapter is on Ultras Ahlawy's campaign for retribution, rights, and reforms in the wake of the Port Said massacre. If chapter 3 demonstrated how the new fans challenged the emotional-political

Fig. 4.2. Murals commemorating the victims of the Port Said massacre on Cairo's Muhammad Mahmoud Street. From left to right: Mahmoud Suliman, Muhammad Gamal Muhammad, Anas Mohyeldin, Ahmed Yusif. The text in the top-right corner reads "Glory to the martyrs." Photo: Hossam el-Hamalawi, 10 February 2012.

football bubble before and immediately after January 2011, this one considers a period of shock and mourning when the old football complex was in disarray and questions about how to rebuild the sport abounded. A wealth of reports and analyses have been published about the Port Said massacre and the speculations, sit-ins, and demonstrations that took place in the months that followed it.[6] Seeking to complement these studies, my attention is instead directed to a handful of events during a slightly later and less canonized period: the so-called Egyptian Super Cup match in September 2012, the player Muhammad Abu Treika's decision to boycott the same match, and two similar yet different demonstrations outside the Presidential Palace in late October. Accounts of Egypt's revolutionary years have rarely emphasized this period. Falling after the dramatic presidential elections in May and June but before the wave of unrest that culminated in the July 2013 military coup, the autumn of 2012 is, for good reasons, thought of as a moment of relative calm. Nonetheless, a variety of lesser struggles continued to bubble in Egypt. Although Tahrir Square remained empty and party politics comparatively uneventful, many powerful institutions and actors felt uncertain about how a Muslim

Brotherhood–dominated government and a new postrevolutionary system would affect the privileges that they had enjoyed under Mubarak. Strikes and sit-ins were common in workplaces (Shenker, 2016:279–325); independent trade unions expanded (Abdalla, 2020); drastic measures were taken within the crisis-ridden Egyptian tourism sector to bring visitors back (Ahlberg, 2017:175–258).

The chapter examines another such revolution at the margins of the main stage and dominant story. As my ethnography shows, UA07's cause was strengthened tremendously at the expense of previously powerful establishment actors. Most of the group's key demands were met; the fans gained widespread public support; in early autumn 2012, the young football supporters seemed capable of changing everything. My narrative locates this moment of unprecedented strength within overlapping nationalist discourses on stability, respectability, order, and violence. In particular, it highlights the fans' balanced use of violence—never geared to their own partial interests, always with a purpose and for the common good—which resonated with deeply rooted working-class ideals for Egyptian manhood. Combined with an aura of middle-class respectability, granted primarily by Muhammad Abu Treika's endorsement, this made the fan groups all but untouchable. Neither accusations of rowdy thuggery and political partisanship, nor appeals to order and national stability, had any effect. In the process, the masculine figure of the Ultra surfaced as a self-confident, emotionally controlled, and highly respectable role model. The football fans staked out a promising vision for the revolution as well as for the nation at large.

THE SUPER CUP

In late August 2012, a couple of days after the Eid al-Fitr holidays, two months after the inauguration of President Muhammad Mursi, and half a year after the tragedy in Port Said, the Egyptian Football Association (EFA) decided to resume its domestic football tournaments. In a short press release, the EFA announced that a Super Cup match between the reigning league and cup champions, al-Ahly and ENPPI, was to be played on 9 September and that the Premier League would commence one week later. Within Egyptian sports media, the decision was widely applauded. Many considered it a sign that the difficult period of political instability and mourning was over. The country had an elected president, demonstrators had been removed from Tahrir Square, and things were getting back to normal: the "return of the football activities" (*'awdit al-nashat*) was a logical step in a broad national restart.

But the football revival would not be as smooth as journalists and EFA officials had hoped. In the early hours of 3 September, a statement was posted on Ultras Ahlawy's Facebook page. Under the title "The League Will Not Return over the Blood of the Martyrs," the proclamation described the EFA's decision as rushed, disrespectful, and motivated by monetary greed:

- The discussion about the return of football and the noise that the corrupted media is making to display it as a religious festival [*'id*] show complete disdain [*istihtar*], not only for the feelings of the martyrs' families and relatives, but also for the young men who were present in Port Said, but whom Allah destined to live [*katab lihum Allah al-haya'*]. [. . .]
- Do you want the return of football? Do you want to reduce this affair to a handful of money? Do you count the value of those who died in money? If there are those who buy and sell among you, then that is your misfortune. We, however, do not perceive that money [*nafis aw ghali*] equals the value of those who died in our arms.

After also portraying the restart as a cynical attempt to "distract everybody from what actually happened" in Port Said, UA07's statement closed on an unwavering note:

- Neither the Super Cup nor the league will be played before *al-qasas* [retribution]. [. . .] Thereafter you can talk about activities and tournaments. Although for now, what you dream about is a black comedy which draws superficial smiles on your faces. But if you insist on going ahead with this tournament, we will fondly wait with the same smiles for what will happen next . . .
- Oh God be our witness.

Initially, the Ultras' defiance did not draw much attention. Preparations for the new season continued as planned. On 5 September, the league draw took place at the EFA headquarters in a ceremony broadcast live on television. Just a few hours later, images from the same building, but of a markedly different drama, filled the airwaves. Hundreds of young men in UA07 attire broke into the EFA premises, burned *shamarikh*, smashed windows, destroyed documents and computers, and displaced some of the national team's trophies. This was Ultras Ahlawy showing that their threats were serious: they would not just sit back and let the new football season start "over the blood of the martyrs."

Later in the evening, I received a phone call from my friend Mido. An upper-middle-class man in his early thirties, Mido had been a member of Ultras Ahlawy from the beginning in 2007. He had traveled to Ahly games all over Africa and even to Japan, and he knew the *capos* well enough to act as what he liked to call an "older consultant" in periods of crisis. "You saw what happened, Carl, didn't you?" he asked in his flawless English, acquired through private language school education and regular trips to England since his early teens. I told him that I had seen the news on Twitter and asked him for his opinion. I was a bit surprised to hear how concerned he was:

> I don't know. Really, I'm not sure. . . . Of course, I understand the boys; that they're angry and want to stop this stupid game. But I fear it could be counterproductive. The attacks are all over the media; it will not help our case. I think we'll lose a lot of the middle people that have supported us since Port Said. I don't like to tell you, but I think this was a big mistake.

The following day, I had dinner with a group of friends who would probably qualify as the "middle people" whose sympathies Mido worried about. University-educated and in their late twenties or early thirties, all of them were devoted football fans who considered themselves "revolutionary" insofar as they had voted for Hamdeen Sabahi, Abdel Moneim Aboul Fotouh, or Muhammad Mursi (i.e., *against* representatives of the former regime) in the recent presidential elections. Throughout our meal, we discussed the resumption of football and the Ultras' attempts to stop it. Mahmoud—the one at the table I knew the best—suggested that this was no straightforward choice between good and evil: "The football media and the FA and the clubs are of course completely corrupt. All of you know how much I dislike them. But at the same time, what the new government needs is stability (*istiqrar*) and time to work. Not more insults and fanaticism (*sha-ta'im wi ta'assub*), like in Port Said or at el-Gabalaya [the EFA] yesterday." But Mahmoud's work colleague Ahmad did not entirely agree:

> I don't know . . . If it just leads to trouble, why do they have to play this match? I'm of course against violence, that's not the solution,

and if it's true that they stole the Africa Cup trophies, then that isn't only bad manners and fanaticism [*illit adab wi ta'assub*] but a crime against all Egyptians. I mean, these cups belong to us [*al-ku'us di milkina*]. But we also have to understand these youngsters. They lost their friends and they haven't got anything back. I understand that they got tired. Nothing happens in this country unless you push for it.

The others around the table nodded silently.

Ultras Ahlawy's attack on the Football Association did not divide just dinner parties. In the following days, a fault line crystallized right across Egypt's national game. While the EFA, all major clubs, and most football media insisted that the Super Cup match on 9 September would be played, the Ultras vowed to stop the match, if necessary by force. As a result, the supporter group became an acute problem for the football establishment. In his talk show *Masa' al-Anwar* on the football channel Modern, Medhat Shalaby described the attack as an act of thuggery (*baltaga*), carried out by a selfish minority who threatened to "destroy national security and stop the national economy" (5 September 2012). Visibly outraged, Shalaby made clear that it would never be accepted that "a small group of fanatics [*muta'assibin*] destroy the joy of millions." As he put it, "Egypt is too strong to crumble for youngsters. All competitions will go ahead as planned. We must remember that Egypt is a state of law [*dawlit al-qanun*] not a state of anarchy [*dawlit al-fawda*]."

On the day of the match—scheduled to be played at the military-owned Burg el-Arab Stadium outside Alexandria without any fans in the stands—the tensions reached their peak. In the afternoon, media reports began to circulate about groups of youths in red T-shirts marching the thirty-five kilometers from central Alexandria toward the stadium, across the desert under the blazing sun. At 6 p.m., a pre-match show came on air on Modern (9 September 2012). Hosted by Medhat Shalaby and featuring former players and regular pundits Mustafa Yunis, Ibrahim Yusif, and Magdi Abdelghani, it resembled an action movie, but with disappointingly little action. Over three anxious hours, the experts in the studio in Cairo tried to interpret scattered, unedited footage from the dark and empty desert roads surrounding the arena. For a full twenty minutes, the al-Ahly team bus's trip from the hotel to the stadium was the center of everybody's attention. Was the coach going to be attacked? Could there be Ultras hiding somewhere in the shadows on the side of the road? Would the players reach the stadium safely? After the bus made it inside the iron gates and multiple cordons of security police, the focus shifted to live footage of one of the stadium complex's entrances. Every few minutes or so a car passed by. As a suspicious *tuk-tuk*[7] drove up to the gates and the driver asked the guard something inaudible, the excitement grew in the studio. "Look! A *tuk-tuk*! Could it have transported the Ultras?" Yunis exclaimed. Twenty seconds later, the *tuk-tuk* returned in the same direction it had come from, disappearing into the night. Whether or not it had ever served the movements of football supporters remained unclear.

Toward 8 p.m., it became clear that the Ultras present in Burg el-Arab were relatively few and that they did not intend to use any violence. For a while, the fans had expressed their anger at the players in front of al-Ahly's hotel, but as the team sneaked out through a back door, the protest dissolved. For the agitated pundits in Modern's studio, there thus was relatively little drama to report. Instead, a more general discussion ensued. Yunis in particular was furious at the supporters' audacious behavior—in one memorable phrase, he urged the police to "send some dogs against those kids so that we can finish off this story once and for all." The consensus among the talking heads was that the national sport had to return, not only for the future of Egyptian football, but also for the stability of the nation at large. "If we let go now of even the smallest of principles underpinning the state of law, they will never learn," Yusif explained. "That would be the same as accepting that thuggery and anarchy rule Egypt [*baltaga wi fawda bitihkum masr*]." Shalaby agreed and continued:

> We must be strong, not for us, but for the five million who football feeds [*illi ta'akkul al-kura al-'aysh*], and for the nation. To show that Egypt is a state of law is a matter of the prestige of the state [*hibit al-dawla*]. The whole world is watching tonight and thinking, "Should we invest in Egypt?" "Should we go there on holiday?" They will laugh at us if we cannot secure a football game. Egypt is a strong state; we are not India.

STABILITY IN REVOLUTIONARY TIMES

The propensity of Egypt's television pundits—as well as many ordinary fans, such as my friend Mahmoud—to pit stability (*istiqrar*) against the Ultras' demands and activities is at the same time noticeable and unsurprising. As anthropologist Dina Makram-Ebeid has detailed in an ethnography from a steel plant in southern Cairo, the valued notion of *istiqrar*—social, moral, national, political, or economic—elicits a complex range of overlapping and generally positive connotations in Egypt, and it played a central role in the governance of the Mubarak regime (Makram-Ebeid, 2012:146–163). Furthermore, in the aftermath of January 2011, conservative forces of all kinds habitually pointed to a lack of stability when arguing that clashes, protests, and strikes had to come to an end. Many times, these claims resonated. Among my interlocutors—as well as in Makram-Ebeid's steel plant (2014)—there was a widespread sense that the revolutionary unrest could not go on forever, and that a bit more stability—security, economic revival, but also moral order—was desirable.

At first glance, it might seem as if these reactionary impulses prevailed on 9 September 2012. Backed up by the security services, the clubs, and the football media, the EFA persisted in their plans to have the Super Cup played. At 9 p.m., an hour late, the match kicked off. Two hours later, al-Ahly had won a lackluster game by two goals to one and added another title to their impressive record. Egypt's football activities had returned; a little bit of stability had been reinstated.

But the stability bloc's victory over the rebellious youngsters was only partial. In fact, a couple of incidents leading up to the Super Cup significantly boosted the Ultras' cause. On 7 September, two days before the match, Muhammad Abu Treika—al-Ahly's team captain and Egypt's most popular football star—announced that he refused to play the Super Cup "in solidarity with the Ultras' martyrs." The following day, the minister of sports, al-'Amri Faruq, partly acceded to UA07's demands, postponing the start of the Premier League until mid-October. That same night—less than twenty-four hours before the scheduled kickoff in Burg el-Arab—several hundred Ultras Ahlawy members broke into al-Ahly's club premises in central Cairo. As *al-Misri al-Yum* reported, the police did nothing to stop them, and the fans organized a large nighttime meeting on the team's training ground (9 September 2012). After Abu Treika and the Sports Ministry's encouraging decisions, the atmosphere was buoyant. The *capos* exhorted their fellow members: "You are calling the shots now. You are making the difference. [. . .] This is just the beginning. We will continue until we have restored the rights of the martyrs [*hatta yi'ud haqq al-shuhada'*]. There will be no domestic tournaments before *al-qasas*." Later the same night, the leaders outlined the group's vision for wide-reaching football reforms:

> We will establish new principles according to which this fascist state, which only thinks about personal interests, will be run. The postponement of the league is the first step in our cause and our

demands. The rest will come. We will fulfill all our demands, which we will not give up. They are: the cleansing [*tathir*] of the Ministry of Interior; the cleansing of the media; the cleansing of the Football Association; preventing [FIFA executive committee member] Hani Abu Reida, [sports pundit] Ahmed Shoubair and the remnants of the previous regime from running in the EFA elections; and the cleansing of al-Ahly Club from the board of monetary self-interest [*maglis idarit al-sububa*] which runs the club. We demand the resignation of [club president] Hassan Hamdy and his board and the appointment of Muhammad Abu Treika as president of al-Ahly Club, because he is the manliest [*argal*] individual in al-Ahly Club.

Yet despite the bold calls for revolutionary action, the overall message coming out of the meeting was one of restraint. Earlier that day, unconfirmed reports had circulated about the Ministry of Interior striking a deal with the leaders of one of the Bedouin tribes who populate the area surrounding Burg el-Arab. Troubling rumors had it that state authorities had urged the Bedouins to attack the Ultras, in case they would attempt to storm the stadium. In light of this development, UA07 decided to cancel their planned all-out operation in Alexandria the following day; only a small, symbolic group of protesters eventually turned up at Burg el-Arab, and no serious attempt was made to shut down the game. It was simply not worth the risks. As the al-Ahly Ultras summarized it on their Facebook page later that night:

> We do not accept any sort of confrontation between us and individuals of this people [. . .] who do not have any relation to this issue, except that the security services have presented them with false information and excuses. Because, we only have an issue with the corrupt Ministry of Interior, which protects the corrupt football organizations, and not with any other Egyptian citizen. (Ultras Ahlawy Facebook, 9 September 2012)

Like many times in the past, Ultras Ahlawy were walking a fine line between bold action and collateral damage in the days before and after the Super Cup (see chapter 3). They voiced their claims publicly and demonstrated their ability to act with force, but when their demands risked clashing with those of "individuals of this people," they backed off, forsaking their own interests for the common, national good. Some twenty-four hours after the match, this delicate tension reverberated further on Yosri Fouda's talk show, *Akhir Kalam* on ONTV, Egypt's most influential political show at the time (10 November 2012). In the studio, Sherif Hassan, the FilGoal.com journalist and Ultras expert, and Ahmed al-Faqi, a leading member of Ultras Devils from Alexandria, were given forty-five prime-time minutes to present the Ultras' case against the resumption of football, their demands for wide-ranging reforms, and the reasons why they had not tried to stop the match after all. The show also featured a call-in from *al-Shuruq*'s senior sports columnist, Hassan al-Mistakawi. In contrast to Hassan and al-Faqi, al-Mistakawi justified al-Ahly's decision to play the game, and he found the club's stern disciplinary actions against Abu Treika to be in order.[8] As he reminded the younger men in the studio, al-Ahly's unmatched status as a nationalist club (*nadi watani*) had always rested on its collective principles (*mabadi'*), which had priority over any individual, regardless of how important or successful he might be.[9] This argument about stability leading to triumphs and acclaim was challenged, however, first by Fouda and later by Hassan. As Hassan pointed out, many of the most memorable episodes in al-Ahly Club's history were in fact remembered as patriotic acts, not primarily because the club had followed its principles and promoted national stability, but because it had done so for a good cause and in *opposition* to an unjust ruling order.

> For example, in 1948, al-Ahly went to play a charity game in Palestine. It was at the time of the '48 War, and the team was led by Mokhtar al-Tetsh [a legendary Ahly player and leader in the 1920s, '30s, and '40s]. At that time, they were forbidden by the Football Association to go and play the match, but they did so anyway. When they returned, the team was suspended by the EFA. [. . .] But Mokhtar al-Tetsh went to the President of EFA and insisted that he was right. [. . .] Today, Mokhtar al-Tetsh is the one who has given the name to the stadium inside al-Ahly Club. At the time, he was punished but history cleansed him. This is a type of example that people do not understand immediately, but they will understand it in a few years' time.[10]

It is perhaps indicative that at the time when Hassan voiced this opinion, al-Mistakawi had already hung up. In the studio, both al-Faqi and Fouda agreed with what Hassan had just said. Strictly following its uncompromising principles might have built al-Ahly's popularity in years gone by, but it was far from certain that it would continue to do so in the current period of revolutionary change. If anything, the Ultras now embodied the principles that looked fresh and appealing; stability, surely, but only after proper transition and reforms. In the privately owned newspaper *al-Misri al-Yum*, a couple of long articles were published that sided with the Ultras against the EFA and al-Ahly (9, 10 September 2012). Many prominent political actors—from the leftist Revolutionary Socialists to the conservative Muslim Brotherhood-affiliated Freedom and Justice Party—announced their support for the group's key demand: "no football before *al-qasas*" (*al-Misri al-Yum*, 9 September 2012; Murshid, 2012). Especially among my younger friends, I noted a distinct surge in support. For many Egyptians in their teens, twenties, or thirties, the media pundits had lost all credibility; their calls for stability, order, and rule-following at all costs came across as reactionary and hopelessly old-fashioned. Change, in contrast, seemed urgently needed, for the national game as well as the nation more generally. In September 2012, it was the Ultras who were staking out the progressive way forward.

ICONIC ABU TREIKA

A couple of weeks later, on a Friday night in late September, I met up with Mido, my veteran Ultras Ahlawy friend. Since the Super Cup match, I had called him multiple times, but Mido had been busy "consulting" the *capos* and canceled several appointments. Meanwhile, Ultras Ahlawy had been very active. In a series of Facebook statements, the group had continued to raise demands for a purge of the EFA, al-Ahly, and the football media, and they had presented statistics countering the widely circulated claim that five million football workers suffered from the interruption of football (13, 26 September, 6 October 2012; see also Saied, 2012). The group had also kept up their street offensive against the resumption of the league: on 23 September, they had attacked and interrupted their team's training session (Maher, 2012a); two days later, they had blocked Medhat Shalaby and Ahmed Shoubair from entering Modern's studios in Cairo's Media Production City, effectively canceling the duo's talk shows that night (Maher, 2012c). Concurrently with this attack, UA07 had published a YouTube video with a sarcastic song titled "I'lam al-sububa" (approximately "The Media of Monetary Self-Interest") (Ultras Ahlawy 07 Media, 2012). With a catchy melody and witty lyrics mocking the corruption and unprofessionalism of Egypt's infamous television pundits, the song had become an instant success.[11] Throughout autumn, the video would circulate widely on social media spurring discussions, jokes, and laughter among football fans across the political spectrum.

When I finally got hold of Mido at his favorite coffee-and-*shisha* hangout in Heliopolis, he was in an excellent mood. Things were going well, very well indeed:

> So, what do you think, Carl? Not a bad couple of weeks? The Super Cup has changed everything! I can't believe it. First, we started to hate all the people in our club, because we saw that they didn't care about the martyrs, only their money and careers. But then—you've been following, right?—we decided to change everything that's rotten in the game. Because after al-Ahly betrayed us, we don't care about the club's reputation anymore.[12] It makes us freer in a way. Now we can really target the corruption, which is everywhere. Everywhere! Did you see when we attacked the training? Or 6th of October [the Media Production City]? No one tried to stop us; no one can stop us! We can push them wherever we want. *Insha'Allah*, we'll stop the league, but that's only a first step. The boys understand that this is the chance to change everything that's old and corrupt: clubs, players, *ittihad al-kura* [EFA], the media—everything!

I asked Mido what he thought would happen next, and he replied:

> I told you before: this media [*sic*] will die. When there's no league, these amateurs will go bust. Young people are already on our side, and so are many journalists. Did you see the video ["I'lam al-sububa"]? Even here at the coffee shop, all these *filul* [remnants of the old regime], everyone has seen it; also people who agree with [Medhat] Shalaby laugh at it. And why are the police not stopping us? Because [President] Mursi doesn't care! Football isn't important to them [the Muslim Brotherhood], so why would they pick a fight with us when people like us? That minister [of sports] is still one of the old guys: corrupt. But he can't do anything; his boss doesn't support him. . . . But in the end, it was of course Abu Treika's decision [to not play] that changed it all. Everybody loves Abu Treika. And of course, he's important for the Brotherhood. As long as he's on our side, people will never go against us.

Later that night, as Mido drove me home along the 6th of October flyover bridge in his black BMW, our conversation returned to Abu Treika's exceptional popular appeal. "There are so many things with Treika," Mido explained, while casually overtaking a microbus on the inside lane.

> You can't reduce it to being Egypt's best player in the last decade. Actually, that's the least important thing. Why is he the only player that we have special songs about?[13] Why do you find so many Zamalek fans who also love him? Because of who he is, as a human being. People don't know, but he helped the martyrs' families so much after Port Said, both with money and inviting them for *iftar* [the breaking of the fast] during Ramadan. There are so many stories. He's much, much more than just a brilliant footballer.

A brief historical detour is required to explain the magnitude of this iconic, larger-than-life persona. Born in Giza in 1978, Muhammad Abu Treika played for the fading Cairo club al-Tersana during his teens and early twenties. Something of a late bloomer, he signed for al-Ahly at the age of twenty-five, and the peak of his career coincided squarely with al-Ahly's and the national team's unprecedented international success. In the late 2000s, Abu Treika proved exceptionally able to step up on big occasions, scoring a string of decisive goals for club and country from his position as offensive midfielder. Still, as Mido stressed, his performances on the pitch were only part of the story; Abu Treika is also renowned for his exemplary behavior. He holds a bachelor's degree in philosophy; he is polite, soft-spoken, and down-to-earth; and he has always led a quiet and pious family life. As the Egyptian satirist Omar Tahir has noted, this layered popularity is captured in his many nicknames, which not only include *harrif* (skillful, talented) and *sani' al-sa'ada* (he who brings happiness) but also *al-qadis* (the saint) (2010:107). Admired for his integrity and at the same time the most talented player of his generation, Abu Treika was and still is almost impossible to dislike, a pristine "saint" to love and revere.

For the same reasons, Abu Treika's class position and ethos never really fit the chauvinist-nationalist masculinities populating the Egyptian football bubble. In contrast to many of his teammates, his lifestyle was far removed from luxurious cars, extravagant fashion, celebrity parties in resorts on the North Coast, and scandalous affairs with pop stars. His sympathies for the Muslim Brotherhood and visible discomfort at President Mubarak's palace receptions rather made him a somewhat anomalous figure. This dissonance crystallized famously during a group stage game in the 2008 Africa Cup of Nations. After scoring yet another goal, Abu Treika pulled the national

Fig. 4.3. Muhammad Abu Treika showing sympathy with the people of Gaza after scoring in the 2008 Africa Cup of Nations. Photo: AP/Themba Hadebe, 26 January 2008.

team shirt over his head, revealing a T-shirt with a printed message in Arabic and English: "Sympathize with Gaza—*ta'atufan ma' ghazza*." The gesture drew huge international attention. Across the Arab World, Abu Treika's already immense popularity was turned up yet another notch. In a full-page interview in the independent Egyptian newspaper *al-Dustur*, he explained that he knew he would receive a yellow card for the gesture and further disciplinary actions for mixing football with politics. But, as he characteristically phrased it, "everything has a price. [. . .] The declaration in sympathy with Gaza will be judged by God only. [. . .] I do not want any compensation for it in this world" (8 February 2008).

For less oppositional media outlets than *al-Dustur*, though, this overtly political manifestation by Egypt's most popular player raised a delicate dilemma. In the state-owned weekly *al-Akhbar al-Yum*, Abu Treika's gesture was, on the one hand, praised as an expression of high morality (*al-khalq al-rafi'*) by an exemplary and beloved Egyptian on the world stage. On the other hand, the paper made sure to stress that the action did not suggest any political aims (*ahdaf siyasiyya*). It was merely an expression of human sympathy (*kan muta'atifan insaniyyan*) with the people in Gaza that would not be repeated, and which the coaches and the rest of the team had not known anything about (2 February 2008). The paper's ambivalence reflected the tense political climate of the era; a T-shirt like this—indeed any reference to the Palestinian cause—was automatically read as criticism of the Mubarak regime's hopelessly uncourageous foreign policies. A pro-Palestine stance from a national football hero with Muslim Brotherhood sympathies was hence highly explosive. It was not possible to incorporate into the otherwise seamless and regime-friendly football bubble that permeated Egypt in the last years before 2011.

If Abu Treika had been out of sync with dominant subjectivities and the powers that be in early 2008, things were different in autumn 2012. Following a series of dramatic events in Khartoum, Tahrir, and Port Said, the Mubarak era's vulgar football masculinity was now seriously questioned. It was instead Abu Treika's respectable, pious, and revolutionary ethos that harmonized with the moment in history. In stark contrast to most other Egyptian football personalities (al-Banna, 2012), Abu Treika had actively supported Muhammad Mursi's election campaign. During the early months of the new presidency, the player gained monumental status. Everybody seemed to love him. In fact, people would often attach unrealistic hopes to his ethics and politics. Many of my pro-Ultras and anti-army friends, for instance, would tell me that Abu Treika had refused to shake hands with Field Marshal Mohamed Hussein Tantawi, Egypt's then de facto head of state, when he visited al-Ahly's players after the Port Said tragedy. Insistent but unconfirmed rumors also claimed that he was boycotting particular television stations and journalists because of their pro-Mubarak politics. Others—like my friend Zizu, a Coptic former football coach, who adored Abu Treika but did not support the Brotherhood or the Ultras—liked to interpret his stances differently. "Abu Treika is a man of high morals and he has a big heart," he told me in early October 2012.

> But sometimes he wants to do too much; he doesn't understand that he is only a football player. He did what he did [boycotted the Super Cup] because he felt for the kids who died, but then he realized that it was wrong, so he apologized to his club and his colleagues and accepted his punishment. What he does has nothing to do with him being *ikhwani* [supporter of the Muslim Brotherhood]. He is a respectable man [*ragil muhtaram*], who knows when he has made a mistake. We all love him.

Regardless of people's politics, it is no doubt that the combination of talent, morals, and persona made Abu Treika almost impossible to dislike.

He epitomized a respectable postrevolutionary football environment in a better postrevolutionary nation, which a vast majority of Egyptians embraced. Akin to stars from the arts world, who have embodied positive visions for the Egyptian nation at particular historical moments (see Armbrust, 2002b; Danielson, 1997), Abu Treika was by autumn 2012 an iconic, unifying figure perfectly in tune with the *zeitgeist*. When he decided to side with Ultras Ahlawy against the resumption of domestic football, his action thus had far more impact than if it had come merely from a star player. It immediately rendered the Ultras immune to the apparatus of Othering as self-serving thugs who threatened national stability and destroyed the "joy of millions," which the pundits on satellite television mobilized as the crisis intensified. These loaded tags simply did not stick to a group that had the endorsement of someone as respectable and loved as Abu Treika. Furthermore, his stance also precluded the authorities from confronting the supporters by force. For the Mursi government, the continuous support from Muhammad Abu Treika was far more important than that of the football industry, which had always opposed the Brotherhood anyway. As suggested by Mido, this was a crucial reason why the police remained on the sidelines as Ultras Ahlawy launched their attacks against the country's football institutions in September 2012.

MARCHING ON THE PRESIDENTIAL PALACE

As September turned into October, the story of the day remained the same. Supported by Muhammad Abu Treika and a steadily growing number of political figures, Ultras Ahlawy's campaign for football reforms gained momentum and continued to attract media attention. In quick succession, several key demands were met: the players in al-Ahly issued a public apology for playing the Super Cup and gave their unreserved support for the Ultras' cause (Said, 2012), FIFA delegate Hani Abu Reida and media pundit Ahmed Shoubair withdrew their joint candidacy for the upcoming EFA elections (FilGoal.com, 3 October 2012), and al-Ahly's club president, Hassan Hamdy, was questioned by the country's Illicit Gains Authority and accused of wide-ranging corruption (Maher, 2012b). And yet, despite vague promises and multiple postponements, UA07's most essential demand—no resumption of domestic football before retribution (*al-qasas*)—was not fully met. On Thursday, 11 October, with the league set to kick off within less than a week, the group thus decided that they had to give it a final push.

It all began as a meeting outside the 6th of October War panorama near the entrance to the Ahly Ultras' section, *talta shimal*, at Cairo Stadium. As dusk fell during the end-of-the-week rush hour, several thousand group members sat down in one of Cairo's busiest thoroughfares, Salah Salem Street, to discuss how to stop the football league's resumption. Half an hour later, a friend and I approached the stadium complex by foot, and the effects of the blocked traffic—chaotic congestion, honking horns, adrenalin, and frustration—were noticeable several kilometers away. When we reached the panorama, the meeting had just ended, and the young men embarked on a march toward the republic's most elevated seat of power: the Presidential Palace at al-Ittihadiyya. The rally blocked all eastbound traffic along the six-lane boulevard. Crisscrossing through the jumble of stationary cars, we soon caught up with a group of teenagers at the end of the procession. I began to ask the participants some basic questions: Why were they here? Where did they come from? What was the aim of the protest? Suddenly, a middle-aged minibus driver, who for a while had tried to squeeze his packed vehicle through the crowds, shouted at us through his open window: "Is this how you show pride in al-Ahly Club, which we all love so much? Is this respectable behavior? To stop the world like this [*bitwa"afu al-dunya keda*]?" The young men around me looked surprised at each other, as if they could not believe what they had just heard. Then, slowly, they turned toward the fuming man in the minibus, smiled calmly, and one of them replied:

> Fuck off, buddy. We do what we want. [*kuss umak ya 'am. 'amilin zay ma 'awzin*]. This is for our friends who died, for the martyrs and for the revolution. It's not we who stop the world, but the petrol crisis and the corruption. But if they decide to play the league, then you will see. *Insha'Allah* we will stop the world for real.

We turned away from the driver and his desperate attempts to navigate his Toyota toward Heliopolis. The group of friends walked on toward al-Ittihadiyya, leaving the stranded minibus behind. Before long, they joined their companions' steady chanting—against the media, the league, and the corrupted al-Ahly Club, and to the honor of their friends who had been martyred in Port Said. Smoke from burning *shamarikh* mixed with exhaust fumes in the warm, early evening air. The rush-hour traffic simply had to adjust to the rhythm of the demonstration, slowing down to the speed of the march. Moving forward in orderly fashion to voice their demands to the president of the Republic, the marchers crossed a hopelessly inadequate police cordon sent out to prevent the fans from approaching the palace. When the line of security police silently stepped to the side, letting the Ultras pass to set up a sit-in right outside the palace walls, it was a sign as clear as any of a new era and a new distribution of power. As night fell, the fans unfolded a couple of huge banners demanding "no league before *al-qasas*" and calling on President Mursi to take action. When a small group of young women approached the area, the young men formed their own right-angled cordons, ensuring that the women could pass through the area undisturbed. In so many ways, the football supporters of Ultras Ahlawy were in complete control: of their emotional performance, of Egyptian football, and of Cairo's streets and traffic flows. And from the way they acted and reacted, sang, spoke, and danced, you could tell that they were aware of and reveled in their strength and influence.

One of the last really hot afternoons of the year came ten days later, on 21 October. Ultras Ahlawy's campaign had by this point won another incremental victory: the start of the Egyptian Premier League had been pushed back yet again, this time until the end of the month, although more and more commentators were predicting that the whole season would be canceled. In the face of this uncertainty, something unprecedented took place: a few hundred professional football players and coaches from clubs in Egypt's first, second, and third divisions decided to make their voices heard in a public street demonstration. Led by two former players and media celebrities Ahmed Shoubair and Khaled el-Ghandour, the players marched from Cairo Stadium to the Presidential Palace, followed by many photographers and journalists. The protesters had one simple request that they wanted to voice to President Muhammad Mursi. They demanded the return of football, so that they could resume their profession.

Although both the location and the issue being contested were the same as ten days earlier, the mood and atmosphere of the protests were very different indeed. A good week earlier, I had seen teenage boys in cheap, skinny track-suit pants and red Ultras T-shirts filling the space in front of the palace. When I arrived at al-Ittihadiyya this day, the scene was instead dominated by well-built sportsmen in their twenties, thirties, and forties, with fashionable haircuts, trademark track suits and trainers, large sunglasses, and the latest smartphones. Furthermore—despite the numbers being much smaller—I observed none of the unity, emotional discipline, and purpose that UA07's march had displayed. Every once in a while, Shoubair, sitting on the shoulders of a bold, big man with a thick moustache, or el-Ghandour, standing on the curb of an old tram line, would start a chant. For a minute or two, people around them would join in, denouncing President Mursi and the Muslim Brotherhood's "betrayal" of the national sport and cowardly concessions to the Ultras. But the chanting would quickly die out again. Before long, Shoubair jumped down from his elevated position, and the demonstrators resumed taking photos of each other with their phones.

Everywhere I went that afternoon, I heard people arguing about the proper way to proceed: was it appropriate to stop the traffic passing the palace, or would that be stooping to the Ultras' stability-threatening behaviors? Should they also go after the EFA, which had officially taken the decision to stop the league, but which many participants were professionally and privately connected to, or should they stick to chanting against the Brotherhood and the government? And what about al-Ahly's players, who recently had showed sympathy for the Ultras, distanced themselves from their colleagues' demonstration, and continued to play matches in the African Champions League? Was it not egotistical, indeed a sign of lacking solidarity, one player rhetorically asked, that al-Ahly was the only club still playing and making money, whereas they, who had nothing to do with the Port Said tragedy or the Ultras, were prevented from carrying out their profession?

In the early evening, the disagreements split the demonstration in two. Whereas one group, led by Shoubair, stayed at the palace and eventually disintegrated, another proceeded across Salah Salem Street to the nearby Hotel Baron. Later the same night, al-Ahly was to play the second leg of the African Champions League semi-final at a sealed-off military stadium in Cairo's eastern suburbs. Incidentally, their opponents, Sunshine Stars from Nigeria, were staying at the Hotel Baron in preparation for the match. Those heading toward the hotel were the most visibly upset with the egotism that al-Ahly had shown. Indeed, they were so angry that they took a joint decision to stop the match by blocking the Nigerian players from leaving the hotel.

The scene that met me as I reached the hotel entrance can only be described as surreal: hundreds of professional football players were swearing at al-Ahly and President Mursi, with the locked-in Nigerian team observing the spectacle through open windows on the third floor. But it would soon turn even more extraordinary. Suddenly, a few dozen Ultras Ahlawy—led by two of their most famous *capos*—emerged out of nowhere and attacked the players with burning *shamarikh* to allow the Nigerians to get to the match in time. In the ensuing chaos, the players retaliated against the fans with sticks, rocks, and even a revolver. As the brawl reached its peak, I took cover behind a car in a side street, from where I watched stones and smoke flying back and forth in the street in front of the lobby. Next to me, behind the car, I found Hani, a reporter for Egyptian state radio's sports channel al-Shabab wi al-Riyada, calling in a live report. When Hani eventually went off the air, he looked at me and shook his head in disbelief. "Very strange," he noted calmly, "this is very strange indeed. The football players want to stop the Champions League match and they fight the Ultras with firearms. And the Ultras fight back for the match to be played. Very strange indeed."

It took Ultras Ahlawy less than twenty minutes to outnumber and chase away the protesting players from the surroundings of the hotel. A short while later, the Nigerian team got on their bus to the stadium, and the match between al-Ahly and Sunshine Stars kicked off with only a couple of hours' delay. Somewhat surprising given that they had played no regular league matches since February, al-Ahly played well, won the game easily, and qualified for the 2012 Champions League final. But the action on the pitch was not what Egyptian football supporters would discuss in the days that followed. In the media as well as in coffee shops, the strange things that had taken place at the Presidential Palace and the Hotel Baron continued to be the leading story.

Unsurprisingly, both sides of the confrontation were keen to voice their version of the event. In a Facebook statement released a few hours after the skirmish, Ultras Ahlawy explained that they had attacked the protesting players with the intent to protect the honor of their beloved club. They also argued and clarified what at first might seem like a contradiction. Whereas they had long insisted that EFA's *domestic* football tournament must be suspended until justice had been restored, they had no problem with *international* competitions organized by the Confederation of African Football (CAF), an organization that had nothing to do with what had happened in Port Said. Moreover, the group was keen to stress that the players had used firearms and a range of other weapons. Aptly, UA07 described their adversaries' violence as acts of *baltaga* (thuggery), employing a derogatory term that for many years had been used against them (Ultras Ahlawy Facebook, 22 October 2012).

The next day, a counterstatement was published on the website of the newspaper *al-Wafd*. Under the signature "Egypt's honorable sportsmen" (*riyadiyyu misr al-shurafa'*), the protesting players justified their actions as a long-overdue response to the Mursi government's "negligence" and unacceptable "fear of a group of youngsters who call themselves Ultras."

Echoing media rhetoric about the Ultras from the last five years, the statement portrayed the fan groups as the cause of all kinds of troubles that the sport was currently facing. It accused them of self-interest (*masalih shakhsiyya*), of corruption (*fasad*), and of having financial ties to the former regime. The text even claimed that it was the fanaticism (*ta'assub*) of the new fans that had ultimately triggered the bloodbath in Port Said (Riyadiyyu Misr al-Shurafa', 2012).

On a day when images of famous football players throwing rocks and fighting supporters with sticks to safeguard their well-paid jobs were all over the media, however, the talk about self-interested and violent football fans threatening national stability rang hollow for many Egyptians. As many of my friends expressed it, Ultras attacking property and stadiums was something they had grown used to. That professional players—a privileged and pampered elite in the Mubarak years—were taking to the street to fight back was significantly more difficult to comprehend, let alone accept. Indicatively, whereas UA07 protecting al-Ahly's interests outside the hotel was recognized in the press as "honorable and noble" (*mushrif wi nubil*) (Fawzi, 2012), one commentator labeled the demonstration of the players "the march of disgrace" (*musirit al-'ar*) (al-Banna, 2012). Especially in contrast to Ultras Ahlawy's purposeful and well-organized demonstration a week earlier, the players' capricious violence made it difficult to portray the Ultras as dangerous and self-serving *baltagiyya*. If anything, the players were now the ones resembling rowdy thugs, whereas the fans' (counter-) violence came across as tolerable, measured, and even progressive and just. The irony that the players had tried to *stop* the Champions League game, whereas Ultras Ahlawy—and not the police—had stepped in to ensure that it could be *played*, was not lost on anyone.

CONCLUSION: PURPOSEFULLY VIOLENT

The power struggle raging between the Egyptian Ultras movement and the football establishment was a revolution inside the revolution, and it climaxed in late 2012. As this chapter has discussed, the Port Said massacre in February, the election of President Mursi in June, and the EFA's attempt to restart the league in September provoked a series of events that saw Ultras Ahlawy seriously challenge and partly dismantle and remake Egypt's football institutions. By autumn 2012, the young football supporters were both an effective catalyst for change and curiously untouchable. They destroyed the Football Association's headquarters, yet circumvented accusations of causing national instability; they suspended television shows and the league without major police interference; they gathered the support of the players on their team, while enemies within the club's management were charged with corruption; their orderly demonstrations and emotional style gained traction among the general public. Although prefaced by an event of terrible bloodshed and the death of more than seventy young friends, 2012 was the year when Egypt's Ultras football supporters reached their greatest position of strength.

How does it happen that a group of young men manage to carve out revolutionary "pockets of alternative, unstable authority [. . .] within existing power structures" (Shenker, 2016:333)? How do they come to embody a radical and most concrete domain of "popular sovereignty," despite counterrevolutionary forces and reactionary media (ibid., 333–336)? In the case of the Ultras, it is important to recognize a long-standing balancing act related to the use of violence. On the one hand, Egypt's Ultras from the outset presented themselves as masculinized, powerful, and disciplined; on the other hand, in distinguishing themselves from hooligans, they insisted that they only used violence in self-defense, and always in a controlled manner, for specific well-defined purposes. In her nuanced master's thesis tracing UA07's identity and politics, Dalia Abdelhameed Ibraheem labels this tension the Ultras' "violence paradox." She shows that although the supporter groups recurrently stressed their nonviolent principles in statements and interviews, they found themselves clashing with the police and other Ultras groups on a regular basis. In fact, Ibraheem suggests, repertoires of violent action form a significant part of the Ultras' affective thrill and masculine ethos. Violence is exciting, it might sometimes be necessary to claim one's rights, and it is a key reason why the groups have attracted so many young Egyptian men; yet it also exposes the fans to public criticism (Ibraheem, 2015:36–39; see also Gibril, 2015).

As I have shown in this chapter and the previous one, this violence paradox has for a long time permeated public perceptions of the Ultras' fan practices, demonstrations, and morals: from the pre-2011 years, when the new supporters were ostracized and portrayed as destructive thugs, over the revolutionary period, when some but not all of their violent actions were justified and tied to the revolutionary cause, and into the post-Port Said era, when UA07 insisted that they would either die or restore the rights of the martyrs. In the month and a half that followed the Super Cup, the same tension was reflected in what, at first glance, might appear as contradictory stances and actions. Ultras Ahlawy clearly did not shun violence: they broke the law and destroyed public property at the EFA's headquarters, they attacked training sessions and television studios, and they took on the protesting players with *shamarikh*, stones, and fistfights outside the Hotel Baron. At the same time, UA07 always insisted that they used violence *selectively* and did not harm outsiders: they canceled their planned assault on the Super Cup after realizing that they ran the risk of hurting innocent Egyptian citizens, and they were adamant about not destroying private vehicles or causing unnecessary harm during their march to the Presidential Palace.

Such an insistence on a *purposeful* and *selective* use of violence, it is well worth noting, resonates with moral codes for Egyptian masculinity, which exceed sports and predate the revolutionary moment. In her ethnographic study of the materialization of masculine subjects in the Cairene work-ing-class district al-Zawya al-Hamra, for example, Farha Ghannam states that "knowing when to use or avoid violence, the right context for its use or avoidance, and the amount of violence to use is an important skill not mastered by all men" (Ghannam, 2013:121). Ghannam argues that it is especially important for an Egyptian man to deploy violence in ways that benefit the collective. Indeed, violence that "further[s] the public good" is by no means a problem or a vice, but a sign of *gada'na* (adjective, *gada'*, *gid'an* [plural]): a highly valued virtue in Cairo's *sha'bi* (popular, work-ing-class) neighborhoods that translates as "a mix of gallantry and 'nobil-ity, audacity, responsibility, generosity, vigor and manliness'" (ibid., 122, quoting el-Messiri, 1978:49).

By using violence selectively when needed, and shunning it when it risked harming innocent Egyptians, Ultras Ahlawy passed as *gid'an*, real men, in autumn 2012. As a matter of fact, many revolutionary friends of mine put hope in the Ultras not *despite* but *because of* their insistence on violence as a last resort. In a period when the revolution otherwise looked stagnant, the Ultras campaign indicated that a measured and controlled use of violence could get things done. It pointed to a way forward, which broke free from stifling valorization of absolute nonviolence without fall-ing outside the realm of respectability. Furthermore, the balanced deploy-ment of violence helped UA07 sidestep a constantly lingering threat: as Ghannam also shows, a man who in contrast to the *gada'* uses violence randomly to "impose his own will" is known as a *baltagi* (2013:121–122). The *baltagi*, in other words, is not only a masculine subject, whose violence locates him on the fringes of legality (see chapter 3). In fact, most men in less well-off parts of Cairo will have to use violence, break the law, and confront the authorities at times in order to get by and make a living. What distinguishes the *gada'* from the *baltagi* is thus not the use of violence per se. It is that the former is an altruistic subject, whose violence is ordered, purposeful, and in the service of the common good, whereas the latter resorts to violence to seek personal gains.[14]

The purposefully violent *gada'* masculinity of the Ultras played an instrumental role in shaping their popular sovereignty. In late 2012, the football supporter movement embodied a rare-yet-realistic vision for bold action and progressive change that many Egyptians espoused. The Ultras were now everyone's darlings; their appeal bridged political and classed divides, and they combined a violent struggle for retribution with a measured campaign for institutional change. The groups obviously threatened the stability of the football status quo, yet both their means and their ends seemed purposeful and controlled enough to make a stint of unrest worthwhile. In combination with the respectable aura granted by Abu Treika's endorsement, this male ethos shielded the fan groups from the establishment's predictable accusations of *baltaga* and *ta'assub*. As a result, figures such as Medhat Shalaby and Ahmed Shoubair found it difficult to argue that they were standing on the right side of history. Portrayals of a self-serving minority threatening the broad national interest simply did not pertain to the well-measured emotional subjectivity of this increasingly popular group of youngsters.

The reversal of the playing field was never as visible as after the players' infamous demonstration outside the Hotel Baron, a confrontation smacking of desperation, disorderly violence, and defeat. In a video published on Yallakora.com, one of the participants expressed frustration and disbelief that he, a professional football player, had to take to the streets to safeguard his basic interests, "like doctors, workers, teachers or garbage collectors." Yet in contrast to demonstrations carried out by these professionals, the football players and television personalities did not achieve any tangible results. Neither the state nor the EFA made any concessions to their demands. Apparently, no one in charge recognized the players' fear of losing their jobs as an "impulse to take action," a blatant lack of support which, according to anthropologist Caroline Humphrey (2013:289), indicates that the players had lost their position as "nice and normal human subject[s]" within the national formation (ibid., 302). If anything, the protesters' somewhat chaotic and undisciplined behaviors rendered them abject emotional-political outsiders, with whom it had become difficult to sympathize. Television pundit Ahmed Shoubair and his fellow players and journalists had taken the struggle to the streets, and they had been bitterly defeated. Being sports people, they should have known better than to play such a decisive match on their opponents' home turf.

CHAPTER 5

The Insurmountable Double Bind of *Siyasa*

It was always a national movement, not a political one.
Anonymous leading member of Ultras White Knights, TRT
World, 2018

On Saturday 26 January 2013, one day after the second anniversary of the Revolution and less than a week before the one-year commemoration of the Port Said stadium tragedy, the long-awaited verdicts in the Port Said court cases were due. Among seventy-three defendants, nine were high-ranking police officers, three were officials from al-Masry Club, and sixty-one were Masry supporters, many of them members of the Ultras group Green Eagles. The prosecuted policemen and the club functionaries faced charges of negligent conduct and of facilitating the lethal attacks. The defendants accused of organizing and carrying out the killings were all football fans from Port Said (FilGoal.com, 21 January 2013; Close, 2019:48–49).

Following an independent investigation based on extensive eyewitness accounts, Ultras Ahlawy (UA07) had long singled out three groups as responsible for the death of their comrades: the al-Masry fans who attacked them in the stands, the police who did nothing to intervene, and the Supreme Council of the Armed Forces (SCAF), Egypt's de facto rulers in February 2012 (Media9313, 2013). The trials against policemen and Masry supporters were thus seen as an important first step toward justice. At the same time, the Ahly Ultras knew that the police investigation had a series of flaws (Close, 2019:48–49) and that no single policeman had thus far been convicted for any crime committed during the revolutionary period. Determined to break this pattern, the group put as much pressure as they could on the court. In the weeks before the verdict, foreboding graffiti calling for "retribution or chaos" (*al-qasas aw al-fawda*) and "blood with blood" (*damm bi-damm*) spread like wildfire on walls all over Cairo. Large demonstrations were organized in the capital as well as in the provinces.

Three days before the court's adjudication, the Ultras were suddenly everywhere in Cairo, all at once: one group of supporters surrounded a police station in Nasser City; another blocked the entrance to the Stock Exchange downtown; yet another raided and interrupted al-Ahly's training session. In the early afternoon, several hundred young men stormed into Saad Zaghloul Metro Station in central Cairo. Descending onto the tracks, they chanted, burned *shamarikh*, and interrupted the subway traffic for a full hour. Shortly thereafter, a similar scenario unfolded on the 6th of October Bridge, causing massive interruptions on the city's main East-West traffic artery. At 4:45 p.m., the coordinated civil disobedience ceased as abruptly as it had begun. Later in the night, two statements were posted on UA07's Facebook page. The first was short, directed to the public, and read: "What happened today was neither chaos [*fawda*] nor *qarsit widn* [lit. a pinch in the ear]. What happened today was to inform you that the chaos is coming." A second, longer message urged all members to mobilize on 26 January and to be prepared to take justice into their own hands should the verdicts be disappointing (UA07 Facebook, 24 January 2013). Ultras Ahlawy had merely flexed their muscles in bringing Cairo to a halt; their full force was yet to be unleashed.

When the momentous Saturday arrived, it was tense with fear and anticipation. In the street between al-Ahly's club complex and Cairo's Opera House, a few thousand UA07 members and families of the Port Said martyrs had gathered to await the judgments via transistor radios. Arriving at the scene shortly before 9 a.m., I found that fifty group members had scaled the walls surrounding the club compound. They were standing in a straight line on top of the main gate, looking down on the mass of people below. Right behind them was a huge billboard, some six meters high and thirty meters wide. In the center of the black placard, the number 72 was printed in bold, red digits. On either side were thirty-six photos and names, portraying the men who had died in Port Said; along the top ran a line of text: *lan nansakum* (we will not forget you). Most of the men by the billboard were dressed in Ultras Ahlawy's distinctive red-and-black T-shirts or hoodies, although quite a few were bare-chested under the bleak January morning sun.

Moments later, the crowds started to move. The verdict was read out, calling for death sentences for twenty-one of the Masry fans, while adjourning the cases against the remaining fifty-two defendants. The

Fig. 5.1. UA07 members celebrating the Port Said court verdicts outside al-Ahly Club, central Cairo. Photo: Helena Hägglund, 26 January 2013.

sleepy morning mood now transformed into celebrations, somewhat out of control. People danced, cried, and hugged each other. *Shamarikh* burned. Insulting sexualized chants against the people in Port Said echoed in the narrow space, leaving the surrounding whitewashed walls shaking. Some of the bare-chested men on top of the wall pushed their hips forward, flexed their muscles, and raised their arms up into the air. Journalists photographed and recorded videos that would soon circulate across Egyptian and international media outlets. The scene oozed of raw retaliation and masculine superiority.

A short while later, the club's gates were opened and the crowds were welcomed into al-Ahly's club premises.[1] On the pitch inside the club's iconic Mokhtar el-Tetsh Stadium, the festivities continued for several hours. The day was an emotional one for everyone involved. Around lunchtime, I got hold of Mido, the senior Ultra mentioned in the previous chapter. He was in an excellent mood, describing the judgment as "in a deep sense better than all our *butulat* [league and cup titles]." Later in the afternoon, al-Ahly's television channel interviewed the mother of one of the murdered boys. She praised God for the verdicts, which were granting her "happiness, like I have never experienced in my whole life." She also expressed hope that the day would mark an "endpoint to violence and insults among Egyptian football fans" and that it would be remembered as the "beginning of a better future for the country's youth." Despite the somber occasion, the day had developed into a massive family event and picnic on the grass where the Ahly players usually train. On the terraces above the pitch, Ultras Ahlawy put on a spectacular set of choreographed *dakhlas*, pyrotechnical shows with *shamarikh*, songs, and chants. A couple of days later, one *Ahlawi* friend of mine described the afternoon inside the club as a "beautiful and well-deserved moment of joy after a long and hard struggle."

The January 2013 court verdicts could be read as Ultras Ahlawy's most triumphant moment. The fan group's protests received ample media attention; their threats to create "chaos" were taken seriously, and the death sentences were celebrated as an important, if partial, step toward retribution (*al-qasas*). UA07's cause also gained vocal support from an unprecedented number of elite actors: state newspapers, like *al-Ahram*, and representatives of the ruling Muslim Brotherhood showed sympathy for the Ultras' actions, even when they effectively closed down central Cairo (Fathi, 2013); al-Ahly Club as well as the EFA considered the verdicts sound and satisfactory (*Masa' al-Anwar*, 26 January 2013); President Muhammad Mursi issued a timely republican resolution (*qarar jumhuri*) officially declaring the Port Said victims revolutionary martyrs (*shuhada' al-thawra*) (EMSS, 2013). Even the talk show host Medhat Shalaby—long one of the group's fiercest critics—was cautiously supportive. In his show *Masa' al-Anwar* on 26 January, he praised the young men's bravery and principles, and he congratulated them on the just court decision. Surely, Shalaby prophesied, the day would be remembered as the end of the "sad story" that had paralyzed Egypt's national sport over the last twelve months.

And yet, with a few years of hindsight, January 2013 rather stands out as the beginning of the end for the Egyptian Ultras. In the months and years that followed, the football fans' revolutionary momentum was gradually lost; by spring 2018, the decline was completed as Ultras Ahlawy took the decision to dissolve themselves. Bringing the story about Egypt's Ultras supporters to a close, this chapter charts the developments leading to this irreversible decision. Initially, ethnographic emphasis is put on an eventful couple of months in early 2013, a period of increasing animosities between the Islamist government and secular opposition. The new sociopolitical fault line pushed the Ultras to be either politically partisan or irrelevant and passive. For many outsiders, the fans became difficult to read. The latter parts of the chapter outline how counterrevolutionary resets have reverberated within the world of Egyptian football in the aftermath of the July 2013 Military Coup. An increasingly hostile media and security climate has thwarted the Ultras' campaigns and fan activities, eventually forcing UA07's dissolution. The chapter's conclusion looks back on the supporter movement's story between 2007 and 2019. It suggests that 2011 and 2012 constituted an exceptional moment of bold, revolutionary action, which came to a tragic end in the wake of July 2013. I also argue that *siyasa* (politics), as a problematic and a set of questions, played a key role in each step of the fans' rise to fame and eventual demise. The Ultras supporters always had to reconcile two disparate ideals for being nonpolitical: a working-class model of masculine bravery and violence that pitted "revolutionary" street fights against "political" deliberation; and a long-standing, broadly middle-class nationalist sentiment that dismissed self-serving partisanship of all kinds as a threat to the common good of the whole Egyptian people. As long as the Ultras fans managed to shun both, their popularity transcended class divides and their masculine ethos looked truly nonpolitical. Yet the double bind would prove insurmountable. Troubling queries about the fan organizations' politics soon became omnipresent and impossible to ignore.

QUESTIONS ABOUND

Cairo was not the only Egyptian city where drama unfolded in late January 2013. As soon as al-Masry's Ultras Green Eagles learned that twenty-one friends had been put on death row, they took a leading role in a series of raging protests that swept through the city of Port Said in the weeks that followed. The demonstrations might have been waged against the unjust court verdicts and the complacent Mursi government, although for many residents in Port Said, they also expressed more long-standing grievances: the Cairo-centric orientation of multiple governments; al-Ahly's financial and media-driven supremacy within Egyptian sports; the social and economic marginalization suffered by provincial cities; and disregard for the Suez Canal region's sacrifices during the wars in 1956, 1967, and 1973 (Attalah, 2013; Tarek and Maher, 2013; Zaki Chakravarti, 2013). The protests soon turned ugly. Snipers fired live rounds at unarmed citizens, who attempted to storm the prison where the convicts were held. In the first forty-eight hours after the verdicts were announced, thirty-seven people were killed and hundreds injured (Attalah, 2013).

Back in Cairo, Ultras Ahlawy did not show much sympathy for this outburst of violence, spearheaded by fans they accused of cold-blooded murder. Much like UA07's leadership, Mido dismissed Green Eagles' reaction as "dumb and idiotic": "More than thirty killed after a death sentence against twenty-one; such fools," he told me with uncharacteristic coldness. The Ahly Ultras were not alone to hold such opinions. Most politicians, club representatives, and football media voices condemned the unrest in Port Said. On one talk show, Medhat Shalaby described the unrest as an illogical, sad, and overly emotional reaction of random violence (*'unf 'ashwa'i*), incompatible with the rule of law (*Masa' al-Anwar*, 26 January 2013). Somewhat paradoxically given their many bitter conflicts over the previous years, the court verdicts and the ensuing protests in Port Said saw Ultras Ahlawy and the pundits on football television forming a united front.

But the broad and unexpected support that UA07 enjoyed from politicians and the sports media was a double-edged sword. Among Egyptians with pro-revolutionary inclinations—people who had typically backed the Ultras project in the past—enthusiasm was rapidly cooling off. Wherever I went those winter days, I heard people pose troubling questions. Why were these "revolutionaries" suddenly backed by the government, as well as large parts of the football establishment? Why had UA07 accepted and celebrated the court's verdict, even though no policeman had been convicted and no one from the military was even put on trial? And most pressing: given Egypt's notoriously corrupt judicial system, why should *this* death sentence against twenty-one young football fans be considered rightful and just? For many of my non-Ultras friends, it just seemed too likely that the men from Port Said had been scapegoated to calm down the Ultras in Cairo while the real culprits walked free. What is more, the clashes between civilians and security forces in Port Said were increasingly seen as a new front line of the revolutionary struggle. As a result, many of Egypt's self-identifying revolutionaries sided with Green Eagles and the people in Port Said against the security state, against the Mursi government, and indirectly also against Ultras Ahlawy in Cairo (see Thabet, 2013:138–145).

The iconic photos of Ultras Ahlawy celebrating the Port Said verdicts outside al-Ahly Club played a pivotal role in this reassessment. The footage of bare-chested men rejoicing at death sentences, gesturing obscenely, and humiliating Green Eagles, al-Masry, and the city of Port Said came across as disrespectful and repellent to a lot of people I talked to. To insult fellow citizens who had just been sentenced to death and whose guilt many Egyptians doubted was difficult to understand, let alone justify. A couple of days after the verdicts, my friend Sayed—a coffee shop owner and outspoken advocate of the secular strands of the revolutionary movement—explicitly brought up the flexing of muscles when explaining why he had found the scene reprehensible. He described the foul language used that day as "shocking" (*fazi'a*), "disgusting" (*araf*), and "not at all appropriate" (*mish mazbut khalis*).[2]

Similar reactions filled social media too. Activists, journalists, and scholars alike expressed disappointment with a group of football supporters they had thought they understood and increasingly come to trust and admire. Did Ultras Ahlawy's impressive campaign against corruption, oppression, and police violence merely boil down to *this* after all those years of struggle? Had it just been a matter of getting revenge against their long-sworn rivals in Green Eagles, and not a fight against the security state after all? An eye for an eye, and all of a sudden the fans showed their real face? In a moment, the Ultras' long-standing "violence paradox" had snapped back and entrapped them. For outsiders, the masculinized, rowdy scenes outside the club communicated precisely the scripts for self-serving *ta'assub* (fanaticism) and *baltaga* (thuggery) that the Ultras had evaded during the previous two years (see chapters 3 and 4). The supporter groups' respectable, *gada'* masculinity—until late 2012 so well suited to the revolutionary moment—was by early 2013 surrounded by many questions and a great deal of doubt.[3]

CRACKS AND RELAPSE IN A DIVIDED NATION

The general perception of the Egyptian Ultras movement changed dramatically in the month or two that followed the 26 January 2013 verdicts. What began as a number of nagging questions had developed into a veritable wave of criticism, accusations, and mistrust by mid-March, when a second round of sentences was passed. This dramatic swing needs to be understood within the context of a concurrent reconfiguration of Egypt's political terrain, a transformation that was instigated by President Muhammad Mursi issuing a controversial constitutional declaration on 22 November 2012. Among other things, the declaration granted the president the right to overturn any ruling by the judiciary that impeded the drafting of a new constitution. While Mursi portrayed this as a vital revolutionary move against an inherently counterrevolutionary court system, his opponents, as well as many Egyptians who until then had considered themselves neutrals, understood it as an unacceptable power grab.

The declaration proved a fatal turning point. Before long, bloody clashes between Muslim Brotherhood supporters and protesters ensued. More generally, the Egyptian polity crystallized along a sharp and bitter secular–Islamist divide, with both sides insisting that they were the true representatives of "the Egyptian people." In the first months of 2013, conversation between the government and oppositional politicians such as Hamdeen Sabahi, Amr Moussa, and Mohamed ElBaradei broke down. Violence between groups of civilians erupted regularly; within families and groups of close friends, individuals on opposing sides of the rift found it increasingly difficult to communicate.[4]

For the Egyptian Ultras, the new divisive landscape would always be difficult to navigate. The Ultras Ahlawy and Ultras White Knights leaders and membership bases were split right across the secular–Islamist divide. Accordingly, the groups could not possibly take sides. Before November 2012, this had rarely been a problem. Being neither Islamist nor secular had by contrast contributed to the fan movement's broad appeal. Now, the very same stance rendered the Ultras increasingly obsolete; the groups' previously proactive Facebook pages turned passive and reactive. The Ultras themselves always insisted that this passivity was logical. The conflict between the Mursi government and the opposition was not their fight; being football fans, they were only protecting their own rights and had no interest in interfering in *siyasa* (Ultras Ahlawy Facebook, 23 November 2012). For outsiders, though, unwavering neutrality was not an option. The new political climate seemed to oblige each and every citizen to take a side.[5] The Ultras' silence vis-à-vis the conflict that engulfed the nation thus rendered the fan groups difficult to read and even somewhat suspicious.

The issue was not only one of irrelevance and inaction. After the Port Said verdicts, with the country split between al-Ahly and al-Masry, Cairo and Port Said, the Mursi government and the opposition, being Ahly supporters and explicitly antagonistic to al-Masry and Port Said insinuated a particular positionality no matter how much UA07 insisted that they were apolitical. A demonstration on 15 February revealed this tension. Marching on the Ministry of Defense, the protesters demanded that members of the Supreme Council of the Armed Forces should be brought to justice for crimes committed during their year and a half in power (February 2011 to July 2012). As the journalist Wael Eskander notes in a reflective eyewitness account (2013a), the march was a deliberate attempt to reunite the efforts of Ultras Ahlawy and other prominent revolutionary activists after weeks of mutual recriminations. But it ended up deepening the same divisions. Eskander reports that friction developed almost immediately, as the participating Ultras sang their songs and accused the army of having facilitated the Port Said massacre, yet fell silent whenever demonstrators chanted against President Mursi. Contending that the demonstration must remain *nonpolitical*—that is, anti-military but neither for nor against the Mursi government—the Ultras prevented other people in the march from expressing criticism against the government, both verbally and at times through physical violence. Unsurprisingly, this interference provoked the activists whose voices were silenced. For them, the military and the Mursi government constituted two sides of one and the same problem: achieving revolutionary retribution against the generals would not be possible as long as the Islamists stayed in power. As such, the day made visible an irresolvable disagreement. A stance that Ultras Ahlawy considered strictly nonpolitical was for almost everyone else proof that the group had sided with the Mursi government (Eskander, 2013a; Shams el-Din, 2013).[6]

A few weeks later, on 9 March 2013, the second round of Port Said verdicts was announced. Just like in the previous case, these judgments might at first have looked like a triumph for Ultras Ahlawy's cause. Not only were the twenty-one death sentences from January confirmed and another twenty-two Masry supporters sentenced to long prison sentences, but for the first time in any trial after 25 January 2011, two police officers were also convicted and sentenced to fifteen years behind bars (*Ahram* Online, 9 March 2013). For a significant faction within Ultras Ahlawy, however, the punishments were not harsh enough. When learning that seven other police officers had been acquitted, groups of angry fans decided that the time had come to take justice into their own hands. They stormed the Police Club as well as the EFA's headquarters in central Cairo, setting both buildings on fire. In the following days, when it became clear that the EFA building was a complete loss, it was difficult to find anyone in Cairo sympathizing with the fans' actions. In the media, within the EFA, in the government, and among oppositional politicians, the attacks were condemned as an outrageous and exaggerated overreaction, or as senseless destruction (see, for example, *al-Kura al-Naharda*, Modern TV channel, 11 March 2013; *al-Masa'*, 10 March 2013).[7] The Ultras now stood on their own. If revolutionary activists and journalists had turned their backs on the groups in previous weeks, then events after the March verdicts cost them their newfound establishment backers too.

When the short Egyptian winter came to an end, it was clear that the Ultras supporters had lost their iconic status as revolutionary darlings. It did not matter how often Ultras Ahlawy claimed they were saying what they had always said and doing what they had always done (Ultras Ahlawy Facebook, 28 February, 2 and 7 March 2013; see also Elgohari, 2013; Shams el-Din, 2013). A seed of distrust had been planted that did not go away. The Ultras' possible pro-government bias was just one of several problematic questions that loomed. The most common objection that I heard from friends was that the fan groups had become *siyasi* (political) in an undefined yet ultimately problematic way. My friend Sayed and I often discussed the Ultras when meeting in his coffee shop that spring. In late March he told me, "First the Ultras were against everyone, then they were with Mursi and against Port Said, right? And now they claim that they are against the police again? Honestly, I am not following any longer. It's all politics [*kullaha siyasa*]." Sayed spoke to a sense of bewilderment that many of my interlocutors would recognize. The supporter groups, which had long seemed the epitome of steadfastness, had suddenly become immensely difficult to read. Their actions were unpredictable. Nobody seemed sure where they stood, whose interests they fought for, and what they really wanted to achieve.

COUNTERREVOLUTION IN THE FOOTBALL ARENA

If winter 2013 constituted a turning point for the Egyptian Ultras movement, the summer that followed fundamentally changed the course of the country's revolutionary process. From early May, pressure mounted against President Muhammad Mursi in tandem with the *tamarrud* (rebellion) campaign, a grassroots movement aimed at collecting fifteen million signatures demanding early presidential elections. *Tamarrud* culminated on the last day of June in enormous demonstrations against the Mursi administration's purported misrule. As the president clung to power, insisting on the legitimacy of the ballot box, the army ousted and imprisoned him. The 3 July coup was led by Mursi's minister of defense, Field Marshal Abdel Fattah el-Sisi, and it was backed by a coalition of oppositional figures and religious leaders. In the weeks that followed, the Muslim Brotherhood organized a series of demonstrations—the main one was a sit-in in Cairo's Rabaa al-Adawiya Square—demanding that the elected president be reinstated. In the secular media, the protesters were demonized in unison, and the army was called upon to find a "solution." In the early morning of 14 August, the junta crushed the opposition by force. More than eight hundred people were killed when the Rabaa al-Adawiya sit-in was dispersed.

The Rabaa massacre proved the endpoint of Egypt's revolutionary era and the launch pad for something qualitatively different. Before long, the security state reestablished the monopoly on violence that it appeared to have lost in early 2011, clamping down ruthlessly on all kinds of opposition. Hundreds of activists and politicians—Islamists and seculars, liberals and socialists—were killed, and tens of thousands imprisoned. With time, the counterrevolution became increasingly formalized. In May 2014, Field Marshal el-Sisi, the country's de facto leader, won a landslide victory in the presidential elections, and he was reelected for a second term in March 2018.[8] In 2015, a new parliament was also elected. Since then the legislature has largely functioned as a rubber stamp, and Egypt's military rulers have been able to implement whatever policies and legislations they see fit.

Among Egypt's embattled football establishment—the EFA, the clubs, and the media—the developments in summer 2013 were widely appreciated. Already on 1 July—one day after the nationwide demonstrations but forty-eight hours *before* Mursi was finally ousted—the EFA issued a statement "in support of the demands of the Egyptian people in their recent demonstrations." The way in which this declaration emphasized a recent, i.e., *post-2011* interference of *siyasa* in the realm of sports is notable. Not only did the EFA condemn the Mursi government's "attempts to insert star players [i.e., Muhammad Abu Treika] in the political process [*al-'amiliyya al-siyasiyya*] and to exploit supporters and bands [*rawabit*, i.e., Ultras] for personal interests [*khidmit masalihim shakhsiyya*]," but their statement also called for a thorough cleansing (*tathir*) of the sport. For stability and some kind of normality to return to Egyptian football, the political interventions (*al-tadakhkhulat al-siyasiyya*) that had proliferated in recent years had to come to an end (Fawzi, 2013).[9]

The Football Association's 1 July statement predicted many subsequent developments. Just like the EFA had hoped for, the years that followed would give the establishment the opportunity to "cleanse" football of disquieting interference, and to retake control over the country's sports institutions. The Mursi-leaning "star player," Muhammad Abu Treika, for instance, was demonized in the media and harassed through multiple lawsuits. In 2017, he decided to emigrate to Qatar.[10] The counterrevolutionary climate also allowed the EFA, the football media, and the biggest clubs to strike back forcefully against the country's Ultras supporter movement. No doubt, the years after July 2013 have constituted an immensely challenging test for Egypt's radical fan groups.

Let us begin at the beginning. Immediately after the coup, Egypt's Ultras groups made clear that they would not take sides in the standoff between the Brotherhood and the army. In a unique joint Facebook statement, Ultras Ahlawy and Ultras White Knights first noted that the nation was witnessing "a bloody struggle between gangs and dispersal between all sections and layers of the nation" (sira' dami bayn al-gumu' wi tashattut fi kull fada'il wi tabaqat al-watan). In this conflict, which provoked "grownups" to lose their minds and "elites to behave like children," Egypt's two largest football fan groups declared that they had no interest in participating. Instead, the statement clarified, UA07 and UWK had two and only two goals: full retribution for their revolutionary martyrs, and assurance of the Ultras' swift return to the *curvas* at Egypt's football stadiums (UA07 and UWK Facebook, 14 July 2013; see also Dorsey, 2013).

As for the first of these undertakings, bringing the Port Said trials to a conclusion proved to be more complex than Ultras Ahlawy might have expected. In February 2014, the Court of Cassation—the highest court in the Egyptian common court system—ordered retrials for sixty-four of the seventy-three defendants originally sentenced in January and March 2013 (Begato, 2014; *Ahram* Online, 6 February 2014). The retrials resulted in two new verdicts in April and June 2015: among the twenty-one Masry fans on death row since 2013, eleven were once again sentenced to death; forty-one defendants, including the two convicted police officers, were given between five and fifteen years of hard labor; and twenty-one were acquitted (*Al-Misri al-Yum*, 9 June 2015). In October 2016, the prosecution argued for another retrial (Ennarah, 2017), yet this claim was rejected, and the 2015 verdicts were confirmed in February 2017 (Youssef, 2017). Throughout these judicial twists and turns, Ultras Ahlawy continued to organize yearly commemorations of the Port Said martyrs on the 1 February anniversary, and they insisted that they would not accept anything but full retribution (*al-qasas*). Until the day in May 2018 when the group was dissolved, Ultras Ahlawy did not consider any court verdict fully satisfying.[11]

The Ultras' second mission—to return to Egypt's stadiums—has developed into an even more protracted battle. As discussed in chapter 4, all domestic football tournaments were put on hold in Egypt after the Port Said tragedy. For a full twelve months, Ultras Ahlawy insisted that this ban should stay in place—their demand, famously, was no return of football before *al-qasas*—but after the January 2013 verdicts, they tacitly allowed the league to restart. It is important to stress that the return of regular league matches did not imply the return of supporters. Following pressure from the Confederation of African Football (CAF), a limited number of fans were allowed into the stadiums at al-Ahly's and al-Zamalek's matches in the African Champions League and the national team's international qualifiers. However, fans were prohibited from attending all matches organized by the EFA for "security reasons."

Ever since, the situation has been gridlocked between seemingly irreconcilable antagonists. On the one side, the EFA and the clubs have given repeated assurances that they would like to see fans returning as soon as improved security measures are in place. The authorities have announced numerous times that the ban on supporter groups was about to be lifted, only to pull out at the last minute. The problem has always been how to ensure that fans refrain from rowdy behaviors and disturbing "political" protests. Or at least this has been the main reason the Ministry of Interior, which is responsible for security at the matches and thus has the final say, has given for not allowing the fans to come back. Pointing to a series of "failed tests"—international matches at which the Ultras acted inappropriately, insulted the police, or accused the military of the Port Said killings—the security services have revoked several preliminary decisions to let supporters back in (see, for example, Al-Din Muhammad, 2014; *Ahram* Online, 10 December 2015, 19 September 2016, and 14 February 2018). At the beginning of the 2019–2020 season, before the coronavirus outbreak interrupted all football activities in the country, a small number of fans were once again allowed to attend matches in the Egyptian League and Cup. But purchasing tickets required having an expensive club membership and going through a special application procedure that effectively shut out "problematic" fan groups.

Among the Ultras, on the other hand, the stalemate has long been considered completely unacceptable. Assuring that they are and have always been nonpolitical, the groups have been adamant that they must be allowed to watch their teams play—not only at a handful of Champions League games at Burg el-Arab outside Alexandria each year, but regularly, at home at Cairo Stadium. That the Egyptian league has been played for television audiences only for more than seven years is for them a perfect illustration of the modern, media-driven, and hopelessly commercialized football that Ultras everywhere in the world oppose. In the first year after the coup, the groups launched a series of street protests to manifest their right to support their clubs whenever and wherever they wanted to. Ultras Ahlawy and Ultras White Knights defied the crowd ban on multiple occasions, storming stadiums that were officially off-limits (e.g., Maher, 2013; Dorsey, 2014). The more the Egyptian security state regrouped, however, the riskier such actions became. Since late 2014, the most attractive games are all played inside military compounds, and several Ultras have been arrested as they tried to approach high-security stadiums (see, for example, *Al-Misri al-Yum*, 1 March 2014). As one would expect, the media have depicted these raids as further evidence of the Ultras' bad intentions and as proof that the supporter ban needs to stay in place for a while longer.

Meanwhile, a separate conflict has arisen between Ultras White Knights (UWK) and al-Zamalek's club president, Murtada Mansour. A controversial lawyer, foul-mouthed media commentator, millionaire, and staunch

Mubarak and el-Sisi supporter, Mansour was elected in 2014 on a clear platform: he promised to bring in investors to boost the football team and refurbish worn-out club facilities, and he vowed to once and for all resolve the problem of al-Zamalek's rebellious Ultras fans.[11] Frosty from the outset, the relationship between Mansour and the Ultras escalated in August 2014, when the president claimed that the group had attempted to assassinate him. Exactly what happened remains unclear (see Nader, 2014), but Mansour used the incident to clamp down on the supporters. Mobilizing his media contacts, his networks as a regime-friendly lawyer, and Egypt's draconian 2013 protest law, he managed to have more than a hundred UWK members arrested, either for the attack itself or for participating in demonstrations in the following weeks. Within a month, he had convinced all Premier League clubs other than al-Ahly and Wadi Degla, to formally denounce Egypt's Ultras groups. In October the same year, al-Zamalek suspended its talented right-back, Omar Gaber, as a direct result of the player's alleged sympathy for the Ultras' project (Maher, 2014).

In early 2015, the conflict took an immensely tragic turn. In an unexpected move, the EFA and the security forces suddenly agreed to allow a limited number of fans to attend Egyptian Premier League games. The first match with supporters was to be played on 8 February between al-Zamalek and ENPPI at the Air Defense Stadium in Cairo's eastern outskirts. My friend Muhammad, the UWK member from al-Sayyida Zaynab whose fandom I described in chapter 3, had looked forward to this day for several years. His local *dawla* had fought hard to ensure the return of fans; finally, their efforts were about to pay off. But when Muhammad approached the stadium, he immediately realized that the organization was terribly insufficient. "There were too many people—ten, perhaps even twenty thousand," he recalled when we met later the same year.

> You see, first they had said that the game would be for free, because it was the first one with fans. But the last day, the club changed its mind and started to sell tickets. Of course, many people came without tickets. I was there with my friend who is a photographer. We scaled an advertisement board to get a good view for photos. We saw everything. All people had to enter through a narrow corridor. At the end of it, there was only one tiny entrance. They called it a security point, but it was like something used for animals. This small [measuring roughly half a meter between his palms]. Barbed wire. It was impossible to get all those people through. Impossible! And more and more people arrived. Of course, people panicked. But the police didn't care. Instead of opening the gates, they

fired tear gas, right into the crowds! It was hell. First, I stayed on the advertisement board. Then I tried to help out. I saw people smashed. Suffocated.

The stampede at the Air Defense Stadium left twenty Zamalek fans dead and several hundred injured. Although none of the victims were members of UWK, the group launched a campaign for commemoration and retribution similar to Ultras Ahlawy's after the tragedy in Port Said. Ever since, UWK members have directed their rage against "the killer" Murtada Mansour, holding him and the Ministry of Interior responsible for the disastrous organization of ticketing and crowd control. They are also unwilling to forgive their club's president for insisting that the match should be played even though he knew that Zamalek supporters had been killed (UWK Facebook, 10 February 2015).[13]

UWK's struggle for justice has been widely recognized and supported. Most, if not all, Zamalek supporters I know blame the club and the police for the stampede, and they are highly critical of Mansour's way of dealing with the calamity and deflecting the blame back onto the Ultras. Yet in contrast to UA07 after the Port Said massacre, UWK has not been able to make their case heard in the courts. To bring football fans from Port Said to justice during the revolutionary year of 2012 was one thing. To charge police officers and well-connected club officials in President el-Sisi's Egypt is much harder. Ironically, and sadly illustrative of the disastrous state of the Egyptian judiciary, the only individuals who have been brought to justice are seventeen Ultras White Knights members and leaders accused by Mansour for having set up and caused the killing (Mar'i, 2015). In September 2017, fourteen of the defendants were sentenced to hefty fines and long prison sentences (*Mada Masr*, 24 September 2017). Since May 2015, all Egyptian Ultras groups have also been legally banned after accusations of breaking the protest law, threatening national security, and plotting terrorism activities. The case was filed in court by Murtada Mansour (*Egypt Independent*, 16 May 2015).

DISSOLUTION

On 16 May 2018—the eve of the holy month of Ramadan—Ultras Ahlawy took the irrevocable decision to discontinue all activities and dissolve their own supporter group. The decision was announced in a short statement on the group's Facebook page and a video showing their famous banner being burned. Within hours, the page with more than 1.3 million followers was deleted (Nathan, 2018). Eleven days later, another video circulated on the internet that purported to show that Ultras White Knights had made the same decision,[14] although it was immediately denied on UWK's Facebook page (28 May 2018). As of January 2021, UWK still formally exists, but the group's activities are sporadic.

What prompted Egypt's largest Ultras group to make this drastic move? Why did Ultras Ahlawy—a fan association famous for the slogan "Together Forever"—conclude that the time had come to give up and let go? The sequence of events presented in this chapter makes the spring 2018 decision easier to comprehend. Already in early 2013—the time of the first round of Port Said court verdicts—most of the Ultras' friends and backers had turned their backs on the supporter movement. The young fans' intentions were questioned; they were portrayed as vulgar, selfish, politicized, and thuggish by media pundits, activists, politicians, and large numbers of Egyptian football aficionados. In the years that followed the July 2013 coup, the pressure on the groups mounted further. As the football establishment and security apparatus reconsolidated, the Ultras found themselves harassed by the judiciary, castigated in the media, and marginalized in public conversation. Multiple pieces of anti-Ultras legislation were passed by Egypt's parliament (Hamama and Mamdouh, 2017); scores of UA07 and UWK members were put behind bars.[15] In April 2017, at the tenth anniversary of Ultras fans in Egypt, the hostile climate constituted an inescapable backdrop. Both UA07's and UWK's celebrations were notably somber. On 13 April, Ultras Ahlawy posted a brief message on their Facebook page, which summarized their current predicament:

- Today, ten years have passed since the establishment of Ultras Ahlawy.
- Ten years behind al-Ahly Club.
- Today coincides with the renewal of the prosecution against eight Ahly supporters who did not commit any crime at all [. . .]
- Until now, there are no answers to the questions: what are the accusations? What did they do? What is the evidence? [. . .]
- Everyone knows that the eight arrested individuals are treated unjustly [*mazlumin*], and that there are no accusations against them.
- We will always continue to be football supporters behind al-Ahly Club. . . . And we will also continue to wait for the justice that is absent.
- Freedom for the fans.

But injustice and repression were only part of the story. Ultras Ahlawy's decision to dissolve the group was also prompted by the sheer impossibility of doing and feeling what the fan groups had been set up to do and feel. In chapter 3, I suggested that the Ultras instituted a novel emotional style of fun combined with freedom. Bringing together meticulous preparations, elaborate songs, ninety minutes of dancing, and blazing fireworks, the fans revolutionized the atmosphere at Egypt's football stadiums in the last years of the 2000s. By May 2018, Ultras Ahlawy had not been able to regularly put together such spectacles for more than six years. Because of the supporter ban, the group had spent a longer time outside their habitat in Cairo Stadium's *talta shimal* than inside of it. Put simply, the Ultras' style of fun and freedom was no more, and it was difficult to envision its restoration in the foreseeable future. In summer 2020, my UA07 friend Mido explained the group's dilemma in the following terms:

> The boys were forced to dissolve the group. Because of all the arrests and laws and security, it wasn't possible to continue. The *capos* have grown older. They have kids, some live abroad. We cannot do or say anything at the stadium anymore. They have managed to turn it back to the atmosphere we had in the 1980s: old men eating pistachios and peanuts. *Khalas*, it's over. They killed it.

As this book goes to press, al-Zamalek's Ultras White Knights is the only Cairene Ultras group that is still in operation. And to be honest, they are a far cry from what they used to be. Even if UWK continues to push for the release of their imprisoned leaders and honor the memories of their martyrs on their Facebook page, their spectacle in *talta yimin* at Cairo stadium has not been resurrected for more than nine years. At the end of April 2019, Muhammad, my UWK-friend from al-Sayyida Zaynab, and I finally found the opportunity to attend a Zamalek match together at the stadium. The game, a semi-final of the African Confederations Cup played at Burg el-Arab outside Alexandria, turned out to be a great day out. The chartered bus from Cairo was packed with fans and anticipation. Zamalek songs played through the loudspeakers. White-and-red flags waved through the open windows. When we entered the stadium *curva*, we found it packed with many thousands of young men, all of them dressed in white, all of them standing up on the chairs. The unified chanting was already deafening an hour before kickoff. When Zamalek scored the game's only goal late in the first half, all of us hugged and jumped and screamed. The collective ecstasy left the stadium concrete trembling.

At the same time, a number of factors made it obvious that we were not attending an Ultras event. Although the crowd chanted without interruption, I did not hear any of the witty and provocative songs that had made UWK so famous and adored; few people around me carried flags or banners; the stadium showed no signs of Ultras graffiti; only one single *shamrukh* burned. At halftime, Muhammad told me that he was disappointed with "the performance of the players and the fans too, to be honest." We watched the second half seated in the half-empty upper tier.

Two days later, I met Muhammad in Cairo. I asked him what he thought of the match and how he perceived the current situation for Ultras White Knights. This was his reply:

> First of all, you have to understand that the group's activities stopped after the Air Defense massacre [in February 2015]. The main reason is Murtada [Mansour]. He has called us terrorists and blamed us for what happened. He's a lawyer. The courts listen to him. All the *capos* are in prison. In fact, there was only one occasion this year when the group attended a match officially [*hudur rasmi*]: a volleyball game in February, when we commemorated the twenty martyrs [from the Air Defense stampede]. It was announced on our Facebook and our banner was in the arena, so it was official. Otherwise, members attend as individuals [*zay afrad*], like the match the other day. There were several thousand group members at Burg el-Arab, but we all went individually. It was not organized. [. . .] Because of that, the atmosphere was different. You saw it: no *dakhla*, no banners, no songs [*aghani*], only simple chants [*hatafat*]. And the chanting . . . the numbers were good, but it didn't sound good. Many people are not used to it [*mish mit'awwidin 'ala al-tashgi'*]. The chanting broke down a lot.

I also asked Muhammad to reflect on the reasons for these changes. The answer he gave me was an analysis of one single match experience, but I like to think that it encapsulates the predicament and prospects of the Egyptian Ultras at the turn of the 2020s.

> If you want to do a proper *dakhla*, people need to be at the stadium several hours before kickoff. This isn't possible these days. Burg el-Arab is a military stadium. We don't have access. For me personally, I don't have time. I haven't seen some of the other people in my *dawla* for years. The activities have stopped. People focus on their

Fig. 5.2. Timeworn Ultras Ahlawy mural in Abdeen, central Cairo, one year after the group's dissolution. Photo: Lena Malm, 6 May 2019.

jobs, they've grown older. Because there are no games, those who are eighteen or nineteen years old today don't join us. But at least we try. We go to games sometimes. Ultras Ahlawy burned their banner and closed their [Facebook] page, but we might come back. Things might get better in the future.

CONCLUSION: AN EXCEPTIONAL MOMENT IN A TIME OF POLITICS

Part II of this book has followed Egypt's Ultras football fans going full circle. Widely ostracized in the last years under President Mubarak, the supporters found ample space to flourish in the aftermath of January 2011. When the security forces retreated, Egypt's football stadiums turned into liberated zones of fun and freedom. The groups' visible participation on Tahrir Square and the martyrdom of seventy-two Ultras in Port Said bestowed unquestionable revolutionary credentials. In autumn 2012, their renown reached its peak with selective use of violence, Muhammad Abu Treika siding with the fans, and a campaign for retribution and reform that spoke of order, action, and purpose. But the moment as revolutionary role models would only last for so long. Questions began to mount in early 2013, and the counterrevolution that followed curbed the Ultras' emotional style, eventually forcing Ultras Ahlawy's self-dissolution.

When looking back at a decade and more of Ultras fans in Egypt, we see a lengthy uphill struggle broken off by a couple of years replete with promises and prospects. In 2011 and 2012, everything happened, and it happened all at once. On the one hand, the supporter movement was pulled into a maelstrom of events beyond their control. As the Egyptian people rose up and more than seventy Ultras were killed, the fans found themselves organizing demonstrations, commemorating martyrs, and lobbying judges instead of attending football matches. On the other hand, whatever the Ultras did, they did it with remarkable effectiveness. Mobilizing as a unified collective with a clear set of goals, they projected a sense that they could achieve just about anything. The result was a football revolution within the Egyptian revolution, a radical revolt inside Egypt's national game. The supporter movement constituted a conspicuous part of a revolutionary generation for whom the possibilities seemed endless and the future bright and assuring. To borrow a phrase from David Scott's ruminations about the 1979 to 1983 Grenada Revolution, the Ultras were "lean[ing] into that coming future with the complete sense that it belong[ed] to [them]" (2014:95).

The first two years after 25 January 2011 constituted the kind of revolutionary moment that Scott has called "exceptional": a period of "crisis and dislocation in which human action, in its capacity to intervene [in history], stands out starkly against established patterns" (Scott, 2014:34). For Scott, revolutionary exceptionality ultimately resides in a radically condensed contingency. In revolution, things are at stake and unpredictability reigns. Exceptional actors, like the Ultras, might step up, grab opportunities, and change everything. At the same time, Scott cautions that whereas political actors can "initiate action," they "cannot entirely calculate its final outcome" (ibid., 51). Revolutionary moments always encompass an "intrinsic 'frailty' [and a] constant vulnerability to tragic hazards" (ibid., 37). The last five years of the story about the Egyptian Ultras composes a tragic development in this sense of the term. The fans always insisted that they were doing what they had always done and saying what they had always said. Yet the outcome of their actions changed beyond recognition once the exceptional moment passed. Just as the Ultras epitomized the revolution's endless possibilities and openings, then, their fate likewise demonstrates the force of the Egyptian counterrevolution. As the nation split in two, the security state regrouped, legislation was amended, and the clubs and the media sided with the powers that be, Egypt's young football supporters found themselves thwarted, marginalized, and back at square one. This counterrevolution in the Egyptian football arena is one of many small and large tragedies that have unfolded in the wake of the July 2013 Military Coup (for other examples, see Armbrust, 2019; Shenker, 2016; Winegar, 2016).

One issue that the history of the Ultras highlights is the unease that surrounds *siyasa* in contemporary Egypt. A variety of anxieties and questions about *siyasa* and about who or what should be considered *siyasi* have arisen in this (counter-)revolutionary football tale. Over the years, the Ultras supporters have been portrayed as selfish, as a minority, as thugs, or as government affiliates—that is, as self-concerned or *politically partisan* in one way or another. The groups themselves, however, have always insisted that they are *nonpolitical*. "We are just football supporters, we don't interfere in politics," has been a recurrent claim.

What do the Ultras mean when they insist that their activities and objectives are located outside the realm of *siyasa*? What kind of politics do they reject? One possible reading would characterize *siyasa* as a future-oriented process of deliberations and game-theoretical calculations. Historian Lucie Ryzova (2020) makes such a point in a recent analysis of the urban battle that took place in Cairo's Muhammad Mahmoud Street in November 2011. Drawing on interviews with underprivileged, lower-income men who fought the security forces in this glorified and brutal confrontation, Ryzova argues that her interlocutors conceive of *siyasa* as an unclean and insincere game played out by actors whom they consider categorically Other: political parties, organizations with particular interests, or the primarily middle-class activists who occupied Tahrir Square while the battles raged. The clashes in Muhammad Mahmoud, by contrast, constituted a pure revolution precisely because of it being everything that *siyasa* was not. It was an existential and affective fight—part riot, part carnival—where the current moment of liminality was all that mattered, and where the sole aim was to "fuck" the security apparatus and "take back one's rights" (Ryzova, 2020).[16]

The Ultras fans' dismissal of politics has often been fueled by the working-class sentiments described by Ryzova. The fact that scores of Ultras participated in the Muhammad Mahmoud clashes—although only as individual citizens, never as a coherent group—is in this regard telling. Similarly, when the supporters insisted that they confined their struggle to the realm of sports and to restoring the rights of their killed comrades (*haqq al-shuhada'*), it reflected an antipathy to *siyasa* as an institutionalized process that Ryzova's interlocutors would recognize. UA07's decision to protest against the SCAF (who they held responsible for the Port Said massacre) but not against the Muslim Brotherhood government (a political player) in February 2013 is a good example too. Still, this classed rejection of politics from below was never all there was. If the Ultras had cared *only* about fighting the security forces and taking back their rights, the Muhammad Mahmoud clashes should have constituted a black-and-white moment of "absolute truth against absolute evil" (Ryzova, 2020:308). They did not. At the time, leaders from both UWK and UA07 saw themselves forced to make statements in the media denying reports about their members participating in the thuggish street fights and condemning "any action that hurts the *interest of the country and its institutions*" (chapter 3). Likewise, when UA07 in September 2012 decided not to attack the Super Cup match by force, the decision was once again framed in broad *nationalist* terms: "we do not want to hurt *any citizens of this country*" (chapter 4). In a documentary produced by TRT World, an anonymous leading member of Ultras White Knights describes this nonpolitical position as a kind of patriotism: "[the Ultras] was always a national movement, not a political one. We are not involved in politics. We just love football very much and we love our country even much [*sic*] more (2018)."

The multiplicity inherent to these stances suggests the limitations of Ryzova's neat distinction between working-class revolution and middle-class politics. Being nonpolitical is not only a way to distance oneself from future-oriented, nationalist deliberations and long-term institutional change. It might also be a requirement for anyone aspiring to enter precisely this forward-looking field of reforms and action. For one thing is certain: queries about *siyasa* are mobilized as a persuasive form of discursive power in a wide range of Egyptian establishment contexts. In his research on state secularism, for instance, Hussein Agrama illustrates how conversations about proper and improper religiosity constantly spotlight delineations between the religious and the political. At one point, Agrama writes that "secular power works precisely by continually politicizing those traditions that it designates as religious [. . .] it is the politicizing of these traditions that renders them irrelevant" (2012:25). In other words, as soon as a religious group or practice is considered "political," it is rendered suspicious and troubling. Moreover, as I outlined in chapter 2, Egypt's pervasive nationalism is endowed with a similar power-laden capacity to politicize in order to render opponents irrelevant and distrustful. To prove one's nationalist, common-good credentials has for more than one hundred years necessitated a nonpolitical image and charisma. To be singled out as *siyasi* has therefore effectively stripped any given actor of his or her national-political relevance.

These ideals and anxieties were ever-present during Egypt's 2011 uprisings too. The Revolution, as well as the Counterrevolution that followed, were always framed as axiomatically nationalist projects carried out by and for the whole Egyptian people. Every political player with ambitions—President Mubarak, the so-called revolutionary youths, the army, President Mursi, the Muslim Brothers, and Abdel Fattah el-Sisi—inevitably claimed that their particular policies best served the national interest (*maslahit al-watan*) and the will of the people (*iradit al-sha'b*) (Schielke, 2015:191–198; Winegar, 2016).[17] An inevitable flipside of this consensus was an instinctive caution vis-à-vis partisanship and *siyasa*. Competing actors routinely accused each other of prioritizing factional demands (*matalib fi'awiyya*) or personal interests (*masalih shakhsiyya*) (see, for example, Brown, 2013a, 2013b; Makram-Ebeid, 2014; Shenker, 2016). The political process was in this sense curiously antipolitical.

In other words, the impetus on the Ultras to stay strictly nonpolitical drew on two distinct genealogies: on the one hand, templates for working-class masculinity that valorized "taking one's rights" and the emotional rush of violence, while dismissing the *political* deliberations and intrigues that occupied the middle classes; on the other hand, a broad nationalist consensus that shunned all kinds of partisan-*political* motives. By juggling these distinct versions of nonpolitics, the Ultras attempted to do and be two things at the same time: sometimes their goal was *al-qasas* against the security state in the moment, and at other times future-oriented institutional reforms of the national sport; sometimes they were working-class fighters, and at other times middle-class activists. During their exceptional moment in 2011 and 2012, the fan groups pulled off this balancing act in spectacular fashion. The darlings of the revolution were accepted as both rebellious fighters *and* solid nationalists. Their aura transcended class divides. No accusation of *siyasa* seemed to stick. By spring 2013, the tensions could no longer be reconciled. The Ultras could no longer be both. When they at times claimed to be all-nationalist and not taking sides, the movement appeared to be not only disloyal and inconsistent but also passive and somewhat irrelevant. But when they narrowed their focus to fighting immediate enemies and claiming precious rights, that did not work either. Celebrating the Port Said verdicts or burning down the EFA headquarters might have been in line with the action-oriented, antipolitical ethos of some working-class men. Yet it certainly looked "political" to those heralding the strict nonpartisanship of Egyptian nationalism. The tragic tale of the Egyptian Ultras in this sense dramatizes a group of football supporters being caught up in developments beyond their control. No matter how hard the fans tried to stay nonpolitical, they ended up acting within a realm of *siyasa* staked out by others.

Conversations about football and *siyasa* permeated more than just the power struggle between the Ultras fans and the football establishment. In the aftermath of the January 2011 Revolution and the February 2012 Port Said massacre, debates about and experiences of *siyasa* also altered how millions of "ordinary" Egyptian football supporters related to and felt about the national sport. This is the topic of part III.

PART III

AFTERMATH

CHAPTER 6

When the Game Feels Like Politics, It Doesn't Feel Like Much at All

So, we are in the moment, watching the game, submitting fully to the present, awaiting the moment of moments, with the future open and uncertain.

Simon Critchley, *What We Think about When We Think about Football*

In the actual event of revolution, its nature was not ideological, intellectual, or imaginative, but physical and emotional.

Samuli Schielke, *Egypt in the Future Tense*

Hamada smiled when I entered the door, but I could tell that he was exhausted. As usual, he was sitting behind the worn-out wooden desk in his small pharmacy at the fringes of Old Cairo (*masr al-qadima*), the sprawling lower-income neighborhood that covers large parts of the capital's southern perimeters. Dressed in a woolen jumper and a turtle-neck shirt to protect against the winter wind, he was finalizing an order of supplies over the phone, while simultaneously directing his assistant to the right packs of pills and syrups on the glass shelves covering the walls around him. A steady stream of visitors was calling for his attention, buying nappies, pain killers, Tramadol, and hair gel, checking their blood pressure, and asking *el-duktur* for all sorts of medical advice.[1] In his early thirties, with two wives and three kids in two separate homes to support, Hamada was familiar with the routines. For the last five years, he had worked five, six, even seven long days per week in the pharmacy. No holiday throughout this period had amounted to more than four or five days.

After a few minutes, the customers cleared for a moment and we got a chance to talk. Hamada invited me to sit down on a chair next to him, and he asked his assistant to make us tea. In the previous months, Hamada had developed into an invaluable interlocutor and a good friend. An obsessive Zamalek supporter for more than twenty years, he was immensely knowledgeable about the sport's past and present. Whenever I had come to see him in the pharmacy, as well as when we had attended matches together at the stadium, he had taken pains to provide me with all the details and anecdotes I needed to know. This afternoon in early February 2012, however, both of us found it difficult to formulate thoughts and feelings. Since our last meeting about a week earlier, the stadium massacre in Port Said had taken place. The killing of seventy-two young football fans had unleashed clashes between protesters and security forces that were bringing central Cairo to a halt (see chapter 4). Being a *Zamelkawi* and of a different generation than the Ultras, Hamada had no personal relation to anyone who had been present in Port Said. Nonetheless, as a devoted football supporter, the tragedy affected him profoundly. In face of the unfathomable that had befallen, we drank our tea in silence; Hamada fiddled with a piece of paper, his gaze remote and tired. For want of words, I came up with a suggestion. Perhaps he could finish early so that we could watch the semi-final in the Africa Cup of Nations between Ghana and Zambia in a nearby coffee shop? Hamada's reaction was first one of slight confusion. But then he smiled at me, almost embarrassed, and said:

> I don't know, Carl, but honestly until you said it, I didn't know that the semi-final was today, and I didn't know who was playing. It's strange. Remember when you asked me about tournaments in the 1990s and 2000s? I knew all the games and all the players, everything, didn't I? I always watched every game and I remembered so many details about each tournament. I'm really good at that. And now, I don't even know who is playing the semi-final; it doesn't matter to me [*mabiyifra'nish ya'ni*]. I cannot think about football any longer. I'm sorry; it just doesn't feel right. Actually, the only one who discusses football with me these days is you.

Hamada's indifference to football on this day was no doubt a result of both coming of age—family obligations had limited his visits to the stadium in the last couple of years—and dealing with the shock of the Port Said massacre, by far the bloodiest episode in Egypt's football history. At the same time, his feelings were not unique. Most of the football-loving men whom I met and talked to in Cairo in 2011, 2012, and 2013 confirmed that their attachments to teams and matches were flagging. Many of my friends proposed personal reasons for why they no longer followed football like they had in the recent past: Mahmoud, the gym instructor, told me that he had decided to focus more on his religious duties and that his daily prayers had to be prioritized; Bilal, the soon-to-be married man from Abdeen (see chapter 2), blamed the work he had to do refurbishing his new flat; Hani, who worked in the reception in my language school, explained that his new evening shifts clashed with the Ahly games that had been the highlight of his week; Ahmed, a call-center employee, let me know that he had stopped following al-Ahly, but that he watched FC Barcelona's "more entertaining" matches as often as he could. These were all perfectly reasonable explanations. Still, the question of why all these excuses for turning away from Egypt's national game were coinciding was left hanging.

The objective in part III of this book is to ethnographically examine affective reorientations vis-à-vis football in the aftermath of the Port Said tragedy. Whereas part I traced the rise, climax, and initial decline of the Egyptian football bubble (1990–2010) and part II accounted for the Ultras fans between 2007 and 2019, my focus is here on the experiences of more ordinary Egyptian football fans during a time of rapid retrenchment and cautious regrowth.[2] The first year after the massacre at Port Said was a pivotal moment for football fandom in Egypt. As the sport's bubbly past was revaluated and conflicts between the Ultras and the old establishment became the dominant story, attachments to football clubs, matches, and tournaments transformed abruptly. Egypt's *national* game (this chapter)— but not *international* matches (chapter 7)—was plunged into a deep popularity crisis from which it has not fully recovered.

In this chapter, Hamada, the pharmacist, figures as the main protagonist. Analyzing both why Hamada had felt so strongly about football in the prerevolutionary years and how that came to change between 2011 and 2013, I highlight a multidimensional process of mix-up, between sports on the one hand and discourses, events, and rhythms conjured by Hamada as *siyasa* (politics) on the other hand. Sometimes the affect of *siyasa* mirrored the game's thrill. At other times it drowned it. No matter what, politics made football immensely difficult to enjoy. All in all, this chapter's ethnography about withering football emotions unearths yet another layer of the problematic that *siyasa* assembles in contemporary Egypt. In the wake of the 2011 Revolution, the political was not only singled out as a perennial problem for the nation and the revolution. It also elicited a host of powerful and visceral anxieties among Egyptian men at the center as well as at the margins of the revolutionary transformation.

HAMADA THE PHARMACIST

In retrospect, it feels natural that I first met Hamada at Cairo Stadium. On a Saturday evening in early autumn 2011, at the very outset of my field research, a friend and I decided on a whim to watch al-Zamalek play Haras al-Hudud in the semi-final of the Egyptian Cup. It was the first Zamalek game either of us ever attended, and we had all sorts of problems locating the right street and gate within the vast and poorly marked stadium area. When we eventually entered the arena and climbed the steep stairs in search of a place to sit, the game had already kicked off. Sweaty and stressed, we grabbed what seemed like the last seats available, a couple of rows from the top of *daraga tanya*, the second-class sector opposite to the main stand.

The match fulfilled all our expectations: the stadium was nearly sold out, Ultras White Knights put on a series of stunning *dakhlas* and pyrotechnical shows, and al-Zamalek advanced to the final after a late decisive goal. The social interaction among a group of men immediately to our right intrigued us a great deal too. For a full ninety minutes, this noisy group of friends, broad-shouldered and chain-smoking, with thick moustaches and shiny track suits, just did not stop. They insulted the referee and the players from both teams, they laughed loudly at each other's sexually explicit jokes, and they complained and gestured at a million things that they found wrong and outrageous on the pitch and in al-Zamalek's club administration. I soon realized, however, that one man, on the seat right next to me, stood out from the rest. He did not sport a moustache; he was not smoking; I never heard him swear. Rather than being furious at everything and everybody, his straight, almost strained posture and concentration oozed tense nervousness. I also noted that in every heated argument, my neighbor always seemed to have some pertinent details to contribute, whether they were about a comparable game in the past, a certain player's previous clubs and achievements, or any kind of statistic imaginable. Despite his reserved looks and manners, he possessed a peculiar authority within the group, and his comrades were keen to listen to his historical mini-lectures once their own outbursts subsided. I was therefore more than happy when this man politely asked me who I was and where I came from. As I told him about my research and he realized that I spoke Arabic, he gave me his business card and insisted that I come to see him in the pharmacy that he ran. He promised to tell me "everything he knew" about the history of Egyptian football. I thanked him and told him that I would love to come and visit. And so it happened that Hamada and I became friends.

Hamada was born in Cairo in the late 1970s. Before retiring in the mid-2000s, his father worked as a physician in the Egyptian Army. This prestigious position secured the family an established middle-class status and an apartment in a sought-after part of Nasser City, right next to Cairo International Stadium. Growing up close to the epicenter of the Egyptian football universe, it did not take long for Hamada to become mesmerized by the game's colors, sounds, and people. At a very young age he would watch from his window as supporters, merchandise hawkers, and snack vendors congregated outside the stadium in the buildup for big Ahly, Zamalek, or national team matches.

The first time Hamada entered the stadium was at the age of eight, when his father, also a *Zamelkawi*, took him to a game. In those early days, Hamada had briefly wanted to disappoint his father and support al-Ahly—"since they were winning all the time"—but in the early 1990s, he shifted his allegiances to al-Zamalek as he found their style of play "more artistic." He now started to visit the stadium on a regular basis, most often on his own. One fond and formative memory was the 1992–1993 season, when Hamada, then in his early teens, saw al-Zamalek win the league and both derby games against al-Ahly. In the two decades that followed, however, the disappointments would be more numerous than the highlights. Al-Ahly—according to Hamada, with due help from referees and a corrupt Egyptian football establishment—almost always came out on top. Despite the setbacks, Hamada continued to follow al-Zamalek as well as the national team closely. He has watched an impressive number of the most iconic games in Egypt's modern football history live from the same Cairo Stadium section where we first met.

After finishing his pharmaceutical studies at Cairo University, getting married, and having a first child in the mid-2000s, Hamada's visits to the stadium became less frequent. His financial situation has not permitted him many indulgences, especially after separating from his first wife and marrying a second, with whom he today has two more kids. Neither of Hamada's wives are working—"they have enough to do at home, it is better that way"—and to support two homes and a total of six people, he has found himself working up to twelve hours a day, at least six days a week. In the late 2000s, he also felt that the atmosphere at Zamalek games began to change. While he insists that *daraga tanya*—his section at the stadium—has always felt like a second home, the way he narrates the past indicates that something was lost in the years just before I met him. In early 2012, he told me:

> In the 1990s, there was a difference in the way people cheered. In those days, the time of al-Khawaga [a popular cheerleader (*hatif*) in the pre-Ultras era], the songs were different and there was more

joking: not so serious. The songs we sang were simple, like the famous *ya Zamalek, ya madrasa, la'b wi fann wi handasa* [literally, Oh, Zamalek, oh, school, play and art and engineering], and people at the stadium were a bit older. Now, the Ultras sing all through the match; we who sit on *daraga tanya* don't sing very much. They are young and unaware [*mish wa'iyyin*] and a bit ignorant [*gahala*]. But they are organized, so everything they do becomes very strong. This is one reason why I have visited the stadium a bit less in the last years. The atmosphere is not the same as it used to be [*al-gaw mish zay ma kan*].

And yet, despite limited spare time and a gradually changing atmosphere, Hamada kept returning to Cairo Stadium all through the 2000s. Regardless of his workload, he would take time off to watch the most important Zamalek and national team matches each year from the stadium section he considered his. While Hamada does have a small television set in the pharmacy and can follow matches while working, he has often told me that for him, a televised game can never match the experience of watching it live. "Real football happens at the stadium," he emphasized once.

The atmosphere [*al-gaw*], all the people on *daraga tanya*, who I know but only meet there. And the sound and the space. That is what I've always loved and come back for. Television isn't the same. It's like *khudar bayit*, vegetables that have been left out for too long. It has a different bad taste. Of course, the football itself could be nice. But there is no atmosphere.

TALKING FOOTBALL AND POLITICS IN THE WAKE OF DISASTER

At first, the January 2011 Revolution did not change Hamada's relationship to his favorite sport and club very much. Although the economic downturn and the security vacuum that followed the Egyptian police's withdrawal from the streets made life more complicated, visits to Cairo Stadium continued to be part of his everyday routines. He did perhaps watch al-Zamalek play a little less frequently than before—"because when security isn't good you want to stay home with your family a bit more"—and at the pharmacy he noted that customers who used to discuss sports spoke about elections and political parties instead. But as he admitted during the first

round of the parliamentary elections in December 2011, "I still begin reading the sports pages in the newspapers. Honestly, I prefer reading about
a Zamalek victory than the number of votes for the Free Egyptians Party
[the liberal party that he voted for]."

The tragedy in Port Said in early 2012 changed things more profoundly. Two days after the atrocity, I called Hamada on the phone. As
always, he was in the pharmacy working; it was clear that he did not feel
like talking. During the short call, he declared that he felt "disgusted by
what had happened and with all of football actually." I also noted him using
phrases that were commonplace in the media at that time: "This is not
football, it is only politics"; "football should make people happy, not kill
people." Hamada's attitude was by and large the same when I came around
to see him a few days later. After my clumsy suggestion to forget about the
horror by watching another game of football, the ice broke, and we found
a way to talk. Matter-of-factly, he explained how the politicization (*tasyis*)
of football had led to increasing fanaticism (*ta'assub*) in the last decade, and
how this had culminated in Port Said. This development, argued Hamada,
was to be blamed on two groups: the Ultras, with their new "radicalized
way of cheering" (*nu' tashgi' mutashaddid*), and the reactionary media pundits on football television. "The media is the biggest problem," he told me
over a second cup of sweet tea.

> They amplify the *ta'assub*. They're like petrol next to the fire, those
> pundits [*humma zay binzin ganb al-nar, al-kabatin dul*]. They aren't
> neutral. For example, it's well known that Medhat Shalaby and
> Ahmed Shoubair are *Ahlawiyya* and Khaled el-Ghandour is *Zamelk-
> awi*. [. . .] And nowadays, they only speak about *siyasa*. We have
> a saying in Arabic: *iddi al-'aysh lil-khabaza* [leave the bread to the
> bakers]. People should talk about the things they know something
> about. This is a big problem in Egypt, not only in football. Every-
> thing has become *mixed up* [using the English expression]: football,
> media [*al-i'lam*], and *siyasa*.

As a result of the mix-up, Hamada felt that it would be difficult to return
to the stadium. The bloodshed in Port Said constituted a breaking point.
"I think it'll take a long time," he told me as I was about to leave. "For me,
football is now without taste [*min ghayr ta'm*]."

In the year that followed this February afternoon in Hamada's pharmacy,
I heard countless Egyptian fans and sports journalists tell me that football

would never be the same. Often, the reasons for turning their backs on the game were couched in emotional idioms, stressing the impossibility of finding pleasure in a sport that had caused so many deaths. Like Hamada, many of those I spoke to saw the massacre as the ultimate proof that something was deeply wrong with the way football had been organized, exploited, and supported in Egypt before 2011. Tropes about the game's deep-rooted *ta'assub* and troubling links to *siyasa*—which at the time of the Algeria matches in November 2009 had been voiced mainly by football-critical intellectuals and Islamists (chapter 2)—now resonated much more widely. Suddenly, supporters from all walks of life critically elaborated on how the Mubarak regime had mobilized the happiness (*farha*, *sa'ada*) of cumulative national victories as a replacement (*badil*) and a drug (*mukhaddarat*). Hamada and I—who previously had spoken solely about players, transfers, and tactics—regularly discussed the folding of football into politics when we met in spring, summer, and autumn of 2012. Like many fans in his generation, Hamada felt disappointed, even betrayed, that the sport that traditionally had represented beauty (*gamal*) and morals (*ikhla'*) had developed into a tool for concealment (*taghyib*), political exploitation (*istighlal siyasi*), and violence (*'unf*). Somehow, he had not managed (or wanted) to see the extent to which the sport had been part and parcel of the Mubarak regime's dirty power game. The massacre revealed what he had always latently known but never fully confronted: that football, which had seemed a nonpolitical pastime for lighthearted enjoyment and pride, had been deeply embedded in politics all along.

While most supporters I met drew on similar themes, reactions varied in accordance with their ideological affiliations. The game perhaps seemed the most problematic for those identifying strongly with the January 2011 Revolution's aims and ideals. For them, the revelations of what football had been and done during Mubarak's reign made their previous attachments deeply troubling. Several interlocutors described feelings of postrevolutionary sobering and reawakening: how the uprisings had made genuine, real-world concerns more visible, concerns which the Mubarak regime had hidden behind the strong but ultimately illusory passions of sports. Bassam, a digital marketing consultant and father of two in his mid-thirties who blogged about Egyptian sports media, was one of them. In December 2011, a good month before the tragedy in Port Said, he explained that it had become embarrassing to take pleasure in matches, tournaments, and club rivalries. Bassam mentioned that he no longer watched al-Ahly's and AC Milan's matches in public places such as cafés. He had also stopped making football-related Facebook updates. The reason, he told me, was that his "revolutionary friends" would accuse him of being "shallow" and not dedicated to Egypt's "real problems." "I still watch matches once in a while, sure, but I sort of hide it," he explained. "You can't say that you're not in Tahrir because you're watching a football match. It's not possible; this is not the time."

At the same time, the period after January 2011 was also one of great hopes and aspirations for people such as Bassam. New revolutionary projects were springing up everywhere; within the world of football, the Ultras' campaign for reform seemed to promise a more progressive kind of fan culture. For a supporter like Hamada, however, who knew no revolutionary activists and never participated in demonstrations at Tahrir Square, the Ultras did not seem like a promising way forward. Hamada instead viewed the new fans as a nuisance at the stadium, and he put the blame for the game's politicization *jointly* on the reactionary television pundits *and* the Ultras' radical campaigns. They were both parts of the same "political" problem. Accordingly, embarrassment over the game's futility in the new and more serious revolutionary era was for Hamada never the dominant feeling. His most common complaint was rather that he "*zahi't min*" the political circus that the game had become. In Egyptian Arabic, *zahi't min* connotes all of being "tired of," "bored with," and "fed up with" something.[3] As more time passed and the immediate shock of the massacre subsided, Hamada's feelings for football developed from fed-up disappointment toward boredom and utter tiredness. By early 2013, after the Port Said court verdicts and the ensuing street violence, the mix-up between football and *siyasa* reached yet another stage. Hamada had now become all but indifferent to the sport that he had once loved.

EMOTION, AFFECT, AND UNPREDICTABLE EVENTS

In the wake of the Port Said tragedy, all my interlocutors knew that Egypt's national sport was going through a severe popularity crisis. There was also a consensus that a mix-up between sports and politics was at the heart of the game's problems. This common-sense interpretation operated simultaneously on two levels. When fans like Hamada talked about football as political concealment, as an emotional drug, or as boring, this "emotion talk" not only described how and why feelings for the game had waned but also curtailed the very experiences that it was naming. Such an interdependence between language and emotion should not come as a surprise. As anthropologists studying emotionality have illustrated in detail, what humans feel is always contingent on how emotions are valued, discussed, and narrated in evolving sociocultural contexts (e.g., Abu-Lughod, 1986; Abu-Lughod and Lutz, 1990; Beatty, 2014; Leavitt, 1996; Rosaldo, 1980). In chapter 2, about the Algeria games crisis, I illuminated one such case. In late 2009, discourses linking the national game to the political sphere diminished the sport's popularity. The situation after Port Said was similar but also much more pervasive. Nearly everyone now agreed that previously accepted demarcations between football and the outside world had become untenable. The discussions that proliferated about the game's politicization and crises were thus both performative and self-fulfilling.

Even so, revelations about the game's political past were just one of several changes that were underway. Discourses alone, no matter how influential, will never determine in full how feelings for football take shape, circulate, and eventually wither. As anyone who has visited an electrifying football stadium will know, something elusive and highly intangible is often in the air; the fans' reactions to goals, wins, losses, and what Hamada would call *al-gaw* (the atmosphere) are immediate and embodied, and are not necessarily discussed nor thought through. To really grasp how feelings for football died in post-2011 Egypt, it is in other words imperative to also pay attention to intensities and energies that evade and overflow symbolic capture. In short, the analysis of how socially and historically coded *emotionality* was shifting must be supplemented by an attention to transformations of nonrepresentational, materially propagated *affect* (see Massumi, 2002; Stewart, 2007; Thrift, 2007; Blackman, 2012:1–25; Gregg and Seigworth, 2010; Malmström, 2019).

Such an inclusive analytical optic has already been applied in this book, although mostly just implicitly. Chapter 1, to take one example, characterized the Egyptian football bubble as inherently emotional *and* affective: a result of the materiality of new stadiums, money, and infrastructures, on the one hand, and a variety of media discourses—talk shows, pop songs, and feature films—on the other. Similarly, I argued in chapter 3 that the unique emotional style of the Egyptian Ultras movement took shape at the intersection of physical space inside stadiums, material objects brought into the stands, international principles, social media content, witty songs and banners, and a whole lot of hard work. Both these cases illustrate that sensorial football experiences are complex and multifaceted. What fans actually feel is the result of a singular interweaving of everyday conversations, media narratives, materiality, space, and crowd dynamics that afford, structure, and circulate feelings in particular spatiotemporal settings.[4] What also becomes obvious is that rigid distinctions between semiotic-linguistic and material-immediate sensations, a split that has fueled many debates between affect and emotion scholars in recent years (see, for example, Leys, 2011; Massumi, 2002), are not particularly useful. If anything, football affect and football emotions are ideal types at opposite ends on a continuum: two sides of the same coin that are inherently intertwined and rarely useful to disentangle.[5]

What can this approach to football feelings add to the story about ordinary, non-Ultras football fans such as Hamada? How can an analysis of emotion *and* affect help us understand how and why passions for al-Ahly, al-Zamalek, and the national team waned during Egypt's revolutionary years? Let us begin by dissecting the charged *events* that football brought together *before* January 2011, in the years of the sport's inflated "bubble." Whenever my interlocutors have tried to explain to me why football dominated their lives so completely in this period, their stories have kept returning to singular *occasions* of rushing, immediate, and upbeat affect: match-winning goals in the last minute, famous victories for club and country, tournaments when the whole nation was brought to a halt, or street parties that swept across Cairo after each of the three Africa Cups of Nations. The event that Hamada—like so many other Egyptians—has liked to bring up as *the* occasion to remember and revel in is the first of Egypt's two games against Algeria in November 2009. Hamada belonged to the lucky minority who had tickets to the game in Cairo, and the dramatic moments before the final whistle constitute an affective memory that he will never forget. Time and time again in our conversations, he has returned to this electrifying night, adding fresh details to the story each time: how his customers talked about nothing but the match for weeks before the clash; how he arrived at Cairo Stadium more than six hours before kickoff to make sure he had a parking spot and his preferred seat on *daraga tanya*; how people in the stands spent the warm but breezy afternoon sharing food and drinks while waiting for the game to start; how Egypt scored the first goal early on and created chance upon chance, but how frustration grew in the stands as the team struggled to score the necessary second; how he encouraged a stranger next to him to keep on believing, keep on cheering, even when things looked desperate and time was running out; how everyone in his section stood for the last twenty minutes of the match; and how, in the ninety-fifth minute, he saw Emad Moteab steer his famous header past the Algerian goalkeeper, felt the stadium's concrete shake underneath his feet, and all but drowned in an unmatched mix of confetti, flags, scarves, and all-out chaotic exhilaration.

Hamada's memories from this enchanted night bestow insight into the range of factors that need to come together for an affective football occasion to unfold in the moment: a match's significance in its particular competition, a longstanding rivalry between two Arab nations, previous match results, spatial features of the stadium, material objects brought into the stands, the weather, and, of course, the dynamic of the match itself. While most evident in a packed stadium, similar dynamics are at play among fans tuned in to broadcasts of such matches too: in front of a television in a coffee shop, at home, or in a pharmacy; when listening to the radio while driving; or when checking live reports on one's smart phone during a job meeting. Hamada's account also illuminates how crucial it is for fans—whether highly organized Ultras or ordinary non-Ultras—to work on themselves, individually and collectively, to make occasions sparkle; how they think about and discuss an upcoming match, prepare mentally and materially, stuff themselves with food and drinks, and cheer and shout in unison at the stadium, to articulate with each other and their inanimate surroundings. To partake in an affective football occasion, in other words, is a complex matter, and it does not happen easily. Although it might happen that passers-by are drawn into a match event they do not know much about, the complete range of affective nuances are not readily available to anybody. Songs and chants, the right behaviors in the stands, previous match results and historical anecdotes—supporters need to learn a great many things to be fully moved by the affective registers that football occasions (for comparison, see Latour, 2004).

The emotional-affective boom that football sustained in the late Mubarak era could not have happened without this preparation and learning. Hamada, like millions of other fans across the nation, allowed himself to be carried away, thus allowing the buzz to happen. And yet there were no guarantees. Contingent as they always are not only on stadium designs, crowd dynamics, history, and appropriately trained spectators but also matches, goals, and results, really thrilling football occasions are rare and intrinsically unpredictable. One can never really know when they will happen, an aspect which no doubt is a key factor behind the intense affectivity that *is* engendered when everything *does* come together at the same time. As suggested in part I, this unpredictability was critical to the affectivity of Egypt's pre-2011 football boom, a hype tied closely to the self-reinforcing euphoria of cumulative national victories. Neither the money that the state sprinkled on the game nor the media that propagated football across the nation could guarantee that Moteab's last-minute header would reach the back of the net, let alone that the national team would win three African

Cups of Nations in succession. Hence, when Moteab scored his goal and the national heroes won their titles, the euphoria was all the more intense. For supporters like Hamada, it was ultimately these open-ended occasions that had rendered football so enticing.[6] Retrospectively, the late Mubarak era seemed almost dream-like in its stream of possibilities, excitement, and thrilling success against the odds. Hamada once likened it to a "long and crazy party that we felt would never end"; another time, he pondered on the emboldening feeling of being "unbeatable" and of "knowing deep inside that we could beat anyone, even the World Champions, Italy."[7] These were the affective registers at the core of the pre-2011 football bubble: a never-ending series of momentary jubilation, dreams, and happiness, which was never possible to fully control.

FLEETING OCCASIONS, FALLING EXPECTATIONS

Egypt's postrevolutionary football crises might be construed as an inversion of the boisterous bubble preceding it. In the years when I got to know Hamada, the well-assembled, affective football occasions of yesteryear almost completely ceased to materialize. The latest Africa Cup of Nations triumph was only a couple of years back, but the "long and crazy party" already belonged to an oddly distant past. While a reversal of fortune had begun when the national team lost the second game against Algeria in Sudan, the Port Said massacre made the situation more acute. Other than the contentious Super Cup match in September 2012, all domestic football tournaments were suspended for twelve months after the tragedy. And when the league was restarted in early 2013, fans were banned from the stadiums for security reasons. When matches were occasionally broadcast on television, there was not much for Hamada to celebrate either: al-Zamalek's performance in the African Champions League in summer 2012 was dismal. The national team failed to even qualify for the African tournaments in 2012 and 2013.

Many times, we all sensed that it just was not meant to be. Even before the tragedy, spectacular football occasions that appeared to be on the horizon typically ended in frustration. The disgruntlement was never as clear as when Hamada and I sat in his car on the crowded Salah Salem Street and tried to talk away our disappointment after the final of the 2011 Egyptian Cup. When we had taken our seats at the stadium a few hours earlier, everything had been in place for a night to remember: the warm and breezy October night, the sold-out stadium, the crowds all dressed in al-Zamalek's white and red colors, the chance for the club to end a humiliating three-year spell without a title, and the relatively weak opponents, ENPPI, a club owned by the government's gas company, completely devoid of supporters. The match had also started well with al-Zamalek dominating possession. It was thus both deserved and logical when, in the forty-seventh minute, Amr Zaky scored the opening goal right in front of the Ultras White Nights' packed *curva*. When Zaky sprinted toward the stands to celebrate with the fans in that beast-like manner that had given him his nickname *el-buldu-zir*, the stadium had erupted in white and red and smoke and fireworks. Hamada and I, with seventy thousand others, had stood up on our chairs, hugged each other, and screamed straight into the night.

But then, not even ten minutes later, a penalty had been called from nowhere and the score was suddenly 1–1. And shortly thereafter, ENPPI had scored a second goal after some sloppy defending—so typically al-Zamalek! The rest of the game had unfolded in panic and silence. The clock had run down all too quickly; before long we had heard the final whistle. And now, as we sat in Hamada's car in traffic congestion, we mourned the loss, mourned the occasion, which had promised so much but not delivered. There was nothing I could say or do to console Hamada, as he told me quietly:

> That was the first time in fifteen years that I saw the stadium like this, only white, no Ahly-fans, only us. For *Ahlawiyya*, this happens all the time, but last time it happened for us was at the African final against Shooting Stars [from Nigeria] in 1996. Do you understand me, Carl? I don't know when there will be a chance to be this happy again.

Football's thrilling moments did not only fade because of a lack of matches with favorable results. Even when al-Ahly surprisingly won the African Champions League in November 2012, the occasion did not really take off.[8] It did not matter that a limited number of fans were allowed back into the stadium for the final versus Esperance from Tunisia; the attendance was disappointing, and the atmosphere remarkably bleak. Even die-hard *Ahlawiyya* friends were not particularly eager to attend the match. When I asked why, many said it was because of the horrendous event in Port Said.[9] But some also mentioned that the atmosphere at the stadium was likely to be "dead" or "a bit boring." The fact that the game was played at the remote Burg el-Arab stadium in the desert outside Alexandria, more than two hours' drive from Cairo, and that only a fraction of the eighty thousand tickets had been sold did not help either. This arrangement precluded the proximity between fans and players that much of football's collective intimacy and affectivity thrives on.

A combination of intuition, facts, and rumors thus triggered a rapid and multidimensional fall in *expectations*: for the quality of the game, for the teams' performance, and for the occasion itself, which did not promise to be particularly exhilarating. As anthropologist Magnus Marsden has illustrated, expectations play a crucial role as emotions are fostered, circulated, and amplified within collective gatherings. When people expect to be emotional, they work on themselves as well as on each other, and feelings materialize as a result (Marsden, 2007). I have argued that such reinforcing interplays between expectations, preparation, and work were key to the intense atmosphere at Egyptian football stadiums in the late Mubarak era. But the reverse dynamics are of course also possible. When people do not expect to be moved, they do not come prepared, and they do not put in the work necessary for feelings to flow. Al-Ahly's 2012 African Champions League final constituted such an occasion. Compared to much lesser matches only a year earlier, the media coverage before the match was modest. As one of some ten thousand fans attending the game at Burg el-Arab, I noted how practices that otherwise are standard, such as arriving early, bringing in flags, and standing up while cheering were not particularly common. That is, if people went to the game at all; most Ahly supporters did not even bother to make their way to Alexandria, leaving thousands of seats empty and dropping expectations yet another notch lower. Consequently, the occasion never truly sparkled. Even when al-Ahly scored a decisive goal late in the game, I found the atmosphere surprisingly restrained.

As a *Zamelkawi*, Hamada was not present at the stadium in Burg el-Arab that night, but he was familiar with the structure of feeling. In 2012 and 2013, it just seemed too unlikely that the sport would match the intensity it had induced a couple of years prior. The games were too few, the results too poor, and the atmosphere just not very appealing. For Hamada and many like him, these lowered expectations would become self-fulfilling. As he did not expect to be moved, he rarely went to the stadium, making the chances to feel in full even less likely. "It's no point," he told me once in spring 2013 when I asked him if he would attend an upcoming Zamalek Champions League match at Burg el-Arab. "You know that I go to games because of the atmosphere and the people I meet. I don't think many people will go to Alexandria. Why should I go alone? And I'll have to work."

NEW RHYTHMS OF THE NATION

After January 2011, the rhythms of Egypt's national game broke down. With weekly matches, year-long seasons, and biannual tournaments such as the Africa Cup of Nations, the sport had long offered a rhythmic backbone to the everyday lives of supporters such as Hamada. That changed abruptly, however, in the revolution's wake. In his short book *Rhythmanalysis*, originally published in 1992, Henri Lefebvre proposed a program for how such rhythmic reoccurrences could be studied (Lefebvre, 2004). Taking off from a definition of rhythms as linear accumulations of longer or shorter cyclical phenomena (ibid., 8, 74–77), the book conceptualized the social world as a "bundle" of social, material, and astronomical rhythms that all interact with each other, as well as with the biological rhythms of human bodies (ibid., 10, 80–81). Lefebvre's somewhat speculative ideas take more concrete shape in the works of the geographer Tim Edensor.[10] Among other things, Edensor turns the discussion of rhythms toward affect and nationhood, suggesting that the "repetition of innumerable quotidian routines and habits" gives rise to distinctive "structures of feelings" and coherent "national temporalities" (Edensor, 2006:528).

Lefebvre and Edensor's vocabularies make it possible to reformulate how Hamada's football experiences were structured in the late Mubarak era. In the period of the sport's bubble, matches and tournaments not only were highly potent affective occasions, but also constituted those "small everyday arrangements [that] merge the local with the national through serialization and [which] underpin a common sense that this is *how things are* and this is *how we do things*" (Edensor, 2006:529). Even as the number of satellite television channels proliferated and programming became more fragmented after the turn of the millennium (see Sakr, 2007), sports events maintained a unique ability to synchronize time and feeling across the Egyptian nation. Drawing millions of citizens to the television sets simultaneously on a weekly, monthly, or biannual basis, al-Ahly, al-Zamalek, and the national team formed a key part of the nation's rhythmic common sense.[11]

At the same time, as Lefebvre also alludes to, even the most entrenched social rhythm tends to be reordered in the wake of large-scale crises and upheavals. At one point he writes:

> Disruptions and crises always have origins in and effects on rhythms: those of institutions, of growth, of the population, of exchanges, of work, therefore those who make or *express* the complexity of

present societies. One could study from this perspective the rhythmic changes that follow revolutions. From 1789 to 1830 [in France] were not bodies themselves touched by the alterations in foods, gestures and costumes, the rhythm of work and of occupations? (Lefebvre, 2004:44)

Within the sociocultural universe of Egyptian football, such a revolutionary reordering of rhythms has been stark after January 2011, and it has touched bodies, like Hamada's, with great effect. Whole seasons have been canceled, and fans banned from stadiums. Egypt's football-only television channels, blossoming enterprises in the prerevolutionary years, have lost millions of viewers, and several networks have been forced to close down. The shifts were most dramatic immediately after the February 2012 Port Said massacre when domestic football was brought to a complete halt. When the array of games was truncated for the most tragic of reasons, a series of results, missed chances, referee decisions, and injuries that since October 2011 had shaped the narrative and emotional momentum of the ongoing season was suddenly rendered a stump, deprived of its former significance. Hamada, who in the late 2000s had visited the stadium many times each month and watched football talk shows more or less daily, stopped visiting Cairo Stadium completely. He could go weeks without turning on a sports channel. "There is nothing to watch on Modern [the biggest football network] these days," he told me in May that year. "No matches, only problems and *siyasa*. If I want to watch politics, I watch another channel."

In the same period that the rhythmic successions of football occasions faded, however, other kinds of serialized events proliferated in Egypt. Elections and referenda dominated the media for weeks on end; almost every Friday, demonstrations mobilized tens of thousands of participants in Tahrir Square or elsewhere in the country. At regular intervals, the protests turned into street fights that brought large sections of the city to a halt. During these periods of urban violence, Cairo tuned in to the rhythms of revolutionary politics. For hours on end, the citizens followed the action live via television, radio, and social media. Even Hamada, who had never been overly interested in "the political circus," made sure to watch the latest news on a small television set in the pharmacy's ceiling. It simply was not possible to avoid. The spectacles of *siyasa* consumed everyone's attention.

The revolution wove together its own affect and emotions, and it was intriguing to note how football-like its rhythms and occasions often turned out to be. The Ultras fans' spectacular emergence on the national-political stage might have constituted the most visible example, but it was not the only way in which sport and politics were conflated. During an interview in December 2011, Bassam, the digital marketer and football blogger, tried to explain to me why football had the ability to move him so profoundly. His way of slipping between two ostensibly distinct contexts was illuminating:

> I don't know if this makes much sense, but football is one of the very few things in life that you can actually watch happening. In a particular moment, no one in the entire world knows what is gonna happen: if [the ball] is gonna hit the post, or if it's gonna go in, or go out. This was the thing with the moments in Tahrir [Square] as well. You can't believe that these things are happening right now when we are standing here, when you're actually out there with the people in the streets fighting against whoever you're fighting against. I think that's the crazy thing about it. We go to the streets together; we fight an opponent together. People form theories and are analyzing stuff, but I don't know what they are analyzing. [. . .] You can't explain passions; when they happen they just happen.

For a year or two after 25 January 2011, demonstrations, sit-ins, and clashes provided a rhythmic and seemingly never-ending stream of those unpredictable occasions for unity and friction, hope and adrenalin, that Bassam alluded to. Indeed, as anthropologist Samuli Schielke has argued, the revolutionary process in Egypt was never primarily "ideological, intellectual or imaginative, but physical and emotional"; it was driven by "embodied act[s] of doing something that could make a difference [. . .] physical move[s] that made the world appear in a different light," and through which "action [ran] ahead of imagination and form[ed] it" (Schielke, 2015:180). That Bassam found the thrill of these moments football-esque should not come as a surprise. The parallels were plentiful. Similar to the affective momentum that had intensified with each football victory in the late Mubarak era, for instance, the bloody cycles of protests and street fights fed chillingly on expectations of more of the same kind. They continued for days without end as death was translated into rage, rage into grief, grief into an urge for revenge, revenge into more fights, more adrenalin, more teargas, more bullets, more death (Schielke, 2015:203–209; see also Butler, 2014).[12] Moreover, the dissemination of these rhythmic events through satellite television was highly reminiscent of the mediation of football. Not only did Tahrir Square, semi-encircled as it is by high apartment buildings with balconies, resemble a stadium on camera; live footage from the clashes was also commented on by experts in a studio, much like how television football pundits analyze tactics and predict outcomes. And just like sports in the recent past, the action downtown became the default program of choice in coffee shops, restaurants, and stores all over the city during the days and weeks when the action in the streets reached its peak (see Armbrust, 2019:53–55).

These observations cast my interlocutors' insistence that football had become "mixed up" with *siyasa* in a new light. At least among fans like Bassam, who identified closely with the revolutionary project, political affectivity interfered with the realm of sports, and the process was to a large extent one of replacement: football lost its lure precisely when revolutionary politics came sweeping in. But the substitution was never merely, as the well-rehearsed cliché about football as an overcome emotional drug would have it, one of rational politics for emotional sports. Rather, one set of affective occasions and rhythms was exchanged for another peculiarly similar one. The feelings of togetherness, unpredictability, collective chanting, media attention, and eventual victory when Mubarak was ousted made Tahrir Square affectively isomorphic with a great victory at Cairo Stadium. And yet the differences between the occasions were also immense. Even for Bassam, who found it helpful to compare the two, the experiences in Tahrir were "of course the most powerful in my life." The revolution had been far more unexpected, its unpredictability much more open-ended, its possibilities vastly escalated pertaining to matters of life and death. Because of that, the conflation of sports and *siyasa* ushered in an overflow and canceling out. The powerful feelings prompted by Egypt's political transformation dwarfed all competing national rhythms and temporalities. Despite—or perhaps because of—the many parallels, sports felt more like a shallow replica of something infinitely more real.

ADJUSTING TO WHAT IS, LONGING FOR WHAT WAS

But what about Hamada? How did he, who was never much involved in events and actions downtown, adjust to a life without football, in which the rhythms of revolutionary politics had become the dominant ones? In the first months after the massacre in Port Said, Hamada entertained a hope that the new era was a temporary one. In July 2012, a week after the inauguration of President Muhammad Mursi, he told me:

I've been going to the stadium for more than twenty years, so obviously there is something that's missing in my life [*fi haga na'sa fi hayati*]. But the strange thing is that it has almost become normal to live without football. I think we all forgot about it a bit, especially with all of the elections. But now when we've a president again, the normal thing would be that football comes back, right? Of course, the security at the stadiums has to be fixed, but I think it's not so difficult. The league will restart soon, *Insha'Allah*.

The months that followed would prove Hamada's predictions wrong. Few things got back to normal; football did not come back. Hamada and I met regularly in autumn 2012 and early 2013, and each time I saw him, I found him more and more discouraged. In March 2013, I paid a final visit to his pharmacy before wrapping up my fieldwork and returning to my university in London. At the time, the Port Said verdicts had been decided, Ultras Ahlawy had aborted the campaign to stop domestic football, and a truncated version of the Egyptian Premier League had been restarted. The national team had also made a promising start to the 2014 World Cup qualification campaign under the new head coach, Bob Bradley, an American. But the football crisis was far from over. The previous week, a faction within Ultras Ahlawy had burned down the headquarters of the Egyptian Football Association after a disappointing second round of court verdicts (see chapter 5). As for the restarted league, no supporters were let into the stadiums, and interest in televised matches remained low. The impression I got this bright and dusty spring day was that Hamada was disillusioned with the course that his life and country had recently taken. He told me that the economic downturn was hitting his business hard, that he found himself working longer and longer shifts, and that he worried about a growing lack of security in the neighborhood. One of his customers had been shot recently; drug use was on a steep rise. For the first time in the eighteen months I had been coming to see him, Hamada insisted that I take a taxi back downtown instead of walking to the Metro station a few hundred meters down the market street. During a Coca-Cola break, he summarized his disappointment and frustration:

You know I told you, most people here in Old Cairo were never into *siyasa* and what happened in Tahrir. I never went to any demonstrations, but of course I hoped that things would get a little bit better [*al-hala bitithassan shiwayya*], also for people like us. But instead everything got worse: there is no security, no money, and the electricity breaks down every day. I'm fed up with politics [*zahi't min al-siyasa*]. Actually, the only thing I'm thinking of now is stability [*istiqrar*]: working and supporting my family. One has to focus on the most important things. [. . .] I try to watch al-Zamalek's games on television, but it's difficult when I'm working. There are always customers coming in, and as you know, my television is small and the sound is bad. And the way the team plays. . . . It's not as nice as before. Many players, like Shikabala, have left, and there are always fights: within the board, between the players and the coach, and with the new fans [i.e., the Ultras]. Everything has become politics [*kull haga ba'it siyasa*]; there is no fun left. I don't really know. . . . Of course, I miss the days at the stadium. But what could one do?

Shortly before dusk, we said our goodbyes. We promised to keep in touch through Facebook, and I took a taxi home as Hamada had suggested. In the car, I kept thinking of his struggle to adjust to the challenges of the era. On the one hand, I found it remarkable how matter-of-factly he accepted that he had to "focus on the most important things," like his job and caring for his family, and that entertainments such as sports could not be a priority. On the other hand, adapting to the predicaments surely was not easy. When Hamada told me that "everything has become politics; there is no fun left," the "politics" that he was talking about was clearly both worrying, distressing, and very difficult to evade. To some extent, his problem was the same one that has recurred over and over in this and several previous chapters: a mix-up between discourses and practices of sports and politics that should ideally be kept separated. But the politicization that troubled Hamada was also more conclusive. The revelation that the national sport had been a tool for self-serving exploitation during the Mubarak years was not his sole concern. And it was not really a case of affective-emotional parallels between match events and thrilling protests either. Instead, for Hamada, *siyasa* was mostly endured as chaos and instability; as dramatically increased feelings of insecurity, as constant violence in the streets and on television, as a slumping economy that hurt his business, as internal power struggles within his beloved club, and as Ultras fans protesting at the stadiums and in the streets. In an ethnography set in the same post-2011 period in a village close to Alexandria, Samuli Schielke has observed a similar range of sentiments and argued that they were a result of people no longer knowing the explicit and implicit rules of the game: "Different people based their actions on highly different understandings of what was going on in the first place. Various forms of paranoid fear towards political opponents, different assessments of what can and what cannot be done, of right and wrong, and a collapse of social taboos and inhibitions created a situation that was confusing, to say the least" (Schielke, 2015:185).[13]

Possibly, it was this sense of a complete lack of rules paired with an all-inclusive uncertainty that Hamada referred to as "everything" having become "politics" that day in early 2013: a radically expanded unpredictability and openness toward the future, which could be exhilarating and heady during a sit-in in Tahrir Square, but which looked very different from a small pharmacy in Old Cairo. Whatever the new political world was understood to comprise, it was a world that evoked anxiety and fear, and which contaminated life's former pleasures. As much as Hamada wanted to embrace the revolution's aims and ideals and did his best to move on to the most important things in his life, his ambivalence was thus always discernible. Whenever I asked him, he admitted that he missed the atmosphere at the stadium: the emotions he had felt, the community he had participated in, and perhaps also the man he had been allowed to be. There was a sense of longing and nostalgia for lost feelings, which he seemed to enjoy cultivating with me, the only person with whom he still discussed football. And perhaps, this longing for football as it once had been might also have been part of a larger nostalgia for a bygone era when his life had been a little bit more predictable, pleasurable, and joyful. In a time when people in Egypt were not supposed to long back, I sometimes think that football worked as an idiom that allowed Hamada to do precisely that: to remember and mourn a less serious and less anxious past, when football had not yet been folded into *siyasa*, and when the nation had moved to a different rhythm.

CONCLUSION: MIXED UP IN *SIYASA*

This chapter has examined how and why large numbers of Egyptian men lost their attachments to football in the aftermath of the 25 January uprisings, transforming an inflated football boom into crisis followed by generalized apathy. Focusing primarily on the experiences of my pharmacist friend Hamada, my material has highlighted a multiplicity of intertwined processes contributing to the disengagement: reshaped public conversations, diminishing emotional occasions, drastically lowered expectations, and reordered spatiotemporal rhythms. A comprehensive mix-up between football and phenomena referred to as *siyasa* (politics) has formed a central theme in my ethnography. *Siyasa* takes different shapes in different spaces and contexts: a revelation of how the old regime used the game *politically*; curiously football-like affective-*political* occasions; or an ever-present uncertainty in an era where everything has become *politics*. Notwithstanding, the sensation that *siyasa*, however defined, was mixing with football affected fans such as Hamada profoundly. Especially in the generation born in the 1970s and 1980s—the cohort who more than any other lived and embodied both Mubarak's football bubble and the January 2011 Revolution—these intrusions made football increasingly difficult to enjoy.

The postrevolutionary predicament of Egypt's non-Ultras football fans can be construed as a broad societal conflation of predictability and unpredictability. In the years of its inflated bubble, the sport thrived on inherently unforeseeable occasions: those rare moments of vertigo, well out of the ordinary, when "you can actually watch it happening" and "no one in the entire world knows what is gonna happen." Despite their singularity, these unpredictable football occasions were always tightly regulated. Matches conformed to well-established rules, and they were serialized into predictable rhythms of seasons and tournaments that gave quotidian life a familiar structure. Football, in other words, spawned an accessible and highly controllable universe of affect and excitement tied to ultimately uncontrollable match results. This carefully contained unpredictability carved out an alternative sphere of joy, possibilities, and dreams within an everyday existence otherwise saturated by boredom, gloom, and despair. For fans in Egypt—and just about everywhere else in the world (see Elias and Dunning, 1986:189–202)—this demarcation between the game and the outside was key to football's inflated appeal.

Egypt's revolutionary process altered this well-balanced distribution. Between 2011 and 2013, Cairo was suddenly filled with even more unpredictable occasions and rhythms, on Tahrir Square and at the ballot box, all taking place within a chaotic present that made the future almost impossible to foresee. Their enthusiasm for the developments that swept the country might have differed, yet Bassam's comparison between revolutionary action in a square and a big match at the stadium and Hamada's lament that "everything has become politics" ultimately point to one and the same transformation: a radically expanded unpredictability within a suddenly omnipresent "political" sphere. One corollary was that the sport's unique distribution of predictabilities and rhythms collapsed. As nearly every aspect of the social fabric looked uncertain, eventful, and possible, the game lost its affective singularity. Hence football, political contestations, and everyday coping were also mixed up in this regard. No matter where one looked—discourse, rhythm, or predictability—football and *siyasa* had become difficult to fully disentangle.

All things considered, the ethnography in this chapter has provided yet another account of where and why *siyasa* arose as a concern during Egypt's revolutionary years. If the chapters about the Ultras movement illustrated a series of reasons why being labeled *siyasi* constituted a burden for an activist group trying to push through revolutionary demands, this one has depicted *siyasa* as a nuisance for more ordinary Egyptian football fans: infringements of the political in the realm of sports foreclosed and ultimately aborted long-term emotional engagements with the country's most popular spectator sport. Such an aversion to phenomena considered *siyasi* has drawn the attention of a number of students of contemporary Egypt. Whether in up-close neighborhood ethnographies (Alkhamissi, 2018; Kreil, forthcoming), in research with factory workers longing for stability (Makram-Ebeid, 2014), or in analyses of the revolution *and* counterrevolution's reactionary valorization of middle-class propriety, order, and cleanliness (Winegar, 2016), we learn that Egyptians from different social classes consider *siyasa* repulsive and disconcerting.[14] As the material in this book emphasizes, these sentiments are not exclusive to the counterrevolutionary polity that has taken shape in Egypt after the July 2013 coup. Among many of the country's football fans, the notion of *siyasa* as a destructive force to be avoided was present throughout the revolutionary period, indeed even as early as the Algeria matches in November 2009. Moreover, unease conjured as *siyasa* is also something that people have experienced *viscerally*, through events, rhythms and more or less regimented unpredictabilities. *Siyasa* is a multifaceted phenomenon, and it has looked and felt differently for different Egyptian citizens in different historical periods. Regardless of its particular manifestations, however, the political has long interfered with and troubled attachments of football fans to Egypt's national sport.

For this chapter's main protagonist Hamada, these multiple rearrangements of sports and *siyasa* produced a curious state of affective discord. Hamada's mindful body had for more than two decades been habituated to be moved by the particular spaces, media, predictabilities, and narratives that came together inside of the Egyptian football bubble. As this constellation broke down and *siyasa* encroached on his enjoyment of football from every possible angle, his "emotional habitus" lost its sync (see Scheer, 2012). As an affective subject and football fan, Hamada no longer fit. In part, his alienation was a result of growing older. Extended family obligations made him unable to watch as many games as he had in his youth, and the emotional style of the younger Ultras fans was never going to be his kind of football. But his detachment went beyond mere coming of age. The sport that Hamada had learned to love was no more; it had become conflated with a kind of politics and fanaticism that he found appalling; as the stadium supporter he had always been, he could not take much pleasure in the matches that were still shown on television. In short, the habits, preferences, and rhythms that for more than two decades had rendered Hamada exceptionally attuned to the game had turned into a problematic inertia. As the football bubble burst, he thus found himself emotionally out of sync, ill-fitted to his former favorite pastime.

CHAPTER 7

No National Significance,
No Political Concerns

*Of course, we play football. Why wouldn't we? It's a very
normal thing.*

Abdu, football supporter and player from Abdeen, February
2013

If you take a walk east from Tahrir Square, along Muhammad Mahmoud
Street—infamous for the clashes there between protesters and security
forces in November 2011, and for the revolutionary murals and graffiti
that for years covered its walls—you will first pass the old campus of the
American University in Cairo, a couple of private schools, and a string of
up-market coffee shops. Moments later, you will find the rear of the ram-
shackle indoor food market in Bab al-Luq on your left, and if you glance
down any of the streets to your right, you might catch a glimpse of a fort-
like complex that until 2016 hosted the Ministry of Interior. At this point,
the character of the neighborhood begins to change. Grand yet fading
colonial-era apartment buildings with restaurants, clothing stores, and coffee shops on the ground floor—so emblematic of downtown Cairo—still
line the street, but in the intersecting alleyways, you find a more eclectic
mixture of new and old buildings housing tailors, print shops, gyms, internet cafés, and shacks selling *ful* and *ta'miyya* (fava beans and falafel). Some
ten minutes from Tahrir Square, Muhammad Mahmoud intersects with
Muhammad Farid Street. Had you turned left here—due north past the
square facing the nineteenth-century royal palace—you would soon find
yourself back among downtown boulevards and the Metro station named
after Egypt's first president, Muhammad Naguib. If you instead turn right,
the street narrows and the elegance of the buildings fades. As is common
in residential neighborhoods, the number of children and women in the

street increases. On your right, you pass a mosque and community center that is always bustling with people; a few hundred meters down the road, you reach the entrance to a bustling vegetable market. You are now in the heart of the working- and lower-middle-class *sha'bi* (popular) neighborhood Abdeen. On your right-hand side, the street widens and a few plants screen off an unusually broad sidewalk. Behind the greenery, swelling out into the street, you find an *ahwa* (coffee shop; plural, *ahawi*), named Ward al-Qahira (Cairo's Flower).

In 2012 and the first half of 2013, I spent a great deal of time in Abdeen, especially watching football in Ward al-Qahira. At first I wanted to explore what role football played in everyday life in the neighborhood, but I soon found myself talking about all kinds of other things too. In Abdeen, I came to meet some truly great people: Ward al-Qahira's owner, Sayed, his friend and waiter, Abdu, Abdu's younger brother, Muhammad, and Bilal, the soon-to-be-married man introduced in the chapter about the Algeria matches, are still among my best friends in Cairo.

The period when I learned to know these people was one when the revolution and its aftermath preoccupied most Cairenes. Just like for Hamada, the pharmacist from Old Cairo, *siyasa* (politics) was an ever-present concern, which made it difficult for al-Ahly, al-Zamalek, and the Egyptian national team to mobilize the fans' passion and attention. Also in Abdeen, football came to be considered either irrelevant or too politicized; there was so much else to think about and care for. "Football is finished, there is no point [*al-kura khalas, mafish fayda*]," as Sayed once told me when I asked him why his café remained empty during a decisive Africa Cup of Nations qualifying match in June 2012.

For Abdu, football seemed an odd anachronism in an era dominated by revolutionary change. In February and March 2013, the Egyptian league had just been restarted after a twelve-month suspension following the Port Said massacre, but Abdu did not really follow it. With fans banned and the stadiums empty, the matches broadcast on television came across as dull and unexciting. And then there was politics. "I tell you something," he told me once that spring:

I was crazy about al-Zamalek before the revolution [*kunt bimut fil-zamalek abl al-thawra*], but it's not the same now. Should I watch these dead matches [*mutusha mayta*], when I've friends being shot at al-Muqattam [a neighborhood in Cairo, which had recently seen of a lot of violence]? It would be ridiculous. Football is dead in Egypt [*al-kura matit fi masr*].

It is worth noting, though, that when Abdu and Sayed proclaimed football to be "finished" and "dead," they were talking specifically about the Egyptian national game. Indeed, the reason why I was so surprised to find Ward al-Qahira empty on the day of the national team's June 2012 qualifier was that the *ahwa* had been packed only a few days earlier when Spain beat Portugal in the quarterfinal of the European Championship. As supporters of Portugal and of Cristiano Ronaldo, Sayed and Abdu had been crestfallen after the final whistle. Ronaldo had missed a golden opportunity close to the end; the prospect of Spain following up their 2010 World Cup victory with another international title was hard to take. And yet later the same night, Abdu had found a way to put his disappointment aside. For several hours, until well after two o'clock in the morning, he, his brother Muhammad, and a few friends had played pick-up football against other groups of young men in a nearby square, winning four competitive matches in succession. In a period when football fans purportedly no longer felt connected to the sport, Abdu had spent a whole evening and a large part of the night indulging in it. For a sport considered dead and buried, some facets of the game were apparently alive and kicking.

This final chapter tells stories about men in Cairo's Abdeen neighborhood. My focus is initially on televised football from Europe watched at Ward al-Qahira; thereafter, I move on to recreational games in Abdeen's biggest square. The chapter's objective is twofold. On the one hand, it intends to widen the perspective on what is meant by the phrase "Egyptian football" through ethnographic explorations of a series of emotions, social milieus, and masculinities that stayed relevant throughout Egypt's revolutionary period. Even among the cohort of men in their twenties and thirties who had become the most detached from Egypt's *national* game, other kinds of football continued to hold an appeal. The chapter's second aim is to deepen my interrogation of experiences and conversations about *siyasa* in contemporary Egypt. As in chapter 6, my focus is on the aftermath of the 2012 Port Said massacre, a period when "political" debates, developments, and events dominated Egyptian society. As I show, *siyasa* was both discursively proximate and geographically adjacent to my interlocutors in Abdeen. Nonetheless, and in contrast to Hamada, the pharmacist, their football activities always resumed as soon as the political realm subsided a little. I argue that the ability of *this* football to stay relevant and joyful rested on a combination of infrastructural specificities and a particularly nonpropositional and transparent emotional masculinity. International tournaments and pick-up matches were "just football," nothing more and nothing less, a characteristic that effectively insulated them from the ever-present intrigues and power struggles. Most crucially, the football that I encountered in Abdeen was never thought of as a *national* game with *national* significance. Because of that, it remained separated from the anxieties and unease of *siyasa*. In Egypt, politics is first and foremost nationalism's problem.

INTERNATIONAL FOOTBALL, ABDEEN-STYLE

Ward al-Qahira's owner, Sayed, grew up in Abdeen, a few hundred meters from the *ahwa* that was to be his. His family origins are in a village in the country's far south, which his grandparents were forced to leave when their lands were inundated after the building of the High Dam in Aswan. Sayed is in other words Nubian, and he has often been outspoken about the racism that his people face in Egypt because of their darker complexions. Just before the outbreak of the 2011 Revolution, he married a Nubian woman who grew up in London and holds British citizenship. At the time I came to know him, the couple had just had their first daughter, and they were living in a small apartment in one of Abdeen's side streets. In his early thirties, Sayed was working hard to improve his English: a couple of years later, he would fulfill his dream to relocate with his family to the United Kingdom.

After graduating from university, Sayed worked for serval years in a friend's company that designs and prints business signs. After saving up a little bit of money, he began thinking of starting his own business. When he learned that the lease for the *ahwa* on the wide pavement was not going to be extended in the summer of 2011, he decided that it was time to give it a go. "My idea was always to have a proper, international football *ahwa*, like Sports Café in [the upscale neighborhood] al-Muhandisin, but cheap, Abdeen-style, and open twenty-four hours," he once explained.

> I spent a lot of money on television screens and sound systems. This makes us special. We've three televisions, two inside and one outside, and two satellite receivers, so we can show two games at the same time. It wasn't cheap. Actually, I'm not sure if it's good business. In Abdeen, people aren't willing to pay anything extra just because you have the best television. But I'm content anyway, because Ward al-Qahira is the only *ahwa* that really cares about football in this part of Cairo. And so far, I'm making enough money to support my family, *alhamdulillah* [praise be to God].

Ward al-Qahira is a typical Cairene *ahwa*. It is one of many thousands of coffeehouses sprinkled across the city, establishments which for centuries have made up "third places," outside work and home, for men to socialize and entertain themselves (Ellis, 2004; Hattox, 1985; Oldenburg, 1999). When Sayed depicted his café as "cheap" and "Abdeen-style," this was a way of indicating that he was *not* running a "coffee shop": a mixed-gender, up-market establishment, like Costa Coffee or for that matter Sports Café in al-Muhandisin, the place which he in many other regards tried to emulate (see de Koning, 2009). Sayed's Ward al-Qahira was instead a *sha'bi ahwa*: a semi-open, mixed-class, but strictly male-only space with wooden chairs, small metal tables, cheap tea, coffee, soft drinks, and *shisha* (water pipes).

Cairo's *ahawi* have long been sites of media consumption. Storytellers performed there in the old days; in the first half of the twentieth century, men congregated to listen to news or music on what was often the neighborhood's only radio (Hourani, 2005:393). Today, every *ahwa* in Cairo has a television, always turned on, and football is a staple of the programming. In contrast to countries in sub-Saharan Africa, where matches from European leagues are watched in most bars (Akindes, 2011; Fletcher, 2010), domestic football has traditionally drawn the biggest crowds to these semi-public television sets.[1] Sayed had always found this bias unfortunate. "People in Egypt don't understand what they're missing," he once complained. "The football in England and Spain is much better, much more beautiful."

In an attempt to change prevailing attitudes, Sayed made sure to make Ward al-Qahira an "international" *ahwa*, focused on the European game. For this, he needed to access the Qatari pay-TV network al-Jazeera Sports and the Emirati channel AD Sports, which, in contrast to Egyptian free-to-air networks, aired football from all over the world and featured an impressive range of Arab and international experts. AD Sports' English Premier League broadcasts in particular made Ward al-Qahira stand out. Between 2010 and 2012, it was actually not possible to legally watch English league football in Egypt, but Sayed had found a work-around: a friend living in Saudi Arabia had brought him the appropriate subscription card and hardware.[2] As one of very few coffee shops in central Cairo to show games from all major leagues,[3] Ward al-Qahira attracted a somewhat specialized crowd, a fact that contributed to its atmosphere and boosted the *ahwa's* reputation as a place where European football was the main attraction. On big Champions League nights, when Sayed carefully lined up chairs in front of his big screen on the pavement, the space was packed well before kickoff. Many customers told me that they lived far from Abdeen—in Nasser City, al-Muqattam, or Imbaba—but enjoyed coming to Ward al-Qahira because of the ambience and the attentive crowd. Sayed had at this point only run the place for seven months. Through his investments in television technologies and a rare piece of imported infrastructure, he had established what he had always aimed for: an international football-focused *ahwa*, Abdeen-style.

The European league for which the stakes were the highest was the Spanish La Liga. Every customer in Ward al-Qahira was either a FC Barcelona or a Real Madrid supporter. Even Sayed, who primarily considered himself a Manchester City fan but also had a soft spot for Real Madrid, admitted that Real's matches had become more and more important in recent years: "It is what everyone watches and talks about; they are simply the two biggest clubs." The Spanish club rivalry—and the corresponding competition between the world's two outstanding players, Lionel Messi and Cristiano Ronaldo—divided the *ahwa* into two distinct halves. In a period when it had become difficult to care for al-Ahly and al-Zamalek, the Real-Barca competition became a complement, for some even a substitute, that in a recognizable manner split passions and allegiances. One day in April 2012, I asked Abdu if he believed that the popularity of the Spanish competition resulted from the way it mirrored the two-horse-race structure of the Egyptian league. At least partly, he agreed:

> I'm sure you have heard that *Zamelkawiyya* support Real and *Ahlaw-iyya* are Barca? Some people say it's because Real and al-Zamalek are royal clubs, but I don't know; al-Zamalek hasn't been a royal club for more than fifty years.[4] It could also be the color: I like al-Zamalek, so I like white teams or something. [. . .] Perhaps you are right . . . we're used to a league with two teams. Every week, there are two important matches. I'm Real, so I support Real, and then I support the team that Barcelona is playing against. Like al-Ahly and al-Zamalek. For us, it's almost better when Barca loses than when Real wins, because it happens so rarely.

Abdu's comments reflected a pattern that was widespread in Cairo at the time. With al-Ahly and al-Zamalek's matches suspended after the Port Said stadium massacre, FC Barcelona's and Real Madrid's games were the most watched and discussed throughout the capital's *ahawi* as well as in Egyptian social media. In spring 2012, the rivalry reached a seasonal crescendo. Real

Madrid was at the top of the league standings, but the reigning feeling in Ward al-Qahira was that Barcelona, the reigning La Liga and Champions League title holder, was on the verge of making a comeback. On a Saturday night in April, however, the tide surprisingly turned; Real Madrid defeated their rivals in the El Clásico game away at Camp Nou, effectively clinching the league title that Barcelona had monopolized the previous three seasons. The night was one of the tensest I ever experienced in the *ahwa*. The place was packed an hour before kickoff; more customers than usual wore match shirts to show their loyalties; Sayed had bought a new television set for the occasion. Before kickoff, I asked around for predictions, and the consensus was that Barca were big favorites. Even the most hardcore group of Real Madrid supporters, who as usual gathered in a corner just inside the door, seemed unable to envision beating Barcelona. When Real scored an early first goal after a corner, and then another, decisive one, on a fast-flowing counterattack by Cristiano Ronaldo, the atmosphere among the café's white-dressed faction turned as electrically jubilant as only happens with a victory that is both momentous and unexpected. People jumped up and down in front of their silent Barca friends; they pushed them around, called them names like *ibn al-wiskha* (son of a dirty woman) and *ibn al-sharmuta* (son of a whore) and mocked Barca's *khawwal* (approximately "faggot") hero Messi who had been duly "fucked" by "Cristiano" (Ronaldo). As the final whistle blew, the die-hard Madrid fans all came together in a triumphant song: *ohohohohohoho . . . al-dawri rah minku* (the league went from you). The chant was directed to Abdeen's Barcelona fans, who quickly paid their bills and hurried home.

Throughout that spring and early summer, the rivalry between Barcelona/Messi and Real Madrid/Ronaldo permeated a wide array of emotional practices and affective registers in front of Ward al-Qahira's television screens. Teasing provocations, heartfelt laughter, brutal insults, and a whole lot of banter were commonplace during matches in La Liga, in the final stages of the Champions League, as well as when Portugal and Spain participated in the 2012 European Championship in June. As anthropologist Mark Peterson has noted, Cairo's *sha'bi ahawi* are remarkably inclusive spaces, bringing together men across age and class divisions in one social milieu. Yet they are also sites where men assert masculinity and various kinds of hierarchies through jokes and insults that tend to be sexually connoted (Peterson, 2011:139–169). Emotionally charged football club sympathies play a central if sometimes overlooked role in these performances of masculinity. There is almost always a match to comment on, always a victory to boast about, always a loser to mock. Traditionally, the Ahly-Zamalek rivalry has fueled the lion's share of these assertions of power and manliness. In the wake of the Port Said massacre, with Egypt's national game plunged in its deepest crisis in decades, male competition instead began to center on the fault line between the two biggest clubs in Spain.

This ability of football to emotionalize, masculinize, and hierarchize is predicated on competition between people that hold each other dear. As Abdu's brother Muhammad—also a Real supporter—expressed it immediately after the final whistle of Real Madrid's famous victory: "when we beat Barca, we beat our best friends. To see them lose, finally, is a really beautiful thing." For the same reason, the feelings that the game elicits are difficult to sustain outside the match event's combative space-time. The emotionality is a product of the ecstatic occasion and as such is inherently fleeting. To extend it through time requires both extensive media coverage and the context of a longer tradition of historic matches, tournaments, and rivalries. This ephemerality—more pronounced, arguably, in the case of Spanish clubs without a long history of support in Egypt—was clear when I returned to Ward al-Qahira with some food half an hour after the match in Barcelona had ended. The group of Madrid fans that had been celebrating wildly a short while ago had now moved outside to the street to get some fresh air. I sat down next to them, and I asked them to elaborate on how they felt. One of them, a short and cheerful young man called Nazif, smiled at my question:

> This was the first time we beat them in a match that mattered since 2007, and you ask me how I feel? I feel great of course, but I don't know how those Barca bastards [*awlad al-wiskha betu' Barca*] are feeling. . . . I cannot see any of them, can you? *Insha'Allah*, this was the day of the death of Barcelona and the first day of dominance for Real.

A quick look around confirmed Nazif's observation: Abdeen's high-profile Barcelona fans were nowhere to be seen. As there was no one around to mock and insult, the atmosphere had cooled down. A sentimental music video was playing on Sayed's new television screen. The Real Madrid fans were playing cards, as they often did when the games of the night were over. There was no one to tease, not much to comment on, and not that much to say. Nazif and his friends simply enjoyed the warm night, the tea, and the *shisha*. I could tell that they were very pleased with the victory. But they would not tell me much about it.

AFFECTIVE OVERLAPS

My first visit to Ward al-Qahira took place in early March 2012. At the end of June that year Sayed decided to let the place go when the owner of the property increased the café's rent by more than 40 percent. My time as a regular in Sayed's *ahwa* was therefore relatively brief. Yet it was an incredibly eventful four months. Spanning the end of the European league seasons as well as the European Championship in Poland and Ukraine, the period was full of charged football nights. Televised football from Europe repeatedly accomplished what Egypt's national game could not; the sport provoked excitement, devastation, and loads of masculine banter in the *ahwa* on the broad sidewalk in Abdeen. Meanwhile, consequential political events were literally around the corner. Tahrir Square's demonstrations took place less than a kilometer away, and protests at the Ministry of Interior were even closer. In May and June, the country's first free presidential elections were also organized. At Ward al-Qahira, the campaigns were followed closely on Sayed's television sets. Before and after the matches, the place was bustling with heated conversations about candidates, ideologies, and tactical voting.

The proximity of elections, demonstrations, and debates rendered Ward al-Qahira's emotional football sociality fragile. *Siyasa* in its variegated guises was just beneath the surface, always on the verge of interfering. One Sunday afternoon in early May, there was a significant power outage in large parts of Abdeen. As Sayed's televisions turned black and silent, the match between Newcastle United and Manchester City—a crucial game in the penultimate week of the English Premier League—vanished abruptly. Initially, everyone in the *ahwa* went quiet, as if listening to the silence that suddenly enclosed us. Without working fans, the room soon became unbearably hot. At this point, Mukhtar, an older gentleman temporarily back in Abdeen after many decades abroad, rose to his feet and began a lengthy monologue. With everyone else listening with astonishment, Mukhtar talked and talked: about how disorganized and backward Egypt had become in recent decades, about the laziness of the Egyptian people, about the disarray and chaos that the revolution had brought, about the futile prospects for democracy given the lack of morals and education, and about how everything in Cairo had been cleaner and better organized when he was a schoolboy in the 1940s, during the reign of King Faruq.

Mukhtar's opinions unleashed a heated discussion. Sayed, Abdu, and Sayed's brother Mazen took turns countering the older man's rant. They did not find much relevance in comparing revolutionary Egypt of today with a despotic monarchy that had been abolished sixty years earlier, and they wondered how anyone could ever be "ready" for democracy without being allowed to try it out first. Another regular, a visibly furious *bashmuhandis* (engineer), questioned Mukhtar's audacity to return to Abdeen after so many years and complain about a society he neither understood nor seemed to particularly like. Why did he not return to Europe, if everything was so much better there? Just as Mukhtar began to answer—assuring everyone that he was "more Egyptian than any of you" (*aktar masri minku kulluku*)—the electricity returned. Mukhtar's voice was drowned in a roar from Sayed: his team, Manchester City, had scored twice in the fifteen minutes we had missed, putting them on the brink of snatching the Premier League title from their local rivals, United. He pushed his brother Mazen, who sat next to him, and grinned at Mukhtar on the other side of the room. Mazen and Mukhtar did their best to avoid Sayed's provocations, staring at the screen in front of them. A minute ago, Mazen and Mukhtar had been opponents in a political conversation that was starting to become fairly heated. With the return of electricity and sound and images from the stadium in England, however, they had once again become Manchester United fans. And they both well knew that they were close to losing the league title to Man City supporters such as Sayed.

The incident illustrates how precarious football's affectivity can be, especially in periods when political sentiments and discourses prevail. Without its infrastructural scaffolding, the game disappeared on a whim, and the revolutionary era's structure of feeling recaptured Sayed's *ahwa*. As the presidential elections runoff between the Muslim Brotherhood's candidate, Muhammad Mursi, and Mubarak's former prime minister, Ahmed Shafiq, drew closer, this fine line separating *siyasa* and sports took new shapes. On 14 June, two days before people went to the polls, I was spending a hot afternoon at Ward al-Qahira when news reached us that the Supreme Court had ruled Shafiq a legitimate candidate, despite his previous posts within multiple Mubarak governments. The verdict itself surprised no one; most people had expected Shafiq to be allowed to run. But the court had gone one step further. Out of the blue, it had also ruled to dissolve the Muslim Brotherhood-dominated parliament. For Sayed and Abdu—who, after the narrow defeat of the Nasserite candidate, Hamdeen Sabahi, in the first round, reluctantly supported Mursi against what they perceived as the greater evil of Shafiq—this was a blow that hurt. The court ruling, they insisted, was nothing less than a judiciary coup (*inqilab qada'i*), yet another sign that the deep state (*al-dawla al-'amiqa*) would not let go of power. "It doesn't matter what we do or how we vote," Abdu told me despondently. "They will never allow Mursi to win."

But the court verdict did not disappoint everyone in Ward al-Qahira. Among Nazif's group of friends—all outspoken Shafiq supporters as well as devoted Real Madrid fans—the reaction was instead cheerful. The men were cracking jokes and laughing loudly, and one of them was humming the "Ahmed Shafiq song," a catchy tune praising the establishment candidate's prowess that had gone viral on YouTube, and which was blasted through loudspeakers from pick-up trucks circulating in Cairo in those days. As soon as they spotted someone they knew was a Mursi supporter, they started chanting "Ahmed Shafiq, Ahmed Shafiq" while rhythmically clapping their hands. At several occasions, they mocked the café's Islamist and revolutionary regulars with a true classic: *ma'salama, ma'salama, ma'salama, yi awlad el-wiskha* (good-bye, good-bye, good-bye, you sons of a dirty woman). This was party politics practiced and felt like a football game. In fact, it was all but identical to the teasing and mocking of losers that the same group of men had directed against Abdeen's FC Barcelona fans after Real Madrid's victory in April. By mid-June, the Spanish El Clásico had temporarily been replaced by Egypt's presidential elections. But the affectivity in the moment of victory followed strikingly similar scripts.

Less than two weeks later, in the afternoon of 24 June, the president of the National Election Authority, Faruq Sultan, was at last ready to announce the election results. Following a full week of delays and prolonged counting of ballots, the occasion was tremendously anticipated and charged. Rumors and speculation were everywhere. Who would be given the victory? How would the Brotherhood react if Shafiq was named the winner? Would the announcement of the results be postponed once again? By noon, most Cairenes hurried home from their jobs, and almost all shops closed. At 2:45 p.m., fifteen minutes before the scheduled announcement, astonishing footage of deserted streets in some of Cairo's busiest business areas circulated on television and social media. Outside the open windows of my apartment, downtown Cairo was quieter than I had ever experienced it when Sultan began to read out the results. Everyone was watching.

The actual announcement took only a few seconds: Mursi had won with a margin of 3.4 percent. Immediately, the summer street outside my windows exploded in fireworks, ululations, honking cars, and exclamations that God is great (*Allah Akbar*). Later in the evening, my partner and I took a walk downtown past Tahrir Square and on to Abdeen. Everywhere we went, we saw families celebrating with ice cream and soft drinks; Egyptian flags were flying from cars, balconies, and statues. The atmosphere made it impossible not to recall a great national football triumph. The tense buildup, the ecstatic moment of triumph, and the pleasure of relief that followed it: the parallels were plentiful. When we reached Ward al-Qahira, the quarter-final in the European Championships between Italy and England was up and running, but this was not a night for Andrea Pirlo and Wayne Rooney. Sayed and Abdu were all smiles, surprised and delighted at the outcome. Alaa, a member of the revolutionary Sixth of April movement, which had backed Mursi in the runoff, was handing out sweets to everyone around. Nazif's group of Real Madrid fans and Ahmed Shafiq supporters, on the other hand, were nowhere to be seen. Possibly, they felt that it was better to stay at home, because this night they were on the losing side. This emotional-political occasion, with its sweetness of victory, was for the other half of Ward al-Qahira to celebrate and exult in.

NIGHTS ON *AL-MIDAN*

Sayed let Ward al-Qahira go less than a week after Muhammad Mursi's election victory, but I continued to frequent Abdeen nonetheless. During the subsequent autumn and winter, I visited the neighborhood regularly to see friends, watch a match at some other coffee shop, or, most often, to play a game of football myself. The person in charge of setting up these matches was Abdu, a man born in the mid-'80s who, like Sayed, is of Nubian origin. Apart from being a devoted football player and fan—Arsenal and al-Zamalek are his teams—Abdu's big passion is novels. Regardless of where I have seen him—waiting tables at Ward al-Qahira in 2012, working in the reception area at a local gym and health center in 2013, or somewhere else completely—he has always carried a book around to read in case he gets some time off. Although deeply attached to his family and friends in Abdeen, Abdu's dreams and aspirations have always been outside Egypt. In October 2013, he had finally saved up enough money to move abroad. Today, he is settled in a big city in Europe, where he is in the process of getting a permanent residency.

Until the day Abdu emigrated, he lived with his parents and his younger brother, Muhammad, in a ground-floor apartment a few minutes' walk from Ward al-Qahira. Despite a seven-year age difference, the brothers were very close, and one thing that they made sure to do together, at least once a week, was play football. Like most Egyptian adults who work or study, the brothers played their football late at night. Abdu would typically call me around 9 p.m. on a Thursday or Friday evening. A couple of hours later, we would meet in a small Abdeen *ahwa* and wait for the other regulars to arrive: Muhammad and a couple of his teenaged friends from high school; a medical doctor named Hassan who worked at the same health center as Abdu, and who sported a beard without moustache that betrayed his Salafi sympathies; Jake, an Eritrean refugee, stranded in Cairo while waiting for a visa to join his wife and daughter in California; a talented Sudanese youngster, Mahmoud, who worked in an internet café; and Abdu's childhood friend Zak, who usually arrived late from his bank job and changed from his sleek suit to the fluffy track-suit pants he always played in. It was typically close to midnight before everyone had arrived and we moved on to the pitch at nearby *al-midan* (the square): a vast, floodlit asphalt rectangle between Abdeen Palace and the Cairo Governorate buildings, where jackets, rucksacks, or cardboard boxes served as makeshift goalposts.

The rules on *al-midan* were simple and well known. A match lasted until one team had scored four goals; the winning team stayed on to play the team that had been waiting the longest on the sidelines. While this system meant that we sometimes had to wait an hour or even two before it was our turn to play, Abdu liked to point out the bright side: as long as we kept winning, we could play on indefinitely. In contrast to many men on *al-midan* who played in slippers or even barefoot, all members of our team wore proper football shoes. Despite Abdu and Zak's habit of intensifying the experience by smoking hashish before kickoff, we were also relatively fit. Consequently, we won more matches than we lost. It was not uncommon that we stayed out in the cold night, playing on the black asphalt under the yellow lights, until three o'clock in the morning.

Playing on *al-midan* was not easy. The ball was rarely very good, patches of the field were poorly lit, the hard surface made the ball bounce around, and it was a challenge not to slip. Given the difficult conditions, the technical level was impressive, especially as far as dribbling and clever finishing were concerned. Such technical finesse was always appreciated. Everyone around knew to enjoy a skilled move past a defender; players who found themselves tricked were inevitably humiliated and mocked. Together with the obligatory and many times sexualized insults that goal scorers directed to goalkeepers and winning teams to losers, these celebrations resembled the performance of competitive masculinity that I had observed between Real Madrid and Barcelona fans in Ward al-Qahira. It did not seem to matter that television sets, satellite receivers, studios in the Gulf, and hundreds of cameras in a packed stadium in Europe had been replaced by a floodlit rectangle of asphalt, a torn plastic football, and four jackets signaling

Fig. 7.1. Young men playing football on Abdeen's *al-midan*. Photo: Lena Malm, 6 May 2019.

where to score a goal. The game of football was sufficiently recognizable as a common denominator for passions and social interactions to follow analogous repertoires.

The relatively expansive, well-lit, and car-free square in Abdeen offered something unique in Cairo in the early 2010s. Almost everywhere else in Egypt's desperately congested capital, pick-up football has in recent decades developed into a hobby that one has to pay for.[5] Spontaneous street football is still widespread among young children (see Hussein, 2011). Yet as older friends have often told me, most public spaces where they used to play as kids have been commercialized, privatized, or converted into parking lots (see Rommel, 2018a). In the last years before this book went to press, the wind of change reached *al-midan* too. In 2015, as part of an ambitious public-private push to refurbish and "beautify" downtown Cairo (Rabie, 2015), the asphalt on the square was replaced by slippery stone tiles. Benches were also added, and the "pitch" area at the center was reduced. In 2019, one still finds groups of young boys playing football at the square. But the teams of grownups have moved on.

In the winter of 2012 and 2013, these detrimental developments were still a couple of years away. The space was open and we played for free; on

weekends the matches continued until dawn. But there were other distur-
bances. In the aftermath of President Mursi's constitutional declaration
in November 2012 (chapter 5), everyday life was far from stable. Clashes
between oppositional demonstrators and Mursi supporters erupted regularly. Rumor had it that Muslim Brothers were kidnapping and torturing
protesters. In early 2013, groups of black-clad and masked protesters—so
called Black Blocs—became increasingly common. Exactly who made up
Cairo's Black Blocs has never been fully explained, and no one has been
able to specify their precise goals and allegiances.[6] What is certain, though,
is that the fear and moral panic that these groups generated were powerful,
real, and added to a widespread sense of chaos. In the winter nights when
the blocs roamed the streets, destroyed property, interrupted traffic, and
clashed with security forces, central Cairo became a place to avoid. On
al-midan, few people came to play. The matches came to an end shortly
after dusk.

For Abdu and me, these developments constituted a topic for endless
discussions. A reluctant Mursi voter in the June 2012 run-off, Abdu had
turned into a strong critic of the new president almost immediately after
his inauguration. In late 2012 and early 2013, he participated in several
antigovernment protests; many friends of his were arrested or injured in
clashes. While Abdu accused the Mursi government of incompetence,
moralism, authoritarianism, and a faltering economy, his most serious
grievance was the hatred that the administration was generating among
the populace. Its policies and rhetoric incited violence not only between
protesters and the police, but also among Egyptian civilians. The latter, he
pointed out, was both new and very dangerous. It could lead to unprecedented levels of material and moral destruction, and it was certain to derail
whatever was left of the revolutionary momentum.

As the communal violence escalated, Abdu stopped following domestic
football completely. As described previously, he considered al-Zamalek's
televised matches dead (*mayta*) in an era dominated by death and destruction. And yet it would not take long after a wave of unrest had passed
before Abdu called me and organized a new round of matches on *al-midan*.
This kind of football kept on happening. For one reason or another, it was
a nonproblematic pastime that Abdu was willing to return to.

To think through this discrepancy, let me first note that football on
al-midan had its own episodes of confrontational anger. In the absence of
referees, every incident of body contact, every shot close to one of the
makeshift goalposts, and every ball passing out of bounds had the potential to cause a quarrel (*khina'a*) over the rules of the game. Over time, I

understood that players were not *ever* supposed to admit that they had committed a foul. Instead, it was accepted that each ambiguous call would instigate a few minutes' interruption as players engaged in a tightly scripted argument. First, the protagonists would swear they had done nothing wrong. They would shout at each other, call each other names, push one another, or pull the other's T-shirts. After a minute or two, senior members of each team would intervene, seeking a solution. Sometimes, such efforts at mediation would merely escalate the drama, as the mediators themselves got animated, but most often it marked the beginning of the end. One of the parties might shout "take it if you want to have it" and kick the ball to the other team's half. The other might reply: "no, you take it, I don't want it, you play," kicking the ball back again. At some point, a player on either team would simply take the ball, and the game would resume.

These eruptions of fury and violence were too frequent to be considered mere nuisance. Having played hundreds of matches on dozens of pitches across Cairo over the last decade, I would contend that tussles with male friends form an integral part of the experience: it is part of what makes playing football enjoyable (see Rommel, 2018a). Let me also make clear that these are ritualized "social dramas" (Ghannam, 2013:111–113). The masculinized violence found on Egyptian football pitches is confined and regulated, it rarely results in injuries, and it follows socially sanctioned scripts.[7] Could it be that these benign football fights provided a soothing contrast to the waves of unpredictable, out-of-control political violence that permeated Egypt's revolutionary years? Did the game's ritualized controllability render the matches in the square especially appealing this very winter?[8] At times, my intuition told me that this was the case, yet Abdu did not tell me much about it. I often asked him to elaborate on why he kept returning to the square to play football with his friends, but he did not find the topic worthy of much discussion. "I have always been playing, all young men [*shabab*] play football; it is normal," he told me once. Another time, he got irritated and asked me: "What do you want me to say, Carl? Why do you play with us? It is fun, right? Arguments and fights are normal [*al-khina'a 'adi*]." At the time, I found his reluctance to talk irritating and odd. When it came to most other topics—al-Zamalek, Arsenal, the revolution, or novels—the Abdu I knew loved to deliberate. With hindsight, however, I have come to think that his atypical silence on the arguments illuminates something crucial about the recreational game's appeal. In an era when so much in the country was debated, problematized, and *siyasi*, the games on *al-midan*—the mocking, the sweat, the skills, and also the quarrels—provided Abdu and his friends with an escape into something that was "just a game."

CONCLUSION: JUST A GAME

Part III of this book has charted different kinds of football developing along distinct trajectories during Egypt's revolutionary years. Whereas chapter 6 demonstrated how Egypt's national game became all but incapable of affecting fans after the Port Said massacre, this chapter has explored facets of football's circumscribed but ongoing presence in the midst of the prevailing sociopolitical crisis: televised matches from Europe, and recreational pick-up games. As my ethnographic material has illustrated, these football activities elicited a range of emotions among my friends in Abdeen. Some men would win and some would lose decisive matches on *al-midan* or in Ward al-Qahira; winners would mock losers; others would be mediators in fights; while some would just play on and let their skilled bodies do the talking.

Proximities and overlaps between football feelings, on the one hand, and a multifaceted phenomenon called *siyasa* (politics), on the other, have formed a core theme across part III. For longtime fans like Hamada, football was exposed as *siyasi*, overwhelmed by similar but stronger emotional-political occasions, and mixed up in the confusion of ever-present *siyasa*. At Ward al-Qahira, the dramatic endgame of the presidential election overshadowed matches, and people celebrated electoral victories as though they were football games. On *al-midan*, the uncertainty of Black Blocs and street violence interrupted the action for nights on end. At the same time, the two chapters have told diverging stories. Whereas Egypt's national sport lost its former popularity, the football activities in which I partook in Abdeen retained their capacity to move and affect. As soon as current events withdrew ever so little, fans yet again congregated in Sayed's *ahwa*. Before long, Abdu and his friends got ready for a new round of matches in the square.

How and why did *these* football feelings linger in a period when the domestic game felt so hopelessly out of sync? Why did *this* football remain relevant, despite repetitive intrusions by the realm of *siyasa*? One answer is found in particular spatial-infrastructural arrangements. Both *al-midan* and Ward al-Qahira were singular spacetimes: the former, a not yet redeveloped public space with decent floodlighting, flat asphalt, and no parked cars; the latter, a unique constellation of Gulf-financed satellite networks, television screens, an imported receiver, and cheap coffee, tea, and *shisha*. As far as European football is concerned, technological superiority also played a role. Compared to the lower-key broadcasts of the domestic game on Egyptian television channels, al-Jazeera Sports and AD

Sports' access to the Arab world's most famous commentators and state-of-the-art image production made European matches more enjoyable.[9] Furthermore, everything on these pan-Arab channels—from the matches themselves to advertisements, studios, experts, and commentators—had a cleaner (*andaf*), some would call it more professional (*muhtarif*) or international (*dawli*), appearance. In contrast to the local pundits, who constantly deviated from the game to make reactionary comments on the latest developments on Tahrir Square or at the ballot box, the Gulf networks' experts stuck strictly to analyses of tactics, results, and players. In short, the *international* game was, by definition, not a *national* one. The questions about partisanship and politicization that bothered Egyptian nationalism in general and Egypt's football institutions in particular were thus not raised. Quite the opposite: European football provided a refreshing distance from events and rhythms indexed as *siyasi*. FC Barcelona and Real Madrid continued to generate laughter, anger, joy, and pride, whereas al-Ahly and al-Zamalek did not do the trick.

But technological sophistication and professionalism do not tell the whole story. How could they, when football still mattered on the asphalt on *al-midan* too? To make sense of this resilience, anthropologist Will Rollason's research with men who play football on a small island in southeast Papua New Guinea is illuminating. Rollason suggests that a main reason for football's popularity in Papua New Guinea is that the game is treated as a phenomenon, "which comes in from the outside and *stays what it is*" (Rollason, 2011:487). It is something unproblematic and "completely transparent"; it is "just football," something people enjoy playing, but by and large take for granted. In the case of football as a recreational game, such a matter-of-factness is almost always present. As ethnographic work of pick-up football illustrates (e.g., Worby, 2009), playing football in a park—or a square—is first and foremost embodied performance. It might generate loads of spontaneity, charisma, and nonpropositional emotionality. But it neither requires nor causes much elaboration.[10]

This primacy of the body in motion might explain why Abdu found it irrelevant to discuss the matches he played on *al-midan*. To sweat, shoot, and run but *not* talk for an hour or two was simply part of the joyful thrill. A similar component of nonverbal embodiment was manifest among the men in Ward al-Qahira too. In contrast to how decades-old Ahly-Zamalek games and victories for the national teams could be spoken about for hours—also in a period when current matches did not matter much—European matches did not generate much contemplation. As a matter of fact, it often struck me how *little* Abdeen's dedicated Real Madrid fans had to say, even after a victory as momentous as the one against FC Barcelona in April 2012. "I feel great, of course," Nazif told me succinctly that night, before continuing to play cards with his friends. His football emotions had a scripted obviousness and transparency to them, which left little room to reflect and discuss.

This taken-for-granted, nonverbal obviousness drew a distinct line of demarcation between the politicized spectacle of national "Football"—be it the bursting Mubarak bubble or the Ultras' rebellious campaigns—and the other, minor "footballs" that I have examined in this chapter. In addition to professionalism and technologies, the primacy of embodiment and unself-conscious engagement rendered the game in Ward al-Qahira and *al-midan* qualitatively separated from the conversations about the Algeria games, television pundits, and Ultras groups that I have detailed in previous chapters. While discussions about the purpose and *siyasa* of football as Egypt's national game—its history, its future, and its crisis—kept on haunting national sports institutions and made it difficult for fans to engage, one key characteristic of the recreational football that kept on bubbling in Abdeen was its nonpropositional quality. It was largely practiced as a realm of its own: a parallel sphere for masculine banter, emotionality, and socializing that was not read as nationally significant, and which thus stood out as incommensurable with the political developments that otherwise encapsulated Egyptian society.[11]

For Abdeen's football supporters and players, this separation in the midst of conflation had a number of tangible consequences. Men like Abdu were perfectly capable of shifting their attention between the presidential elections and Real Madrid, between being an apolitical football player and a political citizen, in ways that were not possible as *Zamelkawiyya* or supporters of the Egyptian national team. And in contrast to the "corrupted" and "politicized" spectacle of professional football in Egypt, it was never a problem for Salafists, like Hassan, to play football on *al-midan* as a means of physical exercise. The way Abdu and his friends used the very same name, *al-midan* (the square), for their nightly football pitch in Abdeen *and* for Tahrir Square, the revolution's unquestionable epicenter, is illustrative of the duality at play. The functions and meanings of the two squares belonged to different realms of action, practice, feeling, and subjectivity. Consequently, *al-midan* as a reference would not possibly cause any confusion.

Between 2011 and 2013—the revolutionary years when there was a consensus that Egypt's national game witnessed its deepest crisis since the 1970s—football never disappeared from the Cairene everyday experience.

Although qualitatively different both to the national football bubble and its various adversaries, playing football recreationally and watching European games on television kept generating leisurely enjoyment and perhaps also a sense of normalcy in neighborhoods like Abdeen. These pockets of normalcy in an era dominated by turbulence and uncertainty were neither a result of a gradual routinization of violence (Allen, 2008) nor of some inescapable adjustment to a perpetual state of exception (Agamben, 2005). Rather, the normalization achieved by material infrastructures, male bodies, club loyalties, feelings, and banter was one of separation in the midst of conflation: a sealing off of political troubles from a confined sphere of familiarity, which did not have any national significance, and where the unease of *siyasa* had no role to play.[12] In this exceptional period of Egyptian modern history, when so much had to be meaningful, proper, and politically useful to count and fit in, international football and the played game remained attractive because of their separateness and nonpolitical meaninglessness. This football stayed outside the revolution's turbulence and seriousness. How could it not, when it was just a game?

An Emotional Revolt Trapped in Politics

Politics does not begin after the boundary between political life and bare life is drawn; rather, drawing this boundary constitutes the object of politics par excellence.

Alexei Yurchak, "Necro-Utopia"

THE EMOTIONAL POLITICS OF EGYPTIAN FOOTBALL

This book has argued that emotions and affect are inherently political and that Egyptian football is a realm where this modality of power is exercised with great effect. The Egyptian game has a unique ability to spawn pervasive structures of feeling and more confined emotional styles, and it interpellates politically charged affective-emotional subjects. The national frame has been central throughout this story. In Egypt—a country where all political leaders and parties pledge that they are nationalist—political conflicts regularly surface as struggles over who and what the idealized Egyptian people (*al-sha'b al-masri*) really is. Egypt's indisputably national sport provides a principal stage for this contest. Again and again, football-related affect and subjectivities establish and reestablish what the Egyptian nation and its citizens are and ought to be.

The book's first part explored this interplay in the sports-crazy pre-2011 years. Bringing together money, media, popular culture, and great results on the pitch, football assembled a nationwide emotional "bubble" that encapsulated late-Mubarak Egypt. The football bubble carried a successful, normal and largely upbeat masculinity—neither too intellectual nor too religious—that wedded the presidential family to the people. In this way, the sport staked out a powerful national "We," one that incorporated but also exceeded banal everyday practices (see Billig, 1995) and imaginaries of a shared community (see Anderson, 1991). The football bubble demarcated how, when, and for what normal Egyptian men should and could *feel*. This visceral nationalism rendered football a highly effective political force.

I have also highlighted a leakiness within this emotional unity. There is a volatility at the heart of every given affective order, an inherent excess that attracts and lures, but also eventually ushers in collapse and break-up. In my story, such unruliness first transpired at the time of the two Algeria matches in November 2009. After the shocking defeat in Khartoum, the inflated bubble of sports, masculinity, and emotions was cast in a new and significantly more critical light: as *muta'assib* (fanatical) and *siyasi* (political) rather than nationalist, unifying, and normal. The loss allowed secular intellectuals and Islamists—two "respectable" groups who had long been critical to the game—to publicly question the emotional-political function of football in Mubarak's Egypt. That the same two groups would dominate much of the national-political landscape in the first two years after 25 January 2011 is noteworthy. The Algeria crisis was in this regard a precursor to shifts pertaining to class, aesthetics, and ethics that would take full force a year or two later.

The inherent recalcitrance of the emotional-political was also a theme in part II, about the Egyptian Ultras. The Ultras not only criticized the structures of feelings that football had hitherto fostered but also staked out an alternative. Introducing a radical emotional style of fun and freedom, the supporter groups revamped the atmosphere at Egypt's football stadiums. Especially in 2011 and 2012, their unorthodox way of being and feeling as fans gained widespread popularity, attention, and respect. Embodying a new national and revolutionary football subject, the Ultras draw thousands of young men to the stadiums as well as into the uprisings. Beginning in 2013, however, the supporters' emotional style was castigated by the media and persecuted by the security forces. Egypt's young and rebellious Ultras football fans have struggled to keep up their activities in an increasingly counterrevolutionary Egyptian nation.

My account of the emotional politics of Egypt's biggest spectator sport has proposed an alternative dramatization of the country's (counter-)revolutionary transition. Like scholars who have incorporated January 2011 in longer political-economic trajectories (Armbrust, 2019:29–45; Bush and Ayeb, 2012; Kandil, 2012) or explored sociopolitical shifts beyond political science orthodoxies (Ahlberg, 2017; Armbrust, 2019; Makram-Ebeid,

2014; Shenker, 2016; Swedenburg, 2012; Winegar, 2016), my narration has featured *actors*—football journalists, club officials, the Egyptian Football Association, Ultras groups, and ordinary fans—and *events*—Africa Cups of Nations, the Algeria matches, the Port Said massacre, the Super Cup, and the Port Said verdicts—hitherto not included in the historiography of contemporary Egypt.

My focus on affect and emotions also recasts the revolutionary struggle's *subject matter*. Over the last decade, several scholars have argued that the Egyptian Ultras' prowess rested on factors such as a strict ideology, an extended tug-of-war with the police, the "All Cops Are Bastards" (A.C.A.B) acronym, innovative ways of organizing, utopian aesthetics, effective use of Facebook, or long experiences of street fights (e.g., Bashir, 2011; Close, 2019; Dorsey, 2016; Gibril, 2015; Ibraheem, 2015; Thabet, 2013). As detailed in part II, these were all important dimensions of the supporters' revolutionary intervention. The experience of combating the security forces mattered a great deal, and so did decentralized structures and dedication. Even so, narratives of this kind need to be advanced with caution. They risk entrenching a circumscribed view of the 2011 Revolution as waged in the name of a set of liberal principles, by a social media-savvy "youth" (*shabab*), against the police, and in the surroundings of Tahrir Square. My account of Egypt's football radicals has intentionally steered away from these pitfalls. Incorporating the rise and fall of the Ultras into a thirty-year tale about the national game's emotional politics, I have told a story that accounts for but also pushes back against identity politics and ideological battles. For if the distribution of sentiments that football circulated in the late Mubarak era was at the core of a hegemonic crafting of the nation, then the Ultras' parallel emotional style of fun and freedom challenged this statecraft. Beginning as early as 2007, the Ultras' independence, energy, and affect contested what football, its spectators, and, in effect, the Egyptian nation had been and should be about. The Ultras' project might now be in disarray. But in the years when they gained momentum, Egypt's radical football fan groups constituted a potent revolutionary factor in the affective-emotional realm.

The story about Egypt's football revolution has also suggested something more general about how football feelings work politically. In the introduction, I noted that the emotionality of spectator sports has most often been analyzed either as concealing opiate or as liberating liminality. As far as football as a political drug is concerned, such tropes are widespread in Egypt, and for good reason. Especially after the Port Said tragedy, it has been acknowledged both that the game *concealed* the Mubarak regime's power play and that its thrills *substituted* for more desperate structures of feeling. Still, the cliché that the prerevolutionary regime cynically *used* the sport's inflated emotionality to distract and mislead needs to be nuanced. Direct governmental interventions—legislation, financing of sports clubs, post-tournament receptions—worked in tandem with exogenous processes—private media, individual talents, pop stars and movies, match results—which the government never fully controlled. The game's affectivity was also reappropriated by subversive Ultras fans. At times, football feelings were overshadowed by even more intoxicating ruses of revolution. Put simply, my ethnography has shown that football has a unique ability to distribute sentiments across national territories and to carve out politically consequential emotional subjects. Rather than covering up an ideal realm of rational politics, however, football feelings act in and on a political sphere that is always already affective, inherently fleeting, and on the verge of being made anew.

The second dominant take on political football emotions—the game as liminal ritual—emphasizes the exceptionality of the football *occasion*. Sealed off from the outside world, we learn, the stadium turns into a carnival, where social boundaries are challenged, sometimes even transgressed. For me, the affective uniqueness of the match event is a no-brainer. The enormously anticipated Algeria games, the Ultras' emotional spectacle at Cairo Stadium, or the controlled unpredictability that a cup final brings together—the sport gives rise to a multitude of singular moments with the potential to change worlds and derail the course of history. But depicting such occasions as liminality or ritual only takes us so far. If the match at the stadium is treated as a detached realm of symbolism where subjects and power are particularly malleable, we risk overlooking vital continuities. For what is a football game, really, without the complex material-ideological scaffolding that affords the ritualist intensity in the first place: media campaigns built up over years, meticulous fan preparations, narrations of historical rivalries, pop songs about the national team's glory? And what about critical events outside the confines of sports, such as a revolution, or a military coup? By examining interdependencies between electrifying games and tournaments, on the one hand, and "external" forces and events, on the other, I have demonstrated how football's intensity extends into other times and different spaces. The exceptional affective-emotional events that the game no doubt fosters rest on discursive, material, and metaphorical relays between a stadium, where it all seems to happen, and a surrounding sociohistorical fabric that enables feelings to flow.

THE POLITICS OF POLITICS

Over the thirty-odd years examined in these pages, football in general and the game's emotions in particular were not only mobilized to great effect for a variety of political projects, reactionary as well as revolutionary. Ethnographically salient notions and experiences of *siyasa* also impacted on how Egyptian supporters engaged with and related to games, fan groups, institutions, and media outlets. While *siyasa* takes different shapes in different spaces and contexts, I have argued that most Egyptians share a general, historically informed antipathy against it. The country's nationalist thinkers and politicians have for more than a hundred years looked upon *siyasa* with suspicion. To be a good nationalist requires that one work for the common good, for the whole people, and for the unity of the idealized Egyptian nation. Political partisanship and actions motivated by self-interested, factional demands are not seen with gentle eyes. The reevaluation of football's past that was initiated after the Algeria matches in 2009 and accelerated in the wake of the 2012 Port Said stadium tragedy unearthed this latent tension. The Egyptians increasingly came to realize that football had been exploited by the old regime and deeply entwined with *siyasa*. For Egypt's national game, this was bad news indeed.

The threats posed by political partisanship are not the only issues that *siyasa* brings to the fore. When a multifaceted mix-up between *siyasa* and football made it impossible for fans such as Hamada and Abdu to keep up their emotional engagement in 2012 and 2013, the "politics" that interfered was talked about in a whole range of worrying terms: selfish interests, corruption, uncertainty, and violence. Only football activities that were not understood as national and which as a result upheld a clear separation vis-à-vis *siyasa* remained unproblematic and affectively charged. One thing that my ethnographic encounters with Egyptian football supporters has illustrated, then, is how *siyasa* is experienced viscerally and what implications such feelings had—or did not have—during Egypt's revolutionary period. As political rhythms and phenomena became ever-present, they rendered al-Ahly, al-Zamalek, and the national team largely obsolete. I often heard people argue that the only way to salvage Egyptian football was to cleanse it of political interference (*tadakhkhulat siyasiyya*).

The chapters about the Egyptian Ultras movements have illustrated how conversations about *siyasa* can turn into a potent modality of power. The Ultras always faced a thorny dilemma. On the one hand, the groups regularly asserted that they stood outside all activities and practices rendered as *siyasa*. At times they distanced themselves from "political" deliberations, quarrels, and intrigues; they frequently insisted that they were nationalists first and foremost and concerned with the well-being of all Egyptians. On the other hand, whenever the Ultras worked to effectuate reforms and change, their actions appeared as *siyasi* to many outsiders. In the media, the Ultras were accused of forwarding their own demands and interests; their distinctive emotional and violent masculinity was labeled fanatic, thuggish, and destabilizing, especially by middle-class observers. It was only during the exceptional moment in 2011 and 2012 that these processes of othering could be challenged. Suddenly, it was the football establishment that had to face questions about personal interests, corruption, and political connections to the ousted Mubarak regime. The Ultras, by contrast, transcended class divides, appearing as nonpolitical champions of the common good. Their novel emotionality and aesthetics were widely perceived as progressive, making them a rare source of hope for a crisis-ridden national game.

It is worth emphasizing that Egypt's Ultras groups partly reached this position of strength by conforming to a prevailing nationalist and antipolitical consensus. Ultras Ahlawy and Ultras White Knights might have been boisterous, violent, and somewhat rowdy young men, but now and then they participated in a game of positions where middle-class respectability was hard currency. Whether at Tahrir Square in January 2011, on Muhammad Mahmoud Street in November of the same year, or during the protests that followed the Port Said massacre and the Super Cup match in 2012, the groups made sure to portray themselves as nonpolitical supporter organizations working for the common good. It is also noteworthy what actions this strategy foreclosed. Some tactics, stances, and emotions were simply out of the question for a fan group determined to retain a nonpolitical profile. Certain allies were too controversial to team up with; some protests should not be joined; violence could be deployed only with moderation. Even if I have argued that the story about the Egyptian Ultras by and large was steeped in contingency—these were football fans caught up in events—this active positioning contributed to the supporters' revolutionary renown. Tellingly, as soon as Ultras Ahlawy no longer prioritized this nationalist nonpolitics—such as when disparaging Masry supporters (fellow Egyptians) on death row, or burning down the EFA's headquarters (a national institution)—their appeal was lost, especially among the middle classes. This development demonstrates that rejecting politics might be politically constraining. It can be a tough challenge to be rebellious and radical if you are obliged to serve the common good.

I would suggest that this dilemma, faced by the Egyptian Ultras throughout their short but eventful history, mirrors a predicament of

Egypt's 2011 Revolution as a whole. The uprising was always framed as unquestionably nationalist. At least in its dominant, media-driven and middle-class incarnation, the revolutionary movement thrived on being factionless, asecular (Agrama, 2012:224–235), and all-encompassing.[1] The revolutionary "We" was always a national one; the movement "dreamed of being the people," as anthropologist Hanan Sabea evocatively puts it (2014). It is no doubt that this was a prerequisite for the revolution's broad appeal and initial success. Potentially mobilizing every citizen and bringing the people together in an undivided, national whole, the revolt in January 2011 built on a long tradition that millions of Egyptians recognized and related to symbolically as well as affectively. And yet the very same principles also rendered the revolutionary moment curiously antipolitical. Partisanship and self-interest had no space in the hegemonic version of the nation; to an extent, *siyasa*—in all its varieties and connotations—was precisely what the people were rising up *against* (see Rommel, 2018b). It is not difficult to envision why such an aversion to the political could render a revolutionary mobilization somewhat toothless. If all actors striving to effect change are required to remain nationalist and nonpolitical, then what kinds of change are possible at all? How do you legitimize the violent tearing down of state institutions that a revolution arguably requires, when facing accusations that you are destroying *national* property? And how do you counteract inequalities based on class, gender, religion, or ethnicity, if every political project needs to forward the interest of *the whole people* to be consider legitimate?

This conundrum might help explain why even in 2011, 2012, and 2013—arguably the most politicized period in Egypt's modern history—socialist or feminist parties and viewpoints were unable to make any significant imprint on the country's national-political stage. Even in the midst of a burning revolt, middle-class notions of nationalism and *siyasa* stayed strong. Since proposals for radical redistributions of resources—from rich to poor or from men to women—could not easily be framed as nonpolitical projects in the service of the whole Egyptian people, they struggled to gain broad traction. Instead, public conversations consistently relapsed to questions about national identity. Are we Egyptians—*all of us*—ultimately secular, or are we religious? How to instigate a project of national reawakening? Who are the real nationalists working for the interests of the entire nation? What actors are merely furthering exclusive, partisan demands?

A similar bouquet of questions has prevailed during Egypt's counterrevolutionary turn too. In recent years, public debates have recurrently pivoted around how to purify and cleanse the nation of deviating opinions and projects (Schielke, 2017; Winegar, 2016). General-turned-president

Abdel Fattah el-Sisi has often highlighted his and the Egyptian Army's superpolitical status as proof of legitimacy. This was particularly true when the army was crushing the dangerously "political" Muslim Brotherhood in summer 2013 (Brown 2013a, 2013b; Armbrust 2019: 157–180), and when el-Sisi was running for the presidency without any "political platform" in spring 2014. Understanding *siyasa* as an object of deep hesitation, fear, and unease among Egyptian football fans makes it a bit more comprehensible why this strategy, at least at times, has proved relatively effective. To challenge even the most marginal aspect of the current order might do more than stir the security state's full-blown vengeance: persecution, torture, disappearance, and harsh sentences. Anyone who raises issues about Egypt's class inequalities, labor conditions, gender discrimination, or HBTQ rights also runs the risk of being labeled self-serving, partisan, and not truly patriotic, that is, *siyasi* in the term's most troubling sense.

Magnificent Mohamed Salah
and the Ill-Fated 2018 World Cup

I'll support Egypt and Salah in Russia, of course. But to be honest, I won't be sad if we lose.
Muhammad, *Zamelkawi* and good friend, May 2018

In spring 2013, a couple of months before Field Marshal Abdel Fattah el-Sisi launches the putsch that terminates Egypt's revolutionary experiment, I leave fieldwork behind with Egyptian football stuck in a deep crisis. League matches are being played at empty stadiums. The Ultras are causing trouble. Friends of mine do not really follow matches and tournaments. In the years that follow, my visits to Cairo will be few and brief, but there is no doubt that the downturn continues. Most crucially, the ban on supporters at domestic games stays in place. By the end of the 2010s, a whole generation of young Egyptian boys has never attended a live football match at the stadium. Second, as it is the security services that ultimately decide where and when matches are played, league games are spread out across the week and teams shift home stadiums constantly. The rhythms of the game—vital, we recall, for building up emotional momentum—are thus hopelessly irregular. Third, the Egyptian national team is an embarrassment. In autumn 2013, Egypt crashes out of the 2014 World Cup qualifications after a humiliating 6–1 loss to Ghana; the following year the team fails to qualify for the 2015 Africa Cup of Nations. After the legendary triple victory in 2006, 2008, and 2010, the Pharaohs have now missed three consecutive Africa Cups, an astounding twist of fate.

It takes until 2016 before a cautious resurgence begins to take shape. Coached by the experienced Argentinean Hector Cuper and spearheaded by AS Roma's speedy winger Mohamed Salah, a young Egyptian team qualifies for the Africa Cup of Nations. When the tournament gets underway in early 2017, expectations are initially low and media coverage sparse. But when Egypt beats a strong Moroccan team in the quarterfinals and then Burkina Faso on penalties in the semis, something is unleashed. Football is once again a hot topic on social media; friends in Cairo report that there are extensive late-night street celebrations. Later in the year, the festivities are even larger when Egypt qualifies for its first World Cup in twenty-eight years. As the tournament in Russia draws closer, the names of football players in general and Mohamed Salah in particular are all over the media and on every Egyptian's lips. The growing momentum evokes memories of the late Mubarak era. A new football frenzy seems to have hit the country.

In this postscript, I examine Egyptian football's recovery during a period spanning the World Cup qualification in October 2017, the tournament in Russia in June 2018, and the Africa Cup of Nations hosted in Egypt in summer 2019. This is a period when I once again live in Cairo, and everywhere I go, I meet people who talk about football with newfound passion and enthusiasm. At the same time, I find many fans are hesitant to fully embrace the sport. This ambivalence is only understandable in light of the longer story told in this book. Thirty years of troubling relationships between *siyasa* (politics) and football have generated a situation where Egyptians hesitate to feel strongly about football, making the recent resurge markedly distinct from the emotional-political sports bubble before January 2011.

BACK ON THE WORLD STAGE

As soon as I move back to Cairo in autumn 2017, I sense the palpable change in mood. The combination of Egyptian fans talking about football and Egyptian teams winning matches is something I have not experienced since my research about the game began seven years earlier. Although both al-Ahly and al-Zamalek draw large crowds to the city's coffee shops, the national team's qualifiers for the 2018 World Cup in Russia are clearly the main events. Egypt has started the campaign in the best possible way, and when the team continues to win while its main rival, Ghana, drops points every so often, a victory against Congo is suddenly enough to achieve what even the legendary team under coach Hassan Shehata never managed to do. One more win, at Burg el-Arab Stadium outside Alexandria on 4 October 2017, is all Egypt needs to qualify for its first World Cup since 1990.

With the showdown drawing closer, reminders of its historic importance flood the public sphere. Egyptian football television broadcasts endless talk shows and news reports, some of them mixing pre-game analyses with iconic archival footage from the tournament in Italy twenty-eight years before. All of the country's mobile network providers, as well as the two soft-drink multinationals, run exclusive World Cup-themed advertisement campaigns on television, social media, and billboards. The commercials' exact words may differ, but the overall message is consistent. To reach the World Cup after almost three decades is the "dream of all Egyptians" (*hilm kull masriyiyn*), a once-in-a-lifetime opportunity for celebrations (*ihtifalat*) and happiness (*farha*) in an era dominated by struggles and suffering.[1]

Finally, the momentous day arrives. Tickets for the match at Burg el-Arab have sold out quickly, but my friend Bilal has a spare ticket that I am more than happy to buy. Bilal and I have not seen each other in four years before he and his friends pick me up at the railway station in Alexandria. The last time we had met, Bilal had been busy planning his wedding, and he often told me about the disastrous match in Khartoum, when Egypt failed to qualify for the 2010 World Cup and football lost parts of its magnetism (chapter 2). Now he has just moved back to Giza with his wife and three-year-old daughter after two lonely but profitable years as a migrant worker in Jeddah, Saudi Arabia. As fate has it and Bilal notes with excitement, we are going to the stadium together to watch Egypt play another decisive World Cup qualifying match.

On our way out of Alexandria, the magnitude of the event is impossible to overlook. The highway is crammed with honking cars, people in match shirts, and souvenir hawkers selling flags, scarves, and noisy plastic horns. When we arrive at the vast stadium complex five hours before the match, it is already packed with supporters dressed in red, white, and black. Bilal and I soon lose track of his friends in the crowds and cannot relocate them after mobile phone reception breaks down. But the two of us manage to keep track of each other across multiple gates and security checkpoints, and we find two seats with a good view in the arena's upper tier. The eighty-six-thousand-seat stadium fills up quickly. In our section, people are drinking tea and eating crisps and candy; we also catch the occasional whiff of hashish. Groups of young men are singing, playing drums, blowing horns, and dancing themselves sweaty under the scorching afternoon sun. After the sun finally sets, the volume of the stadium loudspeakers is turned up, and singer Dalida's melancholy classic "Hilwa ye baladi" (Oh my country is beautiful) is blasted out over the massive concrete stadium and the glowing desert surrounding it. When everyone stands up and starts to sing about Egypt's beauties, to which we all long to return, tears are rolling down both Bilal's and my cheeks.

Minutes later the game is underway. The first half ends goalless, but when the nation's darling, Mohamed Salah, breaks the deadlock with thirty minutes remaining, Egypt is cruising. The team controls the game completely; the fans are partying; the Congolese players look despondent. But qualifying for the World Cup after twenty-eight years is not meant to be that easy. In the eighty-seventh minute, Congo finds space on the right flank, crosses nicely, and Arnold Bouka Mouto slides home the equaliser. Silence and shock now reign in Burg el-Arab. Bilal and I cannot believe what we are witnessing. How on earth could Congo score? Why *now*, with so little time remaining? Is Egypt about to throw it all away *again*? In injury time, though, the home team musters a final push. Salah and the veteran goalkeeper Essam al-Hadary wave to the crowds, urging us to keep on believing, keep on cheering, and the noise level rises once more. In the ninety-third minute, a cross flies in from the right, but the Congolese defense clears it. Immediately, another cross comes in from the left, Egyptian striker Mahmoud Hassan Trézéguet gets a touch on the ball, a defender trips him, and the referee calls a penalty. During the fifty-five seconds it takes Salah to pick up the ball, kiss it, and place it on the penalty spot, I see people crying, laughing hysterically, and praying in the stands. Several fans in our section turn their backs to the field—they cannot bear to watch. A moment later, Congo's goalkeeper, guessing wrong, dives to his right while Salah steers the ball into the middle of the goal. Egypt has qualified for the World Cup, and the crowd's euphoria can finally be released. The pitch is flooded with elated supporters; players and coaches are raised to the sky. High above, Bilal and I hug and cry, sing, scream, and dance. Selfies are taken with strangers next to us. All of us want to stay in the moment as long as we can, but eventually we have to let go. On our way out through the gates, surrounded by honking horns, ululations, and red, white, and black, Bilal tells me: "We did it together, Carl. In those last minutes, the fans, Salah and the team did it together. Egyptian football has been a joke, but we're back now. Twenty-eight years. . . . It's a long time. Finally, we reached the World Cup."

The World Cup qualification gives Egyptian football a massive boost. With the biggest event of all coming up in Russia the following summer, an anticipatory buzz is building steadily throughout the winter and spring. The tournament draw in December 2017 constitutes one exciting step along the way. In the days before the ceremony, many media pundits and fans are not sure what to hope for. While facing one or two really big teams and star players in the group stage is a thrilling prospect, a less competitive group would make qualification easier. In the end, most supporters seem content to see Egypt drawn to face Uruguay, Saudi Arabia, and the hosts from Russia in what appears to be the tournament's weakest group. A cautious optimism prevails: proceeding to the second round should not be impossible. A few days after the draw, I meet my friend Mahmoud, the *Zamelkawi* gym instructor, who tells me: "Everything is possible in football. Everyone has a chance. And we have Mohamed Salah. Because of that, everything is even more possible for us."

Oh yes, Egypt does have Mohamed Salah. In fact, the Egyptians' hopes and dreams are rarely projected onto the national team as such. It is Salah who is supposed to do it, Salah who embodies the feeling that "everything is possible." After a trade from AS Roma to Liverpool FC in 2017, Salah performs on a level that few would have expected. Flourishing in the fast, counterattacking game of his German coach, Jürgen Klopp, he cannot stop scoring. When the season ends in May, Salah not only is the top scorer of the 2017–2018 Premier League, but with thirty-two goals he breaks the all-time scoring record and is awarded multiple prestigious prizes.[2] Moreover, largely due to Salah's brilliance, Liverpool progresses all the way to the final of the UEFA Champions League, outclassing Pep Guardiola's Manchester City and Salah's former club AS Roma en route. In short, there is no question at all about it: Egypt's Mohamed Salah has developed from a promising but somewhat fragile talent into one of the very best footballers on the planet.

Meanwhile, in Egypt, a Salah hype is growing. Images of the player's ever-smiling face are everywhere; his photo hangs on the walls of countless cafés; murals of him are painted in downtown Cairo; he is featured in advertisements for Pepsi, Adidas, and Uber, as well as in a much-discussed state-run campaign countering drug abuse among the Egyptian youth.[3] In spring 2018 I am watching as many Liverpool FC games as I can in *ahawi* in different parts of Cairo. There I talk to men, young and old, who have never followed international football, let alone the English Premier League, before, but who make sure to watch every minute that Salah is on the pitch. Many fans I meet like to discuss how the Egyptian compares to the game's brightest superstars. Does this twenty-five-year-old from a provincial town in the Gharbiyya Governorate even have a chance to be awarded the 2018 Ballon d'Or, the magazine *France Football*'s prestigious prize for the best player in the world, which for the last ten years has been monopolized by Cristiano Ronaldo and Lionel Messi?[4]

The successful representative on the international stage that Egypt has long been lacking, Mohamed Salah and his accomplishments in foreign

Fig. 9.1. Poster of Mohamed Salah outside a coffee shop in Abdeen, Cairo. Photo: Lena Malm, 4 May 2019.

lands are portrayed as a reflection on the nation as a whole. Even many academics, Islamists, and women—demographic groups, we remember, that are not supposed to care about football—watch him and discuss his games, and they share articles about their favorite player on Facebook and Twitter. These pieces about Salah's records and prizes, the way he shatters stereotypes about Islam in Europe, or how he gives the despondent Egyptians something to cherish, are often from foreign media. "He makes us all happy and he makes us proud," is a phrase that I hear over and over again. "Finally, the people here in Egypt have got someone who brings happiness and no problems," a journalist friend explains.

By mid-May 2018, everything is in place for a historic Egyptian football summer. The draw for the World Cup in June and July is favorable. Thousands of Egyptians have bought tickets to follow the team in Russia. And

Egypt has Mohamed Salah, the x-factor who makes anything possible. But things do not proceed according to plan. The game's inherent contingency—alluring for sure, but which no one, not even Mohamed Salah, can wield entirely as he wishes—interferes three weeks before the tournament has even begun. On the last Saturday in May, Liverpool FC faces the reigning champions, Real Madrid, in the UEFA Champions League final in Kiev, Ukraine. The match is both a contest for Europe's biggest club prize and a showdown between Mohamed Salah and Cristiano Ronaldo, the top scorers in the English Premier League and the Champions League, respectively. In the hours before kickoff, Cairo is boiling over with expectations. Virtually every Egyptian I know, no matter how invested in football, wants to see Salah prove, once and for all, that he belongs to the global game's ultimate elite.

It does not take long, though, before the evening turns into a national trauma. In the twenty-fifth minute, Salah is brought to the ground after a nasty challenge by Madrid's defender Sergio Ramos. The Egyptian lands awkwardly, hurts his shoulder, tries to play on, but is unable to continue. He disappears into the dressing room, his eyes full of tears. After the exit of Liverpool's best player, Real Madrid wins the match comfortably, but the result is secondary in shell-shocked Cairo. At the street-corner *ahwa* under two large trees in Abdeen where I watch the drama with Bilal and a few other friends, the initial reaction is frustration over a missed opportunity: for themselves to be happy, and for Mohamed Salah to show the world his potential. Later the same night, reports reach us that Salah's shoulder is dislocated and that he probably will be sidelined for three to four weeks. With Egypt's World Cup opener just twenty days away, it is worrying news indeed. "He is a fighter, of course he will make it," Bilal assures me as we walk toward the Metro station, but I can see that he has doubts. In fact, no one is sure. There is little else to do but speculate, pray, and count the days.

With the injury in Kiev, Egypt's World Cup campaign suffers an irreparable blow. Salah fights desperately to rehab his shoulder, but there is just not enough time; he is unable to play the opening match against Uruguay. Despite the superstar's absence, the Egyptian team performs surprisingly well. They eventually lose after an unfortunate late goal, but the mood is nonetheless positive after the final whistle. At the *ahwa* under the trees, I hear people speak about a team proving that they could put up a fight without Salah: a group of real men who, despite losing, has made the Egyptian people proud.

But any remaining optimism is crushed four days later, when a physically superior Russian team sweeps past Egypt by three goals to one in

Fig. 9.2. Meme posted on Kareem Mrghani's Facebook page, 25 June 2018. The text reads: "Miss it Salah . . . miss it."

Saint Petersburg. Salah plays the whole match and scores on a late penalty, but it is far from enough. Egypt is the first team to be eliminated from the World Cup; in a way, it feels as if the tournament ends before it even began. Among my friends, the disappointment after the elimination is tangible yet also contained. With Salah playing injured, the broken dream does not hurt as much. What really hurts, though, is the loss to Saudi Arabia in Egypt's third and final match. Both teams are already eliminated, but to see Egypt being beaten, and at times even outplayed, by an Arab rival in the World Cup is hard to take. At the *ahwa* under the trees, the mood is now angry, at times even scornful. "We are playing defense against *Saudi Arabia*," a young friend of mine notes in disbelief in the middle of the second half. "It is embarrassing. We are making a fool of ourselves and the whole world is watching." "It is better this way, it shows our real level," another man replies. "This is Egypt. The whole people are a failure." When Saudi Arabia scores the winning goal in the dying moments of the match, every single person in the coffee shop stands and gives the Egyptian team a round of spontaneous, sarcastic applause. Later that night, a sad meme circulates on Facebook. It pictures a time traveler from Christopher Nolan's 2014 film *Interstellar* who looks back at Salah's last-minute penalty against Congo from the future, desperately wishing him to miss it. The message is grim but well taken. No World Cup would have been preferable to *this* World Cup, because then the Egyptians would never have needed to hope and dream at all (see fig. 9.2).

A MOMENT OF AMBIVALENCE

For Egypt, the 2018 World Cup never becomes the forever-remembered event it has promised to be. As I complete this book in January 2021, there is little to indicate that the tournament in Russia will have any of the lasting effects on fandom, infrastructures, finance, and politics that ensued after Egypt's previous World Cup participation in Italy in 1990. Why does the long-anticipated competition come and go without fulfilling the dreams that Egyptian supporters have hoarded over twenty-eight long years? It is easy to blame bad fortune. Had only Salah not been injured. Had only Uruguay not scored that late goal. Had Egypt only had little bit more luck—*then* everything could certainly have been different. But the underwhelming display is not the whole story. In 1990 the results were not great either: the team scored only one goal in three matches and, like the 2018 team, was eliminated after the group stage. Nonetheless, the team that returned to Egypt from Italy did so with their heads high. Just making it to the World Cup after a fifty-six-year absence was enough to turn the players and the coach, Mahmoud al-Gohary, into national legends. The team's three matches are still talked about fondly, three decades later. The homecoming from Russia could not be more different. The team is ridiculed; no public celebrations are staged; Hector Cuper's contract is not renewed. Given how rarely people I meet in Cairo today speak of the 2018 World Cup, it is hard to imagine fans recalling details about the matches in Russia in years, let alone decades, to come.

But if it is not bad luck and poor results, then what is it that does spoil the party? To approach an answer, it is useful to spotlight a profound *ambivalence* that many Egyptian supporters express before and during the World Cup, and which resurfaces as Egypt hosts the Africa Cup of Nations in the summer of 2019. Throughout this period, a deep hesitance is always tangible. On the one hand, something qualitatively new is in the air.

Friends of mine talk and care about the national team and Mohamed Salah to an extent and with an intensity that have not been present for many years. On the other hand, the national team is routinely doubted and met with sarcasm. Even in the hours following Salah's last-minute goal against Congo at Burg el-Arab—ostensibly Egypt's biggest football achievement in a decade—the celebrations I witness come with a caveat. In the car back to Cairo, Bilal and his friends scold Hector Cuper's defensive tactics and laugh at how pathetically slow the Egyptians played in midfield. Later the same night, friends of mine post statements on Facebook that describe the team as "embarrassing," "dull," and "utterly boring" despite having qualified for the World Cup.

In the buildup to the tournament in Russia, opinions such as these are tremendously common. Hector Cuper's national team might be well-organized and solid on defense, but that in itself is not enough to achieve anything, let alone to make the Egyptian people happy. Egypt's friendly game against Belgium, less than two weeks before the World Cup is set to begin, provides a telling snapshot of the prevailing and somewhat schizophrenic mood. At the coffee shop under the leafy trees in Abdeen, people are laughing sarcastically as the Egyptian players—without the injured Salah—fail over and over again to play out of the Belgians' high pressing. A couple of men next to me argue that it is futile to travel to the World Cup with a team as utterly poor as this. When I try to point out that Egypt is defending really well against a team full of global superstars, an older acquaintance rebukes me: "Should we play the World Cup just to defend [*hinil'ab kas al-'alam 'ashan nidafi'*]? No, no, no, mister, if we play like this, there is no point!"

Then the World Cup comes and goes, but the ambivalence remains. Among my closest friends, the defeats in Russia prompt mixed reactions: bitter disappointment, raging anger, black humor, and despondent claims that "it's better this way; it shows our true colors" (see Eskander, 2018). The atmosphere is similar during the Africa Cup of Nations in June and July 2019, another underwhelming tournament in which the Egyptian hosts are eliminated in the round of sixteen. Following the shocking exit after a 1-0 loss to South Africa at Cairo Stadium, the Mexican coach Javier Aguirre is sacked, the board of the EFA resigns, and the team is criticized as lacking the necessary fighting spirit. Yet the resentment is triggered by more than the early elimination. Even during the group stage, when Egypt plays decent football and wins all three games without conceding a single goal, many fans reproach the players. Wherever I go, people tell me that the team is a national shame and that it is embarrassing to see an international star like Salah forced to play with such a mediocre group of "local" (*mahalli*) players. It is as though performances and results do not really matter; the notion that the national team plays poor football has been repeated to the point that it has become the conventional wisdom.

I am not alone in finding the atmosphere odd. On 3 July, shortly after the end of the first round, the television pundit Ahmed Shoubair spends a significant section of his daily talk show, now on the new sports channel ON Sports, questioning what he calls a "case of anger" (*halit ghadab*) in the population that "doesn't make any sense." Perplexed and visibly annoyed, he urges his viewers to stop complaining and to take the team's satisfactory performances and objectively good results into consideration. "If it were a case of general dissatisfaction [*'adm rida*], I would understand it and agree," Shoubair states at one point of his monologue. "None of us is completely happy with the way the team plays. But why this anger [*ghadab leh*]? You have to try to measure your feelings!"

HAUNTED BY THE PAST, HAUNTED BY *SIYASA*

Ahmed Shoubair's confusion summons a reflective pause. Why are the Egyptians so angry at their national team, despite Mohamed Salah's brilliance and the best results in a decade? To resolve this paradox, let us turn back to the words of Mahmoud—the gym instructor, *Zamelkawi*, father of two, and pious Muslim—featured in the opening pages of this book. This, we recall, is what my friend tells me in October 2017, a few days after Egypt qualifies for the World Cup:

> Of course, I'm happy that we reached the World Cup. Finally, after all these failures! It's something that makes us all happy. It's good. There are so many problems in Egypt. But to be honest, no one really likes this team. Salah is great of course, amazing, but Cuper . . . The team plays defensively. Boring football. Not like the team of Hassan Shehata. And then . . . There's also a risk. I mean, if people start loving football again, they might forget our real problems. The regime would like to utilize it politically. Like Mubarak, when that ferry sank, remember? Football can be dangerous, Carl. This people loves football very much.

Let us also listen to Muhammad, Abdu's younger brother. By the World Cup summer, the shy teenager I got to know during late-night matches on

Abdeen's *al-midan* has become an outspoken twenty-four-year-old working for a multinational construction company. His take on the tournament a week before it starts is this:

> I'll support Egypt and Salah in Russia, of course, but to be honest, I won't be sad if we lose. Just look at television. All those pundit bastards [*al-kabatin awlad al-wiskha dul*], they want us to win to make us all crazy and to shore up support for the system [*al-nizam*]. Just like in the past. We know how this works. It can be really bad. But people don't buy it, *alhamdulillah*.

Finally, these are the words of Bassam—the digital marketer and blogger we met in chapter 6—the night when Egypt loses to South Africa and crashes out of the 2019 Africa Cup of Nations:

> The love for a national team cannot be taken for granted. No entity in the world wins the support, fanaticism, and enthusiasm of its people if it isn't consistent [*muttasiq*] with some things that you are persuaded by. [. . .] Support comes from the heart; if the heart is closed, it's closed [. . .] To be honest, I found myself in a state of disinterest [*halit 'adam ihitimam*]. [. . .] I have no connection to this arrogant [*muta'agrif*] national team.

These three remarks elucidate how Egypt's recent football renaissance is haunted by memories of the past. Bygone eras cast shadows both on Egypt's participation in the 2018 World Cup and on the 2019 Africa Cup of Nations, shadows that are difficult to shrug off and illustrate the era's distinctive ambivalence. On the one hand, the problem is an irksome feeling that *this* generation of players does not deserve its historic achievements, and that the "wrong" national team has made it to the World Cup. Many fans cannot help comparing the current squad to the iconic one representing the country in the late 2000s. Hassan Shehata's team consisted of a homegrown and charismatic group of players, born and raised in al-Ahly and al-Zamalek, who won three straight Africa Cups, played a free-flowing, attractive style of football, but failed just as it was set to reach the really big stage. By contrast, most players on the national team today play for decent yet unremarkable European clubs. With the exception of Salah, the players in Russia are little known and difficult to take to one's heart.

On the other hand, the ambivalence is engendered by a haunting specter of vulgarity, immorality, and destructive, self-serving *siyasa*. Too much football and too many good results, my friends fear, risk reinvigorating the pre-2011 bubble of sports, media, celebrities, and political foul play that the revolution thankfully managed to undo. These latent anxieties surface with full force as soon as Egypt exits the World Cup. In the wake of the setback, Egyptian social media are filled with inflammatory stories on such themes as the EFA's opaque decision to locate the team's base camp in Grozny, Chechnya, a site necessitating long and tiring domestic flights to all three matches; board members flying business class while the players squeeze into the economy cabin; and celebrities being allowed into the team's hotel rooms, where they keep the players awake until the early morning hours (see, for example, Gamal, 2018). After the Africa Cup of Nations fiasco the next summer, similar debates rage about personal interests being prioritized over the team effort and national, common good, and EFA board members exerting a baleful influence on the media (e.g., *al-Shuruq*, 7 July 2019). The most sensational story, however, is a sexual harassment scandal centered around the team's offensive midfielder Amr Warda. Warda has already gained a reputation as a womanizer, but when he spends an evening during the Africa Cup sending offensive invitations and intimate selfies to an Instagram model who then calls him out publicly, his questionable behavior is seen as a reflection on the national team as a whole. A couple of days later, the EFA expels Warda from the team, only to reverse its decision after pressure from some senior players. The scandal in general and the reversal of the decision to expel Warda in particular prove a disaster for the national team's reputation. Many fans are extremely upset that players on the national team allow personal friendship to overrule morals, good manners, and the image of Egypt on the world stage. The general opinion is that everyone involved, from the players to the leaders to the board of the Football Association, are hopelessly immoral and far beyond salvation.

An alternative way to grasp how memories of a national game contaminated by *siyasa* continue to cause unease is to consider the ambivalent moment's flipside: the unreserved adoration that virtually all Egyptians express for Mohamad Salah. Being the most successful player in Egyptian football history is of course central to Salah's appeal. But a unique air of nonpartisan purity plays a role too. It is worth noting that Salah is one of very few Egyptian football stars who have neither represented al-Ahly nor al-Zamalek. Leaving Egypt as a teenager, shortly after the February 2012 Port Said massacre, he has always stood outside this defining rivalry running through the country's football institutions and fan communities. Moreover, Salah has made his career in a professional universe that is vastly distant from the Egyptian game's idiosyncrasies. Coming of age in Switzerland, Italy, and England, he has never operated in, nor depended on, the orbit of tabloid television, scandals, celebrities, and political intrigues that typify Egypt's domestic game. Salah instead shares the same shiny media sphere as Lionel Messi and Cristiano Ronaldo, an international realm that will always be untroubled by Egyptian *siyasa* (see chapter 7). Consequently, he remains incredibly likeable, even when feelings for the rest of the Egyptian national team are ambivalent at best.[5]

In the summer of 2018, Salah's status as an untouchable outsider sets off a couple of acrimonious disputes between the Egyptian football establishment and the country's best player. First, the EFA unilaterally decides to use a huge photo of Salah on the national team's World Cup airplane sponsored by a state-owned mobile phone provider, disregarding that Salah already has signed a sponsorship deal with a competing company (Maher, 2018; Omar, 2018). Second, two months after the tournament, Salah posts a series of videos on his Facebook page to criticize the EFA for its "unprofessional" World Cup preparations and draw attention to multiple instances of mismanagement that undermined the team in Russia.[6] In both cases, the EFA—predictably supported by its allied television pundits—call Salah selfish and greedy and insinuate that he is tarnishing the image of Egypt (e.g., Tawfeek, 2018). Several talking heads find themselves forced to backtrack, however, as it becomes clear that Salah enjoys massive support among the population.[7] Indeed, even when Chechen strongman Ramzan Kadyrov awards Salah honorary citizenship during the pretournament training camp in Grozny, his pristine image remains intact. While hobnobbing with a former warlord accused of human rights abuses raises questions in many international media outlets (e.g., Longman, 2018), few Egyptian fans waver in their support. Indeed, Salah's aura shows no signs of cracking until he publicly sides with Amr Warda and forces the EFA to reinstate the ostracized player in the middle of the 2019 Africa Cup of Nations. The way Salah negotiates with the EFA to protect a teammate charged with sexual harassment is not just perceived as a poor reflection on his morals. The episode also pulls him into a troublesome and distinctively Egyptian football world of scandals, intrigues, and *siyasa* that many fans have hoped he could remain high above (see Zidani, 2019).

The specter of *siyasa* also has a direct impact on how Egypt's political leadership relates to the resurging national sport's institutions, players, and passions. Indeed, the emotional politics of football in Abdel Fattah el-Sisi's Egypt is very different from what it was under Hosni Mubarak.

After the World Cup qualification in October 2017, President el-Sisi initially follows the script of his predecessor, inviting players and coaches to celebrations at his palace and awarding the team hefty bonuses. As these "political" gestures unleash a wave of public criticism, however, the regime soon begins to backtrack (see *Egypt Independent*, 10 October 2017; *Ahram Online*, 10 October 2017). This trend continues in the months that follow. Friends of mine repeatedly assure me that the regime will do all it can to promote the World Cup in a way that allows it to bask in the sport's limelight, but in all fairness, that does not really happen. By contrast, I find it striking how *little* the nation's leading political figures engage with Egypt's first World Cup campaign in twenty-eight years. The 2019 Africa Cup of Nations is not much different. Several interlocutors contrast the lackluster atmosphere during the Cup to the last time Egypt hosted the tournament. In 2006, they say, the stadiums were full, everyone talked about the matches, football was ever-present in the media, and the presidential family was in the thick of it all. In 2019, the stadiums are surprisingly silent, even when Egypt is playing. Tickets that are too expensive and a complex online sales system turn the matches into upper-middle-class family events. Real Egyptian football fans with real passions, I am told, are excluded and do not bother to show up.

Now, while some commentators portrayed this conspicuous absence of national unity as a "failure" of the regime to "manage" the unique opportunities that the World Cup and African championships provide (e.g., Springborg, 2018), I would propose an alternative reading. The Sisi regime might exploit the Africa Cup of Nations in the only way it can. Does not the middle-class cleanliness found at the stadium represent precisely the kind of aesthetics and demographics that the Egyptian counterrevolution has always promoted and cared for? (Winegar, 2016). Furthermore, to the extent that the military regime can be said to rely on an affective modality of rule, it is more centered on launching grand investment projects than fostering a sense of togetherness among and with the people (Rommel, 2019). The tournament in 2019 in particular provides ample opportunities for such "stagecraft" (Ahlberg, 2017). After taking over the organization of the Cup from Cameroon in November 2018, the Egyptian armed forces spend imposing amounts of money and manpower renovating stadiums, setting up the online ticketing system, and organizing a fancy opening ceremony in record time. These impressive efforts—"Egypt presenting itself for its brothers in Africa," as President el-Sisi calls it[8]—are all meticulously documented in the media and depicted as an unprecedented feat by a rising nation.[9]

Other kinds of football politics are much harder to put in motion. As demonstrated throughout this book, developments over the last thirty years have made Egyptian football fans tremendously sensitive to any sign of political exploitation (*istighlal siyasi*). Most supporters surely wish their teams and players well, but not if it comes at the cost of a return to the detested old days when intrigue, emotional manipulation, and deceit spoiled the nation's favorite pastime. This sensitivity vis-à-vis the *siyasa* of yesteryear engenders a measure of vigilance among Egypt's once passionate football fans. A heightened watchfulness about political interference is always present, and this alertness effectively preempts whatever manipulative intentions the government might have. In this sense, the football bubble, combined with the revolution that cracked it open, can be likened to a vaccination. Years of debates and worries about football's entanglement in *siyasa* have, at least for the time being, rendered the Egyptian game curiously immune to the particular variety of emotional sports politics that was the norm a decade ago.[10]

This immunization to political exploitation reestablishes the inherently dialectical argument at the core of this book. What I have analyzed as the emotional politics of Egyptian football has not just shaped how *siyasa* is talked about and experienced by Egyptian fans. The ways in which *siyasa* is felt and debated are also essential to the sport's emotional-political prowess. One intriguing aspect of the idiosyncratic bubble that football brought together at the end of President Mubarak's reign was always that although the regime overtly manipulated the game to boost its popularity, most fans still saw the sport as a nonpolitical sphere of untainted, all-nationalist joy. When contrasted to the situation that we witness in Egypt today, there is no doubt that this earlier sense of football as nonpolitical and unproblematic buttressed the sport's inflated emotionality and the important political function that it evidently performed. Just like in other Middle Eastern contexts, then, where football has been actively "de-politicized" (Yildirim, 2017) or carefully severed from threatening "political symbolism" (Sorek, 2007) to advance what could only be called concrete *political* aims, contemporary Egyptian football history highlights the paradoxical imperative of staying nonpolitical for any political project built inside the realm of sports (see also Yurchak, 2008). In a setting such as Egypt, where the nationalist frame is axiomatic and *siyasa* widely despised, a demarcation from whatever people take to be political is necessary for the game to thrive affectively. Such a thriving, in turn, is a requirement for any exercise of power in and through emotions and affect.

Precisely this insight also illuminates why it is apposite to talk about Egypt's pre-2011 football boom as a bubble. Like all bubbles, the football craze that captured the nation eventually burst. As the past was reevaluated between 2009 and 2012, the hype deflated at pace and a comprehensive football revolution was unleashed. But the story does not end there. In the years that have followed since the 2013 military coup, it has proved impossible to reignite full-blown passion for football, despite improving infrastructure, stadiums, media coverage, and eventually even results on the field. The Egyptians are still too aware that football can be dangerous and destructive. A sense of embarrassment for past feelings is certainly present too. As a consequence, there is no obvious way to turn back time and reemotionalize the Egyptian football nation. When bubbles burst, their debris tends to be badly scattered. What is left is rarely easy to stitch together, let alone to reinflate.

NOTES

Introduction

1. After the third historic victory in 2010, Egypt failed to even qualify for three African Championships in 2012, 2013, and 2015; the team dropped from tenth in the world rankings in 2010 to seventy-fifth in 2013.

2. To guarantee anonymity, I have changed the names of all interlocutors. I have retained the original names of public figures, such as journalists, whom I have interviewed.

3. The club's nationalist roots are reflected in its name. *Al-nadi al-ahli* is often translated as "the national club," although as Hassan al-Mistakawi notes (1997:44), this translation is somewhat misleading. The most common translation of "national" in Arabic is not *ahli* but *watani* or *qawmi*. As the noun *ahl* refers to people, family, and kinsfolk, "the domestic club" or "the people's club" are arguably more appropriate translations.

4. Beginning in 1958, the EFA was presided over by Field Marshal Abdel Hakim Amer, the army's second in command and for a time Nasser's vice president. The field marshal's brother, Hassan Amer, was the president of Egypt's second biggest club, al-Zamalek, between 1962 and 1967. Many Egyptian star players were also formally hired by the Armed Forces (Tawfiq, 2010:59–68; Thabet, 2010:88–100).

5. For a succinct English-language summary of Egyptian football history up until the mid-twentieth century, see Gibril, 2018:347–352.

6. Elsewhere, football has expedited the formation of (male) national identity (e.g., Archetti, 1999; Creak, 2015; Goldblatt, 2014), cross-ethnic unity (Walker, 2013), transregional national belongings (Guinness and Besnier, 2016), nationwide grass-roots institutions (Elsey, 2012; Woroniecka-Krzyzanowska, 2020), and fascist mobilization (Kassimeris, 2012; Martin, 2004; see also De Waele et al., 2018; Goldblatt, 2006).

7. For examples of such polarizing tendencies in other Middle Eastern contexts, see Ben Porat, 2001, 2014; Rommel, 2011; Sorek, 2003, 2007; Tuastad, 1997; Woroniecka-Krzyzanowska, 2020.

8. As described in chapter 7, this has begun to change in the last decade. Compared to the globally oriented fan attachments that prevail in other parts of Africa (Akindes, 2011; Fletcher, 2010), however, Egyptian clubs stay very strong indeed.

9. As of January 2021, al-Ahly has won thirty-seven and al-Zamalek twenty-seven Egyptian Cups; no other club in the country has more than six titles. As for the league, al-Ahly has forty-two titles compared to al-Zamalek's twelve. On only seven occasions has the Egyptian first division been won by any other football club.

10. Al-Ahly was from its founding in 1907 a club exclusively for Egyptian members—that is, explicitly *not* for the country's European elites—and several prominent nationalist politicians served as board members during the formative years (al-Mistakawi, 1997:16–32; Jacob, 2011:84–89). On the contrary, al-Zamalek Club's legacy will always be burdened by the fact that it was founded on the initiative of non-Egyptians in 1911. Originally named Qasr al-Nil, the club's name soon changed to al-Mukhtalat (the mixed), denoting both its "mixed" nationality members and its links to Cairo's Mixed Courts, a part of Egypt's colonial judiciary

that passed judgments in disputes between Egyptians and foreign nationals, or between foreigners of different nationalities. Furthermore, whereas al-Zamalek was called King Faruq Club between 1941 and 1952, indicating its allegiance to the flamboyant, British-leaning monarch (al-Mistakawi, 1997:158–159; see also Tahir, 2010:57–71), al-Ahly kept a strict nationalist and anti-imperial profile throughout the 1930s and 1940s (al-Mistakawi, 1997:65, 68, 144–150, 184–186).

11. My *Zamelkawiyya* friends might have a point. As Suzan Gibril has argued, al-Ahly was clearly the team of the people and al-Zamalek the club of the bourgeoisie, foreigners, and royalists in the first half of the twentieth century. After the 1952 coup and President Nasser becoming the honorary president of al-Ahly Club in 1956, however, al-Ahly has increasingly gravitated toward the political establishment (Gibril, 2018:352–356).

12. Challenging a body of scholarship from the 1990s and early 2000s that had depicted the nation as outdated and irrelevant, Abu-Lughod suggested that "'the nation' continues to be a powerful concept . . . [and] the primary context, at least in Egypt, for the everyday lives of most of the people who produce media and constitute their audiences" (Abu-Lughod, 2005:26–27).

13. This scholarship draws inspiration from Victor Turner's famous analysis of the ritual process (Turner, 1969). See also van Gennep, 1960.

14. The subversive potential of carnival was originally examined by Bakhtin, 1968.

15. The power of appropriately structured football affect is a kind of hegemony targeting prediscursive registers, embodiment, and intuition. It contributes to what Laurent Berlant calls collectively shared "bundles of experiences" that provide an underlying keynote of the reigning "historical present" (Berlant, 2011:51–93). For a book-length exploration of counterrevolutionary affect in President el-Sisi's Egypt, see Malmström, 2019.

16. My documentation of the Ultras adds to previous ethnographic research on reconstituted subjectivities after January 2011, e.g., Samuli Schielke scrutinizing self-identifying "revolutionaries" (2015), Amira Mittermaier contemplating augmented ethical-religious subjectivities (2014), Jessica Winegar analyzing a reactionary turn to respectability and cleanliness (2016), and Walter Armbrust exploring counterrevolutionary "tricksters" (2019:181–238).

17. See, for example, Blackman, 2012; Leys, 2011; Lutz, 2017; Navaro-Yashin, 2009, 2012; Stewart, 2017.

18. Max Weber's definition of power as the ability to exercise one's will despite the resistance of actors with opposing interests was presented in *Wirtschaft und Gesellschaft*, 2005 [1922]. Carl Schmitt outlined his famous arguments about the political as a realm of public contestations between friends and enemies in *Der Begriff des Politischen*, 2015 [1932].

19. The masculine adjective *siyasi* takes the feminine form *siyasiyya* and plural *siyasiyyin/siyasiyyat* (masculine/feminine). For simplicity, I translate "political" as *siyasi* throughout this text regardless of gender and numerus. When a whole phrase is translated, I use the appropriate form.

20. The launch of the Egyptian League in autumn 1948 in particular constituted a timely intervention to divert attentions from the disastrous military campaign that a few months earlier had confirmed the creation of the state of Israel (Tawfiq, 2010:55).

21. In the 1960s, Egyptian football media expanded, passions for the national

team were revitalized, and invitation matches against European and South American clubs brought some of the world's biggest stars to Cairo (Erlich, 1989:181; al-Mistakawi, 1997:165–170). Tensions between al-Ahly and al-Zamalek also reached unprecedented levels, resulting in violence and vandalism at derby games, which according to Hassan al-Mistakawi were played in a "fearful atmosphere, as if the two teams were to rush into a war battle [ma'arkatan harbiyyatan]" (1997:165; see also Tawfiq, 2010:64; Di-Capua, 2004).

22. The way in which I subsume ethnographic debates about siyasa into my own analytical notion of politics arguably risks "trump[ing] and discard[ing]" my interlocutors' interpretation of what politics is and does (Candea, 2011:311). I am convinced that this is a risk worth taking, yet it necessitates awareness and specificity about two different levels of abstraction: on the one hand, my ethnographic examination of discourses and practices, which renders some entities and individuals *political* and others *nonpolitical*; on the other hand, my analysis of these processes' *emotional-political* effects in light of my own, likewise partial, definition. Structurally, my argument parallels Alexei Yurchak's ethnography of the explicitly antipolitical Necro-realists in 1980s Leningrad, a movement which, in Yurchak's analysis, played a critical political role precisely because of their positioning outside conventional political discourses (Yurchak, 2008).

23. Elections for the two chambers of parliament were held between November 2011 and February 2012. A new president was elected over two rounds in May and June 2012.

24. The referenda were held in March 2011 and December 2012. Two more followed in January 2014 and April 2019.

25. There are striking parallels between the football crises unfolding after the 1967 war and the 2011 Revolution. On both occasions, a boom was replaced by apathy and disengagement, the national game's sociopolitical function was questioned, domestic football activities were suspended, and international results were poor (Erlich, 1989:191–192; al-Mistakawi, 1997:127–128). Several older interlocutors made me aware of this analogy.

26. Lucie Ryzova (2020) and Walter Armbrust (2019) have used the concept of "liminality" to analyze the same inherent volatility and unpredictability. Armbrust's book constitutes the most comprehensive ethnographic account to date of processes and events between January 2011 and August 2013. A recent effort to bring "the study of revolutions [. . .] into a distinctively anthropological terrain [focusing] on quintessential anthropological themes such as ritual, cosmology and personhood" is found in Cherstich, Holbraad, and Tassi, 2020.

27. For a sample of feature stories about the Port Said tragedy and its politicized aftermath in some of the world's biggest newspapers, see Kirkpatrick and Fahim, 2013; Michaelson, 2018; Montague, 2012; Thumann, 2013.

28. Follow-up fieldwork was conducted in December 2015, October 2016, October to December 2017, March to June 2018, and January to July 2019. Even during periods when I have not been physically present in Cairo, I have followed "the field" closely via Egyptian sports media and social media channels.

29. My attempt to uncover genealogies to make sense of the emergence of contemporary conditions is also similar to what Michel Foucault called a "history of the present" (1977, 1997).

30. As mentioned, fans have been banned from domestic football games in Egypt

since the Port Said tragedy in February 2012. My stadium visits were hence most frequent between September 2011 and January 2012. In recent years, I have attended a handful of international games, most often at Burg el-Arab Stadium.

31. The media sources used include daily newspapers such as *al-Shuruq* and *al-Misri al-Yum*, the weekly sports magazine *al-Ahram al-Riyadi*, the public sports radio channel al-Shabab wi al-Riyada, matches and talk shows on football television channels (Modern, Al-Jazeera Sports, BeIN SPORTS, ON Sports, and Abu Dhabi Sports), and the websites FilGoal.com and Yallakora.com.

32. The three books that I draw on most frequently are Muhammad Gamal Bashir's *Kitab al-ultras* (2011), Muhammad Tawfiq's *Masr bitil'ab* (2010), and Yasser Thabet's *Hurub kurit al-qaddam* (2010). More sporadically, I also use Tahir, 2010; Thabet, 2013; Abdel Shafi, 2010; and al-Mistakawi, 1997.

33. Walter Armbrust notes in reference to the study of another cornerstone of Egyptian popular culture—films—that an anthropologist needs an "orientalist" knowledge of names, dates, and narratives in order "to approach anything remotely like a 'native' ability to understand how Egyptians deploy their common stock of imagery and personalities" (Armbrust, 1996:6). My "orientalist" knowledge about Egypt football was admittedly limited as I began this project; even today, I have only mastered parts of the "enormous corpus of works with which [my interlocutors] grew up" (ibid.). Yet a decade of regular football media consumption has brought me significantly closer to such mastery.

34. Roughly half of my interviews have been recorded. While I have always recorded conversations with football journalists, bureaucrats, and club officials, many supporters did not feel comfortable having our talks taped. In particular, it has not been possible to record interviews with Cairo's notoriously media-skeptical Ultras fans. My accounts of these meetings are based on written notes and voice memos recorded immediately after the interviews ended. About 70 percent of my interviews and almost all casual conversations with interlocutors were conducted in Arabic. A handful of interviews with well-educated football journalists took place in English.

35. Most importantly Bashir, 2011 and Thabet, 2013.

36. One female friend even told me that she avoids going out in public during big football matches. Large congregations of men, she claimed, aggravate Egypt's perpetual problem of sexual harassment.

37. Previous research on football masculinity has typically spotlighted aggressiveness and violence (Marsh, 1978; Smith, 2000) or men using the game to break free from obligations and conventions (Hughson, 2000; King, 1997; but see also Archetti, 1999). Similar foci have dominated the scholarship on Middle Eastern masculinity, where hypermasculine settings, such as the army (Haugbolle, 2012; Kaplan, 2000; Sinclair-Webb, 2000), the *hammam* (Farhi, 2000) or circumcision rituals (Bouhdiba and Khal, 2000) have been given ample attention (but see Hughes, 2017; Inhorn, 2012; Rommel, 2018a and 2018b; for a critique of this scholarship, see Amar, 2011a). Highlighting how the emotionality of sports imbues contestations over the Egyptian nation's male character, my research approaches masculinity from a different angle. My analyses of affect that sometimes reinforces and at other times destabilizes hegemonic-national masculinities have more in common with recent gender studies research on "political masculinities" (see Starck and Luyt, 2019) and studies that, while interrogating the intersection of masculinity and emotions/affect, move beyond clichés about unemotional,

cold, and angry men (see Gottzén and Reeser, 2017; Reeser and Gottzén, 2018).
38. A different version of this chapter has been published in *Critical African Studies* (Rommel, 2014).
39. See, for example, Bashir, 2011; Close, 2019; Dorsey, 2016; Gibril, 2015; Ibraheem, 2015; Thabet, 2013.
40. A smaller section of this chapter was included in an earlier publication in *Middle East—Topics and Arguments* (Rommel, 2016).

Chapter 1. Normal Nationals and Vulgar Winners

1. A similar depiction of Mubarak's Egypt as curiously inward-looking is found in Jack Shenker's book *The Egyptians: A Radical Story* (2016:109–120).
2. Before 1993, when the national team player, Rada Abdel 'Al, moved from al-Zamalek to al-Ahly for the staggering sum of 650,000 EGP, no Egyptian transfer had exceeded 100,000 EGP. A decade later, during the summer transfer window of 2005, the amount of money circulating among the clubs in the league had long since dwarfed the Abdel 'Al deal, reaching almost 80 million pounds (Tawfiq, 2010:163). As for salaries, an EFA employee told me in an interview that in the last season before 2011, the average contract for a player in the Egyptian Premier League was worth 120,000 USD per annum. The greatest stars made more than a million dollars.
3. The last major upset in the Egyptian Premier League is al-Ismaily's title in 2002. Since then, al-Ahly and al-Zamalek have not let a single league title slip away. Al-Mansoura had a surprising and still famous run to the Egyptian Cup final in 1996. The team, full of talented youngsters, eventually lost the final to al-Ahly.
4. In contrast to football in Europe, where the value of broadcasting rights began to spiral in the early 1990s, private football television did not turn into a lucrative business in Egypt before the first decade of the new millennium.
5. Among people I have talked to, the former al-Zamalek board member Abdel Khaliq Yusif pointed to the yearly membership fees from more than fifty thousand members as the club's main source of income. Tarek Mourad at *al-Masa'* suggested that a significant portion of al-Zamalek's revenues stems from a string of shops that the club owns and rents out on the outside of the club premises in the upmarket Cairo district al-Muhandisin.
6. Since the implementation of professionalism, al-Ahly has won the league twenty times in comparison to al-Zamalek's six titles. Since 2004 the dominance is even more striking: thirteen titles for al-Ahly and only one for al-Zamalek.
7. In contrast to its main rivals, al-Ahly has not had a businessman president since President Gamal Abdel Nasser forced the monarchic millionaire Ahmed 'Abbud Pasha to resign in 1961 (Di-Capua, 2004:148).
8. Company clubs have constituted an intrinsic part of Egypt's football scene since the early twentieth century. Indeed, Egypt's oldest football club, al-Sikka al-Hadid, established in 1903, belongs to the national railway company.
9. The most successful company club in the 1970s and 1980s was al-Muqawilun al-Arab, a state-owned construction company founded by the engineer, entrepreneur, and politician Osman Ahmed Osman. Al-Muqawilun won the Egyptian League in 1983 and three Egyptian Cups in the 1990s and 2000s. The club has also won the Africa Cup Winners' Cup three times.
10. Currently the Ministry of Youth and Sports.

11. Since state-owned companies and government offices are loath to allow access to budget details, it is impossible to tell exactly how much the state spent on football teams. Considering the player wages that company clubs had to offer to stay competitive, even as their lack of supporters left them deprived of most external sources of income, sports journalists I met estimated the expenses to be in the range of tens of millions EGP every year for each club. In the same period, the government also channeled vast resources into the building and refurbishment of stadiums in preparation for Egypt's hosting the 2006 Africa Cup of Nations and the 2009 Under-20 World Cup.

12. The differences in state involvement were most significant in comparison to sub-Saharan Africa. The situation in the Maghreb was in many ways similar to the Egyptian case (Amara, 2012; Boum, 2013).

13. The construction of new football stadiums followed this pattern too. Whereas the army built two stadiums in Cairo and Alexandria for the 2009 Under-20 World Cup, Petro Sport Stadium outside Cairo, inaugurated in 2006, was financed by the government's oil and gas industries.

14. Daily sports pages first appeared in Egyptian newspapers in the 1920s (Lopez, 2009). Radio began to broadcast football games in 1934 and television followed suit in 1960 (al-Mistakawi, 1997:179). Dedicated sports magazines, such as the weekly *al-Ahram al-Riyadi*, first appeared in the early 1990s.

15. The broadcasting rights for this season were never sold. Following the outbreak of the revolution, the negotiations were postponed several times. After the Port Said stadium massacre in February 2012, the season was canceled.

16. Significantly, the Egyptian player with the most prolific international career in the 2000s, Ahmed Hossam "Mido," never played a prominent part on the record-breaking national team.

17. Amro Hassan brought this up as one example of late–Mubarak Egypt being a self-contained "bubble."

18. Retrospectively, many interlocutors have drawn parallels between the communal elation that followed these victories and the popular uprisings that swept Egypt in January 2011. Chapter 6 analyzes some implications of these affective similarities.

19. It is intriguing to compare these 1980s football films with prevailing notions of the pre-1990 game as pure and ethically sound. Judging from the portrayal of players, coaches, and managements as greedy, corrupt and scandalous, it is questionable how well today's perceptions of the 1980s as a moral paradise concur with opinions held during the epoch itself. Two other famous movies that in different ways depict football as a primarily joyful force for the good are Muhammad Abd el-'Aziz' *Rajul faqad 'aqluh* (A Man Who Lost His Mind, 1980) and Muhammad Khan's *Al-Harrif* (The Skillful, 1983).

20. For a detailed analysis of the film's wider function in the Egyptian state's battle against Islamists in the 1990s, see Armbrust, 2002a.

21. Some examples are *Ana mish ma'hum* (I Am Not with Them, Ahmed al-Badri, 2007), *al-Zamahlawiyya* (Ashraf Fayiq, 2008), and *Wahid Sifr* (One Zero, Kamla Abu Zakri, 2009).

22. Armbrust's usage of "vulgarity" is analytical rather than ethnographic. His interlocutors do not necessarily use the Arabic equivalents *suqiyya* or *bagaha*, but the concept allows him to identify certain patterns in his material. I will use the

notion in a similar analytic manner, as a means of highlighting characteristics of the Egyptian football boom.

23. E.g., *678* (Mohamed Diab, 2010), *Fibrayir al-aswid* (Black February, Mohamed Amin, 2013), and *Akhir ayam al-madina* (In the last days of the city, Tamer El Said, 2016).

24. Egypt's best and most popular player, Muhammad Abu Treika, constituted an important exception (see chapter 4).

Chapter 2. Fanatical Politics and Resurging Respectability

1. The almost identical match in November 1989, when Egypt had last claimed a spot in the World Cup, constituted the most famous precursor. On that occasion, Algeria had also visited Cairo for a decisive group match, and the game had been surrounded by clashes and troubles. Other famously disorderly matches between the two countries were two World Cup qualifiers in 2001 and a game in Blida, Algeria, in summer 2009 when the Egyptian team allegedly was poisoned in their hotel in the hours before a match in the same qualification group (*al-Shuruq*, 14, 18 November 2009; Thabet, 2010:119–123; Montague, 2009; Oliver, 2009).

2. During the June 2009 Confederations Cup, FIFA's pre-World Cup tournament in South Africa, Egypt beat the reigning World Champions, Italy, and lost narrowly to Brazil in a highly entertaining game. Although the team was eliminated after a disappointing 3–0 loss to the United States, the tournament was generally taken as proof that the Egyptian team was able to compete with the game's global elite. Today, the two matches against Italy and Brazil play central roles in the narration of Egypt's great football successes in the late 2000s.

3. Moteab's goal and the celebrations that followed are well captured in this YouTube clip: https://www.youtube.com/watch?v=UOuRWMCIO_E (accessed 26 April 2019).

4. The chapter primarily considers the privately owned daily *al-Shuruq* between early November and early December 2009. I also use articles from *al-Misri al-Yum* and *al-Dustur* as well as detailed secondary accounts by Yasser Thabet (2010) and Ashraf Abdel Shafi (2010).

5. The Egyptian football website FilGoal.com was a notable exception. The site was criticized for a lack of patriotism after publishing a couple of reports about injured Algerian players and fans (Chief Editor Ahmad Saied, interview, 7 May 2012). In *al-Shuruq*, this side of the story was either neglected or reported in a tone indicating that the Algerians had made it all up (see, for example, 14, 16 November 2009).

6. As I discuss elsewhere, the Egyptians' patronizing attitudes betray traces of a colonial legacy (Rommel, 2014:169–170). For details about the long-standing, problematic (post-)colonial relationship between Egypt and Sudan, see Troutt Powell, 2003.

7. One of Fouad's call-ins is found here: http://www.youtube.com/watch?v=ZWiJhvcz9tI (accessed 30 March 2017).

8. An Egyptian man who I met in Cairo in 2012 provided an example of the intensely toxic atmosphere. Due to his blond hair, he had been taken for an Algerian and almost beaten up inside his local supermarket in Cairo. In *al-Shuruq*, no incidents of this kind were mentioned before 26 November, eight days after the second match.

9. Alaa Mubarak also made a similar phone call to the talk show *Beit Beitak*; see http://www.youtube.com/watch?v=NYTH6Vn7zIQ (accessed 9 April 2015).

10. Linguistically, most Arabic words stem from three-letter roots. In its most basic form, the root *'ayn-sad-ba*, which *ta'assub* derives from, means to wind, fold, tie, bind, or wrap. The transitive verb *'assaba* is associated with the process of winding a bandage or a turban on somebody else, whereas the reflexive derivate *ta'assaba* is used when a turban is wound onto one's own head. But the self-winding can also be figurative: to create a team, clique of coalition; to plot against someone; to gang up or to take sides; to be chauvinist, bigoted, fanatic. The substantiated form of the verb *ta'assaba*, *ta'assub* technically denotes the carrying out of these actions, although it also translates metaphorically as zeal, partiality, and racial or national pride. In addition, words referring to nerves (*a'sab*; singular, *'asab*) are also formed from the same root: nervous (*'asabi*) and nervousness (*'asabi-yya*). The latter can, as I discuss later, be used as a synonym for *ta'assub* (*The Hans Wehr Dictionary of Modern Written Arabic*, 4th ed., 1994).

11. Khaled Fahmy's *In Quest of Justice* is primarily interested in the *siyasa* system, a judiciary-legal complex of discourse and practice that predated Egypt's wide-ranging legal reforms in 1883. For the genealogy that I am tracing, Fahmy's observation that several early twentieth-century nationalist leaders portrayed *siyasa* as premodern, nontransparent and outdated is worth noting (2018:87–88).

12. In Nasser's view, the pluralist parliamentary system that had been in place during Egypt's "Liberal Age" of nominal constitutional monarchy (1922–1952) had been disastrous for the nationalist project. Invested in partisan interests, Socialists, Communists, Muslim Brothers, and the landowner-dominated Wafd Party had made concessions to the British (de facto) colonizers and sown divisions within the national unity. Thus, one objective of the 1952 Free Officers' Coup was to put an end to political intrigues. Workers, peasants, and professionals were encouraged to organize in unions and syndicates that managed the local allocation of state resources. Yet no partisan group or interest was allowed to interfere in the national-political decision making (Roussillon, 1996:20–23).

13. From the 1970s onward, a number of social democratic and liberal parties were allowed in Egypt. By the mid-2000s, when the Muslim Brotherhood won eighty-eight parliamentary seats running as independents and Ayman Nour from the Ghad Party challenged President Mubarak in the country's first multicandidate presidential election, the field of formal politics was more contested than at any time since 1952.

14. These moves harmonized with international trends. Calls for technocratic governments, independent central banks, anticorruption measures and disempowering of political elites have in recent decades been voiced by an eclectic range of actors, including the International Monetary Fund and the World Bank, the European Union, and right-wing populist politicians (see, for example, Fassin and Pandolfi, 2010). The Egyptian development has been analyzed in detail by Sarah Ben Nefissa, 2011.

15. This constellation of sports, class, masculinity, and nationalism was historically specific. In the early twentieth century, another period when sports figured as a pivot for the formation of national and male subjectivities in Egypt, football was associated with the educated and professional *effendi* middle classes (Jacob, 2011).

16. In this regard, the football-critical debates had much in common with sig-

nificantly earlier Egyptian conversations about national middle-class masculinity, rationality (*'aql*), and the importance of emotional control (see Prestel, 2017).
17. Over the last decades, it is intriguing to recall, Egypt's different Islamist movements have often been castigated as *muta'assib* (fanatical) and accused of injecting *ta'assub* (fanaticism) into the religious sphere. When Islamist actors found discursive space to portray the regime-aligned football boom as *muta'ssib* in late 2009, the term used thus added an extra layer to the revenge.
18. According to Gabriel Kuhn, the quoted suggestion was put forward not by Goebbels but by the Nazi regime's foreign affairs secretary, Martin Luther (2011:53).
19. A divergent take, which mobilizes the world of sports to critique philosophical works on event and eventfulness (Badiou, Deleuze, and Derrida), is found in Grant Farred's *In Motion, at Rest* (2014). Farred's orientation is not primarily toward singular matches and results, but to extraordinary occasions that break the rules and exceed the game as such, e.g., the French superstar Zinedine Zidane head-butting the Italian defender Marco Materazzi in the dying moments of the 2006 World Cup final.

Chapter 3. A Revolutionary Emotional Style

1. *Kushari* is a cheap Egyptian staple dish made of pasta, rice, lentils, chickpeas, fried onions, and tomato sauce.
2. *Talta shimal* refers to the third-class stands (*talta*) to the left (*shimal*). The opposite end, where al-Zamalek's Ultras White Knights are located, is called *talta yimin* (right).
3. *Curva* is Italian for "curve." It refers to the typically curved stadium section behind the goal, where Ultras fans congregate. *Shamarikh* (singular, *shamrukh*) are a powerful type of firework flares originally used at sea in times of emergency.
4. In many European countries, these entrance scenes are called *tifo*, an Italian word that stems from *tifoso* (supporter).
5. "Group" (*grub* in Egyptian Arabic) is the term that Ultras use when talking about their own associations. I refer to the Ultras as "groups" throughout this book. The abbreviation UA07 indicates the year (2007) when Ultras Ahlawy were established.
6. E.g., Yellow Dragons (supporting al-Ismaily), Green Eagles (al-Masry from Port Said) and Green Magic (al-Ittihad from Alexandria). In addition, until 2015, al-Ahly's Ultras in Alexandria were known as Ultras Devils and run semi-independently of Ultras Ahlawy.
7. The Ultras' outreach through social media has always been remarkable. At the Cairene group's ten-year anniversary in May 2017, their Facebook pages were "liked" by 1,046,000 (UWK) and 1,317,000 (UA07) users respectively.
8. As Dalia Abdelhamdeed Ibraheem notes (2015:8–9, 84–85), the Egyptian Ultras use a variety of terms when referring to individuals and hierarchies within the groups (capos, actives, the secret group). Terminologies also differ between UA07 and UWK. For simplicity, I tend to use "members" when speaking of individual Ultras, and "capos" when referring to the group's leaders.
9. Individual Ultras sometimes make financial contributions to the groups. In 2013, one UWK-member told me that he was paying 30 EGP per month to his *dawla*. Others have suggested that they only make voluntary contributions.

According to researcher Robbert Woltering, rich members might pay as much as 100 to 150 EGP per month, whereas less well-off fans give significantly less (2013:300).

10. I will return to this match in chapter 5. The politics and effects of the supporter ban will be discussed in detail in chapters 4, 5, and 6.

11. The Ultras' stances stood in stark contrast to those of many famous club officials, coaches, and players, who—to the disappointment of many fans—supported President Mubarak and called on the protesters to return home (Auish, 2011).

12. I will return to this topic in subsequent chapters.

13. Interestingly, the Egyptian security forces also thought of these pre-2011 clashes against the Ultras as a kind of "training exercise for how to disperse political demonstrations" (el-Zatmah, 2012:806).

14. For a nuanced analysis of the crucial, complex, and classed role of martyrs during Egypt's revolutionary period, see Armbrust, 2019:53–139.

15. For parallel examples elsewhere in the Middle East, see Menoret, 2014 and Nuhrat, 2018.

Chapter 4. A Respectable Revolution Measures Its Violence

1. A slightly different account is found on al-Ismaily Sporting Club's website: http://www.ismaily-sc.com/home/index.php/history/1698.html (accessed 24 January 2019). On the rivalry between al-Ahly and the clubs from the canal region, see also Close, 2019:15–16.

2. The first minutes of the attack are covered in this YouTube clip https://www.youtube.com/watch?v=Btu6jAFMWd4&feature=youtu.be (accessed 4 April 2017).

3. According to some accounts, the doors had been welded shut (Mohsen, 2012). Other eyewitnesses claim that the gates had been locked by the police (Dorsey, 2016:80) or by the military (Ibraheem, 2015:82–83). Material from the official fact-finding committee indicates that two out of three gates were welded in the weeks before the game. The third was locked during the course of the match (Close, 2019:50–51).

4. Although the literal English translation of *haqq* is "right," "justice" is sometimes more appropriate. This is especially so in contexts where the *haqq* that is to be claimed or restored belongs to people who are dead. As Farha Ghannam notes, another function of the Ultras' campaign was to establish that the young men had "died doing good deeds," i.e., that their lives had had "good endings" (Ghannam, 2013:157–158).

5. E.g., Yousri Fouda's *Akhir Kalam* on ONTV (6 February 2012).

6. For eyewitness reports, see Biermann, 2017; Ibraheem, 2015:81–85; Fakri, 2018; and The Art of Chaos, 2012. UA07's protests in February and spectacular sit-in outside the Egyptian Parliament from 25 March to 9 April 2012 have been documented in Tarek, 2012; Thabet, 2013:77–87; Close, 2019:35–48. Some of the most thorough attempts to make sense of the tragedy's causes are Badawi, 2012a, 2012b; El Dahshan, 2012; Zaki Chakravarti, 2012.

7. A small three-wheeled vehicle that is used as a taxi in less-developed areas in Egypt.

8. Abu Treika was given two months' suspension and fines amounting to half a million Egyptian pounds for siding with the Ultras. He was also stripped of the team captaincy.

9. It is worth remembering that al-Mistakawi, as the author of the most compre-

hensive account of al-Ahly's history to date (1997), is a main contributor to this historiography.

10. This incident forms a famous part of al-Ahly's nationalist legacy. However, Hassan seems to have confused the year of the trip. As Dalia Abdelhameed Ibrahim notes (2015:26), the contested visit to Palestine actually happened during World War II, in 1943.

11. The song explicitly targeted five pundits: Medhat Shalaby, Ahmed Shoubair, Mustafa Yunis, Khaled el-Ghandour, and Mahmoud Ma'luf. The video is found here: https://www.youtube.com/watch?v=1-rkXFbUN_I (accessed 25 January 2019).

12. When talking about al-Ahly's "betrayal," Mido partly alluded to the decision to play the Super Cup. In part, he also referred to the club neglecting to send any legal representatives to FIFA's appeal tribunal in Zurich in August, which revoked the EFA's decision to suspend al-Masry from the league for two seasons (see Hassan, 2012b).

13. Ultras fans across the world make a point of supporting their clubs rather than individual players, who represent the team temporarily. In the case of Abu Treika, Ultras Ahlawy made a rare exception.

14. This tension reached a turning point with the so-called Battle of the Camels, the dramatic event on 2 February 2011, when protesters on Tahrir Square were attacked by thugs paid by the Mubarak regime (some riding on camels). Among Ghannam's interlocutors, notions of whose violence was ordered and purposeful, and hence a sign of *gada'na*, and whose was random and self-interested (*baltaga*) were drawn upon to make moral sense of what was going on. The event boosted the appeal of the revolution and turned many people in al-Zawya against the Mubarak regime (2013:124–128).

Chapter 5. The Insurmountable Double Bind of *Siyasa*

1. Ultras Ahlawy might be al-Ahly's most dedicated supporters, yet a vast majority do not have the financial means to be members of al-Ahly Club. They are normally not allowed to enter the club premises.

2. More generally, the display of male domination and retaliation seemed to confirm suspicions that the Ultras embodied a problematic kind of masculinity. Many feminists had already been critical of the group's insistence on maintaining traditional gender roles and spatial, as well as temporal, segregation between men and women at sit-ins and demonstrations (see, e.g., Close, 2019:83–84).

3. One telling example of surprise paired with disappointment was found on anthropologist Samuli Schielke's Facebook on 26 January 2013. Commenting on the fact that the Ultras rejoiced at the death sentences of twenty-one youngsters, Schielke stated that he had now "lost hope in the Ultras." Journalist and activist Sarah Carr expressed her feelings more bluntly on Twitter the same day: "Of course Ultras el Ahly [*sic*] are celebrating. They are a bunch of teenagers whose raison d'être is rivalry with other clubs. They just hit gold." Activist Alaa Abd el-Fattah showed more understanding. In a series of tweets, he argued that it was too early to dismiss the Ultras and ridiculous to claim that they had "sold the revolution." If anything, the court's rulings and the Ultras' happiness showed that the revolution was still alive, and that putting pressure on the authorities could pay off.

4. For an incisive recent analysis of the detrimental implications of this secular-

religious rift and of one Egyptian politician, Abdel Moneim Abouel Fotouh, who worked hard but ultimately failed to overcome it, see Mohie, 2020.

5. Hussein Agrama has argued that one key source of strength of the 25 January Revolution was its articulation as an "asecular" revolt. In contrast to what had been the case in the late Mubarak era, questions about different actors' religiosity and/or secularism were rarely asked in the uprising's early stages (2012:231–232). President Mursi's constitutional declaration constitutes the ultimate endpoint of this asecular period. After November 2012, the secular framework's questions about religion in general and its engagement in politics in particular returned with full force.

6. These tensions speak to a general pattern. In early 2013, several commentators insinuated that the Mursi government had struck a deal with Ultras Ahlawy (see, for example, *al-Misri al-Yum*, 18 January 2013). For those looking for it, there were many indicators: the Ultras' no-show at anti-Brotherhood demonstrations in December 2012, say, or the police's reluctance to confront the groups since Mursi had come to power. Even Muhammad Abu Treika's endorsement now turned from a trump card into a burden. Because of his outspoken support for the government, Abu Treika's popularity and nationalist role-model status weakened significantly as the divisions sharpened (a good example is an interview that Abu Treika gave on Misr 25 Mubashir TV channel, 22 November 2012). Inevitably, his well-known connection to UA07 associated the supporter group with the Mursi camp.

7. The contrast between the reactions to this attack and those after UA07's attack on the same building six months earlier (chapter 4) is indicative of the swift and widespread change of mood.

8. Following a redrafting of the constitution in 2019, el-Sisi is currently eligible to run for office for another two terms, i.e., until 2030. The amendments were passed by a referendum in April 2019.

9. Once the military takeover was completed, the latent anti-Brotherhood sentiments turned even more overt. Within a week, Azmi Magahid, the media spokesperson of the EFA, accused the Muslim Brotherhood of having plotted the Port Said massacre in cooperation with Hamas (Hathutalathnayn, 2013). In summer and early autumn, football pundits such as Shalaby and Shoubair spent long sections of their talk shows attacking the Mursi supporters' dangerous "mixing of football and *siyasa*," while praising the army for having returned stability to the country. The football media thus both demonized the Rabaa sit-in and justified its bloody dispersal.

10. Muhammad Abu Treika's ties to Ultras Ahlawy and outspoken support for President Mursi during his time in office have rendered him a divisive figure in post-coup Egypt. On the one hand, millions of Egyptians still love him intensely. On the other hand, his persona and politics have faced relentless criticism in the media, before as well as after he retired as a player in late 2013. In January 2017, as his name was added to a "terror list" (*al-Shuruq*, 18 January 2017), Abu Treika left Egypt for Qatar, where he currently works as a studio expert for BeIN SPORTS. He is not able to return to Egypt, a fact that became painfully clear when he was not able to attend his father's funeral in February 2017. In another famous case from November 2013, Ahly player Ahmed Abd el-Zaher celebrated a goal in the African Champions League final by briefly raising four fingers into

the air—the well-known sign of sympathy with the Mursi supporters killed in Rabaa al-Adawiya Square. This gesture prompted the media to call Abd el-Zaher a traitor to Egypt, a supporter of terrorism, and a disgrace for al-Ahly Club. The EFA banned him from representing the Egyptian national team for twelve months. Al-Ahly deprived him of bonuses, suspended him from the team, and put him up for sale.

11. When this book goes to press, none of the death sentences has been executed.

12. Once again, it is worth stressing that Egyptian club presidents are elected by club *members*. Members are not necessarily football supporters and are very rarely Ultras. Their main concerns tend to be the cafés, swimming pools, gyms, and gardens inside the club where they and their families spend their spare time.

13. The fullback, Omar Gaber, recently back from his earlier suspension, was the only player who refused to play the game. Although currently playing for a rival club, he remains a hero for many Zamalek supporters.

14. The video was published on FilGoal.com's Facebook page (https://www .facebook.com/FilGoal/videos/10155936853740642/), accessed 6 May 2019.

15. See, for example, *Ahram* Online, 9 January 2016; Ultras Ahlawy Facebook, 26 September 2016, 30 January 2017; Ultras White Knights Facebook, 6 October 2016; *Mada Masr*, 26 October 2017, 10 March 2018, 9 May 2018; Close, 2019:60, 173–174.

16. A similar tendency to pit the freedom of "revolution" against the relative order of "politics" has been noted in post-2011 Yemen (Porter, 2017). See also Arendt, 2006. For a nuanced analysis of the Egyptian revolution's inherent but hidden class dimensions, see Armbrust, 2019:124–139.

17. Contrary to understandings of Islamism as a primarily transnational, pan-Muslim movement, a nationalist ethos has been fundamental to the Egyptian Muslim Brotherhood since its establishment in the 1920s (see Geer, 2011:166–169; Arbrust 2019: 157–180).

Chapter 6. When the Game Feels Like Politics, It Doesn't Feel Like Much at All

1. Tramadol is a mild opiate pain killer that many Egyptians consume as a recreational drug.

2. In this, I draw inspiration from aftermath's etymology. The concept originally refers to the fresh grass that sprouts after a field has been harvested (German: *die Mahd*).

3. For other ethnographic analyses of people in the Arab world expressing this complex range of feelings, see Allen, 2008:473–474 and Winegar, 2012.

4. Distancing myself from earlier, problematic analyses of "animalist" and "irrational" crowd behaviors associated with classed, gendered, and racialized Others (see Blackman, 2012:26–53), I refrain from presumptuously approaching "the crowd" as a given entity with certain predetermined potentials. Instead, I consider the dynamics that large congregations of people effectuate one of many variables that together elicit affect and emotionality in and around football matches.

5. This orientation is analogous to that of several anthropologists and social theorists who in recent years have proposed a blurring of the emotion-affect divide (e.g., Blackman, 2012; Leys, 2011; Lutz, 2017; Mazzarella, 2017; Navaro-Yashin, 2009, 2012; Stewart, 2017). I find Yael Navaro-Yashin's theorization of material

objects being "qualified" through language and history particularly suggestive (2009).

6. In a phenomenological contemplation on football's relationship to time, Simon Critchley evocatively depicts such occasions as "moments of moments" of "sensate ecstasy" (2018:22–23). The prolonged waiting for ecstatic moments to occur, he argues, is key to football's unmatched appeal.

7. In June 2009, Egypt beat the reigning World Champions, Italy, in the Confederations Cup in South Africa.

8. The final stages of this tournament took place in the very same months as the Ultras' spectacular campaign against the resumption of domestic football (see chapter 4). Al-Ahly's semifinal against Sunshine Stars was the match that was all but canceled following the players' demonstration outside the Hotel Baron.

9. As discussed in part II, it was a matter of principle for Ultras Ahlawy not to attend football matches before proper justice (al-qasas) had been done. UA07 would only return to the stadium after the Port Said court verdicts in early 2013.

10. For a couple of recent anthropological studies that take the issue of rhythm seriously, see Dobler, 2016 and Jalas, Rinkinen, and Silvast, 2016. See also Henriques, 2010 for an ethnographic analysis of the copropagation of material, corporal, and sociocultural rhythms.

11. In a recent book, Simon Critchley discusses the importance of football's rhythms at some length (2018:55–59). He even suggests that "the essence of football consists of repetition" (ibid., 56).

12. See also Ryzova, 2020:291–296 for a discussion about the Muhammad Mahmoud Street battle and its distinctive rhythms.

13. In her research with shopkeepers in Cairo's tourist market Khan el-Khalili between 2011 to 2013, Karin Ahlberg observed a similar feeling of incomprehensibility of politics in an era when everything seemed to fall apart (2017:264–299).

14. See also Achilli, 2014, for an analysis of the disengagement from politics among Palestinian refugees in Jordan.

Chapter 7. No National Significance, No Political Concerns

1. The dominance of Egypt's domestic game is less pronounced at the time of writing (January 2021) than it was before 2012. Al-Ahly and al-Zamalek are still Egypt's most popular clubs, yet European teams are also watched and supported, especially among the younger generations. In part, this "normalization" of Egyptian fandom by African standards is due to the protracted ban on supporters at Egyptian football stadiums. It is also a result of the rise of the first truly global Egyptian football superstar, Liverpool FC's Mohamed Salah (see postscript).

2. In contrast to al-Jazeera Sports' cheap subscription card, which was compatible with most standard satellite receivers, AD Sports required an expensive encrypted HD receiver, which had to be purchased together with the card. For some unknown reason, however, the governmental company Cable Network Egypt, which has the monopoly on pay-TV subscription sales in Egypt, refused to sell the necessary cards and receivers from the beginning of the 2010–2011 season until autumn of 2012. In 2013, AD Sports lost the English Premier League rights to a new Qatari sports channel, beIN SPORTS, which currently broadcasts all major international competitions throughout the Arab World.

3. Among more than a hundred ahawi that I visited in Cairo between 2011 and

2013, Sayed's was the only one combining *sha'bi* atmosphere and cheap prices with AD Sports' broadcasts.

4. Al-Zamalek was called King Faruq Club, after the Egyptian monarch, between 1941 and 1952.

5. As of early 2019, depending on the location and quality of the surface, renting a five-a-side pitch costs between 150 and 300 EGP per hour.

6. As Wael Eskander suggested in an insightful commentary, Black Blocs should be considered a tactic used by different protesters rather than an activist group per se (2013b).

7. As Farha Ghannam has shown, masculinized skirmishes unfold all the time in Egypt: in shops and markets, in queues in the city's bureaucratic institutions, and in the hectic traffic (2013:111–113). Ghannam depicts this ritualized violence as a core dimension of Egyptian working-class manhood. With the exception of *nas muhtarama* (respectable people from the upper middle classes), men and boys are encouraged to man up, to protect their rights, and to never back off from an argument. Furthermore, men who happen to be in the vicinity of fights are socially obliged to step in and intervene. Like on *al-midan*, Cairo's relatively high frequency of male violence is thus balanced by masculinized social control (Ghannam, 2013:33–39, 111–121).

8. Loïc Wacquant makes such an argument in his analysis of the appeal of routinized boxing training amidst the violence that prevails in South Side Chicago. He depicts the boxing gym as an "island of order and virtue" in an otherwise highly insecure neighborhood (Wacquant, 2004:14–31).

9. At the time, al-Jazeera Sports employed the region's most famous commentator, the Tunisian Muhammad al-Shawali. His incredibly rapid and linguistically elaborate commentary is immensely popular in Egypt, and it was much enjoyed by the men I met at Ward al-Qahira.

10. Loïc Wacquant makes a similar observation in his auto-ethnography from a South Side Chicago boxing gym (2004:100–104).

11. Lucie Ryzova's interlocutors draw a comparable distinction between the pure "revolution" that they engaged in during the November 2011 Muhammad Mahmoud street fights—embodied, masculine, sexualized—and the endless deliberation characterizing "politics" in Tahrir Square and in the Egyptian media (2020). Playing or watching football in Abdeen are of course very different and much less serious pastimes than fighting the police's bullets in Muhammad Mahmoud Street. However, the way both sets of activities base their affective appeal on detachment from an overly elaborate political realm is noteworthy. For an analogous case of nondiscursive antipolitics, see Yurchak, 2008.

12. This argument dovetails with Matei Candea's examination of Corsican school officials' efforts to separate politics and education (2011). Whereas Candea's ethnography primarily highlights processes of boundary making between the political and nonpolitical, my material foregrounds distinctions between national and non-national football, demarcations that in turn specify where the political arises as a problem.

Conclusion: An Emotional Revolt Trapped in Politics

1. For an alternative view of the revolution that draws on working-class, masculine idioms and values, see Ryzova, 2020.

Postscript

1. The most famous campaign was produced by the network provider Orange. While appreciated for its aesthetics and creativity, the campaign is criticized for making fun of Egypt's elderly and their dream of seeing their national team in the World Cup again before dying (see al-Wahaidy, 2017).

2. The English Football Players Association, the Football Writers Association, and the Premier League itself all give Mohamed Salah the prize for best player of the season.

3. The campaign, consisting of large billboards and a high-profile television ad, is funded by the Ministry of Social Solidarity.

4. The Ballon d'Or is awarded to Real Madrid's Croatian midfielder Luca Modri in December 2018. Salah finishes sixth.

5. Occasionally, this pristine aura instigates fans to protect Salah from the ills of his mother country. In the wake of the bitter loss to Saudi Arabia in the World Cup, to take one example, social media are filled with commentators who regret that Salah has to put up with Egypt's entrenched mediocrity. "Salah looks so miserable, it's not fair," a well-known political activist writes on Twitter. "Please, Salah, leave the national team behind, you're too good for this failed country," a researcher and colleague of mine exclaims on Facebook.

6. See https://egyptianstreets.com/2018/08/28/mo-salahs-demands-reveal -shocking-failures-by-egypts-football-association/ (accessed 22 July 2020). See also Walsh, 2018.

7. One example is found in Medhat Shalaby's talk show *Masa' al-Anwar* on ON Sports, 29 April 2018.

8. This statement is made after the opening ceremony on 21 June 2019. See https://www.youtube.com/watch?v=Rrq8M3ems5Y (accessed 22 July 2020).

9. A video posted on the government-aligned twitter account *mashari' masr* (Egypt's Projects) provides one good example; see https://twitter.com/EgyProjects /status/1138952931221352448 (accessed 22 July 2020).

10. Post-1945 Italy provides a comparative case. As John Foot has documented (2006), Benito Mussolini's regime exploited football with great success in the 1930s, bringing home two World Cups in 1934 and 1938 and boosting fascist-nationalist feelings. During the two decades that followed the war, however, many Italians expressed a sense of embarrassment for the game's politicized past, which made it difficult for them to back the national team.

REFERENCES

Abd El Rasoul, A. 2018. "EFA allows some fans at Egyptian League matches, raises number of squad's foreign players." *Ahram* Online, 11 February, http://english.ahram.org.eg/NewsContent/6/0/290802/Sports/0/EFA-allows-some-fans-at-Egyptian-League-matches,-r.aspx. Accessed 25 April 2019.

Abdalla, N. 2020. "From the dream of change to the nightmare of structural weakness: the trajectory of Egypt's independent trade union movement after 2011." In *Socioeconomic protests in MENA and Latin America: Egypt and Tunisia in interregional comparison*, edited by I. Weipert-Fenner and J. Wolff, 145–168. London: Palgrave Macmillan.

Abdel Mohsen, A. 2012. "Ultras: heroes, villains or scapegoats?" *Egypt Independent*, 5 February, http://www.egyptindependent.com/news/ultras-heroes-villains-or-scapegoats. Accessed 12 April 2015.

Abdel Shafi, A. 2010. *Muthaqqafun wi kurat al-qaddam*. Giza: Dar al-safsafa.

Abu Bakr, B., and A. Al-Hamid Sharbani. 2011. "Ultras al-ahli: hagimna al-amn al-markazi li-hatafna didd al-'adli." *Al-Tahrir*, 6 September; available at http://tahrirnews.com. Accessed 12 November 2011.

Abu-Lughod, L. 1986. *Veiled sentiments: honor and poetry in a Bedouin society*. Berkeley: University of California Press.

———. 2005. *Dramas of nationhood: the politics of television in Egypt*. Chicago: University of Chicago Press.

Abu-Lughod, L., and C. Lutz, eds. 1990. *Language and the politics of emotion*. Cambridge, UK: Cambridge University Press.

Achilli, L. 2014. "Disengagement from politics: nationalism, political identity, and the everyday in a Palestinian refugee camp in Jordan." *Critique of Anthropology* 34 (2): 234–257.

Agamben, G. 2005. *State of Exception*. Chicago: University of Chicago Press.

Agrama, H. A. 2012. *Questioning secularism: Islam, sovereignty, and the rule of law in modern Egypt*. Chicago: University of Chicago Press.

Ahlberg, K. G. C. 2017. "'They are destroying the image of Egypt': tourism, statecraft and infrastructures of image making, 1990–2013." PhD diss., School of Oriental and African Studies, University of London.

Ahmed, S. 2004. *The cultural politics of emotions*. Edinburgh: Edinburgh University Press.

Ahmedhassan17. 2011. "Lajnat al-bath tutlub 160 milyun li-bi' huquq idha'it al-dawri al-mumtaz." *Ahmedhassan17*, 7 October, http://ahmedhassan17.com/publicnews/egypt/1943-hassan-efa-100.html. Accessed 12 April 2015.

Akindes, G. A. 2011. "Football bars: urban sub-Saharan Africa's trans-local 'stadiums.'" *International Journal of the History of Sport* 28 (15): 2176–2190.

Al-Banna, M. 2012. "Musirat al-'ar." FilGoal.com, 2 October, http://www.filgoal.com/Arabic/News.aspx?NewsID=95961. Accessed 23 October 2012.

Al-Din Muhammad, D. 2011. "Al-ultras: qabl ma tadammaruhum . . . lazim ta'arrafuhum." FilGoal.com, 28 September, http://s3.filgoal.com/Arabic/News.aspx?NewsID=82421. Accessed 16 December 2011.

———. 2014. "Hasibu al-dakhiliyya wi laysa al-ultras." FilGoal.com, 21 February; available at https://www.filgoal.com. Accessed 25 April 2019.

Alegi, P. 2010. *African soccerscapes: how a continent changed the world's game*. Athens: Ohio University Press.

Alkhamissi, M. 2018. "Transforming the mirage: the union of skilled handicrafts craftsmen of Egypt and their struggle for a better life, January 2011—January 2014." Paper presented at the Cairo Papers in Social Science 26th Annual Symposium, Worlds of work: precarity affect and possibility, Cairo, Egypt, 21 April.

Allen, L. 2008. "Getting by the occupation: how violence became normal during the Second Palestinian Intifada." *Cultural Anthropology* 23 (3): 453–487.

Al-Mistakawi, H. 1997. *Al-nadi al-ahli, 1907–1997: buttula fi al-riyada wi al-wataniyya*. Cairo: Dar al-Shuruq.

Al-Wahaidy, F. 2017. "To Orange: do not humiliate the elderly." *Egypt Today*, 10 September, https://www.egypttoday.com/Article/8/21997/To-Orange-do-not -humiliate-the-elderly. Accessed 24 July 2020.

Amar, P. 2011a. "Middle East masculinity studies: discourses of 'men in crisis,' industries of gender in revolution." *Journal of Middle East Woman's Studies* 7 (3): 36–70.

———. 2011b. "Turning the gendered politics of the security state inside out? Charging the police with sexual harassment in Egypt." *International Feminist Journal of Politics* 13 (3): 299–328.

———. 2013. *The security archipelago: human-security states, sexuality politics, and the end of neoliberalism*. Durham, NC: Duke University Press.

Amara, M. 2012. "Football sub-culture and youth politics in Algeria." *Mediterranean Politics* 17 (1): 41–58.

Anderson, B. 1991. *Imagined communities: reflections on the origin and spread of nationalism*. London: Verso.

Archetti, E. P. 1999. *Masculinities: football, polo and the tango in Argentina*. Oxford, UK: Berg.

Arendt, H. 2006. *On revolution*. London: Penguin.

Armbrust, W. 1996. *Mass culture and modernism in Egypt*. Cambridge, UK: Cambridge University Press.

———. 2002a. "Islamists in Egyptian cinema." *American Anthropologist* 104 (3): 922-931.

———. 2002b. "Manly men on a national stage (and the women who make them stars)." In *Histories of the Modern Middle East: New Directions*, edited by I. Gershoni, Y. H. Erdem, and U. Woköck, 247-275. Boulder, CO: Lynne Rienner.

———. 2019. *Martyrs and tricksters: an ethnography of the Egyptian Revolution*. Princeton, NJ: Princeton University Press.

The Art of Chaos, 2012. "What happened in Port Said as told by @heemalization, English version." *The Art of Chaos: A Poetic Political Personal Blog*, 2 February, http://thatartofchaos.com/2012/02/02/what-happened-in-port-said-as-told -by-heemalization-english-version/. Accessed 14 February 2012.

Attalah, L. 2013. "The end game for Port Said: football case reveals new breadth of politics." *Egyptian Independent*, 28 January, https://www.egyptindependent .com/end-game-port-said-football-case-reveals-new-breadth-politics/. Accessed 24 April 2019.

Auish, A. 2011. "Hujum dari min jamahir al-ahli wi al-zamalik 'ala la'ibin bi-sabab al-ghiyab 'an al-thawra." *Al-Dustur*, 4 March.

Ayoub, Y. 2010. "Jamal 'abd al-Nasir." *Al-Misri al-Yum*, 7 January, http://today .almasryalyoum.com/article2.aspx?ArticleID=239354. Accessed 15 May 2017.

Badawi, A. 2012a. "Making sense of Egypt: part one, in defence of conspiracy as a method." *Open Democracy*, 22 March, https://www.opendemocracy.net /en/making-sense-of-egypt-part-one-in-defence-of-conspiracy-as-method/. Accessed 25 April 2019.

———. 2012b. "Making sense of Egypt: part two, a partial anatomy of insecurity." *Open Democracy*, 22 March, https://www.opendemocracy.net/en/making -sense-of-egypt-part-two-partial-anatomy-of-insecurity/. Accessed 25 April 2019.

Bakhtin, M. 1968. *Rabelais and his world*. Cambridge, MA: MIT Press.

Bashir, M. G. 2011. *Kitab al-ultras: 'andama tata'adda al-jamahir al-tabi'a.* Cairo: Dar dawwin.

Bayat, A. 2010. *Life as politics: how ordinary people change the Middle East.* Stanford, CA: Stanford University Press.

Beatty, A. 2014. "Anthropology and emotion." *Journal of the Royal Anthropological Institute* 20 (3): 545–563.

Begato, A. 2014. "Ghadab min i'adit mahakimit al-muttahimin fi majzarit bur sa'id." *Al Arabiya*, 7 February; available at https://www.alarabiya.net. Accessed 16 May 2017.

Ben Nefissa, S. 2011. "La vie politique locale: les *mahaliyyat* et le refus du politique." In *L'Égypte au present: inventaire d'une société avant revolution*, edited by V. Bettesti and F. Ireton, 343–346. Arles, France: Sindbad.

Ben Porat, A. 2001. "'Biladi, Biladi': ethnic and nationalistic conflict in the soccer stadium in Israel." *Soccer and Society* 2 (1): 19–38.

———. 2014. "Cui Bono? Arabs, football and state." *Soccer and Society* 17 (4): 496–511.

Berlant, L. 2011. *Cruel optimism*. Durham, NC: Duke University Press.

Besnier, N., S. Brownell, and T. F. Carter. 2018. *The anthropology of sport: bodies, borders, biopolitics*. Oakland: University of California Press.

Biermann, C. 2017. "Märtyrer aus der Kurve." *11 Freunde*, 4 November, https:// www.11freunde.de/artikel/al-ahly-ultras-ueber-die-grausame-nacht-von-port -said. Accessed 25 April 2019.

Bilal, M. 2011. "Egypt's 'Ultras' pitch in at Tahrir protest." Al-Jazeera, 29 November, http://www.aljazeera.com/indepth/features/2011/11 /201111284912960586.html. Accessed 12 April 2015.

Billig, M. 1995. *Banal nationalism*. Thousand Oaks, CA: Sage.

Blackman, L. 2012. *Immaterial bodies: affect, embodiment, mediation*. London: Sage.

Bouhdiba, A., and A. Khal. 2000. "Festivities of violence: circumcision and the making of men." In *Imagined masculinities: male identity and culture in the modern Middle East*, edited by M. Ghoussoub and E. Sinclair-Webb, 19–32. London: Saqi.

Boum, A. 2013. "Shoot-outs for the nation: football and politics in post-colonial Moroccan-Algerian Relations." *Soccer and Society* 14 (4): 548–564.

Bromberger, C. 1995. "Football as a world-view and as ritual." *French Cultural Studies* 6 (18): 287–292.

Brown, N. J. 2013a. "Egypt's wide state reassembles itself." *Foreign Policy*, 17 July, http://foreignpolicy.com/2013/07/17/egypts-wide-state-reassembles-itself/. Accessed 15 May 2017.

———. 2013b. "Will June 30 be midnight for Morsi's Cinderella story?" *Foreign Policy*, 27 June, http://foreignpolicy.com/2013/06/27/will-june-30-be -midnight-for-morsis-cinderella-story/#.Uc10J-Uc6CU.twitter. Accessed 15 May 2017.

Brown, W. 1995. *States of injury: power and freedom in late modernity*. Princeton, NJ: Princeton University Press.

Bush, R., and H. Ayeb, eds. 2012. *Marginality and exclusion in Egypt*. New York: Zed.

Butler, J. 2014. "Speaking of Rage and Grief." Leigha Cohen Video Production YouTube Channel, 29 April, https://www.youtube.com/watch?v=ZxyabzopQi 8&app=desktop. Accessed 13 April 2015.

Candea, M. 2011. "'Our division of the universe': making a space for the non-political in the anthropology of politics." *Current Anthropology* 52 (3): 309–334.

Cherstich, I., M. Holbraad, and N. Tassi. 2020. *Anthropologies of revolution: forging time, people, and worlds*. Oakland: University of California Press.

Close, R. 2019. *Cairo's Ultras: resistance and revolution in Egypt's football culture*. Cairo: American University in Cairo Press.

Comaroff, J., and J. Comaroff. 1992. *Ethnography and the historical imagination*. Boulder, CO: Westview.

Creak, S. 2015. *Embodied nation: sport, masculinity, and the making of modern Laos*. Honolulu: University of Hawaii Press.

Critchley, S. 2018. *What we think about when we think about football*. London: Profile Books.

Danielson, V. L. 1997. *The voice of Egypt: Umm Kulthum, Arabic song, and Egyptian society in the twentieth century*. Chicago: University of Chicago Press.

Das, V. 1995. *Critical events: an anthropological perspective on contemporary India*. Delhi: Oxford University Press.

Dayf Allah, K. 2011. "Ishtibak bayn al-amn wa jumhur al-ahli 'aqab nihayyit laqa' kima aswan." Yallakora.com, 6 September, http://www.yallakora.com/ar/News /165393. Accessed 12 November 2011.

de Koning, A. 2009. *Global dreams: class, gender, and public space in cosmopolitan Cairo*. Cairo: American University in Cairo Press.

De Waele, J.-M., S. Gibril, E. Gloriozova, and R. Spaaij, eds. 2018. *The Palgrave international handbook of football and politics*. Cham, Switzerland: Palgrave Macmillan.

Di-Capua, Y. 2004. "Sports, society, and revolution: Egypt in the early Nasserite period." In *Rethinking Nasserism: revolution and historical memory in Modern Egypt*, edited by E. Podeh and O. Winckler, 144–162. Gainesville: University Press of Florida.

Diyab, O. 2011. "Walidat al-shahid: illi matu fi al-tahrir mish baltagiyya." alforsan.net, 26 November, http://www.alforsan.net/newsDetails.aspx?NewsId =897. Accessed 26 November 2011.

Dobler, G. 2016. "'Work and rhythm' revisited: rhythm and experience in northern Namibian peasant work." *Journal of the Royal Anthropological Institute* 22 (4): 864–883.

Dorsey, J. M. 2011. "Egyptian Ultra tactics evident in the battle for Cairo's Tahrir Square." *The Turbulent World of Middle East Soccer*, 4 February, http:// mideastsoccer.blogspot.co.uk/2011/02/egyptian-ultra-tactics-evident-in.html. Accessed 12 April 2015.

———. 2013. "Tactical retreat: Ultras absent from protests in Egypt and Turkey." *The Turbulent World of Middle East Soccer*, 13 July, http://mideastsoccer .blogspot.de/2013/07/tactical-retreat-ultras-absent-from.html. Accessed 15 May 2017.

———. 2014. "Militant soccer fans reassert their key role in protest with storming of Cairo stadium." *The Turbulent World of Middle East Soccer*, 6 December, http://mideastsoccer.blogspot.de/2013/07/tactical-retreat-ultras-absent -from.html. Accessed 16 May 2017.

———. 2016. *The turbulent world of Middle East soccer*. London: Hurst.

Dunning, E. 1986. "Sports as a male preserve: notes on the social sources of masculine identity and its transformations." *Theory, Culture and Society* 3 (1): 79–90.

Edensor, T. 2006. "Reconsidering national temporalities: institutional times, everyday routines, serial spaces and synchronicities." *European Journal of Social Theory* 9 (4): 525–545.

Elassal, M. 2018. "How Egyptians followed the 1934 World Cup?" *Ahram* Online, 12 June, http://english.ahram.org.eg/News/291720.aspx. Accessed 25 April 2019.

El Dahshan, M. 2012. "Egypt's tragedy: this is not just soccer violence." *Foreign Policy*, 2 February, https://foreignpolicy.com/2012/02/02/egypts-tragedy-this -is-not-just-soccer-violence/. Accessed 25 April 2019.

Elgohari, M. 2013. "Egypt's Ultras: no more politics." *Jadaliyya*, 30 June, http:// www.jadaliyya.com/pages/index/12475/egypt%E2%80%99s-ultras_no-more -politics. Accessed 2015-04-12.

Elias, N., and E. Dunning. 1986. *Quest for excitement: sport and leisure in the civilizing process*. Oxford: Blackwell.

Elkayal, H. 2011. "The Ultras White Knights: football hooliganism or social movement?" *Daily News*, 16 September, http://www.dailynewsegypt.com/2011 /09/16/the-ultras-white-knights-football-hooliganism-or-social-movement/. Accessed 12 April 2015.

El Khachab, C. 2016. "Secular preachers: watching television pundits in post-revolutionary Egypt." *Anthropology Now* 8 (1): 117–124.

Ellis, M. 2004. *The coffee-house: a cultural history*. London: Orion Books.

El-Mahdi, R. 2012. Contribution to plenary "Arab revolutions: conflicting narratives." Presented at Narrating the Arab Spring conference, Cairo, 18–20 February.

El-Messiri, S. 1978. *Ibn al-balad: a concept of Egyptian identity*. Leiden, Netherlands: Brill.

Elsey, B. 2012. *Citizens and sportsmen: fútbol and politics in twentieth-century Chile*. Austin: University of Texas Press.

El-Sherif, A. 2012. "The Ultras' politics of fun confront tyranny." *Jadaliyya*, 5 February, http://www.jadaliyya.com/pages/index/4243/the-ultras-politics-of-fun-confront-tyranny. Accessed 13 April 2015.

El-Zatmah, S. 2012. "From Terso into Ultras: the 2011 Egyptian revolution and the radicalization of the soccer's Ultra-Fans." *Soccer and Society* 13 (5–6): 801–813.

EMSS. 2013. "Qarar jumhuri bi-dam dahaiyya majdharit Port Said li-shuhada al-thawra." *Wazarit al-Shabab wi al-Riyada*, http://emss.gov.eg/details_news.php?recordID=20514. Accessed 23 January 2013.

Ennarah, K. M. 2017. "The Ultras Ahlawy: football, violence, and the quest for justice." The Century Foundation, 11 April, https://tcf.org/content/report/the-ultras-ahlawy/. Accessed 16 May 2017.

Erlich, H. 1989. *Students and university in twentieth century Egyptian politics*. London: Frank Cass.

Eskander, W. 2013a. "Clashing with the Ultras: a firsthand account." *Jadaliyya*, 15 February, http://www.jadaliyya.com/pages/index/10204/clashing-with-the-ultras_a-firsthand-account. Accessed 15 May 2017.

———. 2013b. "The black bloc: evolution of the revolution." *Middle East Institute*, 25 April, http://www.mei.edu/content/black-bloc-evolution-revolution. Accessed 25 April 2019.

———. 2018. "Mo Salah, the revolution and Egypt's defeat." *Open Democracy*, 2 July, https://www.opendemocracy.net/en/north-africa-west-asia/mo-salah-revolution-and-egypt-s-defeat/. Accessed 13 February 2020.

Fahmy, K. 2018. *In quest of justice: Islamic law and forensic medicine in Modern Egypt*. Oakland: University of California Press.

Fahmy, Z. 2011. *Ordinary Egyptians: creating the modern nation through popular culture*. Stanford, CA: Stanford University Press.

Fakri, A. 2018. "Tahqiq: ma hadath fi stad bur sa'id bi-riwaya shuhud 'ayan . . . madhbaha mudabbara am infi'al mubara?" Goal.com, 1 February; available at https://www.goal.com. Accessed 25 April 2019.

Farred, G. 2014. *In motion, at rest: the event of the athletic body*. Minneapolis: University of Minnesota Press.

Farhi, M. 2000. "Lentils in paradise." In *Imagined masculinities: male identity and culture in the Modern Middle East*, edited by M. Ghoussoub and E. Sinclair-Webb, 251–262. London: Saqi.

Fassin, D., and M. Pandolfi, eds. 2010. *Contemporary states of emergency: the politics of military and humanitarian interventions*. Brooklyn: Zone Books.

Fathi, M. 2013. "Khittat al-ultras fil-sa'at al-qadima li-i'lan al-fawda" *Al-Ahram*,

24 January, http://shabab.ahram.org.eg/NewsContent/7/99/9010.aspx. Accessed 24 January 2013.

Fawzi, A. 2012. "Khas . . . Tahir Abu Zayd: mawqif ultra *ahlawi* mushrif." Yallakora.com, 31 October, http://www.yallakora.com/arabic/YK_news/details.aspx?id=200375&Catid=1&tourid=255&NewsRegion=1&Selector=true&updated=31102012240&region=. Accessed 31 October 2012.

————. 2013. "Itthad al-kura: an al-awan li-tathir al-riyada...wi kurit al-qaddam masdar al-si'ada lil-sha'b al-misri." Yallakora.com, 1 July, http://www.yallakora.com/arabic/yk_news/details.aspx?id=222173. Accessed 5 September 2013.

Finn, G. P. T. 1994. "Football violence: a societal psychological perspective." In *Football, violence and social identity*, edited by R. Giulianotti, N. Bonney, and M. Hepworth, 87–122. London: Routledge.

Fletcher, M. 2010. "'You must support Chiefs; Pirates already have two white fans!': race and racial discourse in South African football fandom." *Soccer and Society* 11 (1–2): 79–94.

Foot, J. 2006. *Calcio: a history of Italian football*. New York: Harper Perennial.

Foucault, M. 1977. *Discipline and punish: the birth of the prison*. London: Allen Lane.

————. 1978. *The will to knowledge: the history of sexuality*, vol. 1. New York: Pantheon.

————. 1980. *Power/Knowledge: selected interviews and other writings, 1972–1977*. New York: Pantheon.

————. 1997. "Nietzsche, Freud, Marx." In *Aesthetics, method, and epistemology: The essential works of Michel Foucault, 1954–1984, vol. 2*, edited by P. Rabinow and J. D. Faubion, 269–278. New York: New Press.

Gabr, M. 2013. "Egypt's 'political' football." *Mada Masr*, 18 September, http://www.madamasr.com/opinion/egypts-political-football. Accessed 12 April 2015.

Gamal, R. 2018. "Da'wa lil-'awda fi 2022 bil-istifada min durus haqbat kuber." FilGoal.com, 20 June, https://www.filgoal.com/articles/337509/. Accessed 3 May 2019.

Gammerl, B. 2012. "Emotional styles: concepts and challenges." *Rethinking History* 16 (2): 161–175.

Geer, B. 2011. "The priesthood of nationalism in Egypt: duty, authority, autonomy." PhD diss., School of Oriental and African Studies, University of London.

Ghannam, F. 2013. *Live and die like a man: gender dynamics in urban Egypt*. Stanford, CA: Stanford University Press.

Gibril, S. 2015. "Contentious politics and bottom-up mobilisation in revolutionary Egypt: the case of Egyptian football supporters in Cairo." In *Contentious politics in the Middle East: popular resistance and marginalized activism beyond the Arab Uprisings*, edited by F. A. Gerges, 305-330. Cham, Switzerland: Palgrave Macmillan.

————. 2018. "Egypt." In *The Palgrave international handbook of football and politics*, edited by J-M De Waele, S. Gibril, E. Gloriozova, and R. Spaaij, 347–368. Cham, Switzerland: Palgrave Macmillan.

Giulianotti, R. 1991. "Scotland's tartan army in Italy: the case for the carnivalesque." *Sociological Review* 39 (3): 503–527.

Goldblatt, D. 2006. *The ball is round: a global history of football*. London: Penguin.

———. 2010. "The Power and the Passion." *BBC Radio Documentary*. First broadcast on 7 June.

———. 2014. *Futebol Nation: the story of Brazil through soccer*. New York: Nation Books.

Goldblatt, D., and D. Nolan. 2018. "Viktor Orbán's reckless football obsession." *The Guardian*, 11 January, https://www.theguardian.com/news/2018/jan/11/viktor-orban-hungary-prime-minister-reckless-football-obsession. Accessed 25 April 2019.

Gottzén, L., and T. W. Reeser. 2017. "Introduction: complicating the emotions of men and masculinities." *NORMA: International Journal for Masculinity Studies* 12 (3–4): 185–186.

Gramsci, A. 2011. *Prison notebooks (vol. 1)*. Edited and translated by Joseph A. Buttigieg with Antonio Callari. New York: Columbia University Press.

Guinness, D., and N. Besnier. 2016. "Nation, nationalism, and sport: Fijian rugby in the local-global nexus." *Anthropological Quarterly* 89 (4): 1109–1141.

Hagag, M. Y. 2002. *Al-ta'assub wi al-'adwan fil-riyada: ru'iyya nafsiyya-ijtima'iyya*. Cairo: Maktabit al-anglu al-misriyya.

Hakim, M. 2019. "Finding life in football: Upper Egypt girls defy social norms." *Mada Masr*, 12 October; available at https://madamasr.com. Accessed 9 July 2020.

Halabi, N. 2015. "Media privatization and the fate of social democracy in Egypt." *Arab Media and Society* 21. https://www.arabmediasociety.com/post_issue/issue-21-spring-2015/.

Hamama, M., and R. Mamdouh. 2017. "Parliamentary committees approve bill stipulating harsher penalties for sports team fan associations." *Mada Masr*, 12 March; available at http://www.madamasr.com. Accessed 16 May 2017.

Hamzeh, M., and H. Sykes. 2014. "Egyptian football Ultras and the January 25 Revolution: anti-corporate, anti-militarist and martyrdom masculinities." *Anthropology of the Middle East* 9 (2): 91–107.

Hassan, A. 2009. "Egypt: soccer rift makes Mubarak's oldest son a hero." latimes.com, 25 November, http://latimesblogs.latimes.com/babylonbeyond/2009/11/egypt-soccer-rift-reintroduces-mubarak-son.html. Accessed 13 April 2015.

Hassan, S. 2012a. "Khiyanat al-ahly." FilGoal.com, 27 August, http://new3.filgoal.com/Arabic/News.aspx?NewsID=93811. Accessed 28 August 2012.

———. 2012b. "'Ultras' khamsit a'uwam min al-ghumud wi al-ta'thir . . . al-halqa al-akhira." *Al-Misri al-Yum*, 19 April, http://www.almasryalyoum.com/news/details/173220. Accessed 12 April 2015.

Hathutalathnayn, H. 2013. "Magahid: al-ikhwan wi hamas dabbaru we naffadhu madhbahit bur sa'id." FilGoal.com, 8 July; available at http://www.filgoal.com. Accessed 16 May 2017.

Hattox, R. S. 1985. *Coffee and coffeehouses: the origins of a social beverage in the medieval Near East*. Seattle: University of Washington Press.

Haugbolle, S. 2012. "The (little) militia man: memory and militarized masculinity in Lebanon." *Journal of Middle East Women's Studies* 8 (1): 115–139.

Hawkey, I. 2009. *Feet of the chameleon: the story of African football.* London: Anova Books.

Henriques, 2010. "The vibrations of affect and their propagation on a night out on Kingston's dancehall scene." *Body and Society* 16 (1): 57–89.

Hirschkind, C. 2006. *The ethical soundscape: cassette sermons and Islamic counterpublics.* New York: Columbia University Press.

Hourani, A. 2005. *A history of the Arab peoples.* London: Faber.

Hughes, G. F. 2017. "The Chastity Society: disciplining Muslim men." *Journal of the Royal Anthropological Institute* 23 (2): 267–284.

Hughson, J. 2000. "A tale of two tribes: expressive fandom in Australian soccer's a-league." In *Football culture: local contests, global visions*, edited by G. P. T. Finn and R. Giulianotti, 10–30. London: Frank Cass.

Humphrey, C. 2013. "Fear as a property and an entitlement." *Social Anthropology* 21 (3): 285–304.

Hussein, N. 2011. "The social significance of street soccer in Greater Cairo: game structure and social functions." *Journal of the History of Childhood and Youth* 4 (2): 309–328.

Ibraheem, D. A. 2015. "Ultras Ahlawy and the spectacle: subjects, resistance and organized football fandom in Egypt." Master's thesis, American University in Cairo.

Ikram, K. 2018. *The Political economy of reforms in Egypt: issues and policymaking since 1952.* Cairo: American University in Cairo Press.

Inhorn, M. 2012. *The new Arab man: emergent masculinities, technologies, and Islam in the Middle East.* Princeton, NJ: Princeton University Press.

Ismail, S. 2006a. *Political life in Cairo's new quarters: encountering the everyday state.* Minneapolis: University of Minnesota Press.

———. 2006b. *Rethinking Islamist politics: culture, the state and Islamism.* London: I.B. Tauris.

———. 2012. "The Egyptian revolution against the police." *Social Research: An International Quarterly* 79 (2): 435–462.

Jacob, W. C. 2011. *Working out Egypt: effendi masculinity and subject formation in colonial modernity, 1870–1940.* Durham, NC: Duke University Press.

Jalas, M., J. Rinkinen, and A. Silvast. 2016. "The rhythms of infrastructure." *Anthropology Today* 32 (4): 17–20.

Kandil, H. 2012. *Soldiers, spies and statesmen: Egypt's road to revolt.* London: Verso Books.

Kapferer, B. 2015. "Introduction: In the event—toward an anthropology of generic moments." In *In the event: toward an anthropology of generic moments*, edited by L. Meinert and B. Kapferer, 1–26. New York: Berghahn.

Kaplan, D. 2000. "The military as a second Bar Mitzvah: combat service as initiation to Zionist masculinity." In *Imagined masculinities: male identity and culture in the Modern Middle East*, edited by M. Ghoussoub and E. Sinclair-Webb, 127–144. London: Saqi.

Kassimeris, C. 2012. "Franco, the popular game and ethnocentric conduct in modern Spanish football." *Soccer and Society* 13 (4): 555–569.

Kelly, W. W. 2004. "Sense and sensibility at the ballpark: what fans make of professional baseball in modern Japan." In *Fanning the flames: fans and consumer culture in contemporary Japan,* edited by W. W. Kelly, 79–106. New York: SUNY Press.

Kholoussy, H. 2010. *For better, for worse: the marriage crisis that made modern Egypt.* Stanford, CA: Stanford University Press.

King, A. 1997. "The lads: masculinity and the new consumption of football." *Sociology: The Journal of the British Sociological Association* 31 (2): 329–346.

Kirkpatrick, D. D., and Fahim, K. 2013. "A crisis deepens in Egypt after ruling on riot, calls for a military coup." *New York Times,* 9 March, https://www.nytimes .com/2013/03/10/world/middleeast/egypt-sentences-2012-soccer-riot.html. Accessed 25 April 2019.

Kraidy, M. M. 2010. *Reality television and Arab politics: contention in public life.* Cambridge, UK: Cambridge University Press.

Kreil, A. Forthcoming. "Le 'parti du canapé': mise en retrait de la politique et défense du quotidien en Égypte." In *Désirs d'État,* edited by L. Bazin and L. Mehdi. Paris: L'Harmattan.

Kuhn, G. 2011. *Soccer vs. the state: tackling football and radical politics.* Oakland, CA: PM Press.

Larkin, B. 2008. *Signal and noise: media, infrastructure, and urban culture in Nigeria.* Durham, NC: Duke University Press.

Latour, B. 2004. "How to talk about the body? The normative dimension of science studies." *Body and Society* 10 (2–3): 205–229.

———. 2005. *Reassembling the social: an introduction to actor-network-theory.* Oxford, UK: Oxford University Press.

Leavitt, J. 1996. "Meaning and feeling in the anthropology of emotions." *American Ethnologist* 23 (3): 514–539.

Lefebvre, H. 2004. *Rhythmanalysis: space, time and everyday life.* London: Continuum.

Leys, R. 2011. "The turn to affect: a critique." *Critical Inquiry* 37 (3): 434–472.

Lindsey, U. 2011. "Ultras and the revolution." *The Arabist,* 9 September, http:// arabist.net/blog/2011/9/10/ultras-the-revolution.html. Accessed 12 April 2015.

Longman, J. 2018. "Mo Salah, now starring in Chechnya." *New York Times,* 11 June, https://www.nytimes.com/2018/06/11/sports/mo-salah-egypt-chechnya .html. Accessed 3 May 2019.

Lopez, S. 2009. "Football as national allegory: *al-Ahram* and the Olympics in 1920s Egypt." *History Compass* 7 (1): 282–305.

Lutz, C. 2017. "What matters." *Cultural Anthropology* 32 (2): 181–191.

Maher, H. 2011. "Ahly survive Maqassa scare amid sombre mood." *Ahram Online,* 23 December, http://english.ahram.org.eg/News/30071.aspx. Accessed 12 April 2015.

————. 2012a. "Angry Ahly fans storm club HQ, attack players." *Ahram* Online, 23 September, http://english.ahram.org.eg/NewsContent/6/51/53639/Sports /Egyptian-Football/Angry-Ahly-fans-storm-club-HQ%2c-attack-players .aspx. Accessed 24 September 2012.

————. 2012b. "Egypt's illicit gains authority imposes travel ban on Ahly chairman Hamdy." *Ahram* Online, 9 October, http://english.ahram.org.eg /NewsContent/6/51/55162/Sports/Egyptian-Football/Egypts-Illicit-Gains -Authority-imposes-travel-ban-.aspx. Accessed 10 October 2012.

————. 2012c. "Egypt's Ultras Ahlawy storm Cairo's media production city." *Ahram* Online, 25 September, http://english.ahram.org.eg/NewsContent /6/51/53800/Sports/Egyptian-Football/Egypts-Ultras-Ahlawy-storm-Cairos -Media-Production.aspx. Accessed 26 September 2012.

————. 2013. "Preview: defiant fans challenge crowd ban as Ahly, Zamalek clash." *Ahram* Online, 23 July, http://english.ahram.org.eg/NewsAFCON /2019/77150.aspx. Accessed 10 October 2020.

————. 2014. "Zamalek's fan favorite pays price for Ultras-chairman enmity." *Ahram* Online, 4 November, http://english.ahram.org.eg/News/114774.aspx. Accessed 16 May 2017.

————. 2018. "Liverpool's Mo Salah falls out with Egyptian FA over image rights." *Ahram* Online, 27 April, http://english.ahram.org.eg/NewsContent /6/0/298445/Sports/0/Liverpool%E2%80%99s-Mo-Salah-falls-out-with -Egyptian-FA-ov.aspx. Accessed 3 May 2019.

Mahmood, S. 2005. *Politics of piety: the Islamic revival and the feminist subject.* Princeton, NJ: Princeton University Press.

Makram-Ebeid, D. 2012. "Manufacturing stability: everyday politics of work in an industrial steel town in Helwan, Egypt." PhD diss., The London School of Economics and Political Science, University of London.

————. 2014. "'Old people are not revolutionaries': labor struggles and the politics of value and stability (*istiqrar*) in a factory occupation in Egypt." *Focaal-Blog*, 14 November, http://www.focaalblog.com/2014/11/14/dina-makram -ebeid-labor-struggles-and-the-politics-of-value-and-stability-in-a-factory -occupation-in-egypt/. Accessed 13 April 2015.

Malmström, M. F. 2019. *The streets are talking to me: affective fragments in Sisi's Egypt.* Oakland: University of California Press.

Mar'i, A. 2015. "Al-qabd 'ala 17 min muthiri al-shaghab amam astad al-difa' al-jawi." Youm7.com, 8 February; available at http://www.youm7.com. Accessed 16 May 2017.

Marsden, M. 2007. "All-male sonic gatherings, Islamic reform, and masculinity in northern Pakistan." *American Ethnologist* 34 (3): 473–490.

Marsh, P. E. 1978. *Aggro: the illusion of violence.* London: J. M. Dent.

Martin, S. 2004. *Football and fascism: the national game under Mussolini.* Oxford, UK: Berg.

Mason, T. 1995. *Passion of the people? Football in South America.* London: Verso.

Massumi, B. 2002. *Parables for the virtual: movement, affect, sensation.* Durham, NC: Duke University Press.

Mazzarella, W. 2009. "Affect: what is it good for?" In *Enchantments of modernity: empire, nation, globalization*, edited by S. Dube, 291-309. London: Routledge.

———. 2017. *The Mana of mass society*. Chicago: University of Chicago Press.

Mbembé, A. 1992a. "Prosaics of servitude and authoritarian civilities." *Public Culture* 5 (1): 123–145.

———. 1992b. "The banality of power and the aesthetics of vulgarity in the postcolony." *Public Culture* 4 (2): 1–30.

———. 2001. *On the postcolony: studies on the history of society and culture*. Berkeley: University of California Press.

Media 9313. 2013. "Suna' fi Port Said." Media9313 YouTube Channel, 7 March, https://www.youtube.com/watch?feature=player_embedded&v=jfkZWOeaxv8. Accessed 13 April 2015.

Menoret, P. 2014. *Joyriding in Riyadh: oil, urbanism, and road revolt*. Cambridge, UK: Cambridge University Press.

Michaelson, R. 2018. "Six years after the Port Said riot, Egypt's fans return to the stadiums." *The Guardian*, 12 September, https://www.theguardian.com/football/2018/sep/12/port-said-riot-egypt-football-fans-stadiums. Accessed 25 April 2019.

Mitchell, T. 2002. *Rule of experts: Egypt, techno-politics, modernity*. Berkeley: University of California Press.

Mittermaier, A. 2011. *Dreams that matter: Egyptian landscapes of the imagination*. Berkeley: University of California Press.

———. 2014. "Bread, freedom, social justice: the Egyptian uprising and a Sufi Khidma." *Cultural Anthropology* 29 (1): 54–79.

Mohie, M. 2020. "Abdel Moneim Abouel Fotouh: a man apart." *Mada Masr*, 18 August, https://www.madamasr.com/en/2020/08/18/feature/politics/abdel-moneim-abouel-fotouh-a-man-apart/. Accessed 10 October 2020.

Moll, Y. 2010. "Islamic televangelism: religion, media and visuality in contemporary Egypt." *Arab Media and Society* 10. https://www.arabmediasociety.com/post_issue/issue-10-spring-2010/.

Montague, J. 2009. "Egypt versus Algeria: inside the storm." CNN, 27 November, http://edition.cnn.com/2009/SPORT/football/11/20/egypt.algeria.inside.story/. Accessed 12 April 2015.

———. 2012. "In wake of deadly riot, Egyptian team plays on." *New York Times*, 19 December, https://www.nytimes.com/2012/12/20/sports/soccer/in-wake-of-deadly-riot-egyptian-soccer-team-plays-on.html. Accessed 25 April 2019.

———. 2020. *1312, Among the Ultras: a journey with the world's most extreme fans*. London: Penguin.

Mosbah, A. 2015. "Ultras." Al-Jazeera *World Documentary*, first published 2 February, http://www.aljazeera.com/programmes/aljazeeraworld/2015/02/ultras-150202121425449.html. Accessed 12 April 2015.

Murshid, M. 2012. "Taqrir . . . al-qawa al-siyasiyya tatadamin ma' al-ultras. Wa na'ib al-ikhwan yuradd 'ala al-nizam." Yallakora.com, 9 September, http://www.yallakora.com/arabic/yk_news/details.aspx?id=195540&utm_source=dlvr.it&utm_medium=facebook. Accessed 9 September 2012.

Nader, E. 2014. "How Egypt made soccer a national security issue." *VICE*, 7

November, https://www.vice.com/en_us/article/political-football-0000494
-v21n11. Accessed 16 May 2017.

Naeem, M. 2016. "Mother of the world, against the world and outside it." *Mada Masr*, 9 June, http://www.madamasr.com/opinion/mother-world-against -world-and-outside-it/. Accessed 9 June 2016.

———. 2019. "In Egypt, nothing has changed—but perhaps everything has." *Mada Masr*, 13 November, https://madamasr.com/en/2019/11/13/opinion /u/in-egypt-nothing-has-changed-but-perhaps-everything-has/. Accessed 13 February 2020.

Nathan, R. 2018. "Ultras Ahlawy group announce dissolution." Kingfut.com, 16 May, https://www.kingfut.com/2018/05/16/ultras-ahlawy-dissolution/. Accessed 8 May 2019.

Navaro-Yashin, Y. 2009. "Affective spaces, melancholic objects: ruination and the production of anthropological knowledge." *Journal of the Royal Anthropological Institute* 15 (1): 1–18.

———. 2012. *The make-believe space: affective geography in a postwar polity*. Durham, NC: Duke University Press.

Nuhrat, Y. 2018. "Contesting love through commodification: soccer fans, affect, and social class in Turkey." *American Ethnologist* 45 (3): 392–404.

Oakeshott, M. 2006. *Lectures in the history of political thought*. Exeter, UK: Imprint Academic.

Oldenburg, R. 1999. *The great good place: cafes, coffee shops, bookstores, bars, hair salons, and other hangouts at the heart of a community*. New York: Marlowe.

Oliver, B. 2009. "Twenty years on, the 'hate match' between Egypt and Algeria is on again." *The Guardian*, 10 October, https://www.theguardian.com/football /blog/2009/oct/10/egypt-algeria-repeat-hate-match. Accessed 12 April 2015.

Omar, E. 2018. "Egypt star Salah says 'the way of handling things is very insulting' amid dispute with EFA." *Ahram* Online, 29 April, http://english.ahram .org.eg/News/298559.aspx. Accessed 3 May 2019.

Pannenborg, A. 2012. *Big men playing football: money, politics and foul play in the African game*. Leiden, Netherlands: African Studies Centre.

Pearson, G. 2012. *An ethnography of English football fans: cans, cops and carnivals*. Manchester, UK: Manchester University Press.

Peterson, M. A. 2011. *Connected in Cairo: growing up cosmopolitan in the modern Middle East*. Bloomington: Indiana University Press.

Podeh, E., and O. Winckler. 2004. "Introduction: Nasserism as a form of populism." In *Rethinking Nasserism: revolution and historical memory in Modern Egypt*, edited by E. Podeh and O. Winckler, 1–42. Gainesville: University Press of Florida.

Porter, R. 2017. "Freedom, power and the crisis of politics in revolutionary Yemen." *Middle East Critique* 26 (3): 265–281.

Prestel, J. B. 2017. *Emotional cities: debates on urban change in Berlin and Cairo, 1860–1910*. Oxford, UK: Oxford University Press.

Puar, J. K. 2012. "Coda: the cost of getting better: suicide, sensation, switchpoints." *GLQ: A Journal of Lesbian and Gay Studies* 18 (1): 149–158.

Rabie, P. 2015. "The changing face of Downtown." *Mada Masr*, 29 October,

https://madamasr.com/en/2015/10/29/feature/politics/the-changing-face-of
-downtown/. Accessed 25 April 2019.

Rancière, J. 2004. *The politics of aesthetics: the distribution of the sensible*. London: Continuum.

Reeser, T. W. L., and L. Gottzén. 2018. "Masculinity and affect: new possibilities, new agendas." *NORMA: International Journal for Masculinity Studies* 13 (3–4): 145–157.

Riyadiyyu Misr al-Shurafa, 2012. "Al-riyadiyyun: al-ultras tarabbu fi ahdan al-nizam al-sabiq". *Al-Wafd*, 22 October, http://www.alwafd.org/%D8%A7%D9%84%D8%B1%D9%8A%D8%A7%D8%B6%D8%A9/284853. Accessed 22 October 2012.

Rollason, W. 2011. "We are playing football: seeing the game on Panapompom, PNG." *Journal of the Royal Anthropological Institute* 17 (3): 481–503.

Rommel, C. 2011. "Playing with difference: football as a performative space for division among *Suryoye* migrants in Sweden." *Soccer and Society* 12 (6): 850–864.

———. 2014. "A veritable game of the nation: on the changing status of football within the Egyptian national formation in the wake of the 2009 World Cup qualifiers against Algeria." *Critical African Studies* 6 (2–3): 157–175.

———. 2016. "Troublesome thugs or respectable rebels? class, martyrdom and Cairo's revolutionary Ultras." *Middle East—Topics and Arguments* 6: 33–42.

———. 2018a. "All work and no play? economic pressures and bodily pleasures in contemporary Egypt." Paper presented at the World Congress of Middle East Studies, Seville, Spain, 16–20 July.

———. 2018b. "Men in time: on masculinity, productivity, corruption, and youth football in the aftermath of the 2011 Egyptian Revolution." *Men and Masculinities* 21 (3): 341–362.

———. 2019. "Projected futures: notes from contemporary Egypt." Paper presented at the EASA Mediterraneanist Network Workshop, The Future(s) of the Mediterranean between Uncertainties and Resilience, Turin, Italy, 24–26 October.

Rosaldo, M. Z. 1980. *Knowledge and passion: Ilongot notions of self and social life*. Cambridge, UK: Cambridge University Press.

Roussillon, A. 1996. "Le nassérisme à traverse les âges: recompositions de la formule du pouvoir et de la légitimité." *Peuples Mediterraneens/Mediterranean Peoples* (January–June), 74–75: 13–48.

Rubin, J. D. 2014. "Making art from uncertainty: magic and its politics in South African Rugby." *Cultural Anthropology* 29 (4): 699–719.

Ryzova, L. 2011. "The battle of Cairo's Muhammad Mahmoud Street." *Al-Jazeera*, 29 November, http://www.aljazeera.com/indepth/opinion/2011/11/201111288494638419.html. Accessed 13 April 2015.

———. 2020. "The battle of Muhammad Mahmoud Street in Cairo: the politics and poetics of urban violence in revolutionary time." *Past and Present*, 247 (1): 273–317.

Sabea, H. 2014. "'I dreamed of being the people': Egypt's revolution, the people, and critical imagination." In *The political aesthetic of global protests: the Arab*

Spring and beyond, edited by P. Werbner, M. Webb, and K. Spellman-Poots, 67–92. Edinburgh: Edinburgh University Press.

Said, K. 2012. "Fi biyan rasmi . . . la'ibu al-ahli yid'amun ahali al-shuhada' wi yabarrarun la'b mubarat al-suber." Yallakora.com, 2 October; available at http://yallakora.com. Accessed 2 October 2012.

Saied, A. 2009. "Bil-sut wi al-sura: 'a'id min jahim al-jaza'irin fi al-sudan." Fil-Goal.com, 21 November, http://new4.filgoal.com/Arabic/News.aspx?NewsID =61777&fb_source=message. Accessed 28 November 2013.

———. 2011. "Akthar min 90 musaban ba'dihim fi hala' khatra ba'd hujum al-amn al-markazi 'ala al-jumhur." FilGoal.com, 6 September, http://www.filgoal .com/Arabic/News.aspx?NewsID=81767. Accessed 12 November 2011.

———. 2012. "Is'ila 'an huquq al-5 milayin . . . ya fada'iyyin." FilGoal.com, 2 October, http://www.filgoal.com/Arabic/News.aspx?NewsID=95201. Accessed 8 October 2012.

Sakr, N. 2013. "Social media, television talk shows, and political change in Egypt." *Television and New Media* 14 (4): 322–337.

Scheer, M. 2012. "Are emotions a kind of practice (and is that what makes them have a history)? A Bourdieuian approach to understanding emotions." *History and Theory* 51 (2): 193–220.

Schielke, S. 2008. "Boredom and despair in rural Egypt." *Contemporary Islam* 2 (3): 251–270.

———. 2009. "Being good in Ramadan: ambivalence, fragmentation, and the moral self in the lives of young Egyptians." *Journal of the Royal Anthropological Institute* 15 (s1): s24–s40.

———. 2012. *The perils of joy: contesting mulid festivals in contemporary Egypt*. Syracuse, NY: Syracuse University Press.

———. 2015. *Egypt in the future tense: hope, frustration, and ambivalence before and after 2011*. Bloomington: Indiana University Press.

———. 2017. "There will be blood: expectations and ethics of violence during Egypt's stormy season." *Middle East Critique* 26 (3): 205–220.

Schmitt, C. 2015. *Der Begriff des Politischen*. Berlin, Germany: Duncker and Humblot.

Scott, David. 2014. *Omens of adversity: tragedy, time, memory, justice*. Durham, NC: Duke University Press.

Seigworth, G. J., and M. Gregg. 2010. "An inventory of shimmers." In *The affect theory reader*, edited by M. Gregg and G. J. Seigworth, 1–28. Durham, NC: Duke University Press.

Shams el-Din, M. 2013. "Protesters and ultras clash during march reveals a rift and rivalries." *Egypt Independent*, 18 February, https://www.egyptindependent .com/protesters-and-ultras-clash-during-march-reveals-rift-and-rivalries/. Accessed 24 April 2019.

Shavit, U., and O. Winter. 2011. "Sports in contemporary Islamic law." *Islamic Law and Society* 18 (2): 250–280.

Shechter, R. 2018. *The rise of the Egyptian middle class: socio-economic mobility and public discontent from Nasser to Sadat*. Cambridge, UK: Cambridge University Press.

Shenker, J. 2016. *The Egyptians: a radical story*. London: Allen Lane.

Sinclair-Webb, E. 2000. "'Our Bülent is now a commando': military service and manhood in Turkey." In *Imagined masculinities: male identity and culture in the modern Middle East*, edited by M. Ghoussoub and E. Sinclair-Webb, 65–92. London: Saqi.

Smith, T. 2000. "'Bataille's boys': postmodernity, fascists and football fans." *British Journal of Sociology* 51 (3): 443–460.

Sobhy, H. 2009. "Amr Khaled and young Muslim elites: Islamism and the consolidation of mainstream Muslim piety in Egypt." In *Cairo contested: governance, urban space and global modernity*, edited by D. Singerman, 415–454. Cairo: American University Press.

Sobhy Ramadan, H. 2012. "Education and the production of citizenship in the late Mubarak era: privatization, discipline and the construction of the nation in Egyptian secondary schools." PhD diss., School of Oriental and African Studies, University of London.

Soliman, S. 2011. *The autumn of dictatorship: fiscal crisis and political change in Egypt under Mubarak*. Stanford, CA: Stanford University Press.

Sorek, T. 2003. "Arab football in Israel as an 'integrative enclave.'" *Ethnic and Racial Studies* 26 (3): 422–450.

———. 2007. *Arab soccer in a Jewish state: the integrative enclave*. Cambridge, UK: Cambridge University Press.

Springborg, R. 2018. "Egypt's World Cup: a spectacular own goal for Sisi's regime." *The New Arab*, 3 July, https://www.alaraby.co.uk/english/comment/2018/7/3/egypts-world-cup-an-own-goal-for-sisi-regime. Accessed 25 April 2019.

Starck, K., and R. Luyt. 2019. "Political masculinities, crisis tendencies, and social transition: toward an understanding of change." *Men and Masculinities* 22 (3): 431–443.

Stewart, K. 2007. *Ordinary Affects*. Durham, NC: Duke University Press.

———. 2017. "In the world that affect proposed." *Cultural Anthropology* 32 (2): 192–198.

Stoler, A. L. 2004. "Affective states." In *A Companion to the Anthropology of Politics*, edited by D. Nugent and J. Vincent, 4–20. Oxford, UK: Blackwell.

Swedenburg, T. 2012. "Egypt's music of protest." *MER* 265 (42). https://merip.org/2013/01/egypts-music-of-protest/.

Swyers, H. 2007. "The opposite of losses: where lies the soul of American sports?" *International Journal of the History of Sport* 24 (2): 197–214.

Tāhir, O. 2010. *Zamalkawi: album mi'wiyyat al-jamahir*. Giza: Atlas lil-nashr wi al-intag al-i'lami.

Tarek, S. 2012. "Ahly Ultras show patience in quest for justice, but for how long?" *Ahram* Online, 19 February, http://english.ahram.org.eg/NewsContent/1/64/34857/Egypt/Politics-/Ahly-Ultras-show-patience-in-quest-for-justice,-bu.aspx. Accessed 25 April 2019.

Tarek, S., and H. Maher. 2013. "Egypt's political tensions highlight historical rift between Cairo, Port Said." *Ahram* Online, 16 February, http://english.ahram.org.eg/News/64644.aspx. Accessed 24 April 2019.

Tawfeek, F. 2018. "Egyptian Football Association claims accounts involved in Sa-

lah feud are fake." *Egypt Independent*, 29 August, https://ww.egyptindependent
.com/egyptian-football-association-claims-accounts-involved-in-salah-feud
-are-fake-2/. Accessed 3 May 2019.

Tawfiq, M. 2010. *Masr bitil'ab: kayfa tihawwal al-sha'b al-misri illa gumhur?* Cairo:
Dar al-salam.

Thabet, Y. 2010. *Hurub kurat al-qaddam*. Cairo: Dar al-'ayn lil-nashr.

———. 2013. *Dawlat al-ultras: asfar al-thawra wi al-madhbaha*. Cairo: Dar uktub
lil-nashr wi al-tawzi'.

Thrift, N. 2007. *Non-representational theory: space, politics, affect*. New York: Routledge.

Thumann, M. 2013. "Droht jetzt ein Bürgerkrieg?" Zeit Online, 31 January,
https://www.zeit.de/2013/06/Aegypten-Muslimbrueder-Opposition. Accessed
25 April 2019.

Troutt Powell, E. 2003. *A different shade of colonialism: Egypt, Great Britain, and the
mastery of the Sudan*. Berkeley: University of California Press.

TRT World. 2018. "Egypt's Ultras." TRT World Facebook, 8 January, https://
www.facebook.com/watch/?v=2038365766433569. Accessed 28 July 2020.

Tuastad, D. 1997. "The political role of football for Palestinians in Jordan." In
Entering the field: new perspectives on world football, edited by G. Armstrong and
R. Giulianotti, 105–121. Oxford, UK: Berg.

Turner, V. 1969. *The ritual process: structure and anti-structure*. London: Routledge
and Kegan Paul.

Ultras Ahlawy 07 Media. 2011. "Makasa vs Al Ahly Ultras Ahlawy." Ultras Ahlawy 07 Media YouTube Channel, 24 December, https://www.youtube.com
/watch?v=BQQXynQWZXM&feature=share. Accessed 12 April 2015.

———. 2012. "Ultras Ahlawy." Ultras Ahlawy 07 Media YouTube Channel, 24
September, https://www.youtube.com/watch?v=1-rkXFbUN_I. Accessed 13
April 2015.

van Gennep, A. 1960. *The Rites of Passage*. London: Routledge.

van Nieuwkerk, K. 1995. *A trade like any other: female singers and dancers in Egypt*.
Austin: University of Texas Press.

———. 2013. *Performing piety: singers and actors in Egypt's Islamic Revival*. Austin:
University of Texas Press.

Wacquant, L. 2004. *Body and soul: notebooks of an apprentice boxer*. New York: Oxford University Press.

Wahba, D. 2020. "A thug, a revolutionary or both? Negotiating masculinity in
post-revolutionary Egypt." *Middle East: Topics and Arguments* 14: 56–65.

Walker, H. 2013. "State of play: the political ontology of sport in Amazonian
Peru." *American Ethnologist* 40 (2): 382–398.

Walsh, D. 2018. "Egypt's soccer star aims for a new goal: humbling his own bos-
ses." *New York Times*, 29 August, https://www.nytimes.com/2018/08/29/world
/middleeast/egypt-mohamed-salah-soccer.html. Accessed 13 February 2020.

Weber, M. 2005. *Wirtschaft und Gesellschaft: Grundriss der verstehenden Soziologie*.
Frankfurt am Main, Germany: Zweitausendeins.

Weden, L. 1999. *Ambiguities of domination: politics, rhetoric, and symbols in contemporary Syria*. Chicago: University of Chicago Press.

Williams, R. 1977. *Marxism and literature*. Oxford, UK: Oxford University Press.

Winegar, J. 2006. *Creative reckonings: the politics of art and culture in contemporary Egypt*. Stanford, CA: Stanford University Press.

———. 2012. "The privilege of revolution: gender, class, space and affect in Egypt." *American Ethnologist* 39 (1): 67-70.

———. 2014. "Civilizing Muslim youth: Egyptian state culture programmes and Islamic television preachers." *Journal of the Royal Anthropological Institute* 20 (3): 445–465.

———. 2016. "A civilized revolution: aesthetics and political action in Egypt." *American Ethnologist* 43 (4): 609–622.

Woltering, R. 2013. "Unusual suspects: 'Ultras' as political actors in the Egyptian Revolution." *Arab Studies Quarterly* 35 (3): 290-304.

Worby, E. 2009. "The play of race in a field of urban desire: soccer and spontaneity in post-apartheid Johannesburg." *Critique of Anthropology* 29 (1): 105–123.

Woroniecka-Krzyzanowska, D. 2020. "State, sport and resistance: a case of Palestinian sports clubs in the West Bank." *International Review of the Sociology of Sport* 55 (7): 915-932.

Wurzel, U. G. 2009. "The political economy of authoritarianism in Egypt." In *The Arab state and neo-liberal globalization: the restructuring of state power in the Middle East*, edited by L. Guazzone and D. Pioppi, 97-124. Reading, UK: Ithaca.

Yildirim, A. K. 2019. "Patronage and industrial football: explaining the de-politicization of Turkish soccer fandom." *Soccer and Society* 20 (2): 232–251.

Youssef, A. 2017. "Cassation Court upholds final death sentences in Port Said stadium massacre case." *Daily News Egypt*, 20 February, http://www.dailynewsegypt.com/2017/02/20/cassation-court-upholds-final-death-sentences-port-said-stadium-massacre-case/?mc_cid=7d1cc11d5a&mc_eid=64cbecf158. Accessed 16 May 2017.

Yurchak, A. 2008. "Necro-utopia: the politics of indistinction and aesthetics of the non-Soviet." *Current Anthropology* 49 (2): 199–224.

Zaki Chakravarti, L. 2012. "Football and the game of politics in Egypt." *Open Democracy*, 20 March, https://www.opendemocracy.net/en/5050/football-and-game-of-politics-in-egypt/. Accessed 25 April 2019.

———. 2013. "A tale of two cities: blood, football and politics in Egypt." *Open Democracy*, 11 February, https://www.opendemocracy.net/en/5050/tale-of-two-cities-blood-football-and-politics-in-egypt/. Accessed 25 April 2019.

Zidani, S. 2019. "Pride of the Arabs: Mo, mortality, and memes." *Mada Masr*, 26 June, https://madamasr.com/en/2019/06/26/feature/culture/pride-of-the-arabs-mo-morality-and-memes/. Accessed 24 July 2020.

Ziedan, Y. 2011. "Ijhad al-thawra wi ibqa' al-fawra (4/7): al-taqallub fil-taraqqub . . . mafhum al-baltaja." *Al-Misri al-Yum*, 30 November.

Zirin, D. 2011. "Soccer clubs central to ending Egypt's 'dictatorship of fear.'" sportsillustrated.com, 31 January, http://www.si.com/more-sports/2011/01/31/egypt-soccer. Accessed 13 April 2015.

INDEX

Note: Page numbers in *italics* refer to figures.

Abdeen (Cairo neighborhood): men's views of football, 192–210; poster of Salah in, *224*; street football on *al-midan* (the square), 203–209, *204*; torn Ultras Ahlawy mural in, *157*; Ward al-Qahira (coffee shop), 192–203, 207–209

Abdel 'Al, Rada, 241n2

Abdelghani, Magdi, 32, 119

Abdel Satir, Ahmed, 36

Abu-Lughod, Lila, 8, 46, 48, 77, 238n12

Abu Reida, Hani, 122, 129

Abu Treika, Muhammad: 2006 Africa Cup of Nations, 2; 2008 Africa Cup of Nations, 43, 126–128; background and career of, 126; boycott of 2012 Egyptian Super Cup match, 115, 121, 122, 123, 125; class and ethos of, 126–127; disciplinary actions against, 123, 246n8; emigration to Qatar, 149, 248–249n10; impact and influence of, 42, 116; popularity of, 125–129, 247n13, 248n6; support for president Muhammad Mursi, 128, 129, 149, 248–249n10, 248n6; support for Ultras Ahlawy, 116, 121, 128–129, 137; sympathy with Gaza, 126–127

AD Sports (Emirati television channel), 195, 207–208, 250n2

affect, politics of, 8–12. *See also* emotions

affective states, 10, 31, 57, 107

Africa Cup of Nations: 1957 Africa Cup, 6; 2006 Africa Cup, 1, 2, 10, 41; 2008 Africa Cup, 41, 43, 49, 52–53, 55, 126–127; 2010 Africa Cup, 41, 79, 177; 2012 Africa Cup, 166; 2015 Africa Cup, 219; 2017 Africa Cup, 219–220; 2019 Africa Cup, 4, 26, 220, 227, 228, 230, 231, 232, 233

African Champions League, 2, 41, 42, 132, 150, 177, 178, 179, 248–249n10

Agrama, Hussein, 160–161, 248n5

Aguirre, Javier, 228

al-Ahly Club: African Champions League titles, 2, 41; centennial match versus FC Barcelona (April 2007), 89; club premises, 121–122, 140–142; dominance in the 1990s, 34, 37, 241n6; early history and founding of, 5, 237n5, 237–238n10, 238n11; nationalist history and principles of, 123, 246–247n9, 247n10; Red Devils nickname, 87; refusal to host al-Ismaily Club in 1970s, 110; rivalries with al-Ismaily and al-Masry, 110–111, 146; rivalry with al-Zamalek, 6–7, 14, 197–198, 208, 238–239n21; sponsorship contracts, 33, 35. *See also* Ultras Ahlawy

al-Ahly Fan Club (AFC), 89, 90

Ahly Lovers Union (ALU), 89, 90

Ahmed, Shihab, 102–103, 105

al-Akhbar al-Yum (state-owned weekly newspaper), 52–53, 55, 127–128; Africa Cup of Nations supplement (16 February 2008), 55; front page (9 February 2008), *54*

al-Dustur (oppositional newspaper), 53, 66, 67, 68, 127

Algeria. *See* Egypt-Algeria 2010 World Cup qualifiers

al-Irhabi (The Terrorist, Nadir Galal, 1994), 47–49

al-Jazeera Sports, 195, 207, 250n2, 251n9

al-Misri al-Yum (newspaper), 97, 100, 121, 124